# RAIN FOLLOWS THE PLOW

**Also by Robert D. Clark**

*The Life of Matthew Simpson*

*The Odyssey of Thomas Condon*

# RAIN FOLLOWS THE PLOW

## *HOMESTEADING IN HAYES COUNTY, NEBRASKA*

By
Robert D. Clark

Foundation Books
Lincoln, Nebraska

 For information address Foundation Books, P.O. Box 29229, Lincoln, Nebraska 68529.

**Library of Congress Cataloging-in-Publication Data**

Clark, Robert Donald, 1910-
Rain follows the plow : homesteading in Hayes County, Nebraska / by Robert D. Clark. -- 1st ed.
p. cm.
Includes bibliographical references.
ISBN 0-934988-36-6 (alk. paper)
1. Clark, Warren, 1854-1918. 2. Clark, Ada Harris, 1859-1939. 3. Farmers--Nebraska--Hayes County--Biography. 4. Farm life--Nebraska--Hayes County. 5. Hayes County (Neb.)--Social life and customs. 6. Hayes County (Neb.)--Biography. I. Title.
F672.H4C58 1996
978.2'832031'092--dc20 96-3388
CIP

First Edition
Most recent printing indicated by the first digit below.
1 2 3 4 5 6 7 8 9 10

The paper used in this publication meets the minimum requirements of American National Standard for Information Sciences - Permanence of Paper for Printed Library Materials, ANSI Z39.489-1984. ∞

# Contents

To
Mildred Clark Richter
and in memory of
Opal Routh Clark
and
Leah Rodgers Hidy
Daughter and Granddaughters
of
Homesteaders

# INTRODUCTION

The argument over what to do with America's Great Plains west of the 100th meridian is as vigorous today as it was more than a hundred years ago. John Wesley Powell in his *Lands of the Arid Region* urged they be classified as marginal, not suited for agricultural development on the small homesteads of 160 acres authorized by Congress. He proposed they be reserved for grazing and (except for isolated plots that could be irrigated) be allocated to settlers in large tracts of 2560 acres each. Powell lost the argument and in the 1880s settlers poured across the meridian by the tens of thousands.

After a century of alternating promise and failure, good years and drought, successful dry land farming techniques but declining population, questions again arise: Should the plains have been settled? Ought they now be abandoned? Frank and Deborah Popper, land planning experts from Rutgers University, argue that the plains be returned to the primitive state, that they become a vast "Buffalo Commons." Environmentalists applaud. People who live in the area are understandably upset, angry. And some modern scholars believe that Powell was wrong, that the plains, with techniques of dryland farming, have proved suitable for agriculture. The debate is joined.

The story of Warren and Ada Clark does not answer the questions. But it does tell why one young couple, upstate New Yorkers, enlisted in the horde of land seekers and in 1885, at the height of what Nebraska historian, Addison Sheldon, called the great immigration, crossed the 100th meridian to find a homestead in Hayes County, Nebraska.

Warren and Ada were humble people whose lives, like those of their friends and neighbors, would ordinarily occasion neglect, even in our day of concern with social and family history. The neglect is all the more reason to write about them. Fortunately, enough information is available from diaries, bits of journals, an occasional letter, notes from local newspapers, reminiscences, to recreate the kind of daily life they lived in their youth, something of their courtship, of the routine business of their lives as a young married couple in New York, as tenant farmers in Iowa, and as homesteaders in western Nebraska. And to raise questions as to why they left New York, or Iowa. And why they elected to homestead in southwest Nebraska, on the very edge of what they had learned as school children, was the Great American Desert. And what, then, of their fate?

The story is not one of high adventure or dramatic incident, but it is full of drama, nonetheless, sometimes moving and poignant. The narrative is faithful to the facts, allowing them to reveal the inherent drama, sometimes in description or event, or, as in the lone tree, in a natural phenomenon that had powerful emotional significance for Ada, in her early years and in her old age. The diaries, newspapers, and government records make it possible to keep the story contemporary--to allow the people to anticipate the rain, and rejoice, or gloat, when it comes, to keep their hopes high, for they do not know that the inevitable drought is inevitable. The events of their lives are so interwoven with the events of the community that to tell their story is to tell the story of Methodist Ridge, of Hayes County, Nebraska, and of homesteading on the plains, all without losing Warren and Ada in the larger narrative.

To read the account of their early and happy years in New York is to wonder why they ever moved west, why they did not remain in their native communities. The answer lies in the fact that their lives were influenced, indeed, were directed, by the great intellectual and mythological ideas of their century: Jefferson's dream of the yeoman on his farm and the manifest destiny of the nation in the farmers' settlement of the West. And the far more powerful myth of the arid plains of the West, that the rain follows the plow, increases with the planting of trees and the sowing of crops.

Warren and Ada faced the problem that had confronted their grandparents: the land had been divided among the sons until there was no more available for the new generation. They had, like their forebears, to move to the frontier. Everywhere in the West, in Iowa first and then in Nebraska, they saw the transformation of that frontier into the new settled community. And in the first years in Nebraska the myth of the rain and the plow became reality--a causal relationship argued with simple eloquence and persistence by the editor of the county newspaper. The rains fell and the future looked good, despite low prices and the slow conversion of plain to field. Even after the first dry year their faith, faltering only momentarily, was quickened by the wettest year on record. Then came the drought and the anguish, not only over the loss of crops, but over becoming objects of charity, of state aid with required affidavits of need.

They were sustained by the institutions they brought with them from New York: family, neighbors, school, literary society, picnics, 4th of July celebrations, the church, all of which nurtured the sense of community, gave stability to their children and strength to themselves in troubled times. New Yorkers, bred in a land of hills and trees, perennial sufferers from drought in the West, they never lost their love of New York, and in their old age reaffirmed that love in a nostalgic visit. Perhaps surprisingly, they also came to love the plains, to find that the values they had learned in New York and held most deeply were bound inextricably with the land in the West and the years they had lived on it. They survived longer than most first settlers, never quite gave up their dream, held on to their faith and, if nothing more, bequeathed that faith to their children.

Typically the record contains more about Warren and the enterprise of farming than about Ada. But her presence is always there in fragments about her activities and her support of the family, not only as a housewife and mother and occasional worker in the field, but also as entrepreneur. Her commercial ventures extended beyond chickens and eggs to soap making and rug weaving. Far from being reluctant to leave her paternal home, which she held in great affection, she was at least equal with Warren and perhaps the stronger influence, in the decisions to go to Iowa and to Nebraska. It was she, in little but dramatic incidents and simple language, who articulated the love for the plains that both of them came to feel.

## Acknowledgments

My collection of information for this story began many years ago, when I was able to enlist the aid of several family members and neighbors now deceased. I recognize their contribution for the benefit of their families and friends. For an understanding of the New York years, I owe much to Venila De Stephen of Oswego, to John and Sadie Harris of Camden, and to Ada May (Mrs. Adolph) Hering of Cleveland, Ohio, all now deceased. Venila and her husband, James, not only served as hosts to me and my wife but transported us to points of interest in Oswego County, including, with John Harris, Williamstown and the Stone Hill site of the Harris farmstead. Venila, John, and Ada May, nieces and nephew of Ada Clark, reminisced about their early years, gave me access to family records, and Ada May sent photographs and loaned me her out-of-print and rare copy of the Onderdonk genealogy.

For aid in a search that ranged from gathering facts about the early history of Blackwood to an understanding of the way of life of the settlers on the plains, I am indebted to the children and grandchildren not only of Warren and Ada but also to those of their former neighbors. At my request the late Nellie Clark Rodgers, the Clarks' oldest daughter, wrote her reminiscences of homesteading days. Mary Clark Rodgers, also now deceased, added interesting details to them. Arley Clark, the youngest of the children but then in his old age, responded in detail to my many questions about his parents in the years after they left the homestead. Mildred Clark Richter and her late husband, Homer, who for many years lived in Blackwood, Hayes County, not far from the Clark homestead, answered my unending questions about people, places, and ways of the settlers and sought the answers from others when they themselves did not know. As if that were not enough to try their spirits, they were hosts to me for weeks that grew into months while I searched the records in Hayes Center. The late Leah Rodgers Hidy of Culbertson, daughter of Nellie, told me much about the early community, sought information for me from her friends, from county records, and local newspapers. J. Clayton Clark of Alhambra, California, former resident of Hayes County, also provided useful information about people and the customs of farm life. Mildred and Homer, Leah, and Clayton all read parts or most of the manuscript and offered useful suggestions. William and Glora Clark were hosts to me while I searched the holdings of the High Plains Historical Society in McCook. The late Ray Craw and Peggy French, grandchildren who knew Ada intimately in the years after the homestead, contributed much to my understanding of her as a person. The late Wiley Jewel gave me information from his family records and allowed me to have prints made from his photographs. James Wesley Clark, Arley Clark, Jr., Opal Clark Dean and others contributed information that I sought.

Many friends of the family assisted me. Among them were the late Willard (Bud) McMullen. At ninety-one years of age he cheerfully answered my many questions about a family he knew well and accompanied me to Methodist Ridge to identify the location of sod houses of the homesteaders, the school, the grange, the church, all of them now reduced to the earth from which they had been constructed. Also helpful were Mrs. Glen Scott, Mrs. Archie Gruver, Mrs. Fred Wittwer, Charles Mansfield, all now deceased, and Donald Fagerstone, Robert Korell and Van Korell. Alice Lindekugel, former editor of the *Times-Republican*, not only made available to me her file of the *Republican* and *Times* for those early years, but also provided a space in her office for me to work. Several county officers assisted me in my search for information in the public records: clerks–the late William Fowler, Joan Herald Lauenroth, and Irene Gerih; treasurer Stan Rucker, and County Agent Mick Helberg, all in Hayes County and members of the clerk's staff in Lincoln County, North Platte, and Gosper County, Elwood.

Wendell Tripp, editor of *New York History*, kindly gave me permission to reprint from the January, 1985, issue of that journal, the major portion of a paper on Ada Clark. To the several libraries whose collections I have consulted, I am grateful both for the useful materials and the generous assistance of staff, namely: State University of New York College at Oswego, the University of Nebraska, the High Plains Historical Society, McCook, Nebraska, the Onawa, Iowa, Public Library, the New York Public Library and the Library of Congress. The rich collection of local materials at the Nebraska State Historical Society Library, Lincoln, was indispensable. I relied constantly on the excellent collection of Western materials at the Knight Library, University of Oregon, and upon the imaginative and persistent pursuit of publications by the Inter-Library Loan Librarian, Joanne Halgren.

I am much indebted to Lawrence B. Lee, Professor Emeritus of San Jose, California, State University and specialist in United States public land policy and to Frances Lee, well-schooled in critical review of writings in Western American history, for reading and commenting on the manuscript. I cannot in a word express my appreciation to Earl Pomeroy of the University of Oregon. Over the years we have had, for me, illuminating discussions on many topics, including history of the American West. In addition he read the entire manuscript and made helpful comments ranging from matters of fact and style to basic interpretation. I do not, of course, hold Professors Lee and Pomeroy responsible for views and interpretations from which they may dissent.

Lastly, I thank the late Opal Routh Clark for her interest in the project. She accompanied me in my search for materials, read documents, took notes for me and read the narrative with critical eye.

# PROLOGUE

Warren and Ada Clark were New Yorkers from upstate Oswego County, born on farms, he in Orwell in 1854, she in Amboy, near Williamstown, in 1859.[1] They kept diaries, she irregularly in her teens until she was married and again in her old age, he quite faithfully from his 20th year in 1874 until they moved to Nebraska in 1885 and then again, briefly, for nearly three years, beginning in 1888. The entries are brief, terse, with almost no expression of emotion, personal opinion, or judgment. They tell where they were, what they did, whom they saw and, without fail, what the weather was like. Together with the public and family records and the extant newspapers for the period, they provide the structure and the details to reconstruct something of the world in which they lived.[2]

Warren's Uncle Jabez, his father Chauncey's oldest brother, was the first of the Clarks to move to Oswego County, in 1842, from the family home in the southern tip of Oneida County. His brothers James, Austin and Chauncey, and their sister Emma and, perhaps, their parents followed before 1850. Chauncey, 25-years-old in 1853, met, courted, and married Alma Greenwood whose parents lived at nearby Sandy Creek but were about to move to Boylston, north and east of Orwell. Alma's father Henry was a Vermonter; her mother Susan, a native of Onondaga County, New York, but they had moved to Oswego County by 1833 when Alma was born.[3]

In 1855 Chauncey, Alma and their infant son Warren lived with Austin and his family. By 1860 he had purchased a small farm of his own for which he paid $350. It was valued at $1,000 and was about a mile from Jabez's place, some three miles southeast of the village of Orwell Corners. The land was rugged. Towards Orwell Corners, Shatagee Hill (Chateaugay), one of the highest points in the county, rose a thousand feet above Lake Ontario, less than 10 miles to the west. A mile or so to the south the Salmon River cut an irregular course through the rough terrain. With a mighty roar it dropped 110 feet to the rocky chasm below. The hills were covered with trees and tall Shatagee was covered to its very crest with pine, hemlock, spruce, beech, maple, birch, and basswood (linden). The settlers had cleared the lower hills and valleys for their tiny fields, orchards and meadows. Warren began his studies in a little schoolhouse not far from his home where a neighboring farmer's son, Hubert West, later a farmer himself, was one of his first teachers. No doubt in the summers he fished for speckled trout in the creek that ran southward through his neighbor's field or he may have hiked along the dusty Orwell road to his Uncle Jabez's. His cousins Norris and Zetto were older than he but going to see them was something for a boy to do.[4]

Chauncey, a part-time farmer, was a sailor in the summer months on the Great Lakes. In 1866, to relieve the loneliness of his wife when he was at sea, he purchased a place of 50 acres in Boylston near the farms of Alma's parents and her brother Walter. That must have pleased Alma and suited Chauncey too. He was not much of a farmer. He had 10 acres of woods, only four or five acres under cultivation, 15 in meadow and the rest unimproved. But the farm was large enough for subsistence and it had a comfortable frame house. In 1875 the family had two pigs, two horses, four sheep, four cows, probably some chickens--not too much for Alma and their three young daughters to manage with help at critical times from Warren and Alma's brother Walter. Chauncey no doubt expected to earn enough from his summer wages to pay off his mortgage and purchase necessary supplies. In the winter he could sit by the roaring fire and sing to his children the rollicking songs of the sea that Warren, at least, loved and would never forget.[5]

Ada's moderately successful father, Nathaniel Harris, owned a farm of 150 acres which, in 1875, he valued at $3000. Twenty acres were under cultivation, 25 in pasture, 15 in meadow (hay), the rest in woodland. He had a two-story white-painted frame house, a spacious red barn, an orchard, horses, cattle, sheep, pigs, chickens and bees, stock he considered worth

$1000. For the market he produced meat and wool, butter and honey, hay, tanbark and basswood from which barrels and tubs were manufactured. He owned a buggy and a cutter and an adequate supply of tools and machinery. His father, Daniel Harris, in his youth a school teacher, had moved with his wife and three children from Massachusetts to Amboy in 1832. He bought a tract of land, cleared a spot in the wilderness and built a log house. There Nathaniel was born a few months later. In Ada's youth the log house still stood, a couple of hundred yards uphill from the big frame house.[6]

Nathaniel grew up on his father's farm. He was still at home in 1855 when he was 23, but he soon acquired a farm of his own, adjacent to his father's--probably a part of it, for his father had died a year or two earlier. In 1858 he built his frame house and married Amelia Jane Onderdonk. They were both 25-years-old.[7]

Amelia Jane's father, John, and her grandfather, Roelof, had moved their families from Rockland County, New York, to Amboy in May, 1832, shortly before the Harrises arrived. They had settled a mile and a half down the road toward Williamstown. Nathaniel and Amelia Jane grew up in the same neighborhood, may have attended the same school, probably the same church, the Presbyterian in Williamstown, certainly traded for goods in the same stores in the village, but they belonged to different communities of neighbors and relatives. Amelia Jane in a brief history of her family gives no intimation that they were friends or even acquaintances until, after an extended visit to Rockland County and New York City, she returned to Amboy in 1857, a few months before she and Nathaniel were married. Her forebears were chiefly Dutch, Onderdonks and Van Houtens. She could trace her lineage back to her great grandfather, Nicholas Van Houten, who had been baptized in the old Reformed Dutch Church at Tappan. Had she possessed at the time of her writing the records she acquired in later years, she could have followed the line back to the very beginnings of the Dutch colony in New Amsterdam.[8]

Nathaniel's farm was on a gently sloping hillside, chopped out of the woods, good loam intermingled with rocks and small boulders. They called the little community of closely spaced houses and farms Stone Hill. The route to Williamstown village, three and one-half miles away, they called Stone Hill Road. The whole countryside was still heavily wooded, broken only by the small plots of cultivated fields, meadows and homesites. Ada in her diary had no word for a natural setting that was far too familiar and commonplace to provoke her interest. But 35 years after she had gone from home and returned with Warren to the village for a visit, she was overwhelmed with nostalgia. Revived were memories of the brook that ran by her house, the peppermint that grew along its bank, the wintergreen and the ferns, the moss on the trees, the boulders, the sweetbriar bush near the house, the dooryard fence, the white-cheeked little chickadee with his black bib, flitting from bush to bush, the great rock walls that her father and his brother, Uncle Horatio, had built along the road that separated their farms, the piles of rock in the fields, the orchard once ripe with apples, now unkempt, its fertility reduced to a few "nerly" apples, the gentle sweep of Pa's woodland up the hill and the beauty of the hardwood trees in the fall "after the frosts have tinted them." Down the hill at the corner by the schoolhouse she remembered the great elm that spread its branches over the field and the road. Like Warren's home in Orwell, it was a good place for a child.[9]

Warren's Uncle Jabez was an officer in the Methodist church in Orwell. His father, Chauncey, appeared to be friendly toward the church, but not especially devout. His grandparents, the Greenwoods, and probably his mother, were Protestant Methodists, a reformist group that had abolished the episcopacy with its strict rule by the bishops, but remained Methodist in doctrine, form of worship, and rules of conduct. Warren, converted in one of their meetings after he had moved to Boylston, had been baptized in a creek near his home. But the community at Boylston was remote, the adherents few and preaching services infrequent. Warren spent most of his Sundays at the house, loafing, writing letters, visiting a neighbor, now and then hunting or, infrequently when the weather made it necessary, doing a little work in the field.[10]

Ada and her family belonged to the Methodist society in Williamstown. They were strict in attendance at preaching services in the village church and they went to Sunday school on Sunday afternoon and prayer meetings on Wednesday evening when they were held in the schoolhouse at Stone Hill. At family worship her father or sometimes her mother read from the Bible and they all knelt in prayer. Nathaniel had been converted in a Methodist revival when he was 22. He joined the church and was now a pillar and a leader in the Williamstown congregation and would remain so all of his life. "Ma," Amelia Jane, had come out of and was strongly conscious of the traditions of the Reformed Dutch Church. Her grandfather, Roeloff Onderdonk, had joined the Presbyterians and was counted a "staunch" member. It is likely that the whole family belonged to the Presbyterian Church in Williamstown. But Amelia Jane drew her religious sustenance less from the austerity of Calvinism than from the more gentle tradition of the Dutch pietism of Rockland County. Both the Van Houtens and the Onderdonks had come under the ministration of the devout Guilliam Bertholf at Tappan in the 1690s and early 1700s. Both families had passed their faith and practices of devotion along from generation to generation, undiminished one would judge from the intensity with which it burned in Amelia Jane's father and mother and in Amelia Jane herself. She had been converted in a Baptist meeting in New York City but after marriage she went with Nathaniel to the Methodists. Ada was to emulate her mother in adherence to the faith, in her iron will and in the direction she would give to her own children's faith. But all of that is in the remote future.[11]

# 1.
# Ada Harris, Teenager

Ada Harris was thirteen-years-old in January, 1873, seven months from her fourteenth birthday in late July, when she began to post the first of her few diaries that have come down to us. The winter term was in session at the little schoolhouse that stood at the foot of the hill, a quarter of a mile--three city blocks--from her home. She was an indifferent pupil, writing happily in her diary on January 16, "I do not go to school now, I am helping Ma get the sewing done." Indeed, from the first posting in her diary on January 9 to the end of the month, she went to school only twice. She was quite regular in February except for three days when a great storm blocked the roads and forced the closing of the school. And she was present on March 4, the last day of the winter term, when "every scholar was there."[1]

Ada took no note of what she studied but one day in mid-January she wrote that she had learned "to play penny." On February 14 she noted that Allie (Albert) Laing was in school and that she had "some fun" with him over the exchange of valentines. Months later, in the fall term, she recorded that her "per senteage" for the morning was 40 and for the afternoon was likewise 40. She did not indicate the percentage of what (it might well have been spelling!) nor in boldly exhibiting the score did she reflect any sense of remorse or pain.

If she was indifferent in the classroom, it was not so in the kitchen or at her household jobs. She baked "cuckies," bread, apple pies (which she thought hard work because she had to cut up the apples). She sometimes spent the whole day in the "citchen." In season she made raspberry jell, blackberry preserves, sweet apple pickles, and she helped to boil, strain and "sugar off" the sap from the maple trees, a big job that spring. It was the biggest they had ever had because Pa tapped eighty or ninety trees. On Mondays she helped her mother wash, bending over a washboard and tub, more often than not doing the white clothes while her mother washed the rest. Saturday was cleaning day. Scarcely a Saturday went by that she did not sweep and clean or do the mopping ("moping" she always wrote it). Like her Dutch mother she had then, and through her long life, that disposition toward cleanliness through scrub water that prompted Irving's Diedrich Knickerbocker to say that Dutch women had webbed fingers.

She ironed; she knitted stockings and a pair of woolen cuffs for her young cousin, Henry Black; she churned; one day she and her mother dipped 351 candles; she and Ma papered Grandma's room and the "front room" (parlor). She smoked the meat, helped her mother render lard and make soap; now and then she was secretary to her father, writing his letters for him. She worked in the family garden and might even be pressed into helping her father in the field. On April 22, she and her brothers, Albert and Jesse, sent to the Briggs mail-order house for vegetable and flower seeds which they received promptly on April 30.[2] A few days later Ada sowed her vegetables "and all my posy seeds." She weeded, transplanted flowers; she cut and dropped potatoes for her widowed Aunt Charlotte, pausing to sit on the fence to rest and post her diary. She picked strawberries when they were ripe, raspberries and blackberries. She and Albert picked eight quarts of blackberries one morning.

Twice her father drafted her to rake hay in the meadow, once to "mow" it in the barn, and one afternoon he sent her to the field to help his small crew rake oats. Once, at least, she milked a cow. And one morning in the fall she drove horses and sawed wood--for three hours, she said, as if that amount of time in doing a man's work was unusual and significant. She seemed happy enough in what she did, indoors or out, not resentful or put upon, a little proud of doing grown-up work.

She was not always serious, by no means a slave to her work. Only thirteen, she was sometimes a child in her delight in simple things or a giggling adolescent or a young woman heartbroken in her fantasies of love. She was already fourteen when her Aunt Clit (Calista), visiting from north Williamstown, gave her a pipe to blow bubbles, but she was delighted. She was excited when her mother bought her the goods for a new green dress--fourteen yards at thirty-five cents a yard--and happy again a few days later when her mother bought ribbon for the dress, but she was piqued or playfully indignant, "just as mad as I can be at Ale Carley," her cousin, because "Ma finished her a calico dress" before she made Ada's. When Henry, whose last name she knew too well to record, walked her home from school, she was undoubtedly more pleased than annoyed by three younger girls, all cousins of hers, who followed them and "yelled at us all the way."

She wrote and received notes and letters without number, some to relatives in distant villages and states, but many to her school friends in the neighborhood. She engaged and trusted her brothers or cousins or friends or even her parents to deliver her notes and bring back the replies. How else could a teenage girl maintain intimate communication with her friends in an era that had not yet invented the telephone? She wrote to her cousins and aunts—Retta Onderdonk at Cohoes, Vira Secor in Pennsylvania, Aunt Jane Clemons somewhere out in the West—and even to her mother's brother, Adolphus Onderdonk in Iowa. She counted it an event worth acknowledging when she received a new "led" pencil and a box with "lots of paper" and envelopes.

At thirteen she looked upon the church as the dominant force in the world external to her family. In the day-to-day postings in her diary she sought no word to express her faith, none to admonish herself, none to register remorse or hope. She was singularly free from moralisms. But the church was there, a mighty presence that had to be accounted for. Every Sunday she recorded who had gone to "meeting" and often who had not. Only stormy weather kept them all at home: "it snows and blows terrible auffle," she wrote of one of those days. But the meeting was an event, nonetheless, and must be recorded even though they missed it.

Frequently Grandma Onderdonk, who was eighty-years-old on February 27, could not go out into the cold. Often it was Ada who stayed at home with her. Late in the summer, after she had gone to church one Sunday morning, she noted it was the first time she had been to Sabbath school in seven weeks, the first time to church in ten weeks. If the absences reflected a bit of youthful rebellion and a touch of pride in the naughtiness, it was an easily tamed, short-lived rebellion in one whose exuberant youth was to pass quickly and whose life was to be more than commonly devout.

Stone Hill was a congenial setting for the activities of the young, a tightly knit community of fifteen or twenty families, their houses close together, the relationships interdependent and supportive. Uncle Horatio Harris and Aunt Lydia, with Grandma Harris and the children, lived across the road and a short distance up the hill. Stone walls bordering the lane marked the property line between the two places. Aunt Kate Foil and her family lived over the hill, the other aunts and their children down the hill toward Williamstown.[3] Few days passed when some of the Harrises were not at their neighbors or the neighbors at the Harrises. Ada's best friend was Nellie Wilson. They visited each other frequently, walked to school and into the country, indulged in girl talk without end and sat up one night at Ada's house and heard the clock strike one before they went to sleep--which for thirteen and fourteen-year-olds was late enough considering the early hour they were expected to get up.

That the mothers of Stone Hill knew where their daughters were is apparent from a small incident. Ada went frequently to the houses of her friends, most often to Nellie Wilson's and Nellie frequently to hers, always one might judge, from the casual entry in the diary, as free agents, young women who came and went as they chose. But one afternoon when Nellie came to see her they chatted happily together with far too little time to get their business done before the afternoon was suddenly gone. Ada asked Nellie to stay all night. Nellie hadn't made the proper arrangements at home, so Ada dispatched her brother, Allie, to seek the necessary permission. He soon returned with the cryptic report that "her Ma said all right."

Occasionally Ada and Nellie joined with other "young folks" to spend the evening at each other's houses, parties that the record suggests were more spontaneous than planned. In February they went to the Stones, six of them, eight counting Mary and Warren in whose house they gathered. Ada and Nellie were the youngest among them, the others appreciably older.[4] A month later a dozen of them trooped down to the widow Godfrey's. It was the close of the winter term of school and they had come to bid farewell to the teacher, Kate Belden, who boarded there. Although it was Monday night they did not get home until twelve o'clock. It was no doubt less a disposition to be precise than a touch of vanity in being grown up that prompted Ada to be exact about the lateness of the hour on this and other occasions. In April when Retta came home from Cohoes, laid off from her job for a few weeks, the young people found new reasons for parties and they added to their number Louis Stone, who was twenty-three and interested in Retta, and his brother Frank, twenty.[5]

On the Fourth of July Ada had a "cousin party" at her home with the Harrises, the Smiths, the Carleys and the Foils. There were fourteen of them, counting Ada and her two brothers, ranging in age from ten to eighteen, there for fun in the afternoon and supper at night. She gives no hint of what games they played that afternoon or at any of their parties, but they were Methodists, or most of them were, so they certainly did not dance. Once when Ada was not included in the group--her family required her to go to meeting--she wrote a bit mournfully: "all the young folks but me went to Cornelia's exabition [sic] tonight."

With all her socializing, Ada did not go out with boys. She had several admirers, all of them three or four years older than she, boys who walked her home from school or meeting, called at her house or paired off with her at the parties. But when Nellie Wilson wrote her a letter to suggest they go out with boys, she said no. She declined, too, when her cousin Francis Carley, who was eighteen, asked her to go to meeting with him. She noted in her diary that "Francis came near geting [sic] killed." We don't know what she meant. She may have referred to a near accident and her not having gone with him as an act of Providence. Or, in the exaggerated rhetoric of a teenager, she may have alluded to her impulse to do violence in response to an unwanted invitation. But when Widow Godfrey's son, Willie, who was also eighteen, came to call and lingered to talk, she was delighted.

She was certainly romantically inclined, enraptured by the new moon and by a rainbow after a storm. When she was moody she liked to walk in the woods--she went twice one day when her parents were gone and she was "lonesome." When Willie Godfrey's sister Martha and Mary Stone's brother Frank were married, Ada recorded the event in capital letters printed across the top of two pages of her diary. She was pleased the next day when they sent over a piece of wedding cake and delighted--no doubt with the whispering and giggling delight of a schoolgirl--on the following Sunday when "the bride and the bridegroom" came to meeting.

More than romantic, she was the universal teenager, languishing in thoughts of death and sentiments of love. In March she composed and entered on the back pages of her diary a dirge to a dead maiden:

> Let the dead and the beautiful rest
> Let her sleep neath the willow by the stream
> And the windharps do whisper o'er her grave
> Like the songs of angels in her dream.

Two months later she wrote about the twilight, the song of birds, and the love of the young:

> O meet me when daylight is fading
> And darkening into the night
> When the snowbirds are singing their vespers
> And the stars have far vanished from sight.
>
> And then we will meet [in a land]
> Far away from the pressing throng
> And whisper of love to each other
> When we hear the first whippoorwill song.

To make it quite clear that these were her own compositions, whatever sentiment or phrase she may have borrowed, she noted on the margin of the first, "March 4 I wrote these verses." And on the second, after trying and rejecting some lines, she carefully dated the completed poem May 9.

In June Aunt Betsey and Uncle Nicholas Van Houten from Rockland County came to see Grandma Onderdonk and Amelia Jane. Grandma's mother had been a Van Houten. Uncle Nicholas was her favorite and the chief family tie to the Dutch ancestry.[6] Ma and Pa and Ada met them at the depot and Aunt Betsey gave Ada a two-shilling silver piece and a pair of earrings. They stayed only three days, long enough to visit with the family and for Pa to take them, with Ma and Grandma, on a one-day trip to Uncle Porter's.

On July 5, three weeks before Ada's fourteenth birthday, she and Pa, Ma, Albert, and Jesse went to the village and "had our likenesses taken." How delighted we would be to have a copy of those likenesses, the family portrait with father, mother and the three children in their Sunday best, posed stiffly in the manner of the times. If Ada had reached her full growth, she would have been only five feet, one inch tall, perhaps already inclined toward the plumpness that characterized her four years later when she sat for her wedding picture. She had, to judge from the wedding photograph, a pleasant oval face, a high forehead, a nose slightly prominent, her hair dark, her hazel eyes too light to be brown, too dark to be green. With her pleasure in ribbons, she may have had one or more attached to her hair or dress and been wearing ear-drops, perhaps the ones Aunt Betsey had given her.

Aunt Jane Clemons and her daughter Mary, who had once lived in Amboy, came for a visit in August,[7] from their home in Wisconsin. "West Consin," Ada wrote in her diary, not very clear about her geography or distant place names. Pa was kept busy the entire week she was there, taking her and Mary, Ma and Grandma to see the old neighbors, all-day or half-day visits. One day Pa took them to Uncle Porter's. Mary Stone came to spend the afternoon with Ada and because of a heavy rain stayed overnight. Monday Pa and Ada took them to catch "the cars," probably for Rockland County. Willie Godfrey rode home from the depot with Pa and Ada.

With all the guests to entertain, Pa scarcely had time to do his summer's work, but Aunt Jane had been gone only a week when he, Ma, and Grandma took the train for Mill City, Pennsylvania, to see Aunt Eleanor Secor, Ma's sister and Grandma's daughter. Willie Godfrey drove them to the depot and Ada went along to see them off. Left at home, she managed the household and supervised the boys but neglected her diary. In her parents' absence she posted only one entry, noting Jennie Laing's eleventh birthday. Pa and Ma returned in ten days and Ada renewed the methodical record of events.

In the course of the year Ada began to learn the meaning of death and grief. She set out one summer morning to find a ride to the village. She and Ma were papering the upstairs and they needed more wallpaper. She walked down to the Stones' and the Ellis's and others, trying to find someone who was going to the village, but everyone, like her own Pa, was busy at home. She decided to walk. The village was three and a half miles away. She bought the wallpaper but before she could start home rain began to fall. She went to the house of a family she knew at the church, the Grants, whose daughters, Gene and Adellie, were friends of hers. More than that, she wanted to see Mrs. Grant who was reported to be quite ill. When she was ready to go, one of the boys, Adam, borrowed a horse and buggy from Mr. Hunter, the Methodist preacher, and drove her home. The next day Mrs. Grant died from cancer, leaving her husband and ten children. Unbelieving, Ada wrote, "I called on her Wednesday." Pa and Ma went to the funeral. They usually went to funerals and Grandma with them, but Ada almost never went. She did make a record of the deaths in the neighborhood--Mrs. John Chase, fifty-eight, who had been sick about a week; Mr. Brown, who died of the dropsy (now known as "edema"--an excessive accumulation of fluids in body tissues, most often from pneumonia or from a heart disorder); Mrs. Brewer, who also died of dropsy; Mrs. George Wickes; Jennie Albee; and Mr. Crawford, husband of one of Grandma's friends, who was taken with seizures--"fits," Ada wrote--forty the first day, over a hundred by the next afternoon before he died.

Ada went to the funeral when Allie and Jennie Laing's mother died. She was sometimes put out with Allie, as she had been when he came to her house "for something or nothing," stayed for dinner and was there "all day most." But she had been sympathetic when he cut his knee with a wood saw and a few days later entered a note of concern when the knee was worse. She quickly forgot any annoyance she might have felt in her greater concern for Mrs. Laing when she was suddenly "taken sick." She survived only two days and died at the early age of thirty-four years. Pa and Ada and Nellie Wilson went to the funeral. Allie "felt so bad," was so desolated by the loss of his mother, that he begged Ada and Nellie to go home with him after the burial service. They did, offering what comfort they could, more by being there, one must suppose, than by the conventional words they had scarcely learned to say. That evening one of the family took the girls home.

Retta came home again in October, just before Mrs. Laing died. Uncle Arthur, Ma's brother, came on the same day. Arthur was a veteran of the Civil War, a wanderer and a gentle outlaw, the object of his mother's prayers because he smoked and was not "saved."[8] But all of them liked him and welcomed him on his periodic visits. Ada addressed him as "Uncle," but conventional manners did not inhibit her good fun and boisterous play when he had his forty-second birthday, two days after his arrival. Ada and Retta, not about to let the event go unnoticed or uncelebrated, seized him and "whipped" him, working together, each administering the ritualistic spanking.

Uncle Arthur had scarcely joined the family group before Grandma, his and Ma's mother, came down with "a hard cold." That was Friday, October 10, the day Mrs. Laing was taken ill. One can judge from Ada's entries that the whole family worried about Grandma. All of the aunts, many of the neighbors, and Mr. Hunter, the Methodist preacher, came to see her. The doctor said she had "inflammation on the lungs." She was slightly better by Thursday. For three weeks she gained, grew worse, gained again, worsened. They sat up with her in shifts, Ada and Retta one night until 3:30 A.M. when they called Uncle Arthur, Sarah Comstock and Ada all night, Nellie Smith and Ada until one o'clock, Pa until three, Uncle Arthur until morning, Retta more often than the others, Aunt Sarah all night, Ada, Nellie Wilson and Allie Laing until four o'clock, neighbor women all night for several nights, then Mary Stone and Ada until 2:30 A.M., Pa until morning. By the first week in November Grandma, with only brief relapses, began to gain steadily. Retta had already returned to work at the factory; Uncle Arthur went on to his next stop. Ada and Pa then took turns spending the whole night in Grandma's room, sleeping on the floor or on the couch and rousing to keep the fire going. Six weeks after the beginning of her illness, Grandma was up and around and the household back to the routine of daily chores.

The year wound down, the last weeks scarcely less crowded with events than those of the summer and fall. Ada went back to school, attending irregularly, as other events permitted. As soon as Grandma was well enough, she and Albert drove over to see Aunt Julia Onderdonk and Ma's cousins in Oneida County. It was late in the year, the last of November, but Pa trusted Albert and no doubt depended upon Ada to share in the judgment of what to do if they were caught in a storm. He gave them two horses and, presumably, the sleigh, and they set out for Blossvale, twenty-three miles away. They stopped at Camden for three-quarters of an hour, probably to see Ann Onderdonk Mott, Aunt Julia's daughter, and then drove on to Blossvale. They had been four hours on the road, Ada said, not counting the time in Camden. The next morning it was snowing and blowing "very hard," a "ruff day." They had breakfast, spent the morning, had dinner at noon with Justus Onderdonk--Ma's cousin and Aunt Julia's son--and his wife Amanda, and returned to Aunt Julia's for tea in the afternoon. They again stayed overnight, breakfasted, and started home. It was a little warmer, Ada noted, but cold enough so that they stopped to warm up in McConnellsville, five miles on the way, and again at Camden after another five or six miles. They got home at "most 3 o'clock." They had seen no "sights," had no adventures, and evidently had not even found a cousin worth mentioning, even though Ann had a boy, ten, and Justus had two small boys, five and one.[9] But they had a wonderful time playing "grown-up," facing the open road on cold November days and visiting their mother's cousins without the supervision of their parents.

The next week Ada went to school every day. The weather warmed up and the snow began to thaw rapidly. Thursday, water flowed across the road in two places. Ada and probably her brothers and cousins--or others who constituted the "we!"--had "lots of fun" on the bridge by the elm tree close to the schoolhouse. The water was so high that the bridge floated and the children ran delightedly from one side to the other, balancing on the teetering platform and peering down into the angry waters. Fortunately the moorings held. By the next day the thawing flood had drained off, the waters were contained in the creek, and the bridge had settled back on its pilings.

On that Friday Pa "bootchered" Ada's old cow, but with a farm girl's stoicism she recorded no grief or recrimination. Sunday she "wrote off" some "fortune telling" predictions for Nellie Wilson--which she must have copied from a magazine or booklet that had come into her hands. She was in and out of school for the next two weeks. On Tuesday Pa took her, Nellie Wilson, Albert and Jesse to a Sunday school convention in the village. The snow had melted, the road was bare and they had to go in the wagon, which seemed strange to her for a winter's day.

On December 24 Ada went to the village to see Adellie Grant whose mother had died tragically in the summer. That evening they attended the Christmas tree entertainment at the

Presbyterian church. Nellie and Cora Wilson were there but Ada, having arranged to stay overnight with the Hunter family at the Methodist parsonage, did not go home with them. Pa came for her the next morning, Christmas day. Some families in Williamstown no doubt celebrated Christmas with gifts for children, parties and dinners. But not the Harrises. Like many Methodists and other religious folk they might have thought such celebrations secular or pagan. They had no Santa Claus, or Christmas tree; they did not give gifts. They did not set aside the day fc. religious exercises.[10]

But the Harris children got together and the austerity of the parents did not prevent them from having a hilarious time, clearly the most fun Ada had all year. She and Albert and their cousins Charlie, Ella, Cora, and Henry Harris went over the hill to Aunt Kate Foil's. It was the fourteenth birthday of Willie Foil, Aunt Kate's nephew. The children went sledding on a hill near the house and rode downhill "most all evening." Giving way to the physical energy and exuberant spirit of the young, they got into a great snowball fight. Since it was Willie's birthday, they turned on him and had, Ada said, "lots of fun... whiping [sic] him." It must have been moonlight. They did not get home until eleven o'clock.

Saturday, December 27, Uncle Porter and Aunt Clit came down from north Williamstown. On Monday Ada had a very considerable fright. She and Ma had washed the clothes in the morning. Aunt Clit, Aunt Lydia, and Grandma Harris came over to visit in the afternoon. Suddenly at 4 o'clock Ma fainted. "We were all scart," Ada wrote. She found one of the boys in the dooryard and sent him to the woods for Pa in a hurry. Ma came to and said she was sick to her stomach. She was better the next morning but Ada got breakfast. Tuesday was "auffle," the wind blew and it snowed part of the time so that "you could hardly see the barn." Aunt Clit and Grandma Harris stayed over but they did not seem to be especially concerned about Ma. Pa took them back to Aunt Lydia's on Tuesday and to Aunt Lotte's and the Fifields' on Wednesday. By then Ada's alarm had also subsided and she went with Pa and Jesse to prayer meeting that night. The part of her that was still a child did not know and none of the grown-ups told her that her mother was pregnant with the last of her babies, Elmer who would be born in July.

# 12 RAIN FOLLOWS THE PLOW

And so the year ended. Three more would pass before Ada, a much more grown-up young lady, would again post entries in a diary.

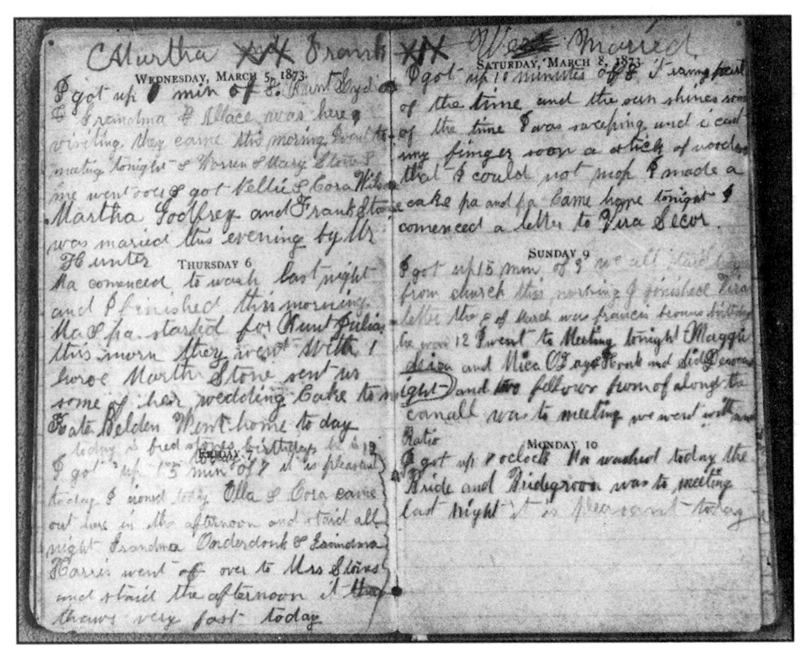

Martha [illegible] Frank [illegible] Were married.

WEDNESDAY, MARCH 5, 1873.

I got up [illegible] min of 8. Aunt [illegible] & Grandma & Allace was here visiting they came this moring I went to meeting tonight & Warren & Mary Stone & me went [illegible] & got Nellie & Cora Wilson Martha Godfrey and Frank Stone was maried this evening by Mr Hunter

THURSDAY 6

Ma comenced to wash last night and I finished this morning Ma & pa started for Aunt Julia this morn they went with 1 horse Martha Stone sent us some of her wedding Cake tonight Kate Belden Went home to day

today is fred [illegible] birthday he is 13

FRIDAY 7

I got up 15 min of 7 it is pleasant today I ironed today Ella & Cora came out [illegible] in the afternoon and staid all night Grandma Onderdonk & Grandma Harris went off over to Mrs Stones and staid the afternoon it thaws very fast today

SATURDAY, MARCH 8, 1873.

I got up 10 minutes of 8 it [illegible] of the time and the sun shines some of the time I was sweeping and i cut my finger on a stick of wood [illegible] that I could not mop I made a cake pa and ma Came home tonight I commenced a letter to Vira Secor.

SUNDAY 9

I got up 15 min of 9 we all [illegible] from church this morning I finished Vira letter the 9 of March was francis [illegible] birthday he was 12 I went to Meeting tonight Maggie [illegible] and [illegible] and [illegible] and [illegible] fellows from of along the canall was to meeting we went with [illegible] Ratio

MONDAY 10

I got up [illegible] oclock Ma washed today the Bride and Bridegroom was to meeting last night it is pleasant today

*Ada Harris diary, March 1873.*

# 2.
# Warren Clark, Farmhand

Warren Clark was 19 in 1874. In the first of the several diaries among his papers, he listed his address as Boylston, his father's home, but he was living with Bell and John Howe, his sister and brother-in-law. The Howes' farm was in Jefferson County, south of Mannsville, near the Oswego County line, about three miles from both villages, Mannsville and Sandy Creek. Chauncey and Alma Clark, Warren's father and mother, lived a couple of miles east of the Howes in rural and sparsely settled Boylston, close to Alma's parents, Henry and Susan Greenwood. In the neighborhood, and spilling over into Richland and Orwell, all within a radius of ten miles, Warren had a host of relatives, among them Uncle Walter Greenwood and down in Orwell his father's brothers, Jabez and Austin, and his older cousins, Norris and Zetto Clark. The Greenwoods and the Clarks were very nearly as tribal in their relationships as the Harrises and the Onderdonks.[1]

In the first two and a half months of the year, before the real farming began, he worked for John Howe, probably for his keep and the chance to be independent from his father--but close enough to help when his father or mother needed him. John was four years older, Bell two years younger than he.

The weather was warm enough in the second week of January for Warren to plow the cornfield, to sow some "wry," and to drag it in. He "drawed" manure, went to Mannsville with a load of grist, the next day with a load of corn. The snow had melted and the crust was thin, rough for "slaying." Several days he "drawed" logs from the woods, sawed and split them; he and John made a log boat, skidded two logs and broke down, mended the boat and spent several days hauling logs out of the woods, one of them a basswood (linden) which they split into boards to make a hayrack.

Three times in January and once in February Warren went to meeting in a nearby school, probably Methodist Protestant.[2] He thought one of them "a good meeting," unusual praise from his laconic pen. One Sunday night he, John, and Bell drove to Sandy Creek to the Baptist meeting. Twice he went to parties at neighbors, but it was cold one night and rained the other, and "there wasn't hardly anybody there." One Saturday he helped John draw wood to Mannsville and they went to an auction. Warren paid 26 cents for a necktie and a pair of sox.

In mid-January, while John was off to Mannsville with a load of corn, Warren and Bell drove the cutter to Sandy Creek and Warren called at the Academy to inquire about enrolling. The school, with nearly 200 students, was housed in a fine new brick building, two stories high. Each floor had an "audience" room and three recitation rooms. All of the classrooms were "surrounded" by slate blackboards and furnished with "patent" folding seats, matters of pride to the school and community.[3]

In ten days Warren returned, apparently for the beginning of a new session. He reported only that he went, and that "the Prof. Rev. B. E. Whipple, the Principal brought me an algebra." After meeting two of his teachers, Miss Mary Munger and a Miss Foster, he concluded that he "liked the school well." He paid his tuition and bought his own copy of the algebra which, he said, "amounted to $3.25." That he also studied arithmetic is confirmed by the examination he took at the end of the term and by his textbook, Davies, *University Arithmetic*, signed with his name and address on the flyleaf. The book, widely used and favorably regarded for its "lucidity," was comprehensive. Beginning with definitions, it led the student through common fractions, decimal fractions, ratio and proportion, percentage, extraction of square and cubic roots, applications to taxes, currency and exchange, business in general, and mensuration--the measurement of surfaces and volumes, all with innumerable questions and a copious supply of problems to be solved.[4] Of his studies Warren recorded nothing and of his social activities only that on the first day at noon he walked down to the village, a half dozen blocks, and later in the term that "I lent my little knife to Rosa Mosier."

Warren was very faithful in attendance. Unless John had an errand in Sandy Creek, he trudged the three miles over the snow-covered road to school and home again, but in the seven weeks before the close of the term he scarcely missed an hour's session. The exceptions he noted carefully. One morning he was late when John and Bell were gone and he had the chores to do; once school kept only half a day. He sawed in the woods that afternoon. He missed two full days, Thursday and Friday, when neighbors brought the word and he, in turn, carried home the mournful news that Uncle Austin Clark, his father's brother, was dead. He as a child with his parents, had lived at Uncle Austin's, and then next door until he was 12, on his father's first little farm. Now Uncle Austin was dead, at age 52. Warren took one of John's horses with him so that his father and mother could go to the funeral at Orwell, some eight or nine miles away. He remained at home with his young sisters, did the chores, helped to shovel out the roads, cut some wood. His parents came home on Sunday, about noon. Neighbors came, they talked for "a while," and Warren went back to John's with the horse.

The next morning the wind blew "hard and cold." Warren walked to school. He was regular for more than two weeks. On a Tuesday morning someone brought word to the Academy that Freddie Johnson, a neighbor's boy, had drowned. Warren finished the session, rushed home and went immediately to the Johnsons'. They sent him to another neighbor's for a buggy. That night he and two others sat up with the body. Hurrying home the next morning, he changed his clothes and drove some of the family to the funeral. He was one of the bearers. The next morning, Thursday, he was back in class.

On school days he did very little work for John, not even the chores, or at least he did not record doing them. One Saturday he hauled straw for a neighbor, nearly always he cut and sawed wood for John or "drawed" logs from the woods. He did not look in at home to saw and chop wood for his father and do chores for his mother. John and Bell did that.

He was equally severe in restricting his social activities. In early January he had called freely at the homes of his friends, or they at his, in the evenings or on Sundays. He had written to his cousins Norris and Zetto and to Angelia, who lived at Florence, in Oneida County. He received an answer from Angelia before the end of the month and a letter from Alice S., but by then he was in school and did not reply, or made no record of replying. He liked to write letters and he liked "visiting" with the young people of the neighborhood. He was a very social being, one must judge from the frequency of his communications. But for the seven weeks he held himself to a Spartan schedule--no letter writing, few social calls, and those chiefly on the weekends, few interruptions of his evenings. After supper he either studied or went to bed to rise early and walk the three miles to school.

At the end of February, encouraged by his instructors, Warren took the Regents' examinations, two sessions in arithmetic, one in geography, and one in spelling. The examinations were formidable exercises, administered by authorities in Albany to students all over the State.[5] By the time the results were available Warren was away at his summer job and did not report to his diary his success or failure.

As the term drew to a close, with the examinations out of the way and only one week to go, Warren caught the train after school on Friday and rode down to Albion station, near Altmar, to see his cousins, Zetto and Norris Clark. He walked out to his Uncle Jabez's, about two miles, arriving a little after eight o'clock. He had two full days with Zetto and Norris. Picking up the hired girl and their young cousin Jenny, Uncle Austin's daughter, who was 12, they called on other relatives, drove to "The Banks" (Sand Bank, now Altmar), went to church on Sunday afternoon at Pineville, and that evening visited some friends in the neighborhood. Warren was up a little after four o'clock on Monday morning. He caught the train at Richland--the same distance from Uncle Jabez's as Albion, but it arrived there a few minutes later. Snow was falling and the wind blowing, but it was not stormy enough for Zetto to get out the horse. Warren walked. The run to Sandy Creek was short, five miles, 15 minutes at most. He arrived about five o'clock and waited in the little station for three hours until the Academy building opened.[6]

Zetto returned the visit the next week, coming up for the last day of school and the exhibition at the Academy on Friday night. Typically, Warren had nothing to say about what went on at the exhibition, except that for whatever purpose he "used" 35 cents. Zetto helped him cut wood until mid-afternoon on Saturday when Warren hitched up the colts, "carried" him to the depot at Sandy Creek and borrowed $1.75 "until the next time I see him."

Monday Warren and John went to Mannsville. Warren bought a trunk for $3.50 and a coat for $13.00. In consequence, he "run in deat" to John, from whom he borrowed the money. That night he went home to his father's place in Boylston. It was March 15 and his summer job would begin soon.

He worked busily for a week, cutting, sawing, splitting wood, repairing the brush fence to hold the stock--the two cows and four sheep his father owned. Chauncey, we can presume, was already weakened from what they thought of as asthmatic cough but which was to develop into "consumption." But on two mornings he took his place with Warren on one end of the bucksaw. Warren called on his grandparents and his Uncle Walter Greenwood. For one day and half of another he and Walter cut wood for a neighbor. In the evenings, after supper, he went to see his old friends. It was spring and time to tap the maple trees. One night friends gave him "warm shugar" to eat. Another he stayed home and wrote a letter to Angelia. Carried away, he inscribed her initials in great capital letters across the page of his diary, A.M.S.

He was at a neighbor's when his father walked over, at noon, bringing a letter. It was from George Norton, in Oneida County, a hop-grower, for whom Warren had worked in the past summer or summers. Mr. Norton wanted him to come to work at once. He went home, got ready, walked over to John's where he had left his trunk, clothes, and other belongings, and spent the night. The next morning John took him to the Sandy Creek station where he caught the train. After a long delay at Rome, over which he complained, he reached Oriskany Falls that evening and walked over to Mr. Norton's, some three or four miles. Mr. Norton picked up his trunk the next day. The trip had cost him $3.60.

Mr. Norton lived in the southwest corner of Oneida County, near the village of Sangerfield. That was the neighborhood in which Warren's father, Chauncey, had been born. Chauncey and George were about the same age and may have known each other when they were boys; certainly the acquaintance of their families or friends must have made the way easier for Warren to get his summer job.[7]

The fertile valleys near Sangerfield, lying between rocky, timbered ridges, were well suited to the region's major enterprise, hop-growing. Mr. Norton, like his neighbors, was a hop farmer. He also cultivated corn, potatoes, hay, peas, beans, and garden produce, largely for his family and his farm animals.[8]

Warren began work on March 27, the morning after his arrival. His responsibilities were general. The first day he hauled hop poles from the swamp and cut a little wood. The day was cold "but quite pleasant," he said, even though the winter chill was not yet out of the air. The next morning, when some snow fell, he chopped wood and threshed beans in the barn. That was Saturday. On Sundays the Nortons, like the Clarks, and most of their friends and neighbors, did no work, other than the chores. Monday morning Warren and the Norton's son Dave, who was his age, sawed in the woods, reducing the fallen trees to lengths they could transport on a skid. It was cold and some snow fell but they worked all day. These spring days, as well as those of the winter, required an enormous amount of labor to feed the ravenous appetites of the cookstove and the fireplace. For five more days Warren and Dave sawed, chopped, and split wood, enough to last until the weather warmed up.

Much of the month, ten days altogether but scattered over the whole of April, Warren split and sharpened hop poles, working often with Dave, and getting more poles, young saplings just the right size, from the swamp when the supply ran out. It must have been tedious work, balancing the ten to twelve-foot poles, swinging his ax to shape the point, one after another all day long, as he did on three of the days.[9] But for the most part his routine of work was broken; if he drew or sharpened hop poles in the morning, he was at some other urgent task in the afternoon. Parts of seven days he boiled sap, gathered from the grove of maple trees; three half days he "drawed" manure, driving a team of oxen as he scattered the fertilizer on the fields. One stormy day he helped a carpenter lay a floor in one of the rooms of the house. A few days later, on a rainy morning, he made a hot bed, putting down the thick layer of manure and the fine top soil to force the rapid growth of vegetable seedlings for the garden. He split, sharpened, and helped set posts and with Dave built a board fence to contain the stock. One cold and rainy morning he and Dave made a "stone boat," a log sledge, and hauled stones from a field. Two full days and half of two others, when the cold wind and snow kept them at the house, they did nothing but chores. On one of those days, the 29th of April, Warren tried to haul manure but gave up and "set in the house the rest of the time."

If Warren's days were crowded with work, his evenings and Sundays were free for social events. The neighborhood was full of young people. The Nortons had two daughters, Mary (Mate) who was 18, Flora (Dolly) 14, a son David 20, and a younger boy, George 8. Two or three times a week, sometimes four or five, after the day's work was done, the dishes cleared from the supper table and washed, Warren and the Norton girls, or Dave, went calling on neighbors.[10]

He was quick to socialize. On the first Sunday he went "visiting" with Mr. Norton over at the "other house" to see old Mrs. Norton, the widowed mother, 80-years-old. Tuesday he, Mate, and Dolly went calling on the DeForests, their near neighbors. Friday he and Mr. Norton drove to the village, Sangerfield Center. Sunday morning he wrote a letter home; he and the Norton girls went calling that afternoon, where he did not record, and Mike Hayden, who was to prove the most frequent visiter, came that evening. More company, unnamed, came after supper on Tuesday. Friday evening Warren wrote a letter to "Angie" (Angelia), but she did not answer--or if she did he took no note of it in his daily record. Mike Hayden came again the next night. And on Sunday morning Zetto Clark drove over from Bridgewater, some seven or eight miles from Sangerfield, where he was working for the summer. Warren took him to the Bangses in the afternoon and that evening Will Denison dropped in. Sometime during the day Warren found time to write to John Howe. The next evening he and the girls, Mate and Dolly, went to Waterville, about three miles distant. Waterville was a considerable village, the largest in the township, with a population of 1100 people.[11] They stopped at Erlies for refreshments. "I used," Warren said, ".70 cts of money." He then had two nights free: no visits, no calls, no letters to write.

Thursday evening the Nortons had a dance for the young people of the neighborhood. Dancing was forbidden by the Methodist Protestant Church as one of those "worldly amusements which do not tend to the glory of God," but Warren danced, apparently without remorse or defiance. He made his entry in the diary, "We had a dance here in the evening," as casually as he noted that same day that the weather was "cold and windy." And he added that he "had a good time." He "used" 30 cents. He was to dance several times that summer, at the Bangses, at Mike Hayden's, in Waterville, and at a place he called Carter's Hollow where he and Harrison Hubbard had taken Dolly and Mate Norton. One night he played "cards" which, like dancing and the theater, was condemned by the church. Socially, as in work, it was to be a busy summer.[12]

The first week in May brought no respite from the cold and windy weather, and Warren awakened on the morning of the 8th to find the ground white with snow. But he and Dave had begun to work in the field in earnest and they must not stop. On the second afternoon and every day for a week, and three days later in the month, half days most of the time, they set hop poles, ten or twelve-foot poles, six or eight feet apart, one pole for six or seven vines, seven or eight hundred poles to the acre. That was hard work--driving a heavy "crow bar" into the earth to the depth of one foot, pulling it out and thrusting in the sharpened pole and tamping it down firmly.[13]

That job done, they "grubbed" the hops, digging out and cutting off the unwanted runners from the main root. They cleaned out the hop barn. Several days they plowed and planted potatoes and corn. The month had hardly started before they had to take a half day from the fields to build fence, and ten days later to "fix" the sheep pasture fence. The restless animals, made more restless by the coming of warmer days and the buzzing of insects, rubbed at the fences, loosened the boards or logs, and sent the boys back to making repairs, two more half days that month. On a rainy morning Warren helped the Norton girls clean out the backroom of the house--where the hop pickers would sleep. And once again he and Dave spent a half day digging out big stones from one of the fields and another half day they laid tile and filled in a drainage ditch. The last four days of the month they began to put up the twine and tie the hops, twisting the spiraling tendrils around the pole or string and tying them gently.

All of June Warren was busy in the hopyards, tieing, cultivating, hoeing, part or all of 20 of the 25 working days. In the remaining time he cultivated or hoed corn, plowed and hoed potatoes, hoed the bean patch, hoed the garden. Two half days

Mr. Norton sent him to work on the public road which was maintained by the cooperative labor of the farmers. One afternoon he and Mr. Norton made a gate and three half days he and Dave or Mr. Norton worked at that never-ending job, fixing fence.

He was faithful in posting the condition of the weather, day by day. And cheerful. It might be "cool and pleasant," or "warm and pleasant," "hot and pleasant," "a cold wind but pleasant," always pleasant. Now and then, exuberant in spirit, he wrote simply, "a great day." By his account, it had snowed eight times in April and rained another eight days. It rained 15 days in May, 12 in June, 11 in July. He never complained. Wet summer days were a way of life for the New York farmer.

In July the work shifted from hops to corn, potatoes, and hay. Warren and Dave were in the field early and late, plodding after the cultivator and hoeing corn and potatoes, uprooting the weeds, loosening the soil on the surface so that it would absorb the rain, what little of it there was in the first weeks of the month. The days were warm, a few "very warm," and rain fell on only four working days in the first three weeks--twice driving them from the field, one afternoon to put pickets on the barnyard fence, and for a full day, on Mr. Norton's order, to help a neighbor put a sill under his house.

In the third week they began to cut hay. The mowing machine with a flexible sickle bar had come into general use in the years after the Civil War, so we presume that Warren's entry--"Dave and I mowed"--means precisely what it says: that one or both of them sat on a mower pulled by two horses. They would have looked alternately at the horses, slapping them with a line to urge them on or tugging left or right to keep them on course, or they would have glanced down at the furiously chattering sickle bar to see that it did not clog with weeds. And all the while they inhaled the sweet scent of the grass, its stems bruised and its fragrant juices released by the flying sickle. But it was not all sweet scent and romance. The days were hot, "good for haying," Warren wrote, and good for gnats and flies that swarmed around the heads of horses and men, got into nostrils and tasted bitter on the tongue. And the wind, even when it blew ever so lightly, raised a cloud of dust, pollen, and leaf fragments that wedged in the corner of a boy's eye, clogged his nostrils, irritated his throat, settled in his hair and in streaks on his sweat-dampened face. But all that was part of a farmer's work, nothing that called forth a protest from Warren.[14]

Farm work was never done. They had not yet finished the haying before they had to return to the fields part of several days to begin the last round of hoeing potatoes and corn and cultivating and hilling the hops. That took four half-days in the last week of July and ten days in August. They spent a week, a little more, getting in the crop of oats. The two fields may have been too small for the mowing machine, or too rocky, or Mr. Norton wanted the tall stems laid out, head to head, in neat rows, ready to gather up and bind in sheaves. So Warren and David "cradled" for three days, swinging the heavy scythe with three oak bars parallel to the blade. They raked, bound and hauled in what they had cut. Two days they worked on the drainage ditch, they spent four days harvesting the peas, they picked wild berries one day, and one morning, for no apparent reason, Warren simply "fussed around the house."

In the meantime, his social life had continued, undiminished. He had no sweetheart or girl in whom he was especially interested. For the most part he went with the Norton girls (girles, he always spelled it), "carrying" them in the family buggy or cart. Once, he took them to the circus at Sangerfield Center, and spent $1.00. One Sunday afternoon he, Mike Hayden, and the girls drove over to Willowvale, eight or nine miles to the northwest. Warren spent $4.00 for an unstated purpose, his most costly excursion of the summer. Theodore Hickox, Dave, Warren and the girls drove or walked to the Sangerfield Center, and Warren bought a pair of fancy boots--they must have been fancy at the price he paid, $5.00. That was one-fourth, or more, of his month's wages, about $18.00, if we judge from the $20.00 a month he earned two years later.

He was with Dolly often. At 14 she was old enough, and jolly enough, to be company but too young for him, at 19, to become romantically involved. They sometimes picked up another girl or two--Clara and Flora Hewett, who were nine and 12-years-old, one Sunday morning when they drove to Oriskany Falls to church; Julia Waterman on a Friday evening when they went to Waterville. Warren spent $2.75 for a hat that evening, nothing for the entertainment of the girls--or nothing that he recorded. He and Dolly drove to the village one Thursday evening and he bought a shirt for which he paid $2.75. One weekend he borrowed Mike Hayden's buggy, washed it

Saturday after work and on Sunday he and Dolly drove seven or eight miles to Bridgewater to see cousin Zetto. He teased Dolly on that trip, solemnly recording in his diary a joke that males since the beginning of time have thought funny: Dolly, he wrote, "was so heavy that she broke down Mike's buggy, thats all."

He went off with the boys, too, to the village for the most part, no doubt to stand around and loaf, banter with the boys, flirt a little with the girls; twice to go to a "show," perhaps an amateur theatrical or a traveling troupe, to which he did not take the Norton girls. One Sabbath he and Dave drove to Bridgewater to see Zetto. He spent small amounts of money as he did when he went with the girls, 40 cents in Waterville, 55 cents in the village once and 40 cents another time. In mid-summer he sent $14.50 to John Howe, most of it to pay for the coat he had bought in Mannsville. He liked to dress well. He had spent, in addition to the coat, $10.50 for clothes--hat, shirt, and boots. And $7.45 for entertainment, including the unexplained and extravagant $4.00 at Willowvale. No doubt he had other expenditures, some for work clothes, small amounts for refreshments, for admission to the shows he attended. He must have repaid Zetto the $1.75 he had borrowed from him in Sandy Creek and the $3.60 it had cost him to travel from Sandy Creek to Oriskany Falls. But he had been prudent. Constantly on the go, he had a good time and spent very little money for entertainment. But his clothes had put a considerable tax on his summer earnings.

The climax of the season's work and of the social activities for the young came with the harvest of the hops. They were ready by the end of August. Earlier in the month Mr. Norton, Dave, and Theodore Hickox had gone to recruit the pickers. They began to arrive on Sunday, August 29, young people from neighboring villages and towns, or counties. Mr. Norton and his neighbors, each with small acreages, had agreed to harvest cooperatively. On Monday morning a partial crew of pickers, Warren, Dave, and the Norton girls among them, started in Hayden's field. With the arrival of more pickers they were at full strength Tuesday morning. The tenders, having already set the empty boxes, pulled a section of poles to let down the vines. The pickers swarmed into the field, a sling or a basket suspended over their shoulder to free both hands. Plucking the cone-like hops from the vines, as free from leaves as possible, and dropping them into the basket, they moved slowly forward.

The pickers were young, full of the zest of life, quick to socialize in the crowded field, but with an eye, too, to their earnings. They dumped the full basket into the boxes, made record of what they had picked, and returned to the vines, to pluck and drop the cones, the same routine, hour after hour.[15]

In the evenings they loafed about the house where they lodged or paired off in couples to walk along the road or down to one of the other houses. Or they danced. They danced on Tuesday night in Hayden's hophouse, after the second day of picking. A hophouse was a good place to dance, a little warm, with the crowd of young people, but a big square building, freshly cleaned for the new crop. What music they had, Warren does not tell us, probably a fiddle, perhaps an accordion, a mouth harp or two. No doubt they danced the country dances: *Sailor's Hornpipe*, *Arkansas Traveller*, *Old Zip Coon*, *Pop Goes the Weasel*, perhaps the half-dancing party games: *Skip-to-My-Lou*, *Needle's Eye*, *Miller Boy*. The caller called the steps, the young bodies surged forward and fell back in a rhythmical beat. It was good exercise, said a dancing master: "all the muscles of the human body are fully brought into action. . . ." Certainly it was a good outlet for the exuberant spirits of the young.[16]

Old Mrs. Norton died on Wednesday, interrupting the nightly festivities. Warren sat up with the body on Wednesday and Thursday nights, and worked both of the following days. The funeral was on Friday. Saturday night the young people danced in the Bangs' hophouse. They danced there again on Monday and Friday of the next week, and the following Tuesday, the third week of picking. On Friday night, the last full day of harvest, they danced at the Nortons. Warren was attracted to a girl by the name of Evelyn, but what he thought about her--all but her name--he did not record.

They finished the hop picking on Saturday, September 19, and by Sunday all of the itinerant pickers were gone. Warren was 20-years-old the next week, but he took no note of it. He remained at the Nortons' another two months, until November 16. There was still some work to be done with the hops--drying, pressing, transporting them. He cut corn, hauled in the stalks, threshed peas, gathered apples, husked corn. He and Dave, sometimes with the help of Mr. Norton, built a pigpen, shingled the hen roost, banked the house against the cold of winter, and built a "storm house" over the front door.

On a Saturday afternoon in November he and the Norton girls went into the village and had their pictures taken, undoubtedly to trade them, for the next afternoon he exchanged with Flora Hewett. No copy remains among his papers. On the next Monday Mr. Norton went with him to the village and helped him pick out a suit of clothes, which pretty well completed his wardrobe. The next week he caught "the cars" for home, stopping off a couple of days at Albion to see his Uncle Jabez and his cousins, Zetto and Norris.

He continued on the train to Sandy Creek, stayed overnight at John Howe's and went home. For two days he threshed oats, piling the sheaves on the barn floor and beating them with a flail. One day he went with his Uncle Walter to Mannsville and bought a saw. While there he paid $25.00 of his summer earnings to Mr. Howe, John's father Elias, on the "book acct." No doubt it was to repay money that he, or his father Chauncey--we could guess from later developments--had borrowed. Then, at home, he plunged into the winter's work, legislated every year by the grim necessity laid on every farmer and household to provide fuel to fight off the winter's cold.

On Monday, December 14, he enrolled in the district school. Apparently, he had not passed all of the Regents' examinations. For two weeks he went steadily. On Christmas day, borrowing a team, he broke a road through the snow into his father's woods, and hauled out what he had sawed earlier in the month. That evening, in the only celebration to mark the holiday, he, and perhaps others in the family, went over to Uncle Walter's to see the Tryons, members of his mother's family from Sandy Creek. In another half dozen years, the name Tryon would figure strongly in his life.

Monday, he returned to school for three days. He had a letter from Dolly Norton on Tuesday. Two days later, December 30, he caught the train for Oriskany Falls. The Nortons met him at the depot. He had come to renew the delights of the summer months. The next evening he and Dave, Mate and Dolly, went over to a neighbor's to celebrate the coming of the New Year.

What he thought of Dolly (Flora), now 15, he does not tell us. But she thought well enough of him to pick from among the sentiments she had collected for autograph books four lines that spoke her admiration. She wrote in his diary, in a fine feminine hand, after he had made his own last entry on December 31.

W.F.C.

Green is the leaf upon the vine
I have chosen you for a friend of mine
I have picked you out from among the rest
Because I thought you were the best.
F.D.N.

As if to reflect his own uncertainty, or simply his big-brother relationship to both of the Norton girls, he entered in large florid script on the next page of the diary, one reserved for "Memoranda," the initials of both Dolly and Mate, and his own: "F.D.N.," "M.E.N." and "W.F.C."

We do not have a record for 1875. If he kept a diary, it is missing. We can only conjecture, with his booklet for 1876 in hand, that he remained for a brief time at the Nortons' and returned to Mannsville to continue the term at the schoolhouse and to do odd jobs for John Howe, his father, and others, until it was time to begin spring and summer work at the Nortons.

He was still adrift, uncertain of his course. He could not count on his father's farm. It was too small to sustain the family, let alone to provide a start for him. But he was young. There was time enough to think about the future.

*Schoolhouse where Ada Harris and her brothers went to school.*
*Courtesy of Ada May Hering*

# 3.
# I Went with Ada Harris

After an interval of a year, Warren in January, 1876, was once again at John Howe's. He was 21-years-old and still adrift, waiting out the winter months until the seasonal farm work began in April. On the first day of the new year, Saturday, after helping John do the chores, he walked down to Sandy Creek and took the train to Richland station to see Norris Clark, his newly married cousin. Norris was 30-years-old but he and his bride lived with his parents, Warren's Uncle Jabez and Aunt Lodelia. With the low wages and inflated land values it was not easy for a young farmer to get a start. The parents had turned over one room in the house which Norris and his bride could call their own. They were gone when Warren came and did not return until Sunday evening. Warren visited them "a little while" in their room and remained for the second night at Uncle Jabez's. Rising at four o'clock, as he had done when he was a student at the Academy, he struck out across the frozen countryside to Richland, two miles away, caught the "cars" to Sandy Creek, walked out to John's, another three miles, and arrived in time for breakfast. That was his major excursion and social adventure for the first three months of the new year.[1]

He worked with John for two days, spreading manure, threshing oats, and then brought old Mr. and Mrs. Howe out from Mannsville, where they lived, to do the chores while he, John, Bell, and the baby, Bernice, went over to the Clarks' at Boylston. For four days Warren and John cut and split wood, fuel for Chauncey and Alma and the girls. The remainder of the month and the first week of February he worked for John, often full days, probably without pay. Early in February he went back to his father's house in Boylston to remain until the last week of March.

He plunged at once into his regular winter's work--cutting and sawing trees in the woods, hauling some to the mill to augment the family's meager cash income. Warren's father came home at the end of the first week but, suffering from poor health, he lent no hand to the sawing and chopping. His presence did make it possible for Warren to formalize an understanding over their financial relationship. In the fall of 1875 Chauncey had mortgaged the farm for $187.70. We do not know why. Warren advanced $113.00 to his father, giving him a total of $300.00 to meet his obligations. On February 14 Chauncey signed a note to Warren--"for the money he has had of me," Warren said, an amount equal to six months of his summer's wages.[2] The weeks that winter were cold and often stormy. "The wind blew and the snow flew" he said of one day, and of another, the wind "blowed from the west like the devill," the second day in a row that he could not let the cattle out of the barn. On five of the stormy days he threshed oats in the breezeway of the barn, beating the kernels out of the husks with a flail, two slender sticks bound together, end to end, with a rawhide thong, thirty or forty strokes to the minute, as long as a man could stand it, hour after hour. Two afternoons the wind blew strong and Warren winnowed the grain, tossing it in the air to blow away the chaff.[3] One stormy day he put new bottoms in his mother's chairs. A couple of days he did only the chores and "set in the house" the rest of the time. Twice he helped shovel snow to clear the road. He went to a party one night with his sister Dell who was 15, and to church on two Sundays, all day meetings held by the Methodist Protestants.

On March 3 he had a letter from Dave Norton, down in Oneida County. He answered a few days later, writing in a store at Sandy Creek while he waited for John Howe to get his trading done. Dave wanted to come to see him. He arrived on a stormy night in late March, with "the wind howling like the verry devil," apparently getting a ride from Sandy Creek with one of Chauncey's neighbors. They sat around the fire the next morning waiting for the snow to stop and then walked over to John Howe's. Warren borrowed a horse, did some errands for John on Tuesday and on Wednesday took his trunk to the depot.

He and Dave went to a party that night and "had a nice time," his finest praise for a party. The next morning, Thursday, March 30, John took them to Mannsville and they caught "the cars" for Rome, Utica, and Waterville.

Warren's summer work was not much different from what it had been two years before. He plowed, grubbed, and sprouted the hops, sharpened and scattered the poles, tied the vines, stretched the twine, cleaned out the hophouse. He planted, cultivated, and harvested the same crops, adding popcorn. And he did the routine jobs of the farm: hauling manure, fixing fence, helping with the chores.

On July 4 he walked to Waterville, some three miles, caught the train for Utica, a considerable city of nearly 30,000 people, there found some of the "boys," and celebrated with them. He "had a good time," he said, and did not get home until "most two o'clock at night." When the Irish held their festival in Waterville a month later he must have had an even better time. He did not get home until 5 a.m. He made no excursions to Bridgewater, for his cousin Zetto, whom he had gone to see two summers past, had died. With Warren's diary missing for that year, there is no record of his sense of loss or sorrow.[4]

He managed to post his diary regularly, or back post it on Sunday afternoon, in ink--which required that he sit at a table or a writing board and dip his pen into the open bottle. He wrote several times, as was his practice when he was away from home, to his family, to John and Bell Howe, to his sisters, Dell who at 15 was planning to come down to the Nortons' to pick hops, to Hattie 10, to whom he sent money for "socks," and to his cousin Norris.

Mr. Norton had opened a new hopyard and increased his planting that summer. With more hops to be harvested, he did his own recruiting of pickers, not relying on his neighbors to join him as in the past. He went up to Oswego County in mid-August and engaged several young people, among them Wallace Harris and Rosa Spink from Kasoag, Warren and Mary Stone and Ada Harris from Stone Hill, all of them from near Williamstown village. Warren 21 and Mary 19, brother and sister, were Ada's friends, neighbors who lived a half mile down the hill, and had grown up and gone to church and school with her. Ada had just turned 17. Wallace 19, Uncle Porter's son, was her cousin and Rosa 15, whom she counted as a cousin, was a niece of Aunt Calista, Wallace's mother. All of them went to the Methodist church at Williamstown village.[5]

Almost at once Warren liked the Williamstown group, or he liked Ada Harris and, as a good tactician, sought to court her by cultivating her friends. They arrived on the 29th of August and began picking the next day, Wednesday. Warren "tended box," putting out the boxes to which the pickers brought their hops, and emptying them into the hop wagon. It was a good job, a strategic post for the exchange of greetings, banter, verbal jousting. He was friendly, outgoing, well-liked by the others, talkative. And a handsome young man, 21, almost 22-years-old, five feet eight inches tall--about average for that era--, slender, lithe, with black wavy hair.[6]

The first evening after the pickers arrived Warren was busy. He borrowed a horse from Mr. Bangs and drove to Oriskany Falls to pick up Mr. Norton and his own father, Chauncey, and probably his sister Dell, although he does not say so. Chauncey was always concerned about the well-being of his children. Dell was only 15 and he had come, probably to accompany her, knowing that Warren was there to look out for her during the harvest.

Social activities got underway at the end of the second day of picking. That evening "we played cards," Warren wrote. He does not say what kind of cards, or who played. The next night, Friday, he took Dell to a dance at the Patricks'. "We all went," he says, but he named no names. "We all went" again on Saturday night, to the Bangses', Mate and Dell with him. Sunday was "cool but pleasant." Four couples, whom he does not name, save that he included himself, walked down to the hophouse. And that evening after supper, narrowing the field, he walked with Ada Harris and Mary Stone. They walked again, three couples of them, on Monday evening after hop picking.

Tuesday he received a letter from Johnny Tryon. That was an event of such significance to him that it foreclosed his interest in noting other social matters for the day. Johnny was his cousin whom he had known when they were small boys, he in Orwell, Johnny in Richland. In the 1860s Johnny's parents had moved to western Iowa, and Johnny wrote from that wild country far out in the West, on the banks of the Missouri River.[7]

Wednesday like Sunday was "cool but pleasant." Warren worked in the house, went to a neighbor's for butter, hauled some hops. He had little opportunity to talk with the pickers that day. But he either had made arrangement earlier with Ada Harris or he talked to her in the course of the afternoon. That evening he took her to the dance. She must have suffered some anguish. Her family was closely knit and loving, her parents seem not to have been unduly strict and arbitrary in their rules of conduct and dress, but they were devoted to the Methodist church and its teachings--and the church forbade dancing. We do not know if she tempered her guilt with defiance, or a love of adventure, neither of which seems likely, or if she acted impulsively, swept away in her emotional response to the young man who asked her.[8]

If she did not suffer remorse then, she did afterwards. More than fifty years later, when Warren was gone and she was an old lady past seventy years of age, she picked up his diary to browse in it, recall old times, and make her own notes for a new day. She came across the entry, dance in the evening,--"I went with Ada Harris." Mortified, she erased the offending entry, in her haste and embarrassment not very thoroughly, and then, holding her pencil on its side, she rubbed the passage with the lead and left a black smudge in the little book. Poor dear, she could not know that in another half century an impious grandson, by then also grown old, would erase what she had blotted out with pencil to learn what his grandfather had written with ink. But in 1876 she was 17. Warren asked her to go and she went.

Friday night Warren walked to the village, Waterville, and back with Ada Harris, Rosa Spink, Mary Stone, and his sister Dell. Saturday the Bangses had a dance. "Lots of us went," Warren reported to his diary. He took Ada Harris, "and had a good time," he added, again without remorse--at least on his part. Saturday marked the end of the second week of picking. The harvest was two-thirds over. One week remained to the pickers--for work and good times.

Sunday was a warm and pleasant day. Warren and Ada and Warren and Mary Stone went for a ride to Oriskany Falls. The warm, sweet air of early fall, or Ada's presence, was mesmerizing--she, her cousin Vira Secor had written, with her "dark and flashing eye and . . prettie little haughty head."[9] Warren had no word for how he felt, but he could not shake off the spell, he could not see enough of Ada or be with her enough to satisfy his need. Later that afternoon he organized another walk, Mary Stone and Ozzie Loomis, his sister Dell and Wallace Harris, he and Ada. They strolled over to the Catholic cemetery, wandered among the stones, stopping, no doubt, to read inscriptions and to marvel at sentiments and carved figures strange to the Protestant eye. They went on into the village to church, a Methodist meeting, we must presume, or he would have identified it.

Tuesday night they had the last big gala party for the pickers, a dance at the Nortons'. Warren recorded no details. Wednesday, after work, eight couples, unnamed but a group that must have included Warren and the Norton girls and the entire harvest crew, walked over to the near neighbors, the Waterman's, for butter, an errand any one of them could have performed. It was, Warren said, a "pleasant evening." Thursday the pickers finished the harvest. They loafed around the house after supper. Warren in his brief record gives us one of those rare glimpses into the kind of person he was. He "buzzed the girls," he said, "in the forepart of the evening." All of the evidence suggests that he, indeed, liked to talk. And then, in a last gesture of tenderness and romance, he "set up a while with Ada." The next day, Friday, September 15, the pickers went home, all but Warren Stone who remained to help Warren Clark and Dave Norton with the general farm work.

On Sunday afternoon Warren wrote to Ada. She had been gone two days. He wrote, also, to Johnny Tryon, his cousin in Iowa. He had no inkling of destiny, on the day of his first written communication to Ada, when he linked together those three names, his, Ada's, and Johnny's and the two states, New York and Iowa. He did not get an immediate response from Ada. The next Sunday he and Warren Stone retreated from the Norton family to an upstairs room and sat together, writing letters. He wrote to his family, to Mary Stone, and to Wallace Harris. That was a flank attack, letters to persons who were quite likely to see Ada and if they saw her, certain to report that they had heard from Warren Clark.

The two Warrens and Dave had a few days' work cleaning up after the hop harvest--vines to burn, poles to stack, hops to press and cap, and miscellaneous work on the farm: corn to cut, shock, and husk, popcorn to husk, peas to thresh, fence to repair and build, stones to draw from a hillside field Mr. Norton wanted cleared. But the big job, and the reason for keeping both Warren Stone and Warren Clark for another two months, was the digging and tiling of a big drainage ditch. They were at the job for five weeks, plowing where they could, shovelling day by day, long hours and, when the tile was laid, shovelling again to fill the ditch.

If Warren thought it hard work, he did not complain to his diary. Nor did he reduce his social activities: evenings with the boys in the village, dances (with Warren Stone's name noticeably absent from the lists of those who attended), an occasional after-supper stroll to one of the neighbors, an oyster supper, a day at the Deanville fair, a Sunday evening at church with a girl he "found" in Waterville. And one afternoon, November 8, when all eligible hands went to vote, he cast his ballot for president. Whether he favored Rutherford B. Hayes or Samuel J. Tilden, he did not say.

He heard from Ada on Thursday, September 28, two weeks from the last evening he had spent with her, eleven days since he had written. He replied on Sunday. The following Saturday he received a letter from Mary Stone. He did not hear from Wallace Harris and he did not again write to him. But he now seemed to have the girls on regular schedules, two-week interlocking cycles that required him to write every week and brought him a once-a-week response. He answered Mary on Wednesday, heard from Ada on Saturday, October 14, and wrote to her on Wednesday, the 18th. He had a second letter from Mary Stone on Tuesday, October 25. Then Ada broke the magic circle. The days went by, grew into a week, and weeks, and a month, and she did not answer. Warren did not write again. And when Mary Stone answered his third letter, he did not reply.

Mr. Norton and the three boys had pretty well completed the fall work by mid-November. On the 16th Warren Stone set out for home, taking Dave Norton with him. Warren Clark remained at the Norton farm for another week to help with the chores and odd jobs while Dave had a holiday. But he had made arrangements before Warren Stone left--at whose initiative we can only guess--to stop over at Williamstown on his way home to Boylston. And he wrote to John Howe to tell him when he would arrive at Sandy Creek.

He finished his work the next week, seven and one-half months at $20.00 a month, $150. He had drawn $75.75 during the summer and fall. Mr. Norton paid him the balance, $74.25, and took him to the depot at Waterville. Mate Norton went with him, glad to have an escort (or certainly her parents were) for her own holiday trip to see her summer friends who had come down from Oswego County. They stopped off at Williamstown and, Warren noted, went to Mr. Stone's house "a visiting." That was Thursday, November 22.

In what at this distance appears to have been a studied neglect of Ada, but might have been a ritual of deference to his host, he went hunting the next day with Warren Stone and his older brother, Louis. How long they were gone and how he communicated with Ada Harris, he does not tell us, but that evening he went up to see her. The Harrises invited him to stay overnight. The next morning was cool and it snowed "like fun," but the temperature was mild enough to thaw the frozen ground. He walked down the "awful muddy" road to the Stones' and he and Warren went to Williamstown. Grandma Stone was very ill and had to have someone with her constantly. In some manner, and again he does not tell us how, he communicated with Ada and they sat up with Mrs. Stone that night. They must have had much to talk about--or have found much satisfaction in being quietly together, in the long hours of that winter's night, whether they were alone or someone else sat with them.

The next morning, Saturday, he walked Ada home up the muddy hill, and stayed a short time until Warren Stone came to drive them, Warren, Ada, and Mate, up to Kasoag to see Wallace Harris and Rosa Spink. Warren Stone dropped them at Uncle Porter's and returned home. For two days they called on cousins and friends, all busy work and small talk, but reason enough for Ada to be there, and he with her. On the Sabbath they went to Sunday school in the afternoon and then Uncle Porter took Ada back to Williamstown. That was to have been the last Warren saw of her on this trip. If the parting was painful, he knew at least that he had made some advance, that he could write to her and expect an answer.

He and Mate spent another two days with friends and returned to Uncle Porter's on Tuesday. There they learned that Grandma Stone had died. Wallace drove them down to the funeral. Warren must have seen Ada, may have talked with her, but he says nothing about it. Crowded for time, he and Mate had to get to the train if they were to reach Sandy Creek when

John Howe expected them. Wallace "carried" them to the depot and they caught the train, Mate to see her friend and Warren's sister, Dell, Warren to go home and to John Howe's to wait out the winter months until spring work began.

*Nathaniel and Amelia Jane Harris. Parents of Ada Harris Clark. Williamstown, New York, ca. 1880. Courtesy of Ada May Hering.*

*Chauncey Clark, father of Warren Clark.*
*Boylston, New York, ca. 1877. Courtesy of Ada May Hering.*

# 4.
# A Ring That Binds Me

Warren quickly settled into his winter's routine. Mate Norton remained a week, visiting at the Howes' and the Clarks', before Warren and Dell put her on the train for Williamstown and on home to Oneida County. Warren stayed at John's most of the winter, with a few days or weeks at home now and then.[1]

He wrote to Ada on the first Sunday afternoon, before Mate had gone. Ada answered promptly, so that when he and John "drawed a barrel" over the snow "to make a track" to get through to Mannsville, he found her letter waiting for him, ten days after he had written. He replied in two days, while he sat in the warmth of the forge at the blacksmith shop in Sandy Creek, waiting for John's horse, "Old Joe," to be shod. That was December 15. Five days later he had a letter from Johnny Tryon out in Iowa--a name once again intruding itself into his thoughts as he wrote to Ada. That same day he picked up his watch, that he had left to be repaired, a timepiece that he cherished. He returned home the next day, to remain a week, chopping, sawing, splitting wood, getting the fuel supply in order, while his father and mother, with a cutter he had borrowed from a neighbor, and John's horse, drove down to Orwell to see Uncle Jabez. On Sunday, December 24, a neighbor brought him another letter from Ada and one from Warren and Mary Stone.

He remained at Boylston until his father and mother came home. On Saturday, after it "snowed and blowed" again, he helped break out the road, drove the horse back to John's, walked to Sandy Creek, and took the train to Williamstown. Again he went to Warren Stone's, not getting there until after eleven o'clock at night. Sunday, December 31, it stormed and blew all day "like fun." All that he did was to go the barn twice and "set by the fire the rest of the time." Monday morning he helped the Stones break out the road. By afternoon he got to the Harris' and he and Ada and her brother Albert went for a ride in the cutter to Williamstown.

Tuesday Mr. Harris took Warren and Ada to the depot and they caught the train for Camden. Her cousin, Retta, married in 1875, lived in the village with her husband, Louis Stone, a brother to Warren and Mary. We have Ada's diary for 1877, as well as Warren's, and on this occasion she recorded more details than he. As soon as they reached the village, they had their picture taken and then went out to "ret's," for dinner. In the afternoon Warren hired a horse and cutter and they drove three or four miles to the hamlet of East Florence to see Lute Whitford, one of Warren's friends who had spent the previous summer in Oneida County and knew them both. Lute's mother served them "tea," Ada reported. They had much to talk about from their summer's adventures and got back to Camden just in time to catch the last train to Williamstown. Ada's father was at singing school that night so they sat in the hotel, the Sage House, until 10 o'clock when he came after them. Warren stayed overnight at the Harris'.

He had planned to go home the next day, Wednesday, and got as far as the Stones', half a mile down the road. But he couldn't pull himself away. "I finely changed my mind," he wrote. That night he spent with Warren Stone--and most of the next day. It was very cold. The snow blew and drifted and blocked the roads. The two Warrens sat by the fire until the afternoon was almost gone. Word came that Ada's friend, Cora Wilson, Nellie's younger sister, was ill and needed a doctor. The boys helped break the road through to the village. That evening they and Mary went over to the Wilsons'. Ada may have been there, but the page in her diary on that day is blank and Warren does not mention her. At last on Friday, after one more short visit to the Harris', he returned to Sandy Creek.

They continued their courtship by mail. Warren wrote to her on Wednesday, January 10, five days after he had returned to John's. Ada did not post her diary that week, so we do not know when she received his letter. She replied on Sunday,

January 21. He received her letter on Tuesday and responded on Sunday, decent intervals, neither hurried nor negligent, when one allows the two to five days required for delivery of the letter, which was dependent not only on the mail service but on how often the correspondents went to the village to post or pick up the mail.

On March 30 Warren made a quick trip to Williamstown. There was no indirection this time. Friday morning he packed his satchel, walked from his home to John Howe's, and on to Sandy Creek, caught "the cars" to Williamstown, and went straight to the Harris', again walking. The next morning Ada did her usual Saturday sweeping and mopping. One can suppose that Warren helped Mr. Harris and Albert with the chores. It was the season for tapping the maple trees and collecting the sap. Mr. Harris had his buckets out. That afternoon they "sugared off." Mary and Warren Stone came over and they ate warm maple "shugar." In the evening while Ma and three-year-old Elmer stayed with Grandma, the rest of the Harrises and Warren, "the whole Load,", went to Williamstown to meeting. It was the first time in three months that Warren had been to church. Sunday morning he and Ada remained at home with Grandma while the others went to church. In the afternoon he went alone to see Warren and Mary Stone. But he was gone only "a few minutes," Ada said. That night she and Warren sat up talking until four o'clock in the morning.

Monday he took his leave of Ada and, on the way to the depot, called once more on the Stones. Warren Stone was about to take over the summer job at the Norton's that he, himself, had held in previous years. And Warren Clark had hired out to work for his brother-in-law, John Howe, to begin the next morning, for $18.00 a month, two dollars less than Mr. Norton had paid him. We can only speculate on why he left the Norton's: perhaps that Williamstown was only 24 miles and less than an hour's run from Sandy Creek.[2]

Warren knew John Howe's farm well. But with all of his doing the winter's chores these three or four years, he had never farmed the land. At Mr. Norton's and from the mean little plots his father planted, he had learned the skills of cultivating crops, but he had not experienced the full rhythm of the season or learned in his bones the tough struggle of grubbing out a few acres from the timbered and sometimes rocky inclines of

Jefferson County. He learned well that summer. He "improved" the land, beginning that first day of his summer's work to drag the big rocks out of the oats and corn ground. Some of the stones were so huge that he had to dig a trench around them and build a fire to break them up. He dug out roots, burned out stumps, and hauled off chunks of wood to clear the fields. He plowed greensward, stubble, cornstalks, the rough, unimproved land, dragged it, spread manure, and with a sling over his shoulder helped John broadcast the seed: wheat, oats, rye, buckwheat. John was a progressive farmer. Four times he or Warren picked up "plaster" (plaster of paris--gypsum) from the village and "sowed" it,[3] whitening the fields with the most generally praised "soil dressing." He and John planted potatoes, they "marked" the ground and planted corn at the intersection of the lines, they built a new fence, moved the barnyard, plowed the old one and sowed it to corn which, later in its thick green growth, they would cut for cattle feed. The plots were small, how large we do not know, but we can estimate from the plantings of other farmers that they ranged from two or three to no more than seven or eight acres per crop. The pressure of the work was constant, unrelenting. They had not finished the planting before, on June 1, Warren began hoeing and cultivating the potatoes and the corn. When, on June 22, he plowed all day--the unimproved land we can guess--he confessed that he was "very tired."

Ada at 13 had been a charming youngster, delighted with child's play, proud, too, of her woman's work, a little boastful, preempting credit, perhaps, for tasks her mother had done or helped her to do. Now, four years later, almost 18, she was mature, independent, competent. She did a woman's work as a matter of course, not with a sense of pride in being grown up, but because it was work to be done. She was full, nonetheless, of an unmistakable zest for the doing, and satisfaction in having done it. Her tasks were not unlike those of the earlier year, but more often she worked independently. She did the washing on Monday, the ironing on Tuesday, frequently the sweeping and mopping on Saturday, while her mother did other tasks and looked after Elmer and Grandma. She took over the whole of the housework when Ma fell and injured her leg "between her ankle and her knee so she can't walk," or when Ma and Pa drove up to Uncle Porter's, or when Ma went down to Camden to attend Retta Stone at the birth of her first child. When Pa and

Ma were both gone she not only did the housework but helped the boys, Albert 16 and Jesse 13, with the milking. And she learned something of the trials of a mother with children. When Ma was gone to be with Retta she left three-year-old Elmer to Ada's care. Her only entry in the diary about that distracting responsibility was not so much a complaint as a sigh: "I washed today and it took most all day for we had to churn and I had to look after Elmer." On the whole she seemed contented and happy. Occasionally she posted her irregular report on the condition of the weather, not at the beginning of the entry as Warren always did, but at the end. And so, after noting that she and Ma had washed on Monday morning, and that she had done some sewing, "stichery," for Vina and had gone to meeting at night, she could write, "It is very pleasant today." It seemed less a statement about the weather than a comment on her satisfaction and joy in living.

She worked where she was needed, regularly at home and, like her mother, at times of illness in the homes of her aunts or neighbors. When old Mrs. Fifield died, Ada took over the household duties. She worked three days and sat up one night with the corpse. She sat up, too, with Cora Wilson, Nellie's sister, when she was ill, with Aunt Lydia Harris, and several times with Grandma Onderdonk when the doctor pronounced her at the point of death (she was to live another eight years, until she was 92).[4] One week she went up to Uncle Porter Harris' in Kasoag to keep house while Aunt Clit, who suffered from a sick headache, came down to Stone Hill for rest. Ada washed and ironed on Monday and Tuesday, cooked the meals for Uncle Porter and Wallace, but she had time to visit her cousins and friends, Rosa Spink, Lilly Wheeler, Emma and Ella Austin. She went to Emma's one afternoon, returned to Uncle Porter's to get supper and do up the dishes. Uncle Porter had gone to Williamstown for Aunt Clit and left Wallace, who was 20, and Ada at home. She discreetly went back to Emma's to spend the night. But she was at Uncle Porter's to get breakfast for Wallace the next morning.

Of all her work, Ada liked best to sew. She took over almost completely from her mother. Early in the year she made a new dress for Ma, the skirt first then the "waste." She bought worsted yardage in the village and made a scarf for Pa, she made a dress for cousin Vina, a wrapper for herself, shirts and two pairs of pants for Albert, shirts for Jesse, shirts for Pa, aprons, dresses, and three pairs of pants for little Elmer. She made a dress for Nell Wilson, and an overskirt, a waist for Grandma, a tablecloth, a pair of pillowcases and sheets for Ma. She sewed for Martha and Cora Wilson, Nell's mother and sister, and for Mary Stone. She made carpets, dyeing and braiding the rags and sewing together the braided cords.

Her social life was simple, but apparently satisfying. They had singing school through January and February, on Monday or Tuesday and Friday evenings, chiefly young people in attendance, but adults, too, Pa among them. When instruction ended they gathered in each others' homes to sing. And one Sunday morning Ada and Mary Stone and two others felt well enough practiced to join the "quire" at church. Parties were rare but the young people saw each other at singing school and at the frequent meetings of the church. Now and then Ada went to church with one of her cousins, Wallace Harris, Charlie Harris, or Eli Austin. Dave Norton came to see her when he was visiting Warren Stone. She still liked to walk alone in the woods, went fishing one day but caught no fish, picked flowers another, saw a snake writhing in the moss and killed it.

She kept up a lively correspondence, not with Warren only (whom she always called Clark in her diary), but with Dave and Mate and Dolly Norton, with the Austin girls in Kasoag, with Retta Stone, her cousins Vina Harris and Vira Secor, and Gene Grant whose mother had died so tragically that summer when Ada learned about death. One evening in January, after she had written to Clark she commenced a letter to Uncle Adolphus Onderdonk, her mother's oldest brother, a bachelor and a wanderer who had lived in Iowa for several years. What prompted her to juxtapose those names, to write letters to both of them on the same night (even as Warren had written to her and to Johnny Tryon), we cannot say.

Her spelling had not improved much over the days when she was a young teenager. She still wrote "moping" for mopping and the fourth day of the week was still "Wendsday"--and would be yet when she was an old lady of 70 years making new entries in an old diary. Like Warren she used idiomatic speech which gives us brief glimpses into the conventional language of her people. She "called to Mrs. Wilson's tonight," she did the housework for a neighbor who had been ill and who was "not smart enough to work yet." She felt sorry for Grandma who was very ill and "stupid and sleepy all of the time." In a girlish impulse she invented a code to protect from prying eyes her diary entries about Warren--and sometimes used it, but more often did not. Taking the rule she had learned at school, that the vowels are a, e, i, o, u, and sometimes w and y, she numbered them in order, from 1 to 7, and substituted the numbers for the vowels. So when Warren came to see her and they called on Nellie Wilson, sat up until two o'clock, and were up again at four, she wrote: "62 62nt 4v2r t4 s22 N21132 1 f26 m3n5t2s. 3 62nt t4 b2d t64 4cl4ck. g4t 5p f45r 4cl4ck." (We went over to see Nellie a few minutes. I went to bed two oclock. got up four oclock)." It was a transparent system but no doubt fun!

Nellie Wilson remained her best friend. They went to church together, to Sabbath School, to singing school. Nellie brought her a book, a novel we must guess, the only book she read--or noted--all year. Nellie often came over in the afternoons while Ada sewed for her. She sometimes spent the night (they sat together writing to their "fellows" one evening before they went to bed), or Ada went to her house, two nights in succession one week when she had gone to Nell's for the night, lingered all of the next day, and finally decided to stay a second night. They had much to talk about. Nell had a new suitor that spring, Henry Devereaux. Hank had grown up at Stone Hill, but he was six years older than Nell and had not been much interested in the gangly teenager until now, at 18, she was suddenly a new and no doubt wonderfully attractive young woman. That spring and summer he worked away from the community. When he was at home, Nell brought him over to the Harris' to see Ada. The three of them went to Sabbath School one Sunday, called on a friend, spent the afternoon at Ada's, and at night went to meeting, probably at the schoolhouse. One night, when Grandma was sick, Nell and Hank came over to sit up with her. Nell, quickly abandoning that plan, crawled into bed with Ada and let Hank and Ada's Pa sit up with Grandma.

If, four years earlier, the church had been the dominant force in the Harris family, it was so now with Ada. The mild rebellion of her first year as a teenager, her pride in missing church services, and her brief fling with Warren and the hop pickers at the Norton's last summer--the exhilaration of dancing feet and the rhythmic sway of bodies, and the disregard of the tenets of the church--all of that was over. Sometime between the hop picking season in September and the first of January she seems to have undergone a religious experience, a confession of guilt, perhaps, and a re-affirmation of her faith.

She went to church regularly and, one must judge, gladly, to preaching in the village one Sunday morning, to Sabbath School that afternoon (she had been elected librarian), to classmeeting at four o'clock where the class leader examined the condition of his charges' faith and received their testimonies,[5] and to meeting at night, at the village church, presumably. And so she spent many of her Sundays. When protracted meetings began in March and ran for three weeks, she missed scarcely a night. She rarely commented on a service, never about the content, only once about the quality when she thought a meeting was "real good." It was the kind of appreciative judgment that would be commonplace with her in later years. We can believe that by 1877 she had accepted the burden of her faith, that like her father and her mother she experienced God as a reality, a living presence that transformed, and strengthened, and sustained her, and that, like her mother, she felt the thrust and strength of the Dutch Pietist tradition. We can judge from her later years that she did not become imperious, did not aggrandize by word, did not scold or admonish, but that like her mother, strong and dominant, she sought to control and direct members of her family and close associates by the pleading in her eyes, by her own faithful, even stubborn, adherence to the tenets and practices of the church. In later years she would adopt the proscriptive rules of the pietists in matters of dress and conduct. But in 1877 she was full of the joy and exuberance of life, not ready to give up her child's delight in the trinkets and baubles, the pieces of jewelry, the new dresses with which she loved to adorn herself, the "finery" in which her father indulged her.

Warren, having last visited Ada in late March and early April, came again on June 9, bringing his sister, Dell, with him. The visit was brief. Hard at work for John Howe, he could not get away on Saturday until he had finished planting corn and he was back in the field cultivating early Monday morning. He and Ada made much of their little time. Saturday evening they spent at the Harris'. Sunday morning it rained hard, so they did not go to church--at least Ada, Warren, and Dell did not--but in the afternoon they went to Sabbath School at the schoolhouse. Afterward they walked down the road the short distance to Mary Stone's, stayed, Ada said, a few minutes and walked home. The rain had stopped, the sky had cleared, it was a pleasant day for walking. And for riding. Albert took them, Warren, Ada and Dell, making two couples, out across the countryside. It was, we can be sure, a languid June day, suited to lovers who were happy with any purposeful activity that brought them together. That evening they went over to the Wilsons' to see Nell and her family. Warren says only that they were there "for a while" and ends his narrative for the day. Ada limits the time to "a few minutes." They returned home and she and Warren sat up, she says in code, until t64 4cl4ck (two o'clock) in the morning. She was up again at four to bid Warren and Dell good-bye, but she let Pa take them to the depot and she went back to bed.

Warren returned less than a month later for a gala celebration of the 4th of July. On Tuesday the 3rd he had worked until "most night" before going into Sandy Creek for the evening train. Henry Devereaux, Nell Wilson's friend, met him at the depot at Williamstown and took him out to the Harris'. Early the next morning he walked into Williamstown, hired a horse and buggy, and he and Ada, Nell and Henry, drove up to Kasoag, stopped to watch the "celebration," and then with a local couple, Ed Whaley "and his girl," drove to "the Banks" (Sand Bank, now Altmar)[6] where they had dinner at the hotel. That afternoon they dropped in to see Uncle Porter and his family, went to a picnic in the grove, and back to the fireworks at Kasoag. They had, Ada said, "a splendid time." They got home at one o'clock. Warren, after a brief night's sleep, drove the horse and buggy back to the village, early enough not to be charged for another day, and then walked back to Stone Hill. He stopped for a few minutes at the Stones' and again at the Harris' for a longer time, and walked back the three and one-half miles to Williamstown to catch the two o'clock train.

He had another six weeks of summer work at John Howe's. On the last Saturday in August he dug the first of the new potatoes and hauled a load of them to Sandy Creek. Monday he and Dell left for the hop harvest at the Norton's. Several young people joined them at Williamstown. Ada Harris was not one of them.

The harvest was much as it had been in years past: the young people picked hops all day and partied at night, two or three times a week. The difference was in Warren. He went to the hophouse "for a few minutes" or "a load of us went down to the hophouse," or "We all went over to the DeForests in the evening to a party." He did not say that the parties were dances. If they were, either he did not dance or he did not record what he had done. But he did go for walks, three couples, unnamed, to church one Sunday and to a spring in the woods that afternoon. They walked again the next Sunday, six couples this time. But it was nothing. His thoughts were on Ada. He wrote to her twice in the first week he was at the Nortons', on Wednesday the third day and, without waiting for a response, again on Saturday.

She wrote to him, less often than he to her, two letters to his four. She had been negligent, or reticent, since his visit in July, had written to him only twice that month, only once in August. We know from entries in his diary that she wrote, but she made no record of it in her own diary. Her reasons are obscure. She was very busy--Aunt Clit had been ill again in Kasoag and she had gone to help, Grandma had been sick, and Aunt Lydia, very sick, so sick that Ada, Pa, and Ma took their turns sitting up with her. But she wrote to others, even to Warren's sister, Dell.

On August 3, when she was at her Uncle Porter's in Kasoag, her cousin, Eli Austin, took her to Pine Meadows to an unnamed function at the schoolhouse, an event she thought significant enough to write in code. And later, while Warren was having a good time with all of the girls at the Nortons', a young man in Williamstown, whose identity we know only from her entry, asked her to go to church with him one Sunday night. "I went," she wrote.

For some reason, again obscure, perhaps her love of simple adornment, she went to the village one day, "afoot" (some three and one-half miles) and bought herself "a new filled gold ring." That, too, was sufficiently significant to warrant recording in code--as was the extravagant price she paid for it, two dollars.

But when Warren and his sister Dell stopped at Williamstown, after hop harvest, she was at the depot to meet them. She was casual enough the next morning, ironed some clothes and "done the housework." In the afternoon she and Clark called on Aunt Lydia Harris, who was much better. That night they sat up late and had, Warren reported to his diary, "a good visit all by ourselves." Ada recorded what they talked about, in code. "3 1cc2pt2d a 0 t4 n3ght th1t b3nds m2 t4 (I accepted a ring tonight that binds me to)." She wrote as if she were relieved and happy at last to be bound. She did not get to bed until three o'clock in the morning. Dell, much neglected, remained a few days with Ada. Warren returned to John Howe's for another six weeks of work.

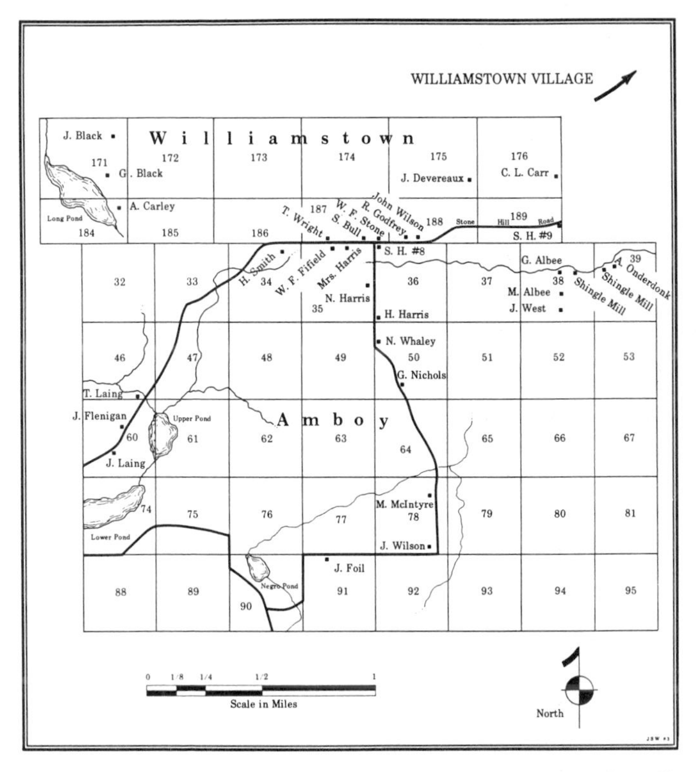


*Map: Parts of Williamstown and Amboy, New York. Adapted from New Topographical Atlas of Oswego County, New York (Philadelphia, 1867), with additions from Ada Harris' diary. Courtesy of New York History.*

# 5.
# A Long Farewell

Ada, busy before, was now feverish with activity. They had set the wedding date for sometime before the close of the year, 1877. She finished a dress for her mother, one she had started weeks before, she quilted, made a tablecloth and four napkins, cut out and sewed an overskirt. She spent a night at Nellie's. Nellie came to stay all night with her and the next day she and Hank were married. "She is Mrs. Devereaux now," Ada wrote. That was Wednesday, October 17. Thursday they all went up to Uncle Porter's where Wallace Harris and his fiancée, Victoria from Sandy Creek, whose last name we do not know, were married. Among the many guests were Warren's parents whom Ada saw for the first time.[1]

She heard from Warren and, no longer inhibited, noted in her diary when she replied. Shortly after Wallace's marriage, on Saturday, she went to Sandy Creek, ostensibly to see her friend, Dell Grant, with whom she corresponded now and then. Clark came to see her that evening and was back the next morning, Sunday, before breakfast. He took her up to Boylston and over to the Howes' to meet his parents and to see John and Bell. She lingered in Sandy Creek for two more days. Clark came to see her in the evenings. Wallace and Victoria, honeymooning in Sandy Creek with Vick's parents, called on her. Sandy Creek, with a population of a thousand people, much larger than Williamstown, had four general stores, one clothing store, two millinery and "fancy goods" stores. She purchased only a ruff for her new dress, a necktie for her father or brother, a white "vale," and some Hamburg lace.[2]

Back in Williamstown, where she could consult with Ma, she bought a new dress and trimmings, a corset, and a pair of shoes. She cut out four chemises and sewed them, one for Ma, three for herself. She made an apron for Ma, one for herself, and two for Elmer, and three pairs of pants for him. She finished a wrapper she had cut out for herself, all but the buttons, and she made herself a pair of "nice" drawers. Her father took her to the village and bought her a new felt skirt, some cuffs, buttons for the wrapper, and another pair of shoes. She cut out and sewed a "busque"--a pleated bodice or corset supported with stays of wood or whalebone--, and an overskirt. For days she worked on a dress, probably her wedding dress, only one day with her mother's help. She cut out and stitched another chemise and a little white underskirt, knitted stockings, made a night dress for herself, and two shirts for Albert. Pa took her to the village again and bought her a new hat, a set of earrings, and a breast pin. He had other business to transact, so she made her own way home, three and one-half miles "afoot," she said.

November had come and almost gone. Nell Devereaux stopped to spend the day with her, Hank came for supper and they both stayed all night. Ada had begun to collect recipes, mostly for pastries, a few for home remedies: for steam pudding, pudding sauce, cookies (which she still spelled "cuckies"), cookies without eggs, ginger cookies, sugar cookies, cream cookies, doughnuts, white cake, marbled cake, surprise cake, fruit cake, jell cake, fried cakes, sponge cake, French fruit cake, dried apple fruit cake, lemon pie, vinegar pie, dried apple pie, currant or berry wine (which must stand, unplugged, for three or four weeks to let it "work"). All of her recipes called for a generous quantity of sugar--from a cup or a cup and a half or two cups for the cookies and cakes to a quart of sugar for three quarts of blackberry pickles. She wrote down how to make yeast, chili sauce, green tomato pickles, cough syrup, ointment for whooping cough.

And as the final entry in her diary--against the day when she might have her first baby, she copied down a recipe for "Parturient Balm," "for the purpose of rendering childbirth more easy."

Take blue Cohosh . . root 4 oz
Lady Sliper root & Spikenard root each 1 oz
Sassafras bark of root & Cloves of each 1/2 oz
bruise all & simmer slowly 2 hours in 2 qts boiling water strain & add 1 lb white sugar
Dose a wine glass full twice a day for 2 weeks or a month before expected confinement.

Warren completed his summer's work for John Howe on November 6, six months and three days at $18.00 a month and 70 cents for each of the extra days, a total of $110.10. He had drawn $38.50 on August 11, an additional $5.00 a little later, leaving a balance due him of $66.60. He does not record what he earned at the Nortons'. On November 6 he settled his account, drew $15.50 of what John owed him and bought a new suit of clothes in Mannsville, perhaps other clothing. That seems to have been the only preparation he made for the wedding.

He worked a few more days for John, irregularly, seven days in all, at 50 cents a day. That brought the total of what John owed him to $54.60. He could not have earned more than $15.00 or $20.00 for the three weeks he worked in the hopyard for Mr. Norton, and from that he had to pay for the ring, his transportation costs, and what other expenses we do not know. He had little hope of being able to collect the money his father owed him. He was about to launch his marriage on savings of less than $75.00.

The wedding was set for Wednesday, December 5. The preceding week, on Tuesday, Ada made two fruit cakes, on Wednesday three more cakes. Thursday night it snowed, and again "by spells" all day Friday. Ada made four white cakes. Saturday through Tuesday she swept the floors, baked bread, did the Monday's washing, sewed "a little," and went to the village.

On Wednesday, the day of the wedding, old Mr. Howe "carried" Warren, John and Bell, and Dell to the depot at Sandy Creek and they took the train to Williamstown. Who met them and who invited them to their home until time for the wedding, Warren does not say. Ada swept the upstairs and the downstairs. It was rainy outside. That was all the she wrote of her preparations, or of the day--nothing of Warren's coming, or of the assemblage of guests in her parents' home.

They were married that evening in the Harris home by the Methodist preacher, the Rev. A. M. Fradenburgh. Henry Devereaux and John Howe signed as witnesses.[3] There was, said Warren, in his only comment, "a great lot of company there." His father and mother were not among them.

Ada, very sober, was rather lovely with her young, smooth, oval face, made longer by her high forehead; her round eyes looked slightly surprised, her hair was in tiny ringlets at her forehead, pulled back severely above her ears, a high comb on the back of her head, a long curl drawn forward over her left shoulder. She wore ear-drops, ribbon bows in her hair, the tips of which showed from behind her head, a lace trimmed scarf and a gold pin to secure it at her throat, a black cord for a pendent, probably her watch. Her wedding gown was a light brown two-piece suit, the jacket over a lighter colored blouse. She used the lovely Hamburg lace she had bought at Sandy Creek to trim her underwear. Warren was handsome in his dark suit, wing collar, and black bow tie, his large eyes deep set, his nose slender, his curly black hair parted on the side and brushed back casually, his mustache full over a rather small mouth. His almost delicate, frail appearance belied his wiry, muscle-hardened body. All of this we know of them, not from any word in the diaries, but from the photograph they had made for their wedding certificate and from the snippets of her wedding dress and Hamburg lace that Ada sent with a note to her daughter-in-law, Kathryn, her son Earl's wife, 55 years later. Indeed, Ada did not even mention the wedding in her diary.[4]

Not for three months, perhaps four, would the demands of spring create a job for Warren. He and Ada had a prolonged honeymoon, not at some far-distant place or exotic resort, but at the homes of their parents, relatives, and friends. They "visited," casually, spending a day or two, or a week, or a month, welcome for themselves and for their help in doing the chores and the housework, both guests and hosts grateful for the shared labors that made communication easier and helped in the business of "sizing up" the new member of the family.

They spent two days at Kasoag with Ada's cousin Wallace and his bride, Victoria, two days with John and Bell Howe, and then old Mr. Howe drove them over to Boylston. Warren's mother, Ada wrote, invited in "our relatives" for supper and everybody had a "nice visit." In the nearly three weeks that followed Warren worked at his winter's chores, in the woods or in the farmyard, chopping, sawing, splitting, piling wood, every day but Sunday, all day occasionally, shorter days when visiting friends, or visits to friends, interrupted him. Ada washed and ironed and knitted and for two days sewed on and completed a pair of pants for Warren that his Ma had cut out. One Sunday morning, when there was no meeting at the church in that remote settlement, she cut Warren's hair which, on the day of the wedding had already begun to look a little shaggy at the edges.

They did not celebrate Christmas. Warren worked in the woods all day with Uncle Walter; Ada and Dell called on Grandpa and Grandma Greenwood. On December 30, Sunday, Uncle Walter drove them back to John Howe's. They went to Mannsville on New Year's eve with John and Bell and the next day drove to Sandy Creek to see Ada's friend from Williamstown, Gene Grant. John and Bell went up to Boylston for two days and left Warren to do the chores and Ada to keep house for him. For the first time they were alone. Monday, January 7, a month after the wedding, Warren "carried" Ada to Sandy Creek and she caught "the cars" to Williamstown. Only 18, away from home longer than ever before and among strangers, even though they were now "relatives," she was no doubt intensely homesick. It is also true, as she penitently admitted in later years, that she had a quick, hot temper. She may have been angry at something Warren had done or said and, overwhelmed by her anger and homesickness, went, as he recorded, "to hir fathers."[5] John had need of Warren for a few days, to help build a rack and to get some logs to the mill. He worked until Friday and then joined Ada at Stone Hill.

They quickly fell into the rhythm of the Harris household: chores and housework, church on Sundays, weather permitting, frequent errands to the village, twice for lectures. They visited much in the neighborhood with Ada's old friends and Warren's new ones: Warren and Mary Stone, Hank and Nell Deveraux, Uncle Ratios, and the neighbors. They saw much of Hank and Nell, spent long evenings with them or stayed overnight together at the Harris' or the Wilson's, where the young Devereauxs lived.

Again Warren sawed and split wood, not for full days as he did at Boylston, but fitfully, working when Mr. Harris did, to reduce to stove size the wood already cut and piled in the yard. He mended shoes, made a "helve" (an ax handle), and one afternoon with no man's work to do, helped Ada quilt. He and Ada "kept house" for the boys when Ma and Pa went up to Kasoag to see Uncle Porter and Aunt Clit. After three weeks at Stone Hill Warren got a job at Uncle Porter's, cutting wood both for him and for one of his neighbors. Ada remained at home but, with Albert, came up to see him one weekend.

Warren then had almost four weeks before his spring job would begin. He had hired out to work again for John Howe. At last, on February 27, Father Harris loaded the young couple's goods into his wagon, tied on behind Ada's cow--that her father had given her to replace the one he had butchered that summer when she was 13-- and, stopping overnight at Richland with Uncle Jabez Clark, drove them the 24 miles to Mannsville. They spent a few days at Boylston, Warren working in the woods, long hours, to get in a supply of fuel for his parents. They returned to John Howe's on March 5. Warren, laconic as usual, merely noted that "Ada and I began work." Ada was engaged, too, for Bell was to have a second child in two months and needed help.

They worked the entire year for the Howes, through the summer and fall and into the winter. It was a good year, but Warren worried about his father's debts and he and Ada were concerned about their future. Chauncey had not paid off the mortgages on his property nor, as far as we can determine, had he made any repayment of the $113.70 he had borrowed from Warren. The annual interest alone on the two mortgages, at seven percent, totaled $35.59, almost precisely equal to two months' wages Warren had earned at John Howe's the preceding summer. In March, for reasons which he did not explain, but probably to protect the farm from any other of his father's debts, he and his father had the deed transferred to him. And in October, with what resources we cannot know or imagine, he seems to have paid off the larger of the two notes. He "took it up," he said, and recorded no further payments of interest on it. Two months later he paid the interest on the other note, $13.14. We can only guess that he farmed for John on shares and had larger returns than wages would have brought him--or, perhaps, that Chauncey had a windfall from his summer work on the lake.[6]

For all their effort, Warren and Ada had little hope that they could make their way in Oswego County. With the inflated land values and low wages, they lacked the capital and apparently saw little prospect of acquiring it. His own father had bought his farm in Richland for $350, sold it ten years later for $1200, and paid nearly $1400 for the 52 acres in Boylston, largely undeveloped. Nathaniel Harris, Ada's father, had tripled his original holding of 50 acres, but he had three sons, and a farmer's lands were for his sons, not for his daughters.[7]

The railroads, however, had broadcast flyers all over the East and the newspapers occasionally published reports of the rich new territory opening up for settlement on the high plains of Kansas and Nebraska, land that was free under the homestead law or available at low costs per acre under the preemption act or the railroad grants. By 1878 John and Bell Howe were caught up in the excitement and Hank and Nell Devereaux had begun to talk about the great West. Johnny Tryon and his parents and Uncle Adolphus Onderdonk, already in Iowa, gave encouragement, we must presume from developing events, to Warren and Ada to join them. Now that he was married, Warren, in the conventional pattern, left the writing of letters to Ada. But in August he joined her in writing to Uncle Adolphus. He made no record of his hopes, nor did she, but there can be no doubt that they shared the American conviction that rural life was the soul of the republic, no doubt that they dreamed the American dream that they should have a farm of their own and that for them, like their grandparents, the future lay in the West. If he and Ada were seriously interested in Iowa, they were unhurried. They did not write again in the remaining months of the year, or if Ada did, Warren made no record of it.[8]

The new year, 1879, offered them no better prospect for the future, perhaps less, than had the first year of their marriage. John Howe had decided to move to Kansas and had no jobs for them. For Warren a fortuitous event of nature intervened, heavy snowstorms late in December and through much of January, to give him, and John, too, unexpected employment. The railroad cuts through the rolling hills near John's place, between Sandy Creek and Mannsville, filled up with snow. The trains could not get through, even with a new snowplow that excited much interest among the farmers, Warren and John included, who gathered on the banks to watch it operate. The railroad hired the men to clear the road with their shovels. Warren worked 18 days over a period of a month in January and early February.

He soon found a place for the summer, with William Bettinger, who lived down by Lacona, close to Sandy Creek. The arrangement seemed a happy one, for Mr. Bettinger, like the Howes the year before, hired Ada as well as Warren. They began work on March 31. It was a good situation but matters quickly went awry. In less than a month Ada was sick. Warren went to the village on Saturday night for medicine. When she felt no better the next morning, he borrowed a horse and took her over to John and Bell's. The days passed and she did not improve. Very probably her father came to take her home. She was gone for over three months, with only two short visits to Mannsville. Warren, in the brief entries in his diary, says nothing about her illness, its cause, or how she was progressing--only that he wrote to her at Williamstown and had letters from her.

In the meantime, John Howe, having put most of his affairs in order, decided to leave for Kansas, alone, as quickly as possible, and to send for his family later. He offered to sell his crops and the part of his stock not yet disposed of to Warren. Mr. Harris, bringing Ada with him, came up from Williamstown. We do not know whether he underwrote the negotiation or simply offered his advice, but while he was there Warren agreed to buy. He did not intend to continue operation of the farm but simply to liquidate the assets he had purchased from John.

Mr. Harris and Ada returned to Williamstown by train, Warren followed with a team, leading Ada's cow back to Stone Hill. The dream of building up a herd and starting out on their own in Oswego County had ended. Warren stayed overnight at the Harris' and returned to Mannsville the next day. He had already quit his job at Bettinger's. On June 4 he took John and his trunk to the train and drove on to Ellis village in Jefferson County to have the bill of sale for his goods and crops recorded. Bell remained on the farm with the children, keeping house for her brother, Warren, and waiting until John was ready to send for her.

Toward the end of June, Warren wrote again to Uncle Adolphus. On July 4, late in the afternoon, he rode the train down to Williamstown, a hurried trip, for he returned the next morning. July was his busy month: corn, potatoes, garden to be hoed and cultivated, hay to cut both at John's and at his father's in Boylston, rye, wheat, and oats to be harvested. By the end of the month he had threshed most of the rye and wheat and in another ten days had finished binding and hauling the oats into the farm lot. Ada came up, alone, on the last day of July to remain for ten days. With the oats in, they drove down to Kasoag, some twenty miles, on Saturday afternoon, to see Wallace and Victoria. They went to Sunday school the next morning and to Uncle Porter and Aunt Clit's for dinner at noon. Warren returned to Mannsville and Ada went on to Stone Hill to remain another month. Before they parted they wrote again to Uncle Adolphus.

Ada returned to Mannsville on September 8, well enough to remain and to take over the housekeeping duties. A week later she and Warren took Bell and the children to the depot at Sandy Creek to start them on their way to Kansas. It took another six weeks to complete the fall work on the farm.

Warren hauled hay and grain to the market or to John's regular customers in Mannsville, he cut and husked and marketed the corn, dug and sold the potatoes, picked the apples. He cut and thrashed the buckwheat and every free day cut and hauled wood, logs to the mill, fuel to people in the village. He traded and sold the rest of the horses and cattle. On October 16 he and Ada wrote another letter, at least the fourth since May, to Uncle Adolphus. A week later Warren hauled away the last of the corn. They packed up their goods, Warren borrowed a team, took Ada to the train, and drove with their goods to Williamstown and Stone Hill.

November and December were a long farewell. Quite clearly by then, Warren and Ada had decided to move to Iowa. None of Uncle Adolphus's letters remains for us to examine, but we can read the record in unfolding events. Guthrie County, where uncle lived, had been settled for a generation and had no free land for homesteaders. But the community was prosperous, the crops abundant, the need for labor constant. They could live with him in his little house until they found a place of their own. Johnny Tryon and his family had lived in Iowa for a decade, Hank and Dell Devereaux probably had already gone west, and the talk, too, of Nell's parents and Hank's father, made the call to Iowa irresistible. Warren and Ada began to make their preparations and to take their last and sometimes tender farewells.

They had not been in Williamstown a week before Warren borrowed a horse and rig to drive over into Oneida County, an almost ritualistic and certainly emotion-laden visit to family and friends. They spent a night with Justus Onderdonk, another with Ann Mott, and drove on the considerable distance, perhaps 30 miles, to Sangerfield, where the Nortons lived. It was there, three years before, that Warren had first seen Ada when she came to pick hops. Dave and Dolly Norton were there and Mary Stone and Lute Whitford, all old friends from the summer when Warren and Ada met. They must have had a great time. Warren wrote only that on Saturday and Sunday he "set around the house and barn all day." On Sunday evening the three couples went down to Patricks'. It was there that they had gone to many lively parties and there that he had taken Ada to a dance. They did not get back to Stone Hill until Thursday, November 13. The next day Albert drove them up to Boylston.

The "visit" to Warren's parents was not much different from all of their earlier ones, save for the constant awareness that it might be, probably was, their last. For three weeks Warren, working with Albert until he went back to Stone Hill and then with Uncle Walter, cut wood, day in and day out, missing only Sundays and two days when the snow fell from morning to night. He thought the weather, on most days, "mild but pleasant," "warm but pleasant," or "cold but pleasant." Evenings they stayed at home to savor the last days with the family, except once when they went to see Aunt Emily and Uncle Kie and twice when they were at Uncle Walter's. On December 3, Warren's father borrowed a horse and "carried" them to Sandy Creek to see Dell and her husband, Frank.

They took the train for Stone Hill on Monday, December 8, three weeks and one day before they would leave for Iowa. Protracted meetings were in progress at the village church. Most of the family went on Monday and again on Tuesday.

A protracted meeting is, in modern parlance, a revival. Its purpose was to convert the uncommitted, or the wayward, to lead them into a religious experience. Typically the preacher's sermon was vivid in language, dramatic in presentation, urgent in its appeal. At the conclusion the preacher called upon those who, to use the language of Ada's mother, had not been "dedicated to the service of the Creator," or those Christians who had grown lukewarm in their faith, to join him at the altar. The preacher pleaded, accompanied usually by an invitation hymn, "Just as I am, without one plea. . ." The congregation shared in the preacher's agony over their loved ones who were unsaved and might be lost. Those who responded to the call gathered at the front of the room, their friends and the leaders of the church around them. The penitent prayed and the forgiveness they felt was real, their spirit unburdened, light and free and joyous. On the second night Warren, as he recorded it in his diary, "went forward." His simple language was the layman's way of reporting the religious experience he underwent. That night he became one with the evangelical spirit of the Methodists--and with Ada. And Ada, gentle and not at all aggressive, but unrelenting in her will, unbending in her faith, had won--or as she would have said, she had "won him to Christ."[9]

The meetings lasted for the remainder of that week and all of the next. The Harrises and Warren and Ada attended them as they were able. Friends came by to see them and they went to see friends. Hank and Nell Devereaux were not among those whose names Warren records--we must presume that they had already gone west. Warren took down boards from the barn and spent several days building a box to ship their goods. They packed it, loaded it on a sleigh, took it to the depot, and shipped it to Stuart, Iowa. The young people of the neighborhood gathered at the Harris' for a farewell party, the girls coming in the afternoon, the boys joining them in the evening. That was Saturday, December 20. On Sunday they went to church.

All of the next week Warren chopped and split a little wood, sat around the house or drove to the village on errands for himself or the Harrises, save on Monday when he and Albert went hunting. The Harrises did not observe Christmas day, but the next night, Friday, December 26, Warren and Ada attended a Christmas tree party in the village with Albert and Jesse and Uncle Ratio's children. Monday they packed their trunks. Tuesday, December 30, Pa took them west to the village of Parish, where they could catch the train directly to Syracuse. Wednesday, the last day of the year, they reached Chicago at eight o'clock in the evening, changed trains, and left two hours later for Stuart, Iowa.

After he had made the last entry in his diary for 1879, Warren closed his book, not to reopen it until later--some days or weeks later we know, because of the change in the color of the ink. As if to emphasize his thought, the pressure of his fingers making the ink flow more freely, he wrote across the page in a strong bold hand the name of a town and the state where it was located: **Culbertson, Nebraska**. Why, out of that vast expanse of western frontier, he picked Culbertson, we do not know. And in any event, on that last day of the year his immediate destination was Stuart, Guthrie County, Iowa.

*Warren Clark. Photograph for wedding, December 1877.*

*Ada Harris. Photograph for wedding, December 1877.*
*Courtesy of New York History.*

# 6.
# First Year in the West

The train pulled up at the station in Stuart, Iowa, just before dark, on Thursday, January 1, 1880, the first day for Warren and Ada Clark in a new land and a new world. Uncle Adolphus Onderdonk was on the platform to meet them. He had brought along a neighbor with a team and wagon to transport them and their trunks to his little house and farm, about four miles from town.[1]

Uncle Adolphus was a bachelor with a bachelor's disregard of the amenities women expect in a household. They reached his place after dark and improvised for the night. The next morning Warren cut a little wood at the doorway and Ada, with her Dutch passion for tidiness, began to clean house. She soon drafted Warren and together they spent the day sweeping, cleaning, undoubtedly mopping, re-arranging the furniture and, Warren said, "other little jobs like that." He and Uncle Adolphus got some straw and made beds--Ada, anticipating the need, had very probably stitched the ticking at home and packed it in her trunk, ready to be stuffed.

They had scarcely put the furniture in place before, on Saturday night, one of Uncle's neighbors, John Kunkle, came to call on them. A farmer, he was the oldest son of Henry Kunkle and Henry, in 1848, had been the second man to establish a claim and settle in Guthrie County. John, now approaching 50 years of age, no longer did the heavy work on the farm but hired a man, or leased his land to him on shares, to put in and harvest the crops while he did the odd jobs, took care of his hogs and cattle, and supervised the farm work.[2] It was a common pattern which Warren understood from his years on farms in New York. Clearly, Uncle Adolphus had talked to Kunkle about this promising young nephew-in-law of his. But John Kunkle was a deliberate man. We must judge, from Warren's entries in his diary, that neither of them approached the subject of his employment on that first evening.

Sunday was warm for the winter, the ground had thawed, the road was too muddy for comfortable walking, and Uncle Adolphus had neither horses nor sleigh. They stayed at home, sat around the house, and wrote letters to their families in New York.

Uncle Adolphus was a cooper by trade, a maker of barrels and tubs, much needed for marketing farmers' produce. He farmed a little on the side, or had others farm his few acres for him. He had free time, or time that he could manage. On Monday afternoon he took Warren over to Mr. Kunkle's. They remained until "most dark." We can surmise that they walked about the farmyard, looked at the barn, the cowshed, the pigpen, the corncribs, the cattle in the corral, the machinery, some of the fields. But Mr. Kunkle did not offer Warren a job and Warren did not ask for one.

By Wednesday, although the day was foggy and damp, the road had dried enough for Uncle and Warren to walk to town. They bought a few groceries and Warren had the broken spring replaced in his much prized watch. There were no letters from home. Continuing the courtship of Mr. Kunkle, Uncle Adolphus asked him that afternoon to draw some wood for him, and the next evening, Thursday, Warren walked over to his place to borrow some flour and butter.

The second Sunday was cold, the ground frozen. Warren and Uncle walked the four miles to the Methodist church in Stuart. Ada, expecting her first child in May, remained at home. Warren, in one of the few times in the many years he kept a diary, recorded the chapter and verse of the text: II Chronicles 14:14: "And they smote all the cities round about Gerar; for the fear of the Lord came upon them; and they spoiled all the cities; for there was exceeding much spoil in them." It was the conclusion of a story of triumph, the victory of Asa over the great hordes of the enemy.

The next morning Warren again split a little wood at the door. In those first days when Mr. Kunkle seemed a good prospect he had not sought other employment, but that morning he walked over to a coal shaft, one of several in the neighborhood, to watch the operation.[3] The day was very cold. It must have made his fingers ache to watch the men working in the cold and to think of grasping the shovel handle with his own worn mittens. He went home and mended them. That evening, January 12, nine days after Kunkle had first come to see him and a week after he had looked over the farm, Warren came to the point--he asked Mr. Kunkle outright to rent him "some of his land" (he had rented a part of it to his brother-in-law, Lou Marlinee). Mr. Kunkle hesitated. He had not yet settled the matter in his own mind. He must think it over a little more. He may have felt uneasy about this young man who had come so far and who had no capital--no stock, no machinery.

Warren visited two more coal shafts the next morning. He went hunting with Uncle in the afternoon and in the evening cut out and began to sew a pair of gloves. Wednesday, in Stuart, he purchased a new cookstove. Mr. Kunkle hauled the new stove home for him. The roads were rough. Warren, fearing that the lurching wagon would throw the stove against the side boards and break the ornate cast iron frame, stood braced against the wagon box and held the stove in place. It was, indeed, the first piece of furniture he and Ada had purchased and he must have been proud of it.

Thursday morning, again at one of the coal banks, Muldoon's, about a mile south of Kunkle's house, Warren hired out to begin work that afternoon.[4] He went home and finished sewing his gloves. That afternoon he sold a little coal and brought a little of it home. The coal shaft was a cut in the earth on the high sloping bank above the stream where the black seam lay close to the surface. There were a number of such mines in the county. Warren's job was to load the coal onto the waiting wagons and collect payment. When trade was slow, he dug the coal out of the bank and piled it on the "dump." One day he had to wheel away the dirt, "lots of dirt," that covered the coal. Occasionally during the week--and it was to be regularly on Sunday--he had to "hoist" water out of the shaft, a job that took two or three hours, sometimes more. One day he sold only two small loads, another the ground was so icy and slippery that the men could scarcely stand up at the shaft and not a team was on the road. But he had many "good" days, some that were "pretty good." One day he sold six "big" loads, another he measured his sales in bushels, 199 of them. He did not record the price of coal but four years earlier the county historian had written that it sold in town for about 15 cents a bushel.[5]

On the first Saturday after Warren had started to work, January 17, Uncle Adolphus, in Stuart on an errand, brought back the first letters from home, one from Albert and one from Ada's mother. And he reported that the box of goods, shipped from Williamstown on December 19, had arrived. Warren arranged with a neighbor, one of the Heaters, Isaac probably, whom he was to come to know well, to haul the box out from town. He brought it to them on Monday night, a month from the day when they had taken it to the depot in Williamstown.

Warren had been at the coal bank a week when he asked Uncle Adolphus to take over for him at four o'clock and he went once more to see Mr. Kunkle. Again they talked over Warren's offer to rent his land, "our bargain," and this time Kunkle agreed to rent--"he made up his mind to let me have it," Warren wrote in his diary. He does not say what the bargain was, but Kunkle must have allowed him less than the two-thirds landlords ordinarily gave to tenants, for he had to furnish not only the land but the horses, the machinery, and even the seed.[6] The arrangement completed, Kunkle gave Warren some meat — advanced it to him against some later reckoning, 21 pounds of pork shoulder, Warren noted in the cash account at the back of his diary.

We can only guess why Mr. Kunkle let Warren have the land. It may have been because they were both Methodists, Kunkle's father the host in his home to the first preacher in Guthrie County, a Methodist circuit rider.[7] Or he may have approved of Warren's work--his wood chopping, his experience as a farmer, his willingness to take up a shovel at the coal bank. Beyond that it may have been simply that enough time had passed for him to get used to the idea of having this young man from New York farm his land.

Spring work on the farm did not begin until March, more than five weeks away. Warren stayed on at the coal bank. He worked long hours, Sundays, too, to hoist the drain water that had collected in the shaft. Very probably, he earned a dollar a day, an amount he was to receive later that year for day work. Uncle's house was close to the coal shaft, a convenient place for the men to have a hot dinner while they waited for Warren to fill their wagons. Ada began to take in boarders, to earn a little extra money.

Twice in January Uncle took Warren's place so that he could go with John Kunkle to the timber to cut and haul wood, probably helping Mr. Kunkle as a means of paying for his own supply. In the last week in February he was at Kunkle's nearly every day. He and John butchered hogs, two for John, one for Warren, which he salted and packed in a barrel. He cut and hauled and split wood for both of them, and one day went into the fields to chop down cornstalks. On March 1 he quit his job at the shaft. He made a cupboard for Ada out of the big box in which they had shipped their goods, helped a neighbor, Tom Shaw, rebuild his shanty, went with John Kunkle and Lou Marlinee to an auction--but bought nothing, and on March 6 borrowed a team from Mr. Kunkle and, with Uncle's help, moved his goods to the farm.

Their house was probably the first one John Kunkle had built on his farm, not much more than a cabin, a "shanty," Warren wrote in his diary. But it was a house of their own, the first since they had been married, save for those few weeks when they had lived at the Howes' after John and Bell had gone to Kansas. It took all day to move and set up the new stove, put the packing box cupboard in place, and arrange, to Ada's satisfaction, the rest of the furniture that they had acquired. At least, Warren said on that Saturday night, "we could live over Sunday."

Kunkle's farm lay four miles north of Stuart, about two miles from the village of Dale City on the South Racoon River, on the open prairie between the undulating hills. A generation before the land had been all prairie grass, tall as a horse's flanks, broken only by the narrow ribbons of trees along the creek beds and the wide band of timber that marked the course of the South Racoon. A creek ran through the farm and a slough, which varied in size with the amount of rainfall, divided the principal fields. Many of the farmers, Kunkle among them, had small holdings of timber on the river where they got their fuel supply. Uncle Adolphus, too, had a plot which he used not only for fuel but for wood from which to make his barrel staves and other products.

Kunkle was a corn and grain, cattle and hogs, farmer. He had some chickens, planted a garden, raised some potatoes and beans, had an orchard. He did the chores, his wife looked after the chickens, Warren was to work in the fields. He shared his responsibilities with Lou Marlinee, a brother-in-law of Kunkle's who farmed some of his land. Lou, eight years the older,[8] and Warren got along well, often exchanged work or worked together, and soon became good friends. They rigged a log to drag over the fields and break off the cornstalks, chopped out the ones that did not break, raked them into a pile and burned them. With Kunkle's help they sowed wheat and oats, and by mid-April had begun to plow for the later planting of corn. Together they chopped and hauled wood, a never-ending demand, and occasionally Warren hauled corn from the granary to Stuart for Mr. Kunkle.

The one unpleasant feature of this new western land was the wind. Warren had seen nothing like it in New York. It blew day after day, week after week, with scarcely an interruption, the last ten days of March, all of April, much of May, and on into June. On the open prairie there was nothing to stop it. Certainly not the canyons cut by the creeks through the prairie or the band of timber in the valley of the Raccoon. Warren noted it in his diary: "windy," "terribly windy," "the wind blew hard and cold from the north," "terribly windy," "pretty windy," " wind blew a gale all day"--these the entries in his diary on successive days in March. On the last of these he yielded to the gale, quit the field and went back to the house before noon. His shoulder ached and he went to bed. April was worse. Despite the rain and mud in early January, the rest of the winter and spring brought little snow or rain. Occasionally the clouds gathered, the skies thickened, and it "tried to rain." No rain fell from the second of April to the 24th, only a few showers on that day, no more for another two weeks, and very little for the remainder of the month of May.

With the fields powder dry, the dust began to rise on the face of the wind. They had an especially nasty time on the 13th of April. "The wind blew so hard," Warren wrote, "and the dust flew so we could hardly see the sun or anything else." He left the field and went to the house. The dust sifted in through the cracks of the shanty and swirled about so thickly they could scarcely breathe and had to get out. Mrs. Kunkle took them into the big house. Late the next afternoon the wind died down and they went home to clean up their place. Ada, reared on the Dutch routine of sweeping, mopping, and cleaning, must have looked on the interior of the shanty with dismay. Putting it in order was "quite a job," Warren said. They had to take almost everything out of the house. That night it rained a little and in the next few days, when Warren could take the time, he and Ada "patched up" the cracks in the house.[9]

Happily, they had a temporary respite from the wind and dust in mid-May. Rain fell on May 8 and in the days that followed only once did the wind blow hard enough for Warren to take note of it. On Friday the 13th a little rain fell toward night. That evening Ada was "taken sick" with labor pains. She suffered all night and through the next morning. The baby was born at noon. They named her Nellie for Ada's girlhood friend, Nell Wilson, now Mrs. Henry Devereaux. Warren, probably Mrs. Kunkle, and a doctor from Dale City, were with Ada until the baby was born. That afternoon Warren was back in the field, and again the next day, Saturday, planting corn. Sunday, he took over the care of Ada and the baby. He "got awful tired," he confessed.

Mrs. Kunkle was a good neighbor. She had no children of her own but that spring, after the death of their mother, she had taken in her two nieces, aged six and eight. The little girls were delighted with the new baby and as soon as she was a toddler, and Ada would let them, they took her to the playhouse by the orchard to make her, along with their dolls, one of their children.[10]

Ada was enterprising. Mrs. Kunkle liked her and soon turned over to her the care of chickens, for which she gave her one-third of the eggs. Nellie, who lived on the Kunkle farm until she was almost three and in the neighborhood for another year, remembered three-quarters of a century later how her mother had divided those eggs, two in a pan for Mrs. Kunkle, one in a pan for herself, and the odd numbers in a third pan, to be distributed the next day.

Warren, too, must have been happy in his new situation. No longer a hired man, he was a renter who farmed on shares. He did not have to "fuss around," as he put it, with the chores. Mr. Kunkle did them. He had odd jobs to do when he was not in the field. He helped Mr. Kunkle clean out the well which they both used, he hauled wood and corn for him, set hedge for a fence, helped him repair his corn shed, for which he received a dollar a day. By the first of April he bought his own cow from old Mr. Kunkle, John's father--to be paid for later; he build a pigpen and bought a pig from Isaac Heater. He planted his own garden, his own melon patch, bought seed potatoes, also from Isaac, and planted them. He liked Isaac, a widower, 20 years his senior,[11] who with the help of his teenage daughter, had managed his household since the death of his wife. He made wooden covers for the glazed pots in which Ada packed fruit and vegetables. In the weeks before and after the baby came he helped Ada with the washing, or took it to a neighbor. Now and then he and John and Lou took an afternoon off and went hunting, for rabbits or prairie chickens. He went fishing with Lou, but caught nothing. And one afternoon he helped John dig out a den of wolves (probably coyotes).

From the time he moved to the farm in March Warren got to church only once, until nearly a month after Nellie's birth. And then he went to meeting in the nearby schoolhouse, Ada and the baby probably with him. The next week he walked to Dale City, undoubtedly alone. But Ada had begun to get out occasionally. She and Nellie went with him the next Sunday to see Isaac Heater, and on the following Saturday, for the first time, she went with him to Stuart.

Once they were located and had time to write to their families and friends they began to hear from them: Mother and Albert and Jesse Harris, but never from Pa; they had letters from Warren's father and mother, and his sisters Dell and Hattie; from John and Bell Howe out in Kansas, from Grandpa and Grandma Greenwood, Norris Clark, Dave Norton, Ada's cousin Wallace Harris and his wife Vick, and from Warren's cousin Johnny Tryon, who lived at Blencoe, Iowa, on the banks of the Missouri River, only 125 miles from Stuart. In mid-April Warren, who had not fully settled his finances with John Howe but who now had a secure situation and some money from his days at the coal shaft, sent a draft to John, paying him what he owed. And in late April he wrote to Hank Deveraux who, with Nell, lived on the very edge of what had been known as the "Great American Desert," in Gosper County, Nebraska, north of Arapahoe, almost precisely on the 100th meridian.[12]

Warren finished planting his corn on May 15, the day after Nellie was born. After the long dry spring, the rains came, a few showers towards the end of the month, rain all of one morning, and then all night on the next to last day of the month, and frequent rains or showers in June and July, even August. The corn prospered. The dry hot days came, too, sometimes after the occasional morning rain, sometimes in succession, three weeks in July, right for the rapid growth of the corn and the harvesting of the grain, the maturing and cutting of the grass. Warren plowed his corn four times over; he and Lou worked together to cut and bind their wheat and oats, and together they made their hay, Lou mowing with a machine, Warren a part of the time with a scythe. They joined others in the neighborhood to thresh, three-fourths of a day at Lou's, and at Warren's from mid-afternoon one day to mid-afternoon the next. And when, at three o'clock, they had finished the hot, dirty job, it was, Warren said, "All hands to the river to wash."

In mid-July a friend of Warren's from Sandy Creek, New York, Merit Widric, who had been out in Kansas with John and Bell Howe, came by to see them.[13] He was a welcome envoy from family and no doubt had much to say about the Kansas plains, and about John and Bell, and sad news to relate. Sometime in late winter or early spring little Elias, named for his grandfather Howe, had died and now lay buried under Kansas sod. He was the baby born in the summer of 1878 when Ada worked for Bell and Warren for John, the first summer of their marriage.

Merit, quite at home with Warren and Ada, stayed a month. Three weeks later they had another visitor from New York, Louis Stone. What a joy that must have been to Ada, to have someone from home. Louis who had lived down the road from her at Stone Hill was the older brother of her close friend, Mary, and the husband of her cousin, Retta, who had grown up in her home. After their wedding, Warren and Ada had called on Louis and Retta in Camden. Like many New Yorkers, and many of Warren and Ada's friends and family, Louis was curious about this western country, and was there to look it over. He did not find it to his liking. In two days he was on his way and when he and Retta moved from upstate New York, they went east to New Jersey.[14]

Generally well situated at the Kunkles though they were, Warren and Ada had little cash income. Warren's earnings from the coal shaft could not have lasted long. He earned a dollar a day, 50 cents for half days, when he worked for Kunkle but that was largely ledger income, not cash, to be balanced against the work John did for him and by the supplies he advanced. Warren worked for Isaac Heater, too, stacked his oats, topped out his wheat stack, helped him thresh, and for Uncle Adolphus and for neighbors, but all of that, like his labor for John, was probably paid for in kind or in trade. He was short of cash. In mid-July he sold his pig, grown to a hog, but two days later he replaced it with several pigs to fatten for the market and to supply his own table. Late in August "Father Harris" sent some money. Warren did not record how much, but as soon as he could get to Dale City he paid the doctor "what I owed him." A week later, to assure himself of his own wood supply when he needed it, he bought a piece of timber from Uncle Adolphus. They went to the river together, got a load of wood for the neighbor who had done Ada's washing, a few hoop poles for Uncle, and measured off the land Warren had purchased. He no doubt paid for it with his services--or deferred payment until his crops were marketed.

By mid-September Warren had begun his fall work. He stripped and cut his small field of cane, hauled it to the mill, and picked up the molasses. He took wheat to the mill to be ground and one load, only one by his record, to the market in Stuart. He plowed, he cut and shocked the corn he wanted for feed. He got poles from Uncle Adolphus and planks that had been replaced in a bridge and built a corncrib. For three days he hauled and spread manure. He dug potatoes, chopped and hauled wood, and picked up a load of coal. He sat with the baby while Ada, who still had the joy of youth in her and the love of the open woods, went with the Kunkles to gather butternuts. A week later he, John, and Lou spent the morning gathering walnuts, and he and Lou picked crab apples in the afternoon.

The last week in October Warren was ready to help Uncle Adolphus husk his small crop of corn. They worked five days, had the help of Lou Marlinee on two days, another neighbor on a third, and they were done. On November 1 he began to husk his own corn. He worked at it for over a month, nearly every day. In that time he interrupted his work only three full and two half days, and Sundays. One day he hau' d corn to town for Uncle Adolphus and cast his vote at the presidential election. One morning he picked up a load of coal, on a rainy day he built a shelf for Ada, helped John repair his cowshed, worked a little more on his own corncrib, and went for more coal. One day when it snowed "by spells" and was "terrible cold," he went to Uncle's timber and got a load of poles for him. One morning he was sick and didn't get into the field until afternoon. The rest of the time he husked corn, banging the ears against the high board day in and day out. Toward the middle of the month John

Kunkle helped for two days, then Uncle came, half days or less, irregularly at first and then in the last week moving over to Warren's house and helping full time. Lou Marlinee, too, came to help the last three days. They finished on December 4. Uncle Adolphus moved back home. Again the day was "terrible cold," 14 degrees below zero.

With his own corn in the crib, Warren spent four days helping his neighbor, Tom Shaw, finish his husking. He hauled wood and coal for himself and Uncle Adolphus, corn fodder for John Kunkle. Twice he went hunting with John and Isaac. The year drew to its close. He had been to church several times in October, not at all in November or December, and Ada, by his record, not since September. Now the last Sunday of the year, the day after Christmas, a mild morning after several days of snow, he and Ada went to church at Dale City, a couple of miles away. They went "afoot," he wrote, and carried the baby.

On Friday, the last day of the month, they had a letter from Hank and Nell Devereaux, from out on the new frontier in Nebraska. And so ended their first year in the west.

*Burlington & Missouri River Railroad Company's land poster. Courtesy of Nebraska State Historical Society.*

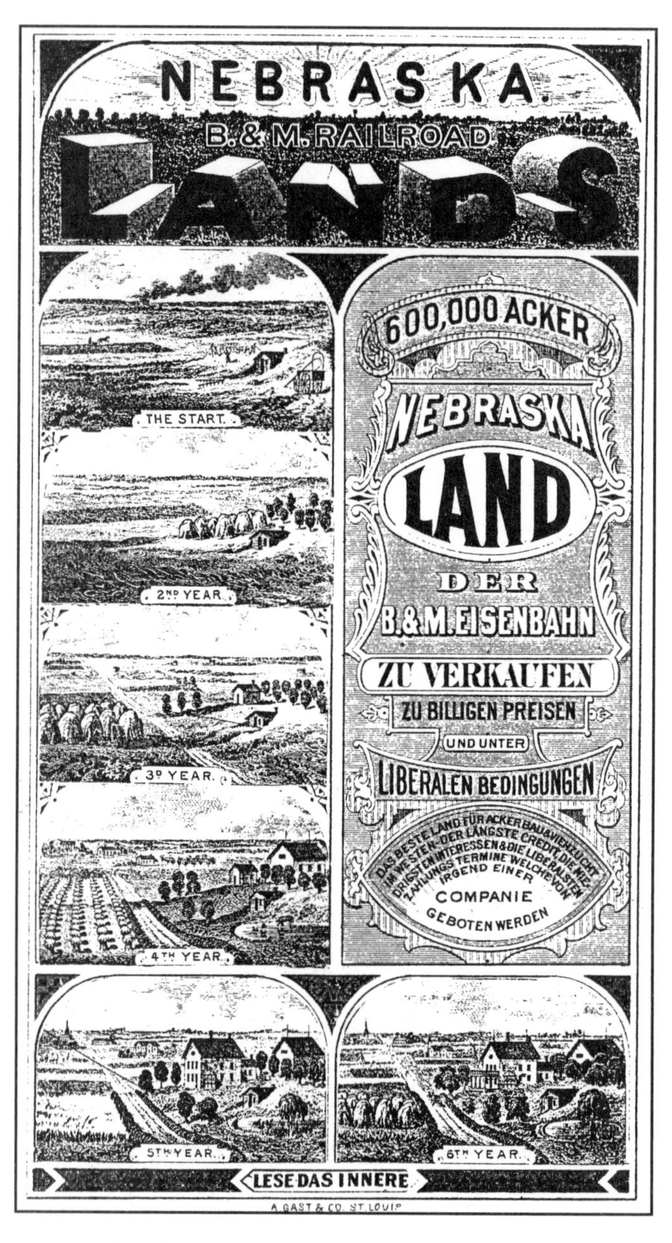


*Burlington and Missouri River Railroad Company's German language land pamphlet, ca. 1881. Courtesy of Nebraska State Historical Society.*

# 7.
# For My Independence

Warren and Ada stayed on at the Kunkles' another two years, until March, 1883, years not much different from the first. The early months of 1881 gave a different taste of weather. January ranged from mild and thawing to stormy and cold. It was "terrible cold" one morning, 25 degrees below zero, the coldest that he recorded. The wind blew and the cold penetrated their warmest clothing and the thin walls of their shanty. One stormy February day drifts of snow piled up until Warren and John had to shovel a path to the farm buildings, throw the snow back from the gates and the barn doors, and break their way through the pasture to the road. But they managed, Warren "setting" in the house on the stormy days, all of them huddled about the fire, no one going out but to do the chores or replenish the pile of wood.[1]

The spring months in these years were wetter than in 1880. Rain or snow fell on 15 days in April, 1881, 13 in May. In that sticky black soil Warren's plow would not scour. He took it down to the creek bed where the soil was sandy and tried to scour it there. But the rains fell and the black earth still stuck to the share. He went to town and bought a new plow.

That was a gesture of his independence, a growing confidence that he could make his own labor more productive by a modest acquisition of stock and machinery. In January, 1881, he struck a "bargain" with John Kunkle to purchase a team of horses, "Old Jim," and "Old Charley." That reduced his dependence on Kunkle and increased his own value in the exchange of work with his neighbors. In some manner he bought or traded for a wagon and got planks from an old bridge, as he had done for his corncrib, to repair the box. He bought harness for his horses. In 1882 he bought a harrow, from whom he does not record, a corn planter from a neighbor, and a cultivator from a merchant in Stuart to whom he gave his note for $34.00 at ten percent interest. He paid up promptly, without recording the transaction in his diary, but he folded the receipt and tucked it into the side pocket of the little book.[2]

He worked hard, constantly, unrelentingly, in the field, or around the house or farmyard when the rain drove him out of the fields, from mid-April when he began plowing for wheat until the last of July when his harvest was over and he had finished cultivating his corn. He took only one day off, aside from Sundays, that one for the Sunday school picnic, the last Saturday in June, and when he got home at five p.m. he went into the field to cultivate corn. He plowed corn on July 4th, Independence Day, the one yearly holiday that he and Ada had always celebrated in New York when they were courting, and even after they were married. But in 1881 he was in the field. "I plowed corn all day for my Independence," he wrote in his diary. The day was "pleasant and quite cool."

His purchase of a cow and pigs in the first year had given him milk and butter and meat. In January, 1881, he bought chickens for Ada, in March he sold a load of hogs in Stuart. In the summer he bought a second cow and another load of pigs. He had his own garden, raised his own potatoes, beans, and garden produce, and stored them in the cave that served both them and the Kunkles. With her share of the eggs and her own chickens Ada could now exchange both in the market at Stuart for groceries and small household items.

The possession of his own stock and crops gave Warren a sense of independence that was reflected simply, as a matter-of-fact, in his diary entries. He referred to "my cow," "my hogs," "my garden," "my cowshed," and "my pigpen," "my wheat" and "my corn." And, indeed, they were his. In the spring of 1881 he began to haul his corn to market, not many loads of it, but a cash return on the harvest of his crops.

Warren's growing independence, particularly his purchase of a team and wagon, and Nellie's growth from baby to little girl, brought some emancipation to Ada, too, some escape from the confining quarters of their little house. The nieces of Mrs. Kunkle, having adopted Nellie as their doll-child, took her to their playhouse by the orchard for endless hours of make-believe. With the team and wagon, Warren and Ada could get about the neighborhood even when the roads were muddy or there was a little rain or snow, and take Nellie with them. They drove to Stuart to have the baby's picture taken. They went to Dale City often, to preaching on Sunday afternoon or Sunday night, and occasionally the longer distance to Stuart. In April, 1881, Warren and Ada helped to organize a Sunday school at the schoolhouse, less than a half mile from the Kunkle farmyard, and from then until it closed for the winter in mid-September, one of them, usually both, were in attendance every Sunday.

Going to church and Sunday school widened their circle of friends. Warren had come to know most of the men in the neighborhood, but until they had their own horses, Ada saw little of the women. Now they frequently dropped in on their friends after Sunday school or on Sunday afternoon. They went to the Knotts for Sunday dinner, Ada stopped at the Batorffs while Warren went to the river for wood and when he returned, they stayed for supper. They stopped at the Baileys for dinner, at the Powells, the Shaws, the Marlinees. The Batorffs came to their house, the Marlinees, the Heaters, and others, all church friends. In late August, 1881, when the harvest was over, they drove with the Baileys to camp meeting at a nearby settlement.

That they had become accepted in the community, that Warren was not regarded as a hired hand but as a farmer in his own right, became apparent early in January, 1882. Lou Marlinee and Isaac Heater, members of the district school board, came by one Sunday afternoon to inform him that they had elected him clerk-secretary to fill a vacancy on the board. Warren must have felt a sense of pride. They were friends of his and he could expect esteem from them, but they were responsible to the community, too, and their choice of him acknowledged both his personal qualities and his better than average education. The nearby town of Stuart had its quota of college graduates but who, other than Warren, in this rural district, would have completed his elementary school, studied for a term at an academy, and taken the Regents' examinations?[3]

His duties were many and varied. Board meetings were casual. Lou and Isaac stopped in at Warren's, or he at one of their houses. They balanced their books, selected items for school meetings, and prepared notices. As clerk, Warren rode about the district to post notices of school meetings and elections, took the school census, wrote letters to prospective teachers, and interviewed them, participated in the hiring, visited the school and observed the teacher. He also had duties less strictly related to instruction. When the grass on the school grounds grew tall, he or one of the other board members mowed it. He and Lou painted the building, and Warren mixed mortar and tended the bricklayer when he put up a new chimney. In an attempt to beautify the grounds, Warren got some trees from Isaac Heater and he and Uncle Adolphus planted them in the schoolyard.

Warren and Ada were soon well entrenched in the new community, but they did not easily let go of the old. Warren was not very good at recording Ada's activities and we must suppose that she did much more writing to their New York family than he did. But he, too, was faithful, not to most of the friends to whom he had written in the early months after they left New York, but to members of the family, his and Ada's alike. In a day when men left the correspondence to the women, he wrote to his mother and to his father, too, and his father to him. There was a strong bond between them, a respect for his father, however incompetent or unlucky he was in his finances, and an affection from father to son. And he wrote to Hattie and Dell, to his cousin, Norris Clark, to his Iowa cousin Johnny Tryon, whom he had not yet seen since he had come west, and to John and Bell.

In the late fall of 1881 John and Bell came by to see them, en route from Kansas to New York. Their venture into Kansas had been neither successful nor happy. 1880, their first full year, had been dry and dusty, and 1881 not much better. They had lost their infant son and now were taking the remains of little Elias with them, back to New York, to be buried near the family home.[4] Warren and John sat in the house the first day, doing no work but the chores. They must have talked much about life on the plains, but Warren recorded not a word of it. The next day Warren worked a little, cut some cornstalks to put on his cowshed, and went over to Ben Williams, from whom he had bought a cow in July, to pay what he owed and take up his note. John went along. The transaction must have given Warren no little satisfaction. They sat around again on

Sunday, worked a little on the cowshed the next day, and Warren took them to the train at Stuart on Tuesday.

Bell and John had been home in New York less than two weeks, scarcely long enough for her to see her family, when her father and Warren's died. He was 59-years-old. Warren, when he received the news, turned back the pages of his diary to December 1 and made a simple entry: "Father died 12 o'clock tonight." Two days before Chauncey died, he and Alma deeded the farm to Bell for $1.00. Alma went to live with John and Bell.[5]

One wonders if Warren thought then of what the doctor in New York had said to him: that he, like his father, would develop weak lungs and contract "consumption" if he did not leave that cold, damp climate?[6] He had been sick several times a year in New York and had spent a number of his Sundays in bed for a part of the day, and now in Iowa, for several days in the cold and rainy winter and early spring of 1881, and in the late summer, and again in the fall. He tried to work through his misery, noting in his diary that he was "most sick," that he "didn't do much work," or "I set in the house the rest of the day." He rarely consulted a doctor but he rode horseback to Stuart for medicine, and when he had been ill for several days Ada gave him a "sweat."

In the fall of 1881 he was "most sick" for the latter two weeks of October, never ill enough to be confined to his bed, but sick enough to take note of it, to do little work, and to sit in the house. But his corn was in the field and had to be husked. He was "most sick" on Monday, the last day of October, but he hauled a load of hay and he and John Kunkle finished building a new privy.

Tuesday was cold and rainy. He banked the house for winter and set posts and put up most of the roof poles for a shed to shelter his cows. Wednesday, November 2, he finished putting up the roof poles on the cowshed and began to husk corn. Uncle Adolphus was on a job over at Corning, some 50 miles away, and unable to help him. Ada let him husk alone that first afternoon, but the next morning she was in the field with him. We do not know whether she was worried about his illness or simply that she was not very busy in the house and knew that he needed help. She dreamed of his "independence" as much as he did, and she was certainly as resolute. She apparently left Nellie with Mrs. Kunkle and her nieces. She would have scoffed at the idea, but there is something heroic about that short, slightly stout young woman, swathed in her great ankle-length skirts, her scarf twisted about her neck, her coat wrapped around her, facing the "cold, raw wind" Warren reported in his diary, trudging after her husband, up and down the rows, wrenching the reluctant ears from the stalks, and throwing them into the wagon. She worked most of the month, some days afternoons only, some of the time all day long. Without the help of Uncle Adolphus, they finished on November 29, almost a week before Warren and Uncle had husked the last of the corn in the previous year, and in time for Warren to husk for a neighbor, to help John cover his cowshed with cornstalks and straw, go hunting several times with John and Lou Marlinee, and catch up with his winter chores of cutting and hauling wood.

Despite his modest success and obvious satisfaction in the possession of goods, Warren had farmed on a very small scale and had harvested in these two years only enough wheat for his family needs, enough oats for his stock. He did not record the acres of corn he planted but it could not have been many. We can make a rough estimate for the summer of 1881, his second year. He spent parts or all of 14 days cultivating his checked corn twice over, down the rows and across. He was interrupted seven of the 14 days by rain. One afternoon because of heat he did not return to the field until three o'clock. He walked behind the cultivator, his heels sinking into the soft, freshly plowed earth, slowing his gait. The hot, humid weather was harder on him than on the horses. He had to stop at every row's end. "It was so warm it nearly used me up," he wrote. It took him, then, about five full days to plow once over. If he plowed four or five acres a day, he would have farmed 20 or 25 acres, given the heat probably a little less. The average yield for Guthrie County, reported in the census for 1880, was 40 bushels to the acre. We can estimate, then, that Warren's total yield was 800 to 1000 bushels. Prices fluctuated from year to year but were reported in the Guthrie *Locomotive* at 43 to 45 cents per bushel for 1882. That would have made his crop worth $360 to $450.[7] Warren had first of all to pay the landlord his share, probably a third of the whole, or more, because John Kunkle furnished the machinery and stock. And he turned over to Kunkle enough of his own share to pay for his team of horses and some of the supplies he had drawn during the year. In the end he had but seven loads of corn to sell in town, or only seven that he recorded. We have no measure of how large the loads were, nor do we know whether the corn was shelled or not, probably not, for Warren's only reference to a corn sheller is a hand machine he borrowed to shell his seed corn. He did a little better the next year, his third, when he acquired a second cow, some calves, and two litters of pigs.

The modest accumulation of stock and machinery was not enough to satisfy Warren with his near subsistence farming. He wanted to rent a larger farm--or buy one of his own. Friends of his, including John Kunkle, seem to have supported him in his effort to do better. Late in August, 1882, after three seasons with Kunkle, he tried to rent a farm at Dale City, but did not get it. In September, with the harvest over, the hay in, and the corn not yet ripe enough to husk, he went with his neighbor, Ben Williams, and two of Ben's brothers, north toward Guthrie Center, looking for a farm to buy. Ben left him with the owner of a country store whom they both knew. Warren looked about the neighborhood, saw a farm for sale and tried to buy it. He looked at another the next day, liked it, walked part way and then caught a ride to Guthrie Center where the agent lived. After extended conversation, he "made some arrangement about buying" the farm. A scrap of paper serving as a receipt and tucked away in a pocket of his diary, records the transaction. He put down two dollars as "earnest money in purchase" of the small farm, 56 acres at $15.00 per acre. He was to pay $100 cash, $168 on February 1, 1883, and assume a mortgage for $200 on or before July 1, 1883.[8] Presumably, he was to have longer to pay the remaining amount due. The farm was about the size of his father's place but all of the land was productive and the price per acre but two-thirds what his father had paid. It was a wild dream. He hoped to make it come true in the same way that he had bought his horses and cattle, his plow and cultivator: by persuading someone to sell him the property against the future, to take his note and let him pay it off with his labor and his crops. The agent's transaction was subject to the approval of the owner. She did not approve, and Warren's dream came to an end.

A month later, October 21, 1882, Warren went to Stuart and on the way home stopped at Sam McMonigal's whose farm, he had heard, was for rent. They bargained for the rest of the day and Warren got the farm. It was larger than Kunkle's, or the acres available for rent were more. Sam would remain on the place but he was through with farming, was about to put his goods up for sale, and wanted a renter to take over. A couple of days later Warren bought a colt for $60, on his note due in one year at eight percent. He borrowed a harness, hooked the colt up with old Jim and Charley, and began plowing at McMonigal's with a three-horse team.

He still had his corn in the field at Kunkle's and his year was not up until March 1. He and Ada remained on the place, with the good will of the Kunkles. John, obviously, liked this young man, approved of his energy and ambition, and thought it proper that he should try to improve his lot. Ada did not help with the corn this fall. She was pregnant, expecting the birth of her second child in December. She had been sick in May and Warren had done the washing and the housework and cooked a few meals. He husked his corn alone that fall, save for help from neighbors on two days, and finished the first week in December. That was in good time for him to get his winter chores done and to take over for Ada when she needed him, to wash the clothes and do the housework. The baby was born on December 24, a second daughter whom they named Mary but over the years were to call Mamie.

The day before the birth of the baby Warren's cousin, Johnny Tryon, came to see him. Johnny was among his favorites, the cousin to whom he had written most frequently, both from New York and since he and Ada had come to Iowa. Johnny had left New York in 1867 with his parents and now lived with them and his own wife and children on the same farm, or an adjacent one, at Blencoe, a few miles above Council Bluffs, not far from the Missouri River.[9] They had prospered on their western farms and were much pleased with the Iowa prairies. Johnny stayed more than a week, days full of exciting talk for Warren, and of hope for the future. But for that winter he had other responsibilities, work enough to do in the next two months at the Kunkles' and a whole year on the farm he had already leased from Sam McMonigal.

He moved on March 1, with John Kunkle, Lou Marlinee, and Isaac Heater each hauling a load for him: household goods, machinery, tools, feed for his stock--and he had to go back another day for some of his tools and what hay he had not been able to sell to John Kunkle. Quite an accumulation for three years. In those last two months he had hauled 11 loads of corn and one of wheat to sell in Stuart, and he had picked up a little extra cash, or credit, with his team and sled by hauling coal from Muldoon's coal bank to town, seven loads in all. But he was still hard pressed to meet the conditions of his lease. The last day of February he spent "most all day" in Stuart "rasing money to pay my rent." To meet his obligation he had to sell part of his corn, pledging next year's crop, we presume.

McMonigal's was a good farm and a pleasant place to live. They were only a mile from Stuart and went there to church rather than to Dale City. They soon had a new circle of friends whom they saw after church or who came to see them. Sam and Martha McMonigal were friendly and loved children. Martha invited Ada to come to her house to sew and she played with the girls and read to Nellie. Mac would lift Nellie to the back of the workhorse where she firmly grasped the harness to ride on his "pony."[10] Warren and Ada held on to their friends in the old neighborhood, went to see the Kunkles, the Marlinees, the Heaters, all of whom stopped now and then on their way to or from Stuart. In March, when Mary was three-months-old, they drove to town to have pictures taken of both babies, "the children," for the family back in New York.

Warren was busier than ever in the field that summer. To judge from the days he cultivated corn, he had, perhaps, planted half again as many acres as in the years at Kunkle's. In June he sold "Old Jim," one from his first team of horses, and in August traded the other, "Old Charley," for a cow and calves. To do his farm work he must have acquired another horse without recording the transaction in his diary. In November he traded some cattle for a colt to match the one he had bought the previous fall. By the end of summer he had sold oats, hay, hogs, and cattle, and had all of his corn to sell.

When he had put up his hay and finished his fall work about the farmyard, and before it was time to begin husking the corn, he took the train to Blencoe to see his cousin, Johnny Tryon, and his Uncle John and their families. He went, too, to work for pay and, perhaps above all, to look over the place and see what it might have to offer him and Ada.

The Tryons owned their farms, cultivated cane as one of their principal crops, and operated a molasses mill. They processed their neighbors' cane, on shares, as well as their own, and produced molasses for the market. Warren spent a month with them, from September 20 to October 22. He worked two days at the mill helping to make repairs and get the machinery ready to run, for over two weeks he hauled cane to the mill, and he spent five hot, sticky days at the "boiling works," where the stalks were pressed and the juices cooked. But he also had five or six days to "visit," to look over the farms, and the flat prairies between the great bluff to the east and the river. The land had been settled a few years later than in Guthrie County so that even late comers like the Tryons had been able to secure good farms. From the sale of their New York property, the Tryons must have had some capital to invest in land, to give them a start.[11] And there can be little doubt that at the sight of their land and their growing prosperity, Warren was aroused to a new determination to have his own farm. Before he left for home the two Tryons, Uncle John and Cousin Johnny, offered him a job or a chance to farm on shares with them. In a new country there might be new opportunities.

Back at McMonigals' Warren caught up on his general farm work and began to get his corn out. Uncle Adolphus helped him. They were at it nearly all of November and through most of the third week of December. He had a good crop of corn, a few oats, and a large amount of hay to sell. Stuart, for this new settled country, was a large town with a population of about 2,000 people.[12] Many families had their own horses and a milk cow. The local market for feed was good.

Warren gave notice to McMonigal and began to liquidate what he had in crops and livestock. He hauled five loads of oats to town, 22 loads of hay, and sold some in the stack, and 29 loads of corn. He sold off his hogs and most of his cattle. In the slack days of January and February, as he had done in the winter after he had acquired his own team, he hauled coal to town, eight loads in as many days. He had burned coal that winter, had chopped very little wood, and now he paid for what he had burned and made a bit of money, too.

By what little evidence we possess, we must judge that he had a profitable year, the best that he had experienced in Guthrie County. But he had determined not to stay another year. Possessed of a dream, a farm of his own, he would do what he could to make the dream come true.

# 8.
# Rain Follows the Plow

On the 21st of February, 1884, Warren and Ada began packing to move to Blencoe. Ada and the children would go by train, he would ship most of his goods by freight but drive through himself, taking what he could in his wagon. Sam McMonigal helped him haul his goods to the depot. Warren and Ada drove over to the Kunkles' to spend Saturday and most of Sunday with their friends in the old neighborhood. On Sunday night Warren went back to McMonigals', alone, and the next morning, with Sam's help, loaded his wagon and started out. It took him eight days, including the Sabbath when he stopped over, even though he was only a day's drive from the end of his journey.[1]

Ada and the children arrived long before he did. Nellie, who was almost four, would remember some of the events. Her cousins had measles. Ada could take the children to the hotel, their relatives said, but measles were all over town and they would probably catch them anyhow. Or they could go to Johnny Tryon's, Ada could help take care of the sick children, and the Tryons would help look after her children when they were sick. They went to Johnny's. And they caught the measles, the children and Ada, too.[2]

Warren began work almost at once, back to the old routine of cutting wood, this time at the sandbar near the Missouri River, hauling it to the house, chopping and splitting it. He helped with Ada and the girls when they were sick and sat up a "good part" of one night. "When [we] were ill," Nellie said, "Papa was always good at caring for Mama and we children."

They were to move into the Tryon granary, which Nellie thought amusing, as soon as Johnny got his machinery out of it and Ada and the children got over the measles. The children were soon well, but it was a month before Johnny emptied the building so that Warren could clean it out, cut a hole for the stovepipe, make a few repairs, and move in the furniture. The granary was big and roomy, Nellie judged, as she looked back on their experience, for it accommodated not only the four of them, but relatives who from time to time stayed overnight with them. To Warren, whenever he referred to it in his diary, it was "the house," never, after they moved into it, the granary.

There were only a few things that Nellie remembered from that year, for one the molasses cookies that her mother made, and the pumpkin butter sweetened with sorghum, "Oh, so good." They had lots of sorghum molasses. Warren brought it into the house by the barrel. And Nellie remembered the Indians who, so recently dispossessed of their open prairie, wandered about the community and the farmstead, picking up property that Nellie thought not rightly theirs: pies, for instance, freshly baked, that Mary Tryon had put on her window ledge to cool. But Mary only laughed. Her sister-in-law, Ida Cook, after a hostile exchange between settlers and Indians, had shown kindness to an Indian who came to her door wet and hungry. The Indians had reciprocated with a gift and had become friendly to the whole family. They often took Mary's pies, she said. Warren, too, encountered the Indians and reacted to them as casually as he would to other men, noting simply that he had helped them pick up their loads of corn.[3]

Little in Warren's experience, at least in the record he made of it, suggests that he thought of himself as being on the frontier, or close to it, nothing to indicate that he advanced his dream to have a place of his own, or even that he continued to dream. He farmed for the Tryons, principally on shares, cultivating and harvesting his own crops, a little wheat, a few acres of oats, larger crops of cane and corn. Some of his fields were on the "prairie," an expanse of flat land between the Missouri and a high bluff along the Little Sioux River. If he tried to bargain for the purchase of a farm he made no record of his effort. Sometimes he worked directly for the Tryons, for wages one must presume; now and then he and Johnny helped one another, as in harvest. Ada occasionally worked in the field with him, two days in the harvest when she helped him bind the wheat and oats, a few afternoons and once all day in the fall when she helped shuck corn. Warren did not attempt to feed hogs or buy and sell cattle, as he had at Stuart, but he had his own potatoes, beans, pumpkins, and garden. And he worked three weeks at the sorghum mill, the "boiling works."

And so the summer passed. And the fall. They saw much of Warren's cousins, the Tryons, the Samsons, the Cooks, went to church quite regularly, to town when they chose. They must have enjoyed being with family. Ada could borrow a sewing machine, and did, from Ida Cook, had some place to leave the children, could throw a pad on the floor for the young cousins when they came to spend the night. Warren abandoned his correspondence with friends--probably relying on Ada to take it over, and wrote infrequently to his mother and sisters, once to his grandmother. As in the past he made no accounting of what Ada was doing unless she helped him. We can judge from the years when we do have a record that she continued to write to family and friends and kept the dream alive. Warren, despite the terse notes in his diary, undoubtedly dreamed the dream with her.

Whatever the record, they certainly remained conscious of Nell and Hank Devereaux on their homestead in Gosper County, Nebraska, north of Arapahoe. Nell Wilson Devereaux was Ada's dearest friend at Stone Hill and Hank was one of the two witnesses to sign Warren and Ada's marriage certificate. Nell's mother Martha and sister Clara had followed them west and lived in the village of Arapahoe. There was free land in Nebraska for farming it and living on it for five years. New counties were opening for settlement west of them.[4]

The appeal was to the great American dream, Jefferson's dream romanticized--the farmer on his own plot of ground surrounded by his fields and his orchard. Charles Dana Wilber, a Nebraska land speculator and amateur scientist, circulated a sprightly written pamphlet to tens of thousands of prospective settlers who lived in Iowa and other states east of the Missouri River touting that dream: a "happy home filled with . . . merry . . . children," and half-concealed by the trees the "barns, pens, coops, granary, shed for wagons, plows and machinery. . . . Farther away . . . in a grassy plot shaded by two elms was a white school."

"This is the last chance," wrote L.D. Burch, a Chicago editor, in his immigrant guide, "for the enterprising and landless poor to secure a free farm and home within the great agricultural belt of the United States." But, he warned, "there are thousands who look to the homestead as their last hope of acquiring independence and to such there is no time to waste . . . ."[5]

Agents, working for the railroads or land companies, distributed the circulars in the states east of the Missouri or put them in the hands of new settlers who sent them to their friends in older states. If Nell Devereaux did not send along any of the pamphlets about southwest Nebraska or clippings from the newspapers, Warren and Ada would have received them from others. Even for those who did not subscribe to a newspaper the advertisements were readily available, passed from hand to hand, talked about in gatherings around the stove in the general store. And right in Blencoe and Onawa they had much to remind them of the opportunities in the West. All that fall, the Monona *Gazette* reported, despite the heavy rains, the prairie schooners continued "to sale [sic] through Onawa" on their way to Nebraska and the Dakotas. Iowa was a prime target for the Nebraska propagandists. Hundreds of immigrants like Warren and Ada had come west looking for a new opportunity only to find the lands already priced beyond their limited means, "increasing in value rapidly" in Monona County, the *Gazette* said. And now the sons and daughters of the first settlers, members of the second generation, were too numerous to be sustained on the farms of their fathers. Like Warren and Ada they had to move on. Among them was at least one of their friends from Guthrie County, Isaac Heater.[6]

As for the dream, Warren had no need to be persuaded of its reality. He had only to recall the experience of his own family: his father, his uncles, Austin and Jabez Clark, Ada's father and her uncles, Horatio and Porter Harris, Uncle John Tryon in Iowa, and countless others whom he had known in his boyhood, had moved or been born into families that moved westward.

He may have had some concern about drought on the plains, wondered if the rainfall was too little, too uncertain to produce crops. That may have been the reason his brother-in-law, John Howe, nurtured in the abundant rainfall of upstate New York, had abandoned his farm in Republic County. The years he spent there, 1880 and 1881, had been dry in some parts of Kansas and Nebraska and in Iowa too. Warren and Ada well knew that from their effort to keep the dust out of the house at the Kunkles in that first year in Iowa.[7] But it may have been more grief than weather, sorrow over the loss of little Elias, that had sent John and Bell back to their loved ones in New York.

There had been much argument about the suitability of the plains for farming. The tide of immigration had halted at the Missouri River, or just beyond, in the decade of the 1860s, but after the Civil War had rolled on west, pouring into the valleys of the rivers. Men warned that it must stop at the 90th meridian, or the 100th: beyond lay the Great American Desert.

But a curious phenomenon occurred. As the settlers moved west, the rain increased. John Wesley Powell, director of the Survey of the Rocky Mountain Region, thought it merely a cyclical fluctuation--the rainy years would be followed by dry ones. Publicists and promoters scoffed at him and even scientists, including Ferdinand Hayden, of the Geological and Geographic Survey of the Territories, and those at the fledgling University of Nebraska disagreed. They found reasons for the change: the planting of trees, of corn, and other crops, the plowing of the land so that it absorbed the rain rather than allowing it to run off the impervious buffalo grass into the gullies and creeks. These changes, they argued, resulted in increased evaporation, more moisture in the atmosphere, and increased rain. Wilber condensed the argument into a brilliant aphorism: "The rain follows the plow." Railroads, land agents, travelers spread the word, and local newspapers and settlers embraced it gladly. Said the Plum Creek (Lexington), Nebraska, *Pioneer*, in 1883, experience had demonstrated that "as the sturdy farmer takes possession of and cultivates the soil the Great American Desert moves still further west, and soon we may look for it to entirely disappear."[8]

If Warren had a moment's doubt about the threat of the desert, if he reflected on why John and Bell Howe had given up in Kansas and gone back to New York, he did not let his doubts check his rising interest and hope. Wilber's magic phrase, or the sentiment it expressed--"the rain follows the plow"--was by 1884 known everywhere in the West and must have been known to Warren. And it must have seemed obvious to him, from reports in the press and the talk of everyone, that as the settlers pushed on across the Missouri and beyond the 100th meridian, they had rain enough for their crops.

Whether Nell Devereaux sent pamphlets or not, she certainly would have reported some facts. The Burlington and Missouri Railroad, which had not yet reached Arapahoe in 1880, had pushed on to Indianola and Culbertson and, in mid-July, 1882, all the way to Denver. The railroad had selected a site near Fairview, a village with only a store and a post office, made it the division point between Lincoln and Denver, and gave it the name McCook. In 1883, the federal government had opened a land office there--for settlers seeking homesteads or preemption claims. And now, in 1884, the state had authorized the organization of Hayes County and the federal government would soon open the public lands to settlement. Hayes County was only a dozen miles from the railroad at Culbertson. Culbertson--that was the name Warren had entered with vigorous pen on the last page of his diary for 1879, after he and Ada arrived at Stuart, Iowa.[9]

From subsequent developments, we can judge that Warren and Ada, in the summer and fall at Blencoe were thinking seriously about migrating to Nebraska. It may be that no opportunity for acquiring a farm at Blencoe presented itself; it may be that, once having begun to think seriously about homesteading in Nebraska, Warren no longer searched for a place for them to buy in Iowa.

Toward the last of November, 1884, Ada's parents, the Harrises, came out from Williamstown to visit their children and grandchildren. Warren met them late one night at the depot in Blencoe and brought them and their son, Elmer, Ada's brother, out to the granary-house. There was plenty of room to accommodate them. Ada made up beds on the floor for ten-year-old Elmer and Nellie, who was four and a half, and for a young cousin, Rube Samson, who came a day or two later to spend a night with them.

Warren had one more day in the field to finish his cornhusking. Father and Elmer helped him. And in the manner that Warren had once busied himself at Stone Hill, Father Harris now worked with him: hauling wood from the sandbar, cleaning out a granary for his corn, fixing fence, building a new outhouse. They went to town, they drove to Ida

Cook's to borrow her sewing machine. Ada and her mother made clothes for the children. Grandma, taking Nellie on her lap, and with needles flashing, taught her to knit. They went to church on Sundays, with Grandma sometimes staying home with the children. All of them went visiting, to Warren's cousins, the Samsons and the Cooks, and to neighbors, and they no doubt saw much of the Tryons who lived in the big house in the same farmyard. The weather outside was cold, 22 degrees below zero, Warren noted one day. Many days he had only chores to do and they sat in the house the rest of the time around the fire and talked.

They talked about New York and their family and relatives in Williamstown, and about Iowa, and the Devereauxs and Nebraska. Ada's mother, Amelia Jane, and Martha Wilson, Nell Devereaux's mother, had been neighbors before their daughters were born and friends longer than that, possibly since they, themselves, had been children. Amelia Jane was a good correspondent, more faithful even than her daughter, Ada. We can be sure that Martha Wilson and Amelia Jane had been in correspondence and that Martha, learning that the Harrises were coming to Iowa, had urged them to come on to Nebraska.

They remained with Warren and Ada for a month, until after Christmas--not that Christmas was a day of celebration, for they seemed to regard it, in the manner of past years, as no different from any other day in the week. But a month was a well-measured period of time, long enough to justify a trip from New York to such a far distant place. On Monday, December 29, Warren took them to Blencoe where they caught the train for Nebraska. Elmer chose to remain with Warren and Ada, so they took Nellie with them.

Gone for two weeks, the Harrises returned on Tuesday, January 13. They remained in Blencoe only a week before leaving for New York and home. But that was time enough to report on Nebraska. They had visited Martha Wilson in the rapidly growing village of Arapahoe and, no doubt, Hank and Nell at their homestead on the rolling plain north of the village. What they had seen they apparently liked.

Warren, anticipating that conclusion, and beginning to wind up his affairs, had already hauled four loads of his corn to Blencoe. Two loads in the next two days were enough for him to "settle up" his affairs and pay what "was owing:" for advances in groceries and supplies. In the next few weeks he hauled a load of wheat and a dozen loads of corn, perhaps more, but his record is incomplete, for during one week in February he was too busy to make entries in his diary.

Altogether Warren seems not to have done as well in the year at Blencoe as during the last year at Stuart on Sam McMonigal's place. He had not engaged in the trading of cattle and building up a herd and he had not fattened hogs for the market. But he had done reasonably well in his five years in Iowa. A handbook for immigrants estimated the cost of equipment necessary for the homesteader to begin his farming: a team of horses, $160 to $220, a wagon, $75, a cow $25, two plows $35, other tools, $20, temporary house, $50 to $100, cash for current expenses, $100; and household furnishings, with no amount stipulated.[10]

Warren had it all: a fine team of young horses, a colt which the young mare had borne, a good cow, a wagon, a plow and a cultivator, both nearly new, a drag, some other tools and machinery, household goods, and whatever cash remained to him after he had sold his corn, settled with Uncle John Tryon for his labor and his rent, paid his freight bill to Arapahoe, and bought a ticket for Ada. He was debt free. And he apparently had promise of an abandoned homestead he could occupy until he was ready to move onto his own place. On February 2, he heard from Hank Devereaux. Either he or Ada wrote to say when they would leave Blencoe and the approximate time when she and the children, traveling by passenger train, would reach Arapahoe.

Through the first week of the month Warren continued to haul corn to Blencoe. He chopped down trees for logs for the Tryons, cut and hauled and split wood to burn. Some days were so bitter cold that he did nothing but the chores. On Thursday, February 26, he took his tools and machinery to Blencoe and began to pack his goods for shipment. With the help of Dick Samson, his cousin Martha's husband, he finished moving and packing on Saturday and that night they stayed with the Samsons. They remained over the Sabbath and went to church with Martha and her boys on Sunday. Monday morning, March 2, Warren finished loading his stock and goods into the emigrant car and the train pulled out for Nebraska. Ada and the children were to follow by passenger train.

# 9. Finding a Homestead

Warren, riding in an emigrant car with his household goods, his farm implements, and his stock--the team of horses and the big white cow--reached Arapahoe on Wednesday afternoon, March 4, two days after leaving Blencoe. The train had gone south on the Iowa side, crossed the river to Blair, Nebraska, and spent the night on a sidetrack. It did not get away until ten o'clock the next morning. The run to Omaha was short, the afternoon long before they started west at eight o'clock. They ran all night and all the next morning until two o'clock in the afternoon. The gently rolling, almost flat landscape reaching into the far distance was, except for the reduced number of trees, not unlike the prairies he had become accustomed to in Iowa. With the dotting of farmsteads and the clustered buildings of villages, it had already begun to take on a settled look. The rhythm of change, the transformation of wilderness into habitable and prosperous farms, had been bred into the westward moving Americans through generations of experience until it had become an expectation, an assured reality. Warren had time for long thoughts in those two days but, to judge from the matter-of-fact entries in his diary, he dwelt on the practical details of the enterprise before him and did not indulge in fantasies of hope or uncertainty.[1]

Ada and the children, traveling by passenger train, started after he had left Blencoe and reached Arapahoe long before his slow-moving freight could get there. The Devereauxs or the Wilsons met them. After five years of not seeing her dearest friend, Nellie, and the family she had known so well, that must have been an exciting reunion, even to Ada who was not much given to expression of her feelings. Nell's mother and sister, Mrs. Wilson and Clara, lived in the town, Hank and Nell a dozen miles north in Gosper County. Ada had time to look around before Warren came.[2]

Arapahoe was a shining example of the miracle of the frontier, lustrous with success and enterprise, more substantial and less vulgar than the towns of the cattle frontier. A bustling place of five hundred people, it had been founded only 15 years earlier at the intersection of the east-west, north-south wagon roads. The coming of the Burlington and Missouri railroad had increased its importance as a distribution point. Freighters and a stagecoach line served the wagon road from Plum Creek (Lexington) south through Gosper and Furnas counties to Norton, Kansas. An enormous hotel, the Arapahoe House, ninety-two feet long, stood at the intersection of the roads. The town had four livery stables, a four-story brick flour mill, a creamery, a broom factory, two brick kilns, a small sawmill. It had numerous false-front stores and shops. The street corners were lighted at night by enclosed kerosene lamps that rested on posts, a little higher than a man's head. The Catholics, the Baptists, and the Christians all had churches, frame structures, the Baptists' with a high spire that could be seen from far away, and the Methodists, organized two years earlier, were putting up a brick church. Trees grew along the Republican River, cottonwood, box elder, and hackberry, and along the banks of the four creeks that flowed southward from Gosper County to the Republican River. Even the countryside, as Warren and Ada would discover, looked well populated, with frame houses and barns beginning to replace the soddies in which the homesteaders had first lived. North to the Devereauxs on the road that followed or paralleled the canyon, they probably were never out of sight of trees along the creek and of small patches of cultivated fields on the plain or in the canyon.[3]

There had been little in the setting to suggest a barren waste or the Great American Desert to Nathaniel and Amelia Jane Harris when they visited Arapahoe in December, or to suggest it now to Warren and Ada. There was much that spoke of hope for the future, that promised equally miraculous change in the new frontier a short distance to the west where Warren and Ada would look for their homestead. "Progress was in the air," the

Nebraska historian, James C. Olson, was to write, three quarters of a century later. "The good crops, the railroads, the growing population all suggested great things. . . . Raw villages indulged in rosy dreams of greatness, and gaslights twinkled where the coyotes should have been left undisturbed."[4]

Once the emigrant car was spotted on a sidetrack, Warren and Hank began to unload it. Getting out the team and wagon first, they filled up both Warren's and Hanks' wagons with goods, sealed the car, and at a late hour left Arapahoe. It was eleven o'clock, Warren noted, when they pulled into the farmyard. The next day both men drove their wagons into town for second loads, an all-day trip. On Friday Warren repaid Hank by helping to haul corn and wood. Saturday they went back to Arapahoe for the last of Warren's goods.

Sunday morning Warren and Hank, answering the need of a neighbor, helped get a cow in from the canyon. That afternoon all of them, the Clarks and the Devereauxs, went over to see the little house, "our place," Warren wrote in his diary, where they were to live for the summer months. It was a sod house, the first dwelling of an early settler. Some land, what little Warren could use, was available for planting. If Ada were dismayed at what she saw, which is unlikely, she did not communicate any sense of dismay or hardship to Nellie. With Warren to be gone staking out his claim, the house was a good place for them, not far from Nell and Hank, and even closer to other neighbors, a half dozen of whom were to make their way into the pages of Warren's diary or Nellie's reminiscences.

The next morning, Monday, Warren shelled corn for a neighbor, building up exchange labor for himself or for Hank, and hauled corn for Hank. On Tuesday and Wednesday he went back to the sod house, cut some wood, cleaned out the well, tidied, or helped Ada to tidy up the house, cleared a place to store corn, and hauled in some corn and potatoes. Thursday, Friday, and Saturday he "fixed up" Hank's plow and his own and did some plowing for Hank. On one of those days he moved his goods and his family into the sod house. Sunday, March 15, they were "at home" all day, happy to receive a neighboring family that called on them.

On that date, March 15, plunged into the absorbing business of securing and settling on his homestead, Warren broke off writing in his diary, not to write in it again, so far as we can determine from the record, for nearly three years. We must reconstruct his story from Nellie's reminiscences, the remembrance of others, from official records of the federal and county governments, and from newspapers.

The Clarks and the Devereauxs had much to talk about: the New York days and homesteading--where to look for the land, how to file on it, how to prove up, what gamble they might be taking on the high plains. Hank obviously had no doubt, for he had persuaded his father, Joel, to come out from New York with his family. He was on his way, intending, despite his sixty years, to stake out a claim. Richard Roberts, Hank's brother-in-law, had already come and had hurried on to the land office at McCook to have a look at what was available. Richard had married Henry's sister Emma in the fall of 1879 while Warren and Ada were at the Harrises at Stone Hill, preparing to leave for Iowa. Ada had known Emma, who was three years younger than she, all of her life and had gone to school with her. Emma died in the first year of her marriage, in childbirth, and the child died, too, leaving Richard alone. He decided to follow the Devereauxs to Nebraska.[5]

At McCook, Roberts was directed to continue some 25 miles west and a little north to the newly organized Hayes County where he would find plenty of open land. His study of the government survey or the word of the agent or of a settler led him to Blackwood Township where he sought out John Hughes, a young farmer, one of the first settlers in the township. He had been there for more than five years, had proved up on his homestead of 160 acres in section five, and was happy to serve as a locator for others, for a fee we can presume. He had also filed on a tree claim of 160 acres a mile from his homestead and his mother, in 1884, had taken a homestead bordering his own. Quick to seize an opportunity to profit, he offered to relinquish the tree claim to Roberts, for whatever the going price might be. All of the other sections in the township, save one, and that an undesirable location, had already been registered for a tree claim and government policy permitted only one per section. Roberts liked the idea. He wanted the tree claim for the extra land and for the prospective wood supply. It was adjacent to the property he had picked out for his homestead, giving him the entire western half of section three. On the east and the north there were open quarter sections, one of which Joel Devereaux could choose. Roberts would build his own house on the northwest corner of his homestead, which would be close to Joel, whichever plot he chose. There were four or five other quarter sections nearly as close, from which Warren Clark could choose.[6]

Having picked out his land, Roberts with Hughes rode back to McCook. On March 21, 1885, Hughes signed the release on his tree claim and Roberts filed immediately on both the tree claim and a homestead. He was the tenth to file that week in Blackwood Township; about half the claims had been taken. The day was Saturday. With his papers signed and his fees paid, Richard apparently caught the train back to Arapahoe, borrowed a horse from the Wilsons, or hired one from the livery stable, and rode out to Devereauxs that afternoon.

Warren probably saw him the next morning, Sunday. That would explain the abrupt breaking off of the diary, for Warren often waited until Sunday to post his entries. The record for the week past is blank; he had no time for the posting. He would have talked with Roberts the whole of the day, Ada and Nell and Henry joining them, hearing his report in full, canvassing every detail. And he would have been much too busy the next couple of days, getting ready to travel. Undoubtedly he took his team and wagon, Roberts joining him, so that they could carry a load of supplies, some of which, including tents or canvasses, they must buy in Arapahoe. They had reason not to delay. 1885 was the beginning of the great migration into western Nebraska, 150,000 people in the next five years, the best of the lands being rapidly taken up by the newcomers. Warren and Richard had sixty miles to drive to the land office in McCook and another twenty-five miles to John Hughes' place, which they must have reached sometime on Friday. They rode about the countryside on Saturday and a part of Sunday, perhaps Monday, John Hughes serving as locator. Warren, like Roberts before him, had learned in McCook that the best land in the valleys of the Frenchman River and the Red Willow and Stinking Water creeks, had been taken up a decade earlier and that the timbered sections of the Blackwood, a dry creek, had also been filed on. What remained was the nearly level plain of buffalo grass, the high "divide" between the streams and gullies, surveyed and marked off in quarter sections, approximating 160 acres. Some of the plots were scored by ravines that had been gouged out of the deep topsoil by the rushing water from the occasional spring or summer downpour of rain. Hughes, who called himself a sheep farmer, had spurned even the timbered sections of the Blackwood to choose, both for himself and his mother, nearly flat quarter sections, matted with the nutritious buffalo grass, only one corner of each eroded by the beginning of a canyon.[7]

After examining the available sites, Warren chose the northwest quarter of section 11, a mile east and a mile south of Roberts' building site. His land, like that of John Hughes', was nearly flat, all of it arable, except two ragged, shallow cuts. He was too unacquainted with the plains to know that the grasses grew more rankly in the canyon bottoms. The land east of his claim sloped upward to a long ridge that marked the line of the horizon, less than two miles away. To the west and south the plain dipped gently and then rose to a more distant horizon.[8]

The advertising flyers of the land agents and the newspaper stories had said that a black loam, ten to fifteen feet thick, underlay the buffalo grass. Warren could judge for himself that the statements were true, that the land agents were not idle boasters, for there at the edge of the homestead he had chosen he could see the thickness of the loam where it was exposed by the eroding canyon. After the years of his boyhood and young manhood in western New York cutting timber, burning out stumps, hauling, sometimes blasting, the stones and rocks to clear a small patch for plowing, he must have looked on that gently sloping expanse with deep satisfaction and pride. If he were ever a dreamer, he must have dreamed then of the house that he would build and the barns and pens; he must have seen the trees and garden, the chickens and pigs, cattle and horses, the fields he would plow, the crops he would plant and harvest, he must have thought of Ada and the children and the new world they were about to enter. His own father, on his little farm, had eighteen acres of cultivated land, Ada's father, forty-five, none of it loam like this. If, in looking out over his treeless land, he had some misgivings, he must have reassured himself in the manner of the fliers and the newspapers that along the creeks there was ample wood for everyone for ten years or more and that by then they could grow a new supply of timber. On his quarter section he had space enough for his own wood lot.

On Tuesday he went back to McCook and on Wednesday, April 1, 1885, paid his ten-dollar fee and filed for a homestead in Blackwood Township, on the northwest quarter of section eleven. He had five years to "prove up," to build a house, to occupy and farm the land, before he would receive the patent assigning the title to him.[9]

Warren returned to Gosper County to be with his family as his responsibilities permitted and to attend to what little farming he could do. He was to divide his time between the two places that summer. The little soddy where his family lived, happily situated close to Ada's girlhood friend, gave him a garden and fresh vegetables for the summer, no doubt potatoes and other root crops for the winter's food, and seed for spring planting.

From Nellie we get brief glimpses of his presence at home. Once he was plowing some distance from the house, but not too far for Ada to call to him that Mary, then two and a half years old, had wandered off and was lost. He came hurrying across an unplowed field towards the house and found her, picking wild flowers, holding up her apron filled with blossoms. That was in the summer, Nellie said, late May or June, the most likely time for wild flowers.

He was at home when a neighbor's house caught on fire and he joined others in trying to put it out. In that settled community, it was a frame house with wooden floors, occupied by a widow and her children. She was baking bread and had stoked her fire to get the oven hot. The end door of the stove sprang open and live coals fell to the floor. The young mother, busy with her children, did not notice until the wood was ablaze. She shouted for help and the neighboring men came running but the little house, tinder dry, burned to the ground.

Warren must have been home, too, on some Sundays when, Nellie remembered, the Devereauxs or other neighbors came by after Sunday school in the schoolhouse, or they went to friends for dinner and lazy talk for the adults in the kitchen or the barnyard and play for the children. But he clearly was not there when they walked to the schoolhouse which to Nellie seemed quite a distance but not too far to walk.

As much of the summer as possible Warren spent at the homestead site. Joel Devereaux came six weeks after Warren had arrived and filed on his claim on May 9. He chose the quarter north of Roberts. Warren and Richard worked together, Nellie says, to build their houses and stables, and Richard, undoubtedly, also worked with Devereaux, perhaps when Warren was in Gosper County.[10]

They must have purchased, or borrowed from John Hughes, a plow especially designed to cut sod in a long ribbon, usually twelve to eighteen inches wide at an even depth of four inches. Nellie says that the walls of their house were two and one-half feet thick, so the cut of the blade was ten or fifteen inches wide. The practice of the homesteader was to pick a low spot where the water had gathered and the grass was thickest. Plowing only what he could use in a day or two, he took his spade to cut the long ribbon into equal lengths, building blocks, prairie granite, the settlers called them, piled the blocks on his wagon, with the sideboards removed, and hauled them to the building site. Buffalo grass made better turf in the early fall after the summer's growth. That may be why Warren built his stable first, to have some shelter as soon as possible, and to build his house when the better turf was available and after he had some experience in construction.[11]

Commonly the homesteader in aligning his house fixed the corners by sighting to the north star. He then drew the inside line of the wall from corner post to corner post, carefully leveled the earth where the blocks were to lie, marked an opening for the door, and set and braced a frame. Richard or Warren handed the blocks from the wagon to the wall, and the other laid them, grass side down, two or three, side by side, lengthwise. With a spade they trimmed the upper side to remove the bumps, filled in the cracks and low spots with dirt. The end blocks of the second layer were only half length, in order to break and overlap the joints, in the manner of laying brick or stone. To bind the whole they placed the third layer crosswise, and so built the wall upward to the level of the windows. As with the door, they set and braced the frames and then laid blocks snugly against them. From Nellie we know that they partitioned the barn into two compartments, each large enough for three or four horses. It must, therefore, have been eighteen or twenty feet long, as long as the house he had marked out, but probably not as wide. Once they had completed the walls, they would have laid a plate along the outer edges--poles from the Blackwood or the Red Willow--to hold the weight of the roof and prevent the rafters from cutting into the sod. At each end they set poles, forked trunks of trees, on which the ridge pole was to rest. Fitting the pole into the forked notches of the end posts, was a considerable job that required the help of several men. Against the wall they slanted long poles that, reaching to the height of the forks, served as skids. Some of the men with ropes attached to the ridgepole and thrown over both walls pulled the pole up the skids while others guided it until it settled into place in the forks. They then attached rafters, smaller poles, from ridge to plate and, for the barn, filled in the open spaces with brush on which they piled hay and laid sod, again filling in the cracks with dirt. The windows in the side wall, "holes," Nellie called them, Warren hung with shutters, attached above with hinges so that he could lower them to close the openings.[12]

The summer passed quickly. Camped in their tents, probably staying at first one place and then the other, as the work demanded, they did their own cooking and chores. They had to haul water from John Hughes' well, a mile or a mile and a half when they were working at Roberts', two and a half miles when they were at Warren's. They washed their own clothes or persuaded Mary Hughes to do it for them. Both of them would have thought it prudent to break a fireguard and a little prairie for next spring's planting. Nellie, when she came to write her reminiscences, wondered where her father got hay to feed his stock when the snow fell that winter. No doubt he and Roberts both took their scythes and cut grass, down in the ravines on the unclaimed sections or on the school section a couple of miles from them. They may have bought and hauled in some corn or oats. Certainly, even for their summer's cooking as well as in anticipation of their winter's need, both men, New Yorkers, would have cut and hauled some wood. They were well prepared for the winter.

*McCook, Nebraska, ca. 1882. Courtesy of High Plains Society.*

# 10.
# The Lone Tree

The law required that a homesteader move onto his place within six months from the date of filing, for Warren by November 1. As the date approached, he had finished his barn and had the walls of his house part way up, with not enough time remaining for him to complete the job. Late in October he took his team and wagon down to Gosper County to get his family.

Nellie, who was five-years-old, would never forget the vivid details of that trip by wagon from the summer farm to the homestead. Jesse Harris, Ada's brother, 23-years-old, had come out from New York to help them move and get settled, and to look over the new country. He and Warren packed the wagon with the goods that remained to be transported. Warren and Ada, with three-year-old Mary between them, sat on the wagon seat, Jesse and Nellie behind them, pressed against the sides of the wagon. Nellie had no remembrance of what goods they carried, save one precious box that held the two kittens that belonged to her and Mary. They led the cow behind the wagon, the big white cow they had brought from Iowa, the best milker Nellie ever saw, two big pails full at each milking. The days were short, but October in western Nebraska is often warm and clear. Warren thought it unnecessary to put a cover on the wagon.[1]

They drove the short distance to Arapahoe the first day and spent the night with their old New York friends, the Wilsons. They went from Arapahoe to McCook, 42 miles or so, in two easy days. The cow led well but Warren did not want to hurry her.

They stopped at noon to picnic and Warren milked the cow to make it easier for her to walk. One day he gave milk to another family, traveling with children, that had stopped near them for lunch. They stayed that night in a farmhouse. Jesse slept by the wagon to watch the goods. The rest of them stayed in the house, and Nellie played with a little girl about her own age. She was wide-eyed and unbelieving when the girl brought out a doll so large that she dressed it in the clothes of her baby sister who had died.

On the next night they stopped at a livery barn in McCook where the owner let Warren put down hay in his office so that they could sleep on the floor. Again, Jesse made his bed under the wagon. If they had time to walk about the town--or seeing it as they drove in--Ada would again have been reassured by the rapid transformation from open plain to substantial village. Established only three years before, as the division point between Lincoln and Denver on the Burlington and Missouri Railroad, McCook already had a population of over 2,000 people and was the largest town in southwest Nebraska. It boasted of several brick buildings--the depot and roundhouse, the splendid Menard Opera House and the newly opened First National Bank. Main Street (now Norris Avenue) had sidewalks, there were three churches, one of them Methodist, and a weekly newspaper, the McCook *Tribune*.[2]

They started early the next morning, the last day of the trip, for the long drive to Blackwood Township in Hayes County, some 35 miles away. The main road west out of McCook followed the Republican River but divided at Culbertson where a branch road ran northwest along the Frenchman River to numerous trails, traces of wagon wheels, some of them leading into Hayes County. Nellie inadvertently suggests the route that they traveled, after they left the Frenchman, by telling us that they stopped overnight at the Hughes', and then drove on to their place the next morning. The Hugheses, in fact, lived beyond the Clarks', two miles west and a half mile north, in the northwest corner of the township. Warren, driving west from McCook, would have to turn back to his own place the next morning. It is important, for what it was to mean to Ada, to establish the route quite clearly.[3]

In 1885, most of the homesteaders were newly arrived, and the roads had not yet been established. John Hughes had taken out his claim in 1879, the first homesteader to settle in the township. He would have picked a route that best suited his convenience. The southeasterly flowing Frenchman had been settled early and the road along the valley was well traveled. It seems reasonable to believe that Hughes would have followed it, upstream, northwest as far as he could go to his advantage and then would have swung north out of the valley onto the divide, angling across the plain to save distance, but choosing a route that avoided the canyons as much as possible. So, he probably entered the township at a point south and a little east of his homestead, angled northwest two or three miles, and then north to his place. Almost all of the settlers in the next four or five years filed on claims in the western part of the township; they would have found his trail convenient, even if they had to turn back to the east a mile or two.

The Clarks spent most of that long day on the much-traveled valley road. There was little to distract them from the monotonous plop of the dust under the horses' hoofs or the rising of the dust on the rim of the wagon wheel and its falling back in ragged gray cascades. Some place they stopped to picnic and to water and feed and rest the horses and the cow. Ada must have thought the country not unlike that where she had spent the summer in Gosper County, a plain broken with streams and creek beds, narrow bands of trees reaching back from the banks, now and then a frame house, or in the towns a store, among the sod huts, giving promise to the change that was to come. She had not yet seen the limitless expanse of the divide. Nor had Jesse.

Mid-afternoon or later they turned from the valley road toward the palisade that bordered the Frenchman and climbed the steep hill to the plateau beyond. Before them stretched the great treeless plain, mile after mile of gently rolling short gray-brown grass, reaching endlessly towards the horizon. The low buildings were scattered widely in that vast landscape, the walls of sod and the grass roofs of the few that existed blending with and all but disappearing into the land. Above, and all around, the blue sky, crystal clear, darkened at the edge of a cumulus cloud and faded imperceptibly into the blue haze of the undulating horizon. In few other places on earth does the conventional figure of a great bowl so aptly describe humankind's relation to the earth and the encircling sky. Francis Parkman, brilliant young eastern historian, looking out over the valley of the Platte from the summit of a low ridge thought the plains a monotonous waste without "one picturesque beautiful feature,"[4] but others among the early travelers experienced in that boundless space a sense of infinity. Jesse Harris was deeply moved, struck by the beauty of the plains. They had a "grandeur more sublime," he thought, than his native, wooded hillside in New York. "The prairies, the canyons, the hills, have each a charm for me," he sang in verse. "With love my heart now fills, as their beauties all I see."[5] Jesse wrote his verses in May, 1886, after he had spent a winter and spring on the plains, but he soon went back to New York, married his sweetheart, and lived most of his long life in Cleveland, Ohio. Ada left no record of what she thought or felt that late October afternoon, or that first winter and spring. But 50 years later, after Warren's death, and after she had been gone from the plains for 20 years, she returned, rode over the plains with her son, Earl, in his automobile, and exclaimed over the beauty of the canyons, the hills, and the prairies.[6]

They would have crossed two or three of the canyons that afternoon, on their way to the Hughes'. The road, angling to avoid the deepest cuts, dipped nonetheless, and the wagon crowded the horses as Warren held the reins tight and the horses pulled back on the neck yokes to slow the descent. The horizon narrowed to rest on the opposite bank and as they crawled up the long slope the plain widened again and to the eye leveled and sealed up the canyon they had left behind, and those that lay before them, leaving only the unbroken plain of limitless space. At some point, as the wagon climbed up a canyon wall, they would have seen on the horizon a small, roundish, not very substantial object, not a soddy or a dugout, certainly in this unharvested country not a haycock, although it was yellow-brown in color; too broad for a bush, it might have been a clump of bushes. As they moved forward behind the slow plodding horses the clump grew, rose against the horizon, heightened into a tree, a cottonwood, they were to learn later. In all that vast expanse it was the only tree on the plain, the lone tree, the settlers came to call it, visible for miles in every direction. Ada from her homestead four or five miles away, standing in her yard, just outside the door of her sod house, would be able to see it. Fifty years later, she would be delighted to see it again, or its successor, green against the blue of a May sky.[7]

The Clarks would have passed the lone tree late on that October afternoon. It was probably off to the left of them, perhaps very close to their route. Christian Schielke had already filed on the land where the tree grew and his son, Andrew, on the quarter to the west, both of them in the week that Warren had taken his claim. There must have been some kind of sod structure on Christian's quarter, perhaps a dugout in the canyon wall that lay several hundred yards to the west of the tree, out of the Clarks' line of vision.[8]

The sun dropped beneath the horizon and twilight began to thicken into dusk when Nellie cried out. The box was open and the kittens were loose. One of them had crawled over the goods to Nellie, but the other was gone. Knowing the anguish of the children, Warren stopped the wagon and he and Jesse walked back along the road, searching and calling. In the half darkness they were unable to find the kitten. Weeks later they saw it at the home of a neighbor, Mrs. Mary Gruver, a widow, who with her six sons and one daughter had come west to homestead. Nellie recognized it at once, although it had grown, and knew that it was hers, for the Gruver boys said they had found it along the road. She was too shy to say anything about it and later her parents persuaded her to let the Gruvers have it, for they were good Christian people. That seemed to her then, and many years later, an entirely satisfactory reason.

It was dark, or near-dark, when they pulled into the Hughes' farmyard, and wearily crawled out of the wagon. Warren had wisely arranged to bring them here for their first night in Blackwood Township. John Hughes was a substantial and well-regarded member of the new community. At 31 years, he was Warren's age, his wife Mary, 27, one year older than Ada. Their oldest child, Fannie, was nine, their boy, Johnnie, who was to be in Nellie's class at school, seven, two years older than she. John had proved up on his place, he and Mary had been in their sod house for some years, had dug a well, built, we can presume, a barn and other outbuildings, had stock and farm machinery. John was highly enough regarded by his neighbors to have been elected that winter as one of the first three county commissioners.[9]

We know nothing of that evening, of what they talked about, of John's boasts of his accomplishments (only from later incidents that he was a vain man),[10] or Mary's confidences about life in a sod house or what assurance she offered. Ada was probably too weary to talk much at all (she was pregnant with her next child, who was to be born in May), and the next morning too eager to get on to their own place. And one doubts, however much she may have relished reassurance, that she needed it. Her own mother, and her father, too, had been born in log huts on farms chopped out of the wilderness, the fields cleared in small plots, then acre by acre the stumps of trees burned out and the rocks gathered and piled in heaps or laid one on another to make a dividing wall, a fence. There were, she could not forget, just such fences between her father's place and Uncle Ratio's, and a pile of stone on which she, herself, had tossed rocks when she worked in the garden and struck one with her hoe.[11]

She had seen the place where her mother had been born. The log hut where her father had spent his childhood, enlarged to a house, was in plain view of the large white-painted frame house where she had been born and had grown up. She knew the process of transition from pioneer to farmer, from rude cabin to frame house. She had seen it in New York, in Iowa, where they had lived in the shanty that the farmer with his family, now in his fine new house, had so recently occupied, and she had seen the marks of change in Nebraska, in the village of Arapahoe and in Gosper County. She did not dream the American dream, the myth of the garden, it was not fantasy for her, it was reality and she was a part of it.

They left John Hughes' farm the next morning, alert to every detail in the landscape, for the hour's drive to the new homestead. There was not much to see. They went east over the open plain for a half mile, dipped down into the canyon of the Little Blackwood where it cut through a tree claim, as yet undisturbed by any activity of its new owner. To the south was the extensive holding of Russell Watts, three full quarters, 480 acres, stretching for a mile and a half along the Blackwood. He had quarters in the canyon by the creek, but they were hidden from view, and he, a cattleman from North Platte, did not live there. A half mile beyond the canyon, on the plain, they came to the edge of Richard Roberts' tree claim. They might have been able to see the low line of his sod house, three quarters of a mile to the north on his homestead, but it is not likely. To the south, Charles Andrews, adjoining Roberts, and Charles Boyd had filed on homesteads the day before Roberts had entered his claim. There were no fields, no fences, no corner posts to mark their homesteads, only Warren's knowing, from his trip to the land office, and his casual encounters of the summer, where they were. He might have pointed out the holdings to Ada but with the scarcely visible or totally hidden houses, and the broad sweep of the unbroken, uncultivated plain, she must have thought the whole countryside quite uninhabited.[12]

One mile more and they came to the northwest corner of their homestead, as uncultivated and barren as the others. There Warren turned south for the last half mile. We know from the testimony of a homesteader's son, who as a boy had lived on the adjacent claim, that Warren had located his buildings on the western border.[13] As they moved forward, beyond the slowly bobbing heads of the horses, Ada may have searched for and found, off to the southwest in the far distance, the lone tree rising above the horizon to cut a yellow-brown arc in the blue sky. They drew up and stopped before the long, narrow, low barn, its roof thatched with sticks, grass, and sod, and the unfinished walls of the house. Ada knew from their conversation what to expect. It would have been quite unlike her to have voiced either disappointment or hope. She accepted the situation as it was, knowing that it would be better.

They moved the furniture into one section of the barn. Warren and Jesse put the stove in place, running the pipe and a protecting sheath through the brush and dirt of the roof; they set up the cupboard and table and Ada unpacked her goods. Either Warren had already cut some grass or she put him to the task, and they stuffed the ticks for mattresses and spread the beds on the floor, or on a bedstead if they had brought one with them, stacking, during the day, all of the ticks and pallets in one corner to conserve space.

Warren and Jesse began immediately to complete the house. But before they could move out of the stable a heavy snow struck, the wind piling drifts around the stable, driving snow through the hay and sod roof. They must have huddled about the stove for warmth. The fact that Nellie had no memory of suffering from want of fuel, or of the animals suffering from lack of pasture or hay, suggests that Warren had been prudent enough to put in supplies of wood to warm their room, and hay to feed his stock.

October storms in southwest Nebraska are frequently of brief duration. Despite the short days, the high drifted snow quickly dissolves in the bright midday sun. And so it must have been that October. Warren and Jesse, working steadily, soon finished the house. Warren built painstakingly, with greater care and at greater cost than he had taken with the barn. The walls rose evenly, the sod fitted snugly against the frames of the door on the west end, the windows on the sides and on the east. He bought lumber for the roof, planks for the plate on the top of the wall, a ridgepole, rafters, boards which he laid tightly side by side and nailed to the ridgepole and the plate. He covered the whole with sod and dirt, probably after he had put down a layer of tar paper, but we cannot be certain, for Nellie tells us that the roof often leaked, and leaked badly when they had a three-day rain that soaked through the loose dirt he had used to chink the sod. But even tarpaper could not stop the leaking. The Keith County *News* to the west of Hayes County, estimated in 1886 that it cost $75.00, a very considerable sum, for lumber, doors, and windows, for a sod house 16 by 24 feet, a figure that may have included the floor. The cost of the lumber and the windows had sufficiently strained his resources so that Warren did not put in a wooden floor. For that matter, most of his neighbors, perhaps all of them, for some years to come, had dirt floors and found the tightly packed earth quite satisfactory, at least to the men.[14]

We can judge from a photograph, made many years later, with Ada standing at the door, that the house was about 14 feet wide and 20 feet long. The outside door led into the first room, the larger of the two, which served as kitchen, dining room, living room, and sometimes as bedroom. They put the cookstove there, the cupboard, the table and chairs or stools or benches, the lounge they had acquired in Iowa and, undoubtedly, a whatnot or shelves in the corners for lamps and small articles, a board fastened to the wall to hold the hooks for coats and caps, the outdoor clothes. The glass windows, set even with the exterior surface of the walls, made deep ledges where, on the north, Ada kept her water pail and wash basin, and on the south, after the first winter, she nursed her house plants and flowers. A sod partition, with an opening for a door, set off the second, smaller room from the first. Ada hung a curtain in the doorway and another to divide the room into two, each large enough for a double bed, and each lighted by the single window on the east.

Warren and Jesse must have finished the house and moved the family into it shortly after the big snowstorm, for Nellie remembered nothing of the severity of that winter on the windswept plain except the first snowstorm when they were in the stable. The sod house was warm. They had only the cookstove to heat it, but that was enough. The thick tight walls kept out the cold and held in the heat. And Warren had put in a good supply of wood. With the outdoor temperatures frequently at zero and now and then 20 below, it was not often then, or in the years to come, Nellie said, that ice formed on the water bucket and Ada's plants on the window ledge rarely froze. They were comfortable enough for the beginning of a new life on a rugged frontier.

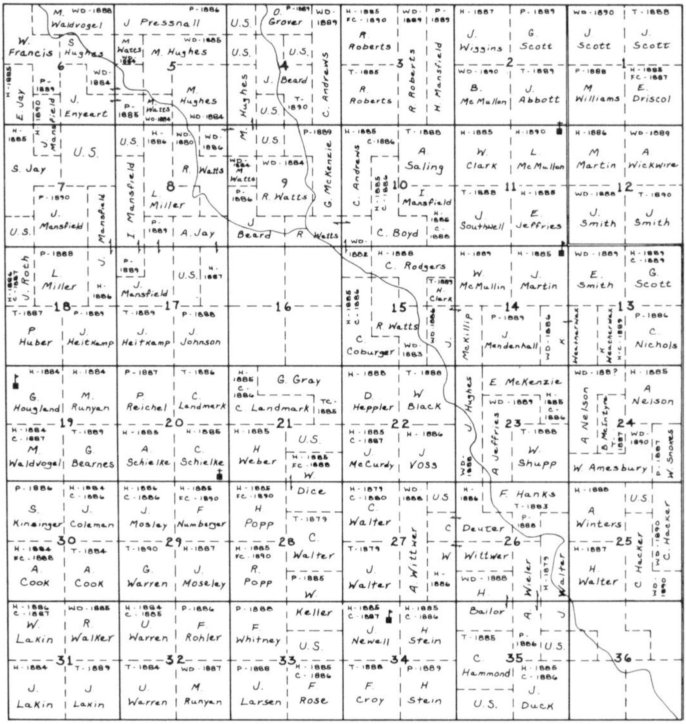

*Blackwood Township, T5N, R32W, Hayes County, 1890. Compiled from US Land Office Tract Book, Vol. 81, McCook; Hayes County Deed Records. Courtesy of Nebraska History (Spring, 1985) and the Nebraska State Historical Society.*

*Clark Homestead, Blackwood Township, 1902. Left to right: Warren, Flora, Jennie, Arley, Jesse and Ada.*

# 11.
# Hope

Once the house was completed Warren had no major jobs facing him until the ground thawed and he could break sod for planting and for blocks to build a chicken house and other out buildings. With but two horses and one cow his chores were light. He had wood to haul from the Blackwood, and to saw and chop into small enough pieces to fit into the cookstove. He undoubtedly built some furniture, stools, shelves, bedsteads for the house, stalls, feed racks, harness hooks for the barn. He may have brought in posts and logs to build a temporary pen for the pig or pigs he knew he would buy in the spring.[1]

Twice a week, sometimes oftener, he hauled water, at first from John Hughes who lived two and a half miles to the west across the deep canyon of the Little Blackwood, where it was difficult to keep the water from splashing. He soon found another neighbor with a well, probably Jacob Case who lived in section one on the ridge, a half miler closer than Hughes and no canyon to cross. Jake and his wife, Ellen, were loyal Methodists, and so were Elisha and Mary Driscol, who had homesteaded in the same section. The Methodists, strangers in a new land, had a way of finding each other out. Warren and Ada had learned almost at once that the Widow Gruver and her sons and their families were Methodists, and had gone to Sunday school at her sod house. Perhaps that is where they met the Cases and the Driscols, and Harlan and Emma Martin, and Harlan's mother Mary.[2]

The Martins also lived on the ridge, a mile and a half southeast of the Clarks. Harlan, a year younger than Warren, and Emma, Ada's age, were to become the Clarks' closest friends. They built a soddy on the north line of their property, across from Ellsworth Jeffries. He and Warren had filed on the same day, probably had gone to the land office in McCook together, for they had successively numbered receipts. Jeffries' northwest corner touched the southeast corner of the place on which Warren Clark filed two weeks later. Ellsworth, a young bachelor, twenty-two-years-old, returned to Pennsylvania in December, 1886, to marry his twenty-year-old sweetheart, Maggie McMullen. He would bring back both his bride and his sister, also Maggie, who was a year older than his wife and a year younger than he. They were United Brethren, a sect Methodistic in its origins and forms that had sprung up among the Germans of Pennsylvania and Maryland. Ellsworth and the two Maggies were used to Methodist ways and at home with their new neighbors in Blackwood.[3]

In the meantime, in January, 1886, Ezra McKenzie had entered his claim for a homestead on the quarter section adjoining the Clarks on the west. Ezra and his young wife were sympathetic to the Methodists and promptly set aside three acres on the northwest corner as a site for a church and cemetery. Richard Roberts had married a Methodist girl from Williamstown, a friend of Ada's who had died in childbirth. He was friendly to the church, and so were others, somewhat farther removed from the Clarks.[4]

Trying to bring to this raw frontier the traditions and values of the communities they had left in the east, the families perceived as primary needs the establishing of a school for the children and a church for all of them. Harlan Martin offered a site on the corner of his homestead where it bordered on the line that quickly became the Ridge Road. The men joined, in the spring of 1886, in putting up a sod building for a school. Pressed with the need to break prairie on their own homesteads, they built quickly and not too substantially, with sod walls, a dirt floor, poles, brush, hay, and sod for the roof, crude benches and desks nailed together, probably out of scrap lumber and packing boxes. Children brought their own books, ones their parents had used or that they were able to buy in Culbertson, unmatched, save by chance, for any of the subjects or levels. The term, as Nellie remembered, was for three months. The first teacher was her uncle, Jesse Harris, and among the first board members were both Warren Clark and Richard Roberts. They moved the Sunday school from the Gruvers' to the new schoolhouse and in another year they would organize a church, one of three stations on the circuit of Hayes County's first Methodist preacher, the Rev. E. L. Hutchins. The federal government appointed Newton Wemple rural postmaster, the mail to be received and distributed at his sod house. He lived on the Ridge, a half mile beyond Jacob Case, in Logan Township. The people, in a spirit of buoyant optimism, called their community and church Pleasant Ridge and their post office Hope.[5]

In the late spring, May 23, 1886, Ada gave birth to her third child, a boy, whom they named Earl. At last, after eight years of marriage, Warren had his first son. Mary Martin, Harlan's mother, who had borne five children of her own, served as midwife. And young Maggie Jeffries came over from her brother's house to take care of the baby and do the housework until Ada was strong enough to do it for herself. We can judge from a later experience that Warren was proud of the birth of his son. He may have rocked on his heels, thumbs in his waistband, and boasted a little as he stood in a circle of men at the schoolhouse church, or at Gull's general store in Hayes Center. But it is unlikely, despite the common practice, that he passed cigars. He could buy them at the drug store of his Methodist friend, Dr. Meredith, and he smoked on rare occasions to celebrate with friends. But Ada disapproved, with the stern disapproval of her Dutch Pietist mother, and in any event, cigars cost money, of which there was very little in the Clark household.[6]

Warren did reasonably well in the first two years. Like his neighbors he had, each fall and spring, plowed a little of the plain to put more land under cultivation. The rainfall, consistently above average, seemed to confirm Charles Dana Wilber's catchy maxim, "The rain follows the plow." The black sod and the bright green of the tiny fields had begun to break the monotonous expanse of the gray-green plain.[7]

It was slow work converting the prairie into cultivated fields. A man walking behind a plow, the lines tied behind his back, resting on one shoulder and under one arm, both of his hands tightly gripping the handles to guide the plow, could turn an acre of sod a day, or at best an acre and a half--and do his other chores. We can estimate, from the number of days it took Warren to plow and cultivate his fields, that by 1888 he had about twenty-five or thirty acres under cultivation. That was more than Father Harris had in Williamstown, or John Howe at Mannsville, but it was not enough for the homesteader's market economy--crops to sell for the purchases he must make.[8]

He had meat and bread and garden produce for his table, grist for his bread, and a little wheat and corn and some eggs for the market. He could do better, he believed, and his neighbors and most of Nebraska believed, if he increased his livestock--cattle, hogs, chickens--fed them the grain from his fields, and put them, not the grain, on the market. But he dared not increase his stock until he had water. As it was, with his few animals, he invested an enormous amount of time, parts of seven or eight days every month, even in the winter, to haul water for his stock and family.[9]

He now got his water from Mary Martin, Harlan's mother, "Old lady Martin," he wrote in his diary, not that he intended any disrespect. He was, after all, only 33-years-old, and she was 58. She lived a mile east, across his and Ezra McKenzie's fields, a little farther if he went along the section line. From January 16 to the last of February, he went for water 11 times. He had by this time acquired three or four fifty-gallon barrels, undoubtedly the wooden casks used to ship kerosene by freight, and he had some kind of water tank or wooden trough for his horses and his cattle, a barrel, perhaps, for the house. The timing of his trips was governed by need, storage facility, the weather, and the demands of other work. Once there was an interval of eight days between his trips, once only two days. Even in these winter months when the stock needed less water, it was a time-consuming task, requiring parts of twenty-five percent of his working days.[10]

It was a hard work, getting the water, cold and nasty in the winter, with the water slopping on his clothes and freezing. He may have turned the windlass by hand, winding the rope around it and drawing the bucket upward a hundred and fifty feet or more to the surface. Even if Harlan had rigged a hitch for the horse to pull the bucket, he still had to swing it wide from the high windlass to the waiting wagon and empty it into the barrel. The bucket, Nellie remembered, held 15 gallons, which weighed 125 pounds. To fill, or nearly fill, four fifty-gallon barrels, he guided and emptied the bucket a dozen times or more. Then he would have removed the top hoops, put cloths over the barrels, and replaced the hoops to hold the cloths and reduce the slopping of the water. Once at home he had to carry the water to his stock and his storage barrel, splashing it if he hurried, getting colder by the moment, but he must empty the barrels and lift them off the wagon before he needed it. He must have a well but he apparently saw no prospect for getting one.[11]

In 1888, after three years of neglect, Warren resumed posting his diary. He had no standard booklet of the kind he had used for so many years, marked out in the days and weeks and months of the calendar. But he felt a compulsion to write, to make note of what the weather was like, of what he had done that day--only rarely how much he had done--, where he had been, who had been with him, or had come to his house. Either he could not buy a diary in Culbertson or he could not bear the expenditure of the few cents that it would have cost him to purchase it. So he used little paperbound "Memorandum and Account" books, put out by Dr. Pierce, dispenser of patent medicines, for "Farmers, Mechanics, and All People." One half of the first thirty-six pages were blank, the other half, and all of the remaining twelve pages, and the inside covers, were filled with testimonials, descriptions of symptoms and diseases and accounts of the marvelous cures wrought by Dr. Pierce's patented remedies. Warren filled the blank pages of three of the booklets, from January to October.

He had little of farming that he could do in these winter months. Aside from water, getting firewood was his most demanding task. On January 12, he and Harlan Martin had almost been caught in the biggest snowstorm of the winter, long remembered as the blizzard of eighty-eight. It took several lives and evoked many acts of heroism, particularly on the part of young schoolmistresses. Warren thought the morning mild when he did his chores. He and Harlan hitched up their teams and started for loads of wood on the Red Willow, eight or ten miles away. The clouds hung low and shortly the temperature dropped and snow began to fall, fitfully. When it persisted they turned back, thinking not so much of themselves as their families and the stock that had to be watered and fed. There was no danger to the children of the neighborhood for in these first years, when they were small and the farms widely scattered, the school board at Pleasant Ridge contracted for fall and spring terms only.[12]

The next day, Friday, was very cold, "verry," Warren spelled it, as if the doubling of the r reflected the emphasis in his voice and the cold in his bones. He stayed at home, and Saturday, too, doing only the chores. But the storm passed without dramatic incident or any sense of alarm that he communicated to Nellie about a great or terrible blizzard. It had snowed several times in the early winter, and from January 11 to March 1 it again snowed three times, was cold fourteen days, very cold on three. Twenty-seven days Warren thought pleasant or mild and what he meant can be judged by his note that after the third day of pleasant and mild or pleasant and warm, the temperature rose enough to thaw the frozen earth.

Sunday after the big blizzard was "pleasant but cold." He went to Sunday school, alone, but only four people came. The preacher, the Rev. E. L. Hutchins, who lived in Hayes Center, had not been able to make it through the snowdrifts, or had not tried. Monday was pleasant and a little warmer. Warren split some wood at the schoolhouse for the use of the church.

On Tuesday he and Harlan were able to go to the Red Willow, Harlan hauling for him. They went again on Wednesday. Altogether he hauled wood on eight days from January 11 to March 1, ten loads in all, counting the two Harlan hauled for him. That was enough to last through the rest of the season. Unlike the typical settler on the plains, the Clarks depended very little on cow chips for fuel. They did not, like the Gruvers, have an attachment to the stove for burning hay or straw. The fliers, urging homesteaders to come, had said there was an ample supply of wood for ten or fifteen years, by which time the farmers could grow their own trees for fuel, and for shelter as well. Warren, a New Yorker who had grown up with the sawing and chopping of trees and burning of wood found the supply adequate. He planned for the future by planting more trees, and when he had corn enough to shell he burned the cobs to augment his supply of wood. He kept the house warm.[13]

Warren's chores were not much more demanding than they had been in that first winter. He had two horses, a cow and a heifer, a few pigs and chickens to feed and water, and almost daily he sawed and split wood for the stove. But he was still in the field on these raw, cold days "gathering" and husking corn, as time permitted, eleven days or parts of them, until

February 13th, when he finished the job. Much of the corn he cut with a corn knife, shocked it in the field, hauled it in as he needed it, and husked the ears in the farmyard or the barn. Apparently he "gathered" some of it in the field from standing stalks, for earlier he had put high boards on one side of his wagon. Presumably he broke the ear from the stalk and threw it at the high board in a swinging rhythmic routine practiced by generations of farmers on the prairies and plains.

He spent the better part of six days late in February and the first two weeks of March building a pigpen and shed to replace the temporary shelter he had put up that first winter. He took a load of his corn to John Hughes, to pay for some unnamed service, and another load to the Red Willow, that certainly to pay for the wood he was burning. In exchange for Harlan Martin's labor, he helped him saw wood down on the Blackwood Creek and he spent one full day breaking sod for him. Occasionally he exchanged work with others, particularly Richard Roberts, who remained a good friend, but in the course of the year Richard married Maggie Jeffries, sister of Ellsworth, and the family tie brought the two men together in their work.

One day Warren went to Culbertson and back, 25 miles each way, a long trip by team and wagon on a winter's day. Twice he went to the mill on the Red Willow to have his grain ground into meal and flour. That was a trip Nellie liked to take with him, for she could play with the little girl whose father ran the mill. Late in February he took the whole family with him as far as the Jacob Cases on the Ridge, and left them until he could get back from the mill late in the afternoon.

Warren was justice of the peace for the Blackwood Township. He had been elected in 1886, or appointed in midterm by the commissioners, at the same time Richard Roberts had been named assessor for the township. Both newcomers, yet among the first to arrive in this new community, they had quietly achieved good standing. Warren, so far as we can determine from the incomplete record, served almost continuously as justice for twelve or fourteen years, unusual in a new country that limited most of its elected officers to one term, or at best two. His office required him, one afternoon, to make out some legal papers for his Methodist friend, John Coleman, and Doras [sic] Baker, both of whom lived in section 25 on the border of Highland Township. They seemed to have reached an amicable agreement in their negotiations and to have come to Warren simply to have him fill out and sign the proper paper. Another afternoon he went searching for Andrew Boyd, who must have been a brother or relative of his neighbor in an adjoining section, Charles Boyd. He found Andrew and collected some money from him for, we can surmise, payment on a note, or on the interest. He was to have more trouble with Andrew before the summer was over. Again, in a long afternoon, "till most night," he talked with another neighbor, Harry (Isaac) Mansfield, who faced a legal problem that would require Warren's later assistance. To serve as justice did not require much of his time, but the effort to resolve his neighbors' conflicts was serious business.

However crowded their days, Warren and Ada did not allow their work to interfere with their devotion to the church. Only illness, an unusually severe storm, or the birth and postnatal care of a new baby interfered with their attendance at Sunday school and preaching. It had not always been so with Warren. But since that night in the fall of 1879 at the Methodist church in Williamstown when he had "gone forward" to declare publicly to the congregation his intent to renew his faith and rededicate his life to God, he had been without serious fault. Chastened, perhaps, by Ada's greater piety, and now as a homesteader on these lonely plains, he found in the church satisfaction for both his spiritual and his social needs.

Weather permitting, they held Sunday school every week, preaching services once or twice a month and prayer meeting on Wednesday or Thursday evening. They had organized a "society," the Pleasant Ridge Methodist Church, in 1886, and formed a "class" which met regularly, after the manner of John Wesley and the Methodists, to examine the spiritual state of the members and to share testimonies. Harlan Martin was class leader and Warren Clark superintendent of the Sunday school. Warren ordered supplies from the David C. Cook Company in Chicago, publisher of religious materials for the Sunday school and the home, including: twelve quarterlies (commentaries on scriptural lessons) for the Bible class, ten for the intermediates, twelve duplicate "lesson leafs," one page reprints for visitors or those who forgot to bring the quarterly with them. He ordered, too, several papers and children's stories: eight copies of *Church and Home Illustrated*, ten each of *Our Sabbath Home*, *The Giant Killer*, *Truth Seekers*, and *Dew*

*Drops*. The totals suggest that there were not less than a dozen families--about twenty or more adults and at least that many children who attended the Sunday school.[14]

In the winter months when, as they said, the farm work was slack, the Methodists often held a "protracted" meeting, a revival. The services were scheduled nightly, with the exception of Saturday, for two or three weeks, with the regular minister doing the preaching. The sermons and the concerted interest and effort of the members served the purpose both of strengthening the faith of the committed and of bringing in new converts. It was in such a meeting that Nellie would be converted when she was eleven, and that other children and adults were "gathered in."

A meeting was scheduled to begin at Pleasant Ridge on January 17, 1888. That was the Sunday after the big blizzard when the preacher, Brother E.L. Hutchins, was unable to drive or ride his horse the ten miles from Hayes Center to the Ridge. Postponed three days, the meetings began on Wednesday. With the birth of her fourth child imminent, Ada did not attend, nor did the children who were too small to go out in the cold weather. But Warren was there, for every meeting through Thursday night of the second week. On the next day, Friday, Ada's labor pains began. Warren bundled up Earl and the girls, took them to a neighbor's and brought back Mrs. Case and Mrs. Driscol, fellow Methodists and close friends. The baby was born between six and seven o'clock that evening, January 27, the third daughter whom they named Flora.

Warren did not go to meeting that night or for the next three days. On Saturday he "helped some in the house," drove to Mary Martin's to fill his water barrels, picked up the children, and husked a little corn. The neighbor women went home and he did the housework and took care of Ada on Sunday. On Monday morning he got breakfast, looked after Ada and the baby, saw that the other children got dressed, and again did the housework until Mrs. Case came. He went back to his chores and to husking corn. Tuesday and Wednesday another neighbor woman came, a Mrs. Burner whom we know only by the entry in his book. Warren husked corn, collected some money in his role as justice of the peace, and Wednesday night again went to church. He took Mrs. Burner with him and brought back her daughter, Amanda, who was to do the housework until Ada could manage for herself. The next morning Warren went to prayer meeting at Mrs. Martin's and to preaching at night. On Friday morning, the baby not yet a week old, they held prayer meeting at the Clarks' so that Ada could be present and see her neighbors and they her baby. The meeting ended that night and Warren was again present. In the two and a half weeks, he had missed only four services.

Churches had been organized at Pleasant Ridge and Hayes Center in 1886. When the Presiding Elder of the Indianola District, the Rev. P. C. Johnson, came to Hayes Center in December of that year to hold the county's first quarterly conference, Warren Clark and Harlan Martin were the delegates from Pleasant Ridge, and from Hayes Center Dr. J. T. Meredith and William Sears, soon to become good friends of Warren's. The preacher assigned to the circuit, the Rev. E. L. Hutchins, was a promising young man who had been "admitted on trial" to the West Nebraska Conference. In the fall of 1888, the Hayes Center quarterly conference, with Warren as one of the delegates, voted to recommend that he be ordained a deacon. By the end of the summer, 1888, Hutchins could report thirty-eight regular and eight probationary members and fifty-one Sunday school scholars in his two stations. We can be quite certain that the membership at Pleasant Ridge was the larger.[15]

Pupils.

Charley Abbott
Nellie Abbott
Rose Jeffries
Maurice Kuhn
Cleve Scott
Willie Martin
Earl Kuhn
Harlan Abbott
Mamie Bright
Roy McMullin
Jennie Clark
Mable Martin
Bertie McMullin
Claten Scott
Otto Smith
Bertha Jeffries
Etta Abbott
Blair Scott
Asa Smith
Earl Clark
Earl McMullin
Flora Clark
Willard McMullin
Calvin Abbott
May Scott
Rosetta Bright
Genopha Clark
Dewitt Clark

SOUVENIR

Pleasant Ridge School
HOPE DISTRICT NO. 8,
Hope, Nebraska.

Oct. 3, 1898—Mar. 31, '99.

PRESENTED BY
Hiram Pickett,
TEACHER.

SCHOOL BOARD
J. S. McMullin J. H. Martin
W. F. Clark

# 12.
# We Finished the Well

For Warren and Ada the cost of having a well dug was prohibitive. Their friends Jacob Case and Elisha Driscol, and several other neighbors, had mortgaged their homesteads, Jake for $300, Lish for $400, to pay for improvements and equipment, including a well. But not Warren Clark. He had had enough of mortgages, making payments during most of the years of his young manhood against the loan his father had taken out on the little farm in Boylston, New York.[1] He would not mortgage his homestead.

He and Ada must have puzzled over the matter for months. When the way opened to pay for the well, it was probably fortuitous, more luck than cunning or foresight. The Timber Culture Act permitted only one tree claim per section and the available land in Blackwood Township had long been taken. Since those who filed were not required to establish residence, the act proved a bonanza to speculators. They made entry on a quarter section and held it until they could sell, "relinquish," for a profit. Most of those who filed on timber claims in Blackwood were speculators, only five of the original 34 taking title. One of the absentee claimants, Bib Bomar, in 1884 had filed on the quarter section immediately west of the Clarks. For reasons not in the record he did not "relinquish" his rights but, without announcement to anybody, canceled on August 18, 1887. How Warren, and no one else, found out, we do not know. He wrote to Jesse Harris in New York, urging him to take up the claim. Jesse, responding at once, filed on September 17, less than a month after the cancellation.[2]

It seems probable that Warren and Ada had hoped to induce Jesse to return to Nebraska--otherwise, Warren would have filed on the property himself. Jesse decided to remain in New York. Warren then offered to buy the rights. Lacking funds, he would give Jesse a note (or two notes as it was finally arranged), which he would pay off when his crops came in. It is possible, of course, that Bib did relinquish his claim and that Warren, lacking funds, persuaded Jesse to pay for it.

In any event, Warren thought he knew how he could get the well dug. Absolom Saling, Elisha Driscol's brother-in-law, had recently preempted a quarter section in Logan Township, on the Ridge Road, a mile north of Jacob Case's. The Salings, in the months before the building of the sod church, along with the Driscols, attended Sunday school and Methodist preaching at the Martin schoolhouse. Warren came to know that Ab was something of a mechanic and engineer and had either dug wells or intended to. Ab was interested in acquiring additional land, or Warren suggested the possibility to him and offered to arrange for Jesse Harris to relinquish his claim if Ab would dig the well for Warren.[3]

Sometime in February, after whatever conversations were necessary, he and Ab came to an understanding. Confirming the bargain, Jesse canceled and Ab filed on the same date, March 13, 1888. Warren had enough cash on hand, or crops to sell, to purchase the necessary supplies to begin digging the well--rope, tackle, bucket, lumber--or, as in Iowa, he knew that he could borrow on credit against the next crop without taking out a lien or a mortgage. He got timbers from the Willow and "dressed" them for the superstructure to hold the windlass, the rope, and the bucket. Twice in the first two weeks of March, as the weather and their other duties permitted, he and Saling went to Culbertson and purchased rope and other supplies--"and stuff," Warren wrote in his diary--"to dig the well." The night of the second trip they went to a party at Driscol's. On Wednesday, March 24, Warren built curbing for the surface area at the mouth of the well and began to build the drum, the windlass around which they would wind the rope for lowering and raising the bucket. The Martins had a party that night. On Thursday Harlan helped with the drum.

That day, Thursday, an ominous tragedy occurred in their neighborhood. One of the Gruver boys, Levi, also a well-digger, down 169 feet into the earth, was smothered to death when the sand on the side of the wall began to run and caved in on him. The Driscols had a prayer meeting that evening. Warren and Ada and the children went. It took a day and a half to recover Levi's body. Only 22-years-old he had left a wife and two small children.[4]

But wells must be dug and Saling was undeterred. He and Warren finished the drum on Friday and he began digging--the hole three or four feet across and square, so that where the soil was loose he could peg posts in the corners and curb the sides with boards.[5] With the rope wrapped around the drum, a bucket on one end--probably iron-bound and holding 15 gallons--and a horse hitched to the other, Warren hauled out the dirt and dumped it. On Saturday morning they went to Levi's funeral at the little cemetery on Methodist Ridge and that afternoon they resumed their digging.

Spring was a busy season. Warren had farm work to do and so did Saling. In the first six weeks they worked at the well as they could. March was a wet month, seven days of rain or snow. On Monday, after four days of digging, they had a snow storm, heavy enough so that they suspended digging and Warren sat in the house until the wind died down and then had to shovel his way to the barn and the outbuildings. Saturday was foggy and wet all day, with snow that night. Brother Hutchins came out from Hayes Center in the afternoon, stayed all night with the Clarks, and went with them the next morning to preach to his congregation at the schoolhouse. So much snow had drifted in through cracks in the ceiling and chinks in the walls that they moved Sunday school and preaching to Harlan Martin's.

Warren had water to haul, wood to saw and chop, he killed a hog, hauled and spread some manure. But for the most part in the last two weeks of March they dug at the well, six full days and another six days for a part or most of the time, equal to ten full days of digging. Averaging eight and one-half feet a day, they were by the first of April 85 feet down, Ab Saling at the bottom of the shaft, Warren at the surface with his horse, pulling up the dirt and emptying the bucket. They encountered no sand and no rock.

April, May, and June were the planting months, April for wheat, oats and corn, May and June for corn and sorghum cane. For the first two weeks of April the men did no work at the well. Warren had plowed his fields for wheat and oats in the late summer and early fall. Now he harrowed them and his fireguard to loosen up the soil. Very probably he used a spike tooth harrow. And if so, it is likely that he had made it at home with a triangular wooden frame hewed out of timbers he had hauled in from the Red Willow and through which he had fitted wooden pegs or driven long iron spikes the blacksmith in Culbertson or Hayes Center had made for him. Harrowing was, Harlan Garland said, farming for his father in western Minnesota, "even more wearisome than plowing." A man had no handles to hang onto, he had to lean back to hold the lines taut, and his heels sank deep into the soft loam, stretching the tendons of his legs "until he could scarcely limp home to supper." Warren's practice in those early years was to plant wheat on wheat ground, corn on corn, for that fitted better into his cycle of work. He could plow for wheat after the harvest, while the unripened corn still stood in the field, and for the corn the next spring, after he had finished his shucking.[6]

In the late summer of 1888 it would take him six days to plow for next year's wheat, three days for oats. A man working long hours, walking behind his team, could do a little better than in breaking prairie, perhaps two acres on a good day. We can judge, then, that in the spring he planted about 10 or 12 acres of wheat, five or six of oats.[7] He sowed the grain broadcast, dipping his hand into a sling suspended from his neck, spreading the seed with a rhythmical sweep of his arm as he walked slowly across the field and back. Then he harrowed the ground again, throwing a light cover of loose soil over the seed. The work went more quickly than the plowing, three days for the wheat, one and a half for the oats. It rained the day after he finished with the wheat, a good omen for the harvest. It would not rain again for three weeks, not until the month was almost over, but then the rain would fall for three successive days, one evening and all night, a little the next day, and on the third day, rain and snow. It looked like another good year for small grain.[8]

Along with putting in his wheat and oats Warren managed his chores and other farmwork--matters that he could not put off. He plowed his garden and potato patch and planted his potatoes, sowed his oats and harrowed in the seed, set out some trees, box elders, went to the mill on the Willow, commenced "backsetting" for corn--plowing back the sod he had broken in the fall while Ada, following, dropped the kernels in every third furrow. And after each interval of three or four days he drove his team a mile and a half to Mary Martin's to fill his fifty-gallon barrels with water.

He also had pressing business as justice of the peace. He spent one long day at the county seat in Hayes Center to support Harry Mansfield, his neighbor in section 10, in his troubles with his Uncle James, and did not get back until two in the morning. Harry, who had canvassed the problem with him in several long sessions in February and early March, had decided to bring suit against his uncle. The issue, never made clear by the record, was not settled until the May term of the court when Warren was again present. The jury, described by the clerk as "of good and lawful men," after hearing evidence, arguments, and instructions of the court, brought in a verdict for Harry. He had, the jurymen concluded, "right of property and right of possession of said property." Harry had been greatly agitated but the jury was amused. Everybody knew that the Mansfields were a contentious lot whose family quarrels not infrequently afforded entertainment to the whole community. They assessed Harry's "damage in the premises" at five cents and suspended all costs.[9]

Uncle James had a much more serious problem before the court than Harry's suit. For reasons not disclosed by the record, he was suing his wife, Harriet, for divorce. The court granted his suit and awarded him custody of their son, Abraham, but gave custody of their daughter, Marie Ann, to Harriet and assessed the costs to James.[10]

On April 5, the day after he had gone to court for Harry Mansfield, Warren had another neighbor at his door, Arza Nicholson from Highland Township, three miles to the east. Arza had a grievance against two of his neighbors who were under Warren's jurisdiction, Charles Nichols and Juniper Slater, both in section 13, Blackwood. Warren listened to Arza's story, made out replevin papers for the recovery of goods unlawfully taken, or unlawfully held, and went with him to see Nichols and Slater. They discussed the matter at some length, taking the whole of Warren's day, and finally "settled up their troubles." But Arza, like James Mansfield, had a problem far more engrossing and serious than the rights to property. Six weeks earlier, in mid-March, his wife Kate had purchased 160 acres in sections 13 and 14, adjacent to Charley Nichols' tree claim. She paid $1000 for it, a sum which included two mortgages totalling $450. Whether she had money in her own right or Arza purchased it for her, the record does not show. But apparently she moved onto the property. She soon discovered, or had already known, what an attractive young bachelor Charley Nichols was. Arza charged that Charley moved in with Kate, or she with him, and brought suit against Charley for adultery which, his formal charge asserted, was "contrary to the form of the Statute . . . and against the peace and dignity of the State of Nebraska." The court found Charley guilty and fined him $100 plus $110 costs, for a total, of $210. It also fined Kate $300 which would be remitted if she appeared in person at the fall session of the court. There had never been such a scandal in Blackwood, perhaps in all of Hayes County. Arza, deeply grieved, gave notice or pledged himself that he would sue for divorce.[11]

Monday morning, April 16, Ab Saling and Warren were at last able to put aside their farming and other obligations and begin anew to dig at the well. They worked with only minor interruptions for the next three weeks, for at least part of all but five days, two of which were Sundays. Harry Mansfield plowed for Warren on three days. One day while Saling put in curbing, to keep the sidewalls from caving in, Warren plowed and planted some more potatoes near the house. Another day Saling went to Culbertson to get his drill sharpened and Warren shelled seed corn with his hand operated sheller. One morning Warren went over to Richard Roberts' on an unnamed errand, another he took his heifer to pasture with Harlan Martin's herd, twice in the late afternoon he planted more potatoes. One day he and Harlan "fixed" his planter, getting it ready for him to put in his corn. But most of the time they dug at the well.

Slowly the shaft went downward. Morning after morning Saling descended to the bottom of the narrow, dark, square tube, three or four feet across, over a hundred feet down. He worked steadily, chopping into the tightly compacted soil with his pick, drilling with his hand auger, twisting the great bit with what strength he could muster, and shoveling the loose earth into the big bucket. He checked his plumb lines to keep the sides vertical, waited for the long haul of the earth to the surface, looked up at the remote and tiny square of light, and watched the slow descent of the empty bucket. Day after day he gouged out a foot of earth an hour, less than nine feet a day. By the first of May they had driven downward more than 150 feet. Some neighbors struck water sooner, some near the surface, like his new neighbor, Jim Scott, some went much deeper, 200 feet or more. Ellsworth Jeffries south of him was to go to 218 feet, a neighbor to the east on the upward slope of the ridge, 244. Warren was luckier. After two months, the equivalent of 21 full days, they struck water at 180 feet.[12] Warren was laconic. "We finished the well," he noted in his diary and then, without comment or word of celebration, "and I finished planting potatoes."

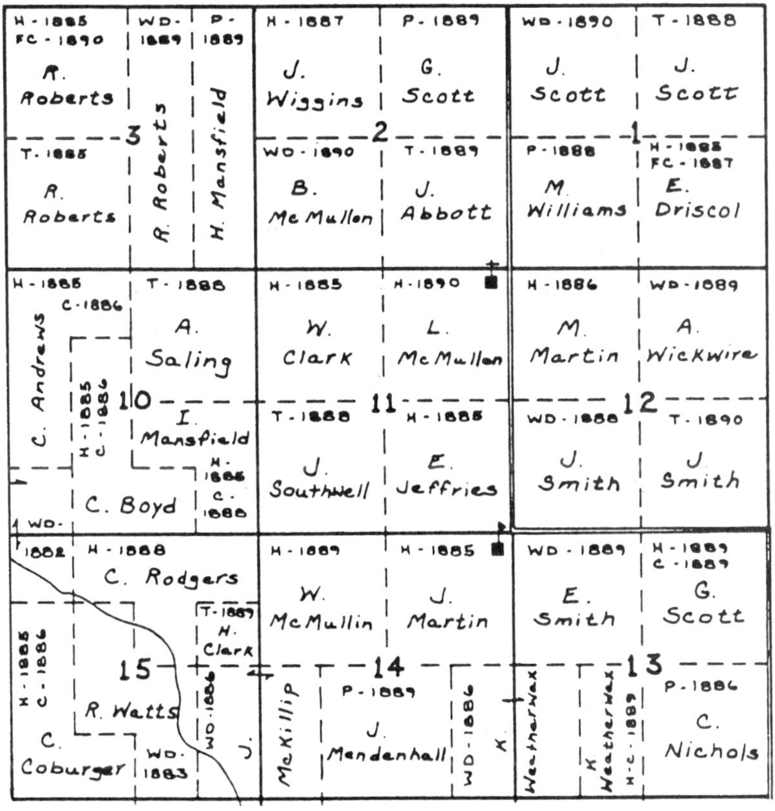

*The Methodist Ridge area of the Blackwood Township, Hayes County, Nebraska, 1890.*

*Clark family, ca. 1888. Left to right: Earl, Mamie, Flora with Nellie standing in between*

*Clark children, ca. 1898. Left to right: Jesse, Earl, Jennie and Flora.*

# 13.
# Summer

There is a relentlessness about a farmer's work. He cannot put off until tomorrow what he must do today. He must plant his wheat when the season says it is time to plant, and his corn and his oats. He must cultivate his corn, his potatoes, beans, and garden at the right moment, after a rain or before a rain, to nip the weeds or to loosen the soil. He cannot harvest his crops until they are ready, the kernels of wheat or oats or corn mature, full and hardened; but he must not wait too long, lest a hard rain level the slender stalks or a hot sun dry the husk and let the grain fall at the first blow of the cutting blade. He must water and feed the stock, repair the barn and sheds, fix the fence, keep the machinery in order, see that the sows and cattle are bred, attend to the calves and piglets, meet the needs of his family, take care of a thousand exigencies, all crowded into a schedule that he can expand only as the hours of daylight increase, or he quickens his pace, or begets sons, buys better machinery, or accumulates enough substance to hire someone else to work for him.

In New York Warren had been the hired hand, the man to work the fields, only occasionally interrupted by the never ending demands of chores and upkeep. Mr. Norton and John Howe had done the chores and attended to the little jobs that through neglect grow into big ones. Now on the homestead, his own farm, Warren had it all to do. Ada helped when she could arrange for the children, four of them--Nellie eight, Mary five-and-a-half, Earl, his only son, two, Flora less than six months.

May came in with rain, four days of it in the first week. They had finished the well on Friday. The next day, Saturday, after an all night rain, was cold and windy. Warren went to the mill on the Red Willow, ten miles distant, for the second time in three weeks. Brother Hutchins, the Methodist preacher, and his family came to spend the night. Warren was sick the next morning, but they all went to Sunday school and "meeting," in the rain. Monday it rained again. Warren was still sick, too sick to do anything but the chores. They had to be done. May was to be a rainy month, twelve days in all, three times rain all day, four all night, five times a part of the day. But two of the rainy days were on Sunday and the night rains soaked into the soil or ran off so quickly that only one of the showery days interrupted, even so much as half a day, his imperative schedule of plowing and planting. He was well enough to be back at work on Tuesday, fixing a pigpen in the morning, and in the afternoon beginning to plow his fields for corn and cane. He plowed and harrowed for eight days, or parts of days, getting the ground ready for planting, taking time out only for the Sabbath. Richard Roberts helped him half days twice and one full day. He took one half day off from the plowing to backset his sod and plant it to corn. Ada dropped the seed for him.[1]

He finished his plowing on May 16. The planting went much more rapidly. He used a check-row planter, an ingenious machine that he knew well from his New York years, designed to make cultivation possible lengthwise or across the rows. He borrowed a marker from Harlan Martin and pulled it across his freshly harrowed field, leaving shallow furrows, "marks," at regular intervals, customarily three and one-half feet in Nebraska. He then plowed across the marks with the planter, walking behind it, his lines taut to control the horses and keep the rows straight. Ada, her baby Flora not yet six-months-old, sat on the planter seat and pulled the lever to release the corn at the cross marks. Two cylinders, reaching down from the seed boxes, made it possible to plant two rows at a time. We can assume that Ada kept Nellie, who was eight, out of school to watch the younger children, Earl and Flora, for the three days it took to do the planting. In another few years Nellie, and later Mary, would sit on the planter seat and pull the lever. It must have been tedious and arm-numbing work, sitting there, eyes-down, watching for the cross mark and pulling the lever every three and one-half feet, hour after hour, all day long. At least Warren had Ada sit on the seat and he walked behind her. The son of another farmer in the county sat on the seat and his sister walked, pulling the cord to drop the seeds at the marked line.[2]

He finished planting his corn on Saturday, May 19, just before an all night rain. The rest of the month was a kaleidoscopic crowding of events--farm work, duties as justice of the peace, family responsibilities. On Monday, Tuesday, and Thursday he was at court in Hayes Center. Ada went with him and they stayed with Brother William Sears and his family, fellow Methodists and farmers who lived on their homestead at the edge of the village. They had arranged for someone to look after the children and the stock, probably Richard Roberts for whom Warren would do the chores in a couple of weeks. Warren went home on Tuesday afternoon, after having heard the Mansfield divorce trial and Arza Nicholson's suit against Charley Nichols. Ada stayed until Wednesday and then came home with a neighbor to relieve Warren so that he could return to court on Thursday for the trial of Charley Coburger. Charley, a young bachelor living on a homestead in section 15, had failed to make payment on a debt, money he had borrowed or credit advanced to him, for equipment or building materials. He did not appear to defend himself. The court reasoned, therefore, that he was guilty, awarded the plaintiff $73.60, with interest at ten per cent, and attached Charley's homestead to secure the judgment.[3]

Friday and Saturday Warren helped Harlan plow and plant. Sunday was wet and cold and Warren was sick. The whole family stayed home. He was still sick the next day. Tuesday all day and Wednesday morning Harlan broke sod for him, he dropped cane seed and Harry Mansfield harrowed it in. That brought him to the last day and a half of the month, Wednesday afternoon and Thursday. He broke prairie for himself on both days. Thursday afternoon he and Richard Roberts, both members of the school board, drove over to see Ross Beard, the third member, who lived two miles west of Warren in section 9, to determine how much money they owed the schoolteacher, and to authorize Warren to collect it from the County Superintendent in Hayes Center. That evening Aubrey Nelson, the other justice of peace in the township, came by. They talked over the case of Ezra McKenzie, whose property joined Warren's on the east. Ezra was in distress, not well, scarcely able to do any farming, and his wife was sick. The justices, mandated by law to oversee the poor in their precinct, called on him, assessed his need, and wrote out an order on the county for the purchase of food and supplies. It was a simple system, based on trust in the judgment and honesty of local officers, that the primitive society used to take care of critically needy families. The action was subject to review by the county commissioners, so that the merchant, too, if he was to be reimbursed for the goods he advanced, must assess the honesty of the justice of peace and, in turn, mete out an honest measure of goods.[4]

In the first two weeks of June Warren did very little farming for himself, one day in his cornfield, three and part of an afternoon breaking sod. Friday, the first day of the month, he went to the county seat at Hayes Center to get the money the district owed the schoolteacher. Ezra McKenzie, already an ill and defeated person, rode in with him to pick up the meager supply of food and clothing that Warren and Aubrey Nelson had authorized. Warren hurried home in the afternoon, did his chores, and that night went to a lawsuit at Nelson's. He tells us nothing of the suit, nor whether he or Nelson presided, only that he was present. The next day, adding his own labor to his official judgment of need, he plowed and planted for McKenzie. Sunday was pleasant and warm. They went to Sunday school and preaching, to Harlan Martins' for dinner, to Sunny Hill in Highland Township in the afternoon to plan for children's day.

On Monday he harrowed his corn all day, the first cultivation. Tuesday he hitched up his team and drove off to Culbertson to trade and was gone all day. One morning he did Richard Robert's chores and planted some trees for him, went home and put in trees for himself, and one afternoon and the next morning he planted corn for Harry Mansfield. He took time off from the field another morning to help the sheriff hunt for Andrew Boyd, from whom, last February he had collected money on his debt. This time he did not trouble to record whether they found Andrew or not. On Friday afternoon he took the family to the Gruvers' to practice for children's day--he always had time for the children--and the next afternoon and again on Sunday he and the family drove down to Sunny Hill for the Methodist Quarterly Meeting. He broke prairie one afternoon, Ada planting in the sod for him. He went to Hayes Center again to see the commissioners, for what reason he does not tell us. He plowed his potatoes and garden, and he took his cow, ready for breeding, off to pasture with a neighbor's herd.

On Saturday, June 16, he began plowing his corn, the first time over. He quit at noon to take the family to the Gruver's, once again to practice their exercises for children's day. Later that afternoon Isaac Heater, neighbor, friend, and fellow Methodist from their days in Iowa and now a homesteader in Hayes County, twenty miles northwest of the Clarks, and his daughters, and the Methodist preacher, E. L. Hutchins and his family, all came to spend the night. One can imagine the crowded state of the two-room sod house that night, but it was summer, the blankets could be folded and put on the floor for pallets, and quite likely some of the guests slept in the shed Warren had built for grain. Sunday they all went to neighboring Sunny Hill schoolhouse for a joint children's day program. They were gone, Warren noted, "most all day." Brother Hutchins and his family went back to Hayes Center after the exercises and the preaching but Isaac, who was a widower, and his girls returned to the Clarks for another night and more "visiting." Warren put a lively and happy weekend into that wonderfully inclusive word, "visiting,"--reminiscences of Iowa, bits of gossip, talk about the weather, crops, prices, politics, the church, problems with the children and neighbors and the livestock, and whatever else might drift into the unending flow of conversation or chatter. The Heaters went home early Monday morning.

In the second half of the month Warren was again in his fields. He cultivated corn for a day and a half, catching up on the growth of weeds since the last plowing. For two full days and half of another he plowed and harrowed the fields he had reserved for his sorghum cane. All one morning Ada planted the sorghum seed for him. As if it were in compensation, he went that afternoon to Arza Nicholson's to get a sewing machine, one that must have belonged to his rebellious wife, Kate. Warren might have bought it, for Kate was gone, and sometime in these years Ada acquired a machine of her own and no longer had to borrow from her neighbors. It rained the next morning, Saturday, and Warren went to the Salings for flour. When the fields dried off, he plowed corn. All of them were at Sunday school the next morning. Monday he and Richard Roberts took their marketable hogs to Culbertson. That was a good day--in two years to have an increase in his herd of swine so that he could write it so casually in his journal. They did not get home until about ten o'clock at night. In the five days of the month that remained he plowed corn, all day save for one morning when he plowed and hoed his garden and part of another when he had to see Richard. On the last afternoon of the month he finished cultivating his corn for the second time. It had taken, roughly, about six days over two weeks.

The first of July fell on the Sabbath. The family went to Sunday school and preaching. Whatever the demands of the farm, there was no neglecting the church. They had not missed a Sunday in June and only one in May when Warren was sick and the day so cold and rainy that they all stayed home. They were not to miss any of the five Sundays in July. Nor were they to neglect their family prayers, morning and evening, after breakfast and after supper. Warren customarily read the Scripture in the morning, Ada in the evening, and after the reading they knelt at their chairs and both prayed, the children, too, when they were old enough or after they had been "saved" in the protracted meeting.[5]

With the second plowing of his own crop out of the way, Warren spent most of the first two weeks of July working for others. With no water to haul and Nellie at home to look after the children, Ada could do the chores and the work around the house: milking the cows, feeding the pigs and chickens, hoeing a bit in the garden. If water for the stock ran low, she had to "hoist" some from the well. That was a hard, slow job, turning the crank handle, twisting the rope around the drum to lift the big bucket from the bottom of the well, 180 feet to the surface. The land sloped down from the well to the tank in the barnyard so she had only to empty the bucket into the trough that led to the tank. But she had to carry what she needed for the pigs and chickens and what she wanted at the house.

On the first Monday of July, Warren began to work for his neighbor, John Coleman, a fellow Methodist who lived a half dozen miles towards Culbertson in section 25. He stayed the entire week, plowing corn and a little cane, from Monday morning until "most night" on Saturday, when he came home. He might have worked for wages, more probably for goods. Not many homesteaders had money to pay out for labor. And it was Warren's custom, Nellie said, to work for others when he had his own field work done. That way, she said, he often got hay or corn that he needed for his stock.

The next week he broke prairie for Saling. Ab had not yet built his sod house on the quarter that Warren, using Jesse Harris' title, had traded to him for digging the well. He worked at that job a day and a half and then broke off to take his family to the Jeffries', less than a mile away but too far to walk with the babies. He may have wanted Ada and the children out of the house before two of his neighbors, Merady Williams and Jacob Wiggins, came over to try to settle a dispute. Jake, perhaps the most successful farmer on the Ridge, was something of a political figure (Abbott called him the "democratic chieftan"). A vain man, he liked to boast that in New York people thought he had "a striking resemblance" to General Grant. "The resemblance ceased," Abbott wrote, "the moment Jacob opened his mouth." Surprisingly, he agreed to arbitration. Warren heard them out, leaving us no hint as to the substance of their quarrel. He sifted the evidence and rendered his judgment on what ought to be done. With whatever haggling over details or meanings might have ensued, they accepted his decision. We made, he said, "a settlement." The men drove off to their homesteads and Warren went after Ada and the children.[6]

The next day he again broke prairie for Ab Saling, finished the job, he thought. All of the farmers made rough calculations of what they owed each other in labor exchange. But Ab Saling was a precise man who traded his specialized labor, in this instance the digging of wells, for cash or a stipulated product, not a rough guess. He came over, got Warren and together they measured the amount of prairie Warren had broken. He was short. Late that month, when his crops were out of the way, he plowed another half day, this time working with Saling to complete the job.

Those first few days of July had been warm, "very warm," Warren wrote in his diary, and "warm as ever." It had been warm most of June, but had rained four times and the warm weather had been good for the crops. By July in southwest Nebraska the corn is reaching upward, eighteen inches tall, or more, the broad dark green blades curving back from the stalk, gently rustling in the wind. To any one who lives in corn country, but above all to the farmer himself who walks behind or rides his cultivator, up and down the rows, the sight of that dark green field against the gray-black soil stirs the blood. It is a thing of beauty--although he would not admit to such a sentiment, or even think it, directly. But without doubt it is a source of satisfaction and pride, and of beauty, too, which he puts in characteristic understatement: "Looks like a good crop this year, if we get rain."

July is the month when the hot winds blow out of the southwest, parching the fields, curling the leaves of the corn, searing the edges, turning the green to yellow-brown. One wonders whether, even in those confident years, if Warren and his neighbors grew anxious when the days turned from "very warm" to "warm and very windy," never less than "warm and windy" or "warm as ever," day after day for nine successive days, eleven days without rain. But it had rained on June 25, two days before the hot weather began and it rained again at the end of the first week in July, only a little, but on two successive days, and rained again a week later after five more days of warm or very warm and windy weather. The prospect for both corn and grain was good.

How could they, these homesteaders, escape feeling a sense of reassurance, that the weather was after all pretty reliable, as Warren and Richard and Harlan had observed, for four years in a row, nine years, men like John Hughes said. Had they read and did they remember the predictions of the boosters and even the professors in the University: "the rain follows the plow?" We can guess, from expressions of relief in the Hayes Center press when the rains came, that the community had not been without some apprehension. But we can guess, too, that Warren, and his neighbors, took the weather as it was, without much thought about what the boosters and the professors had said, and without much worry for, whatever others told them, they had never experienced a drought or a crop failure.[7]

Warren got to his own cornfields for the third cultivation on July 12. He plowed steadily, Sunday excepted, for five days and finished the job, about fifteen acres. He hoed weeds out of his potatoes and garden, he mowed his oats, mowed some weeds, again hoed the garden and the potatoes. Jim Lakin and his family, Methodists who lived eight or nine miles southwest, in section 31, near the village, Palisade, came by to see them. They attended Sunday school at Hougland schoolhouse, on the western line of the township, but knew the Clarks. With the oats already cut and not yet dry, there was no farmwork really pressing and Warren and Ada were so delighted to see them that they put aside everything else and "visited most all day." Warren allowed his fresh cut oats to dry another half day in the warm sun and then hauled them in. A neighbor with a binder came, unexpectedly. Warren, just starting for Hayes Center, pulled up his team, showed the driver where to start cutting, and went after Harlan Martin. It took a day and a half to bind the wheat, he and Harlan following the whirling spindle, grasping the tied bundles and setting them, heads up, in shocks, little round tepees. He then moved into his hayfield--the grama grass grew tall on the divide that summer with the abundance of rain. The mower broke down, he "fixed" it, mowed for the remainder of that day and the next morning, borrowed a hayrack, and hauled it in. They had a good rain that night and he went to town the next morning, the trip he had postponed from the day the binder had come to cut his wheat. Even after he had allowed a day for drying out, the ground was still wet when he got back into the field, but not too wet for plowing. He had broken the lay on his own plow and had taken it to a blacksmith over on the ridge for repair, so he borrowed Saling's, turned over some of his extended garden plot, and planted turnips. It was late, July 27, but early enough for turnips, he reckoned. He cultivated his planting of late potatoes and put in the extra half day he owed Saling for breaking sod. Sunday they all went to church. Brother Hutchins, he thought, preached a "good sermon," one of the few judgments Warren entered in his journal.

The last two days of the month he and Richard Roberts hauled and stacked wheat, first his own and then Richard's. Warren did the stacking--he usually did, Nellie said, for he was good at it. They put up the stacks side by side, spaced so that when the threshing machine came men could stand, one on each stack and toss bundles onto the long conveyor belt. And so ended the month of July.

In early August Warren began to plow his wheat ground and pull weeds from it, taking advantage of slack days to get ready for next year's crops. On the first Sunday he and Ada and the children went home from Sunday school with the Harlan Martins, had dinner, and in the afternoon all of them, a wagon full of grown-ups and children, drove over to John Coleman's. They and other neighbors were meeting once again to practice singing, this time for the coming Sunday school picnic. Monday Warren went back to his plowing, breaking off to go with Saling to look at his hay in the canyon. The next morning he drove over to the ridge to pick up his plow share and plowed until sometime in the afternoon when Lou Marlinee, his closest friend and associate in Iowa, came by. They renewed old times while Warren did the chores, and during and after supper, but Lou was in a hurry and could not stay overnight. Warren returned to his plowing for a day, helped Harlan stack hay for a very long day, until eleven o'clock at night. At last on Friday, ten days into the month, he finished plowing his wheat ground. He had worked at it, with several interruptions, parts of seven days, the equivalent of five, and had plowed, perhaps, eight or ten acres.

The next day, Saturday, the whole family loaded up in the wagon and drove off to the Heaters, 25 miles away, as far as Culbertson but in the opposite direction, north of Hayes Center, to repay their recent visit. Both families went to Sunday school the next morning. That afternoon and Monday they called on other friends in the neighborhood, including several Iowans who had joined Isaac in the move to Nebraska. The Clarks, gone for four days, got home late Tuesday afternoon. It must have been a lark for the children, a pleasure for the parents, the only overnight trip for the family that year. Warren does not record who did the chores while they were away, Harlan Martin, probably, or Richard Roberts.[8]

There was scarcely time in the remaining days of the week to do any work for himself. He looked in on his neighbor to the east, Ezra McKenzie, found him sick and despondent, and his wife sick, too. He hauled some water for him. He had some unstipulated business that took him over to see John Hughes. And then on Thursday they were off to Kleven's grove for the Sunday school picnic.[9]

The grove was on the Blackwood, seven or eight miles to the southwest, a natural park on the banks of the dry creek, shaded by huge cottonwoods and scraggly hackberries. For two days the weather had been very warm but rain had fallen on Wednesday night. Thursday, the day of the picnic, was "warm and pleasant," one of those mild and lazy August days Nebraskans know very well, a mesmerizing warmth that seeps into the pores and infuses the spirit with a sense of well-being. Nellie remembered picnics with joy. Men hung ropes from the trees to make swings for children, set planks on barrels and kegs to make tables and benches, and the women put out cool lemonade. One of the men organized running and jumping games and contests for the boys. Some of the men pitched horseshoes, some, like "Papa" Nellie said, "just visited." Women chattered happily, as they could find time, what with looking after small children or supervising their pre-teen daughters who did the actual caring, bringing out the tableware, tending the fire, making the coffee, and heaping the table with food. Older girls strolled off with their beaus or, if they were unattached, helped their mothers, and young teenagers huddled in small circles, giggling at their own remarks or at the antics of the boys.

The next day, Friday, Warren and Harlan Martin drove their wagons to the Red Willow, ten miles away, to haul wood for McKenzie. On Saturday Warren had to get flour for Ada. With his own supply of wheat exhausted, he picked up some at Fred Smith's, over at Sunny Hill. The route was circuitous--he had to angle off seven or eight miles towards Culbertson, and then turn back northeast to the mill on the Red Willow. But Fred had wheat, they were friends and fellow Methodists, and they had undoubtedly seen each other at the picnic and worked out an exchange.

Sunday they were back at Kleven's grove for preaching. At last, on Monday morning, Warren found time to get to his oats stubble and for three days he plowed steadily until he had finished the job. It was the 22nd of August. Thursday morning he drove the mile across the plain east of his house to the McKenzies' to see how they were. Ezra's wife was quite ill. Warren could not easily dismiss the matter from his thinking, but he had work to do. He dug some potatoes, loaded them into his wagon, got ready to take them to town. Off to Hayes Center, he was gone the whole of the next day. He sold his potatoes, traded for goods, had dinner with his old friends, the Cases, who had recently moved to town from their homestead on Pleasant Ridge. He did not get home until eleven o'clock at night.

He did his chores the next morning and then, no doubt at Ada's urging, went over to see how Mrs. McKenzie was doing. She was sick, very sick. If anyone went for the doctor, or if any other neighbor were there, Warren did not say so. But her case seemed quite hopeless. He sat with her all day, went home long enough to do the chores, came back and sat all night. Again on Sunday morning he drove or walked the mile back to his place, did his chores, and returned to the McKenzies. He sat until afternoon when others came from the church services to relieve him. Mrs. McKenzie died about ten o'clock that night. As soon as the word came to him Warren started for Culbertson, 25 miles away. He picked up John Coleman on the way, they drove all night, purchased a coffin, and were back by noon. The funeral was held that afternoon. In the early days of the frontier society in the heat of the summer there could be no delay in performing the last rites for the dead.

He puttered around for four more days, "fixing" a sled to haul his water and heavy equipment from place to place in the farmyard, building a pig shed and a bin for his grain, and August was gone. The first two weeks of the month had been mostly hot and dry, but rain had fallen on the night of the 15th and on the 18th, again at night. "Now the crops of all kinds are safe," said the Pleasant Ridge correspondent to the Hayes County *Herald*. Before the month was over some of Warren's neighbors had threshed their wheat with yields of 18 to 30 bushels to the acre, very high indeed, when the national average that year was only 11 bushels. Warren's wheat, which looked as good as the best, was still in the stacks waiting for the threshing machine. Rain, good for the corn and the cane, "a pretty rain," he called it, fell again on August 30, in time to benefit the corn and the cane. "A bountiful crop," said the *Herald*, quoting the Hebron *Journal*, is assured, "ample . . . grain and fruit to supply the country for the next two years."[10]

# 14.
# Harvest

September brought little of autumn crispness to the Nebraska air. Summer lingered on. The first ten days were warm, six of them by Warren's record "very warm," one succeeding another with scarcely a breath of moving air. September 5, a temporary break in the oppressive calm, was "very windy," followed by another warm, still day. Rain fell that night but it brought no relief from the heat. The next day was again "very warm"--sultry, it must have been--clammy and uncomfortable to men and women used to the dry atmosphere. But no one worried about crop failure. The August rains had nourished the corn, made certain that there would be full kernels and a good yield, and the September rain was a welcome bonus, a benefit to the late-planted cane and turnips, insurance against the hot dry days that were to follow.[1]

However much the weather spoke of summer, it was autumn and Warren began to reap the product of his spring and summer's labor. He had a few miscellaneous jobs to do, scattered over the whole month: weeds to cut, manure to haul and spread, a half day of plowing, hogs to shift about in the pens and the shed he had built for them; and the major jobs: harvesting the cane and the corn he wanted for fodder, getting in the hay, threshing the wheat, oats, and beans, digging his turnips and potatoes, marketing what he could spare, storing the rest in his granary or pit.

Neither the weather nor demands of harvest interrupted their attendance at church services. All of them went to Sunday school on the first Sunday but in the afternoon Warren drove alone to Hayes Center to the Quarterly Meeting and was entertained by three local delegates. He had supper with William Sears' family, returned to the schoolhouse for evening preaching, and went with George Barda to spend the night. The conference continued its business Monday morning, hearing reports, examining the preacher, the class leaders, Sunday school superintendents, and other laymen, and adjourned at noon. Warren had dinner with Richard May, like the other two men a farmer near the town, but in a few years to become publisher of the local newspaper. The next four Sundays the Clarks had Methodist friends for dinner, after Sunday school or preaching at the Pleasant Ridge schoolhouse. Ab and Alice Saling, and their five girls, came on the first Sunday. The Salings would soon move into their new sod house, a hundred yards or so west of the Clarks, on Jesse Harris' tree claim.[2]

The next Sunday it was Ezra McKenzie and his motherless children and the John Theovalt family. Ezra, sick and discouraged, was about to move off his place and the Theovalts were taking it over, homesteading the relinquishment they apparently had purchased from him. They were active, dedicated Methodists and, with their house only a mile away, the Clarks' closest neighbors on the east and soon to be among their best friends. On the following Sunday Hank and Nell Devereaux attended Sunday school and came home to dinner with the Clarks. Nell, Ada's dearest friend and confidante when they were children and adolescent girls in Williamstown, and her husband Hank, witness at Warren and Ada's wedding, had welcomed the Clarks to Nebraska and to their Gosper County farm, north of Arapahoe. With much to talk about they stayed all afternoon, Hank no doubt helped with the chores, Nell with the dinner and supper, they spent the evening, stayed all night, and did not leave until the next morning. They had come to see Joel, Hank's father, some two and a half miles northwest of the Clarks.[3]

Early in the month Warren spent five days at John Coleman's, getting his molasses mill ready for the fall press. From his years of making sugar in New York and two seasons working in the molasses mill of his uncle, John Tryon, in Iowa, he knew what to do. He began by cleaning out the molasses house, a dirty, messy job. The arch that held the pan had crumbled and had to be rebuilt. That first night the Colemans had a "social." Only a few came but it must have quickened Warren's memory of the evenings in New York when the young people, after a busy, tiring day, picking and hauling hops, gathered for a "social," going from one farmer's hop house to another. One can be sure, however, that there was no dancing at John Coleman's Methodist home!

The next morning, Friday, Warren finished cleaning the molasses house and began to lay the stone for the arch that would hold the pan and control the flow of the boiling sap. He went home for the Sabbath, and on Monday brought Harlan Martin back with him. In the next two days they completed the arch and "got other things ready" to make molasses, a dozen little things, no doubt, checking the sweep and the hitch, clearing out any clutter from the circular path the horse must follow, adjusting and oiling the gears. Warren would bring his own sorghum cane to the mill, but he had planted late, it would not be ready for nearly a month, and he had much to do.

He ground his sickle and cut hay on Emma Saling's tree claim, over on the Ridge, two miles to the east. Emma, Ab's unmarried sister and the fourth claimant on that quarter section, had filed on it, undoubtedly for a fee, on the day it was relinquished by her predecessor.[4] Her success must have prompted Warren to think that his sister Hattie might be able to acquire land in the same manner. After finishing at Emma's, he cut hay for the next day and a half for Ab Saling, on his new place across the road from his own farmstead. Both Emma and Ab had canyon hay, blue stem and grama grass that grew tall and thick that year. He raked and shocked the hay, borrowed a rack and, with Harlan's help, hauled some of it to his farmyard. This time, his debt to Saling apparently paid, he was cutting on shares. He hauled water for Ezra McKenzie. He gathered a little corn, leaving the barren stalks standing in the field; and with his huge knife cut some cane and corn for immediate use. He plowed a half day.

Then he began to cut corn in earnest. It was backbreaking work. Grasping the stalk with one hand, the farmer swung his big knife to strike and sever it, with a single blow, just above the ground; he dropped it parallel to the row so that it would be easy to pick up and shock, and seized another stalk. The job took him three days, with half a day off to help a neighbor thresh.

At last on Thursday, September 20, the neighborhood west of the Ridge plunged into threshing. They went to Elisha Driscol's first, on Thursday afternoon. Lish was a mile and a half east of Warren's, a half mile beyond the Pleasant Ridge (Culbertson-to-Hayes Center) road. It had rained the night before and was warm and too wet to thresh in the morning. Warren moved his hogs and gathered some corn. That afternoon, with the moisture dried off from the stacks, they began threshing for Driscol, finished his job Friday morning and dragged the big separator a mile and a half south on the Ridge road to Harlan Martin's. They set up in time to do a little threshing that afternoon, finished sometime Saturday morning, moved across the road to Ellsworth Jeffries', and threshed for him on Saturday afternoon.

The weather had been typical for threshing--warm on Thursday, "pretty warm" on Friday and "very warm" on Saturday. The machine was powered by horses, with four or five teams hitched to long poles that, like spokes on a wheel, stretched out from the central core of gears. The horses plodded steadily in a big circle, turning the gears in the hub, setting the machine in motion, shaking and rattling noisily, in a great cloud of dust and chaff. A man on each stack pitched bundles down to a conveyor belt, another at the separator cut the twine and fed the loosened bundles into a revolving cylinder where the grain was shaken free from the straw. Rapidly vibrating screens sifted out the grain, a fan winnowed out the chaff, and conveyor belts carried the straw to a growing stack, the grain to a waiting wagon. One man, sitting on a platform atop the hub, drove the horses on the sweep, another forked back the straw to keep it from clogging up the conveyor spout, others loaded their wagons with grain, hauled and scooped it into the owner's granary, and returned for another load.[5]

The men worked long hours, from the time the dew was off the stacks until darkness overtook them. It was hard and nasty work, especially on a hot day, with the sweat streaking down their faces, the taste of salt in their mouths, salt smarting in their eyes, wind blowing the sharp-edged chaff into their faces and down their necks, the beards of the wheat sticking through their sweaty shirts, making their bodies itch. The work for the women was demanding, too, food to prepare for the men, not less than a dozen of them, meat and potatoes and bread and pie and whatever vegetables they had grown in their gardens, they, too, perspiring, over a hot stove on a hot summer's day. Two or three neighbor women came to help, Nellie said, exchanging labor like the men, buying help that they would need desperately when it was their turn to feed the threshers. But with all the hard work, it was a good time for socializing, when the women could "visit" as they hurried about the kitchen, and the men, too, as they lounged on the ground after the noonday meal, or at the stacks when a belt broke or the machine got clogged, or when they had to reset for another pair of stacks.

They moved to Warren's on Monday morning. It was a short distance, about a mile on level ground, and they were ready to start threshing at an early hour. They finished at noon, had dinner, pulled the rig over to Richard Roberts', a little over two miles, and did his threshing that afternoon. The next morning they retraced the route to Ab Saling's, across the road west from the Clarks. They finished his job, did another one that afternoon, "took all day," Warren said. But he was through, he had met his obligations for exchange, eight jobs in four and a half days, all from small plantings. Everywhere the pattern was much the same, a half day's threshing for each homesteader, the product of ten to fifteen acres. Only Lish Driscol required more than a half day, and he had two sons big enough to help him cultivate his crops. The farmers on the Ridge who threshed earlier had reported that their yields ranged from 18 to 30 bushels an acre. Warren did not record his own yield. The typical threshing machine of that period had a capacity of about 750 to 800 bushels a day. If Warren, in a half day, or a little less, got 300 or 350 bushels of wheat from the ten or eleven acres he had harvested, he had a yield of about 30 bushels and was one of the more successful farmers on the Ridge that summer.[6]

On the last afternoon at Saling's Warren pulled his wagon under the spout, loaded up with oats and, the next morning, Wednesday, September 27, hauled it to Culbertson for Ab. Thursday he worked all day for Harlan, helping to sow rye. The next day he gathered corn for his stock, threshed a few beans, no doubt flailing them as he had done on his father's farm in New York, did his chores, and loaded the wagon with his own wheat and oats to take to town.

He set out for Culbertson early on Saturday, September 29. That undoubtedly was to be for him one of the most satisfying days since he had come to the homestead. He started early, before daylight. The fall morning was cool, the first frost of the season. He had 25 miles to drive. One wonders what he thought of southwest Nebraska that morning. A few moments before sunrise the autumn sky would brighten at the eastern horizon, the edges brushed with pink, would fade to light blue on the south and the north, darken to blue-black on the west. The coyotes would be yapping, the cries of one or two, augmented by the echo, sounding like a whole pack. There was no wind for him to take note of, or clouds. In the clear atmosphere of a fall day on the plains space seemed infinite, the spirit unconfined. That was the "grandeur sublime" Jess Harris, Ada's brother, saw and wrote about. With the coming of daylight, the well-defined line of the horizon emerged, a great circle, undulating gently at the margin to conform to the pattern of the land. Warren could see before him, a dozen miles away, the rugged palisade at the valley of the Frenchman and, much closer, off to the right, a couple of miles, the tall cottonwood, the lone tree, that stood out of the canyons, on the open prairie, isolated from its kind, rising above the short buffalo grass, a source of wonder and a welcome landmark to the early settlers. The road to the village of Palisade, swinging off to the west, passed close to the tree. Here on the Culbertson road he could see its upper crown. And he no doubt could remember, if his mood were right, when he and Roberts first saw it as they came out from McCook, driving into that new, wild country, searching for a spot to stake out his claim, or when Ada saw it, that late afternoon, when he first brought his family out of the canyon onto the divide, and to his new homestead and half-built sod house. The road ahead of him to Culbertson turned southeast. It dipped a time or two into canyons, the horizon narrowing sharply, then drawing back into the great bowl as the team pulled the wagon over the crest of the canyon wall.

At last, after seven or eight hours on the road, behind the slow, plodding horses, he came out on the hillside overlooking Culbertson and the valley formed by the confluence of the Frenchman and Republican rivers. From the time of the early travelers men had exclaimed over the great expanse of the plains. A few praised the unexpected beauty of the river bottoms, with the green and reddish-yellow fringe of cottonwoods and willow bushes. Many more scorned the scraggle of brush and the shallow slither of a stream that passed for a river. But who could fail to note the blue haze hanging in the branches, fading into the atmosphere above them, or the steep banks, some of them barren, some grass or shrub covered, standing a half mile or more back from the stream, rising sometimes to palisades. If Warren were moved by any of it, he had no word for his sentiments, left no record of how he felt. But he affirmed his satisfaction and faith in the new country by what he had done. He had encouraged or persuaded his sister, Hattie, to come to the West and file on a claim. If Emma Saling could do it, and other women, why not Hattie? She was 23-years-old, single, uncommitted. Hattie would be on the cars headed west in a couple of days, would arrive in less than a week.

Warren sold his load of wheat and oats, the wheat, if Hayes Center prices prevailed in Culbertson, for 55 cents, the oats for 20. Not good, but better than some years. He then went to the bank, had a draft drawn to the credit of Jesse Harris, and sent him the money to pay in full one of the notes he had given him for the tree claim which he, Warren, had traded for the well. He picked up what provisions he needed and headed for home, late in the afternoon.[7]

Again we would like to draw back the curtain--to know what sense of well-being must have possessed him. That day, September 29, he was 34-years-old. Reared in a family that had lived always on the margin of poverty, he could not forget his father's little farm, heavily mortgaged when he, as a boy and young man, had paid the interest to prevent foreclosure. Now he was more than half way through the years required to make his homestead his own. He still had little money, less than he had earned in a summer as a hired man. There were not enough marketable crops for a cash flow. But that was also true of his neighbors. And his land was free from mortgage, he had increased his holdings in cattle and hogs, he owned his team and wagon, a plow, a planter, a harrow, a cultivator, his household furniture. He had a well and a garden and young fruit and shade trees growing. In a few years he would have his own orchard and his own woodlot. Ada was twenty-nine-years-old, well, a strong and able worker, outdoors as well as in. They had four children. And in less than a week Hattie would be coming, gambling that she, too, could make a good life in the new west.

Darkness overtook him before he got home. The stars hang low in the western Nebraska sky, the configurations stand out brightly. Warren taught his children those configurations, the major ones, and they in turn, their children: the north star, the big dipper with its pointers and bent handle, the little dipper, the seven sisters, even the weak star bright enough to see easily on a clear night. Only a few weeks hence Dock Gruver, looking up into that dark and sparkling sky, would see a falling star, the brightest he had ever seen, and think it remarkable enough to talk about, and the correspondent on the Ridge uncommon enough to include in the items from Hope, printed in the Hayes County *Herald*. It was a long ride that September evening and night, from Culbertson to the homestead in Blackwood, an occasion for long thoughts for a man riding alone. But whatever thoughts Warren may have had, whatever he may have seen of the countryside or of the day or the night, he limited his entry in the diary to comments on the weather and the record of his payment of the note drawn to Jesse Harris.[8]

On October 1 Warren sowed and harrowed in his rye, the last of the fall planting for next year's crop. The rest of the month's work was the harvest of the summer's growth. He gathered a little corn, cut some sorghum cane for fodder. That took two days. He dug some potatoes and put up a load of grist--wheat to be ground--to take to town.

On Friday the 5th of the month he took the grist to the mill at Culbertson and went to the train to meet Hattie. He had not seen her for nine years, or any member of his family since his sister and brother-in-law, Bell and John Howe, had stopped off in Iowa in 1881 for a couple of days, en route back to New York from Kansas. But he had no word for the record of the greeting, or of the talk on the long ride back to the homestead, or of his recollection of his boyhood years, or their plans for Hattie's future on the great plains. Presumably she was included in his entry for the Sabbath: "We all went to Sunday School." In time he would make casual reference to her tree claim, a forty-acre abandoned plot near Warren's on which she filed, and to the plowing and seeding he had done for her or the hay he had cut on her land for himself.[9]

Saturday Warren began stripping cane for the sorghum mill. Farmers had learned a simple technique and the work went rapidly. While the cane stood in the field they broke the leaves from the stalk with the downward swing of a hayfork. Then bending the stalk they cut off the head with one "clip" of the cornknife and with another blow severed it at the base. They tossed the head aside to be picked up later for feed and, as with the corn, dropped the stalk parallel to the row. That expedited the loading of it into the wagon, likewise in parallel rows, thus making it easier to feed the stalks into the mill. It took Warren all of one day and parts of two others to strip and cut his sorghum, enough to make four wagon loads.[10]

In a long day he could haul two loads of cane stalks the five miles to Coleman's, extract the juice, and boil it down to syrup. The process was simple enough. The basic components of the mill were two rollers which stood on end and were geared to each other by cog wheels. A long wooden "sweep" was attached at a declining angle to the top of one of the rollers--much like those for a threshing machine, but with less power needed. A horse or a team hitched to the far end of the sweep moved round and round the mill. A man sitting on a stool thrust the cane stalks between the rollers in somewhat the same manner that his wife put her wet laundry through a wringer. The juice, wrung out of the stalks, was cooked in a long galvanized or copper pan, the evaporator. It was mounted on an arch (which Warren had built for Coleman) over a grate and a fire. The curved arch gave the operator control of both the direction and rate of the flow. He stood with dipper in hand to skim off the green scum. The thrifty farmer took home not only the sorghum for his family but the scum and the crushed stalks to feed his cattle and hogs. We cannot easily judge how much syrup Warren realized from his four wagon loads of cane. Manufacturers boasted that their mills could produce 25 to 30 gallons per hour, but the figure was not very reliable, and it seems apparent that John Coleman's mill was a small one. We can guess that it required at least an hour to process each of Warren's four loads and that he took home an ample winter's supply of several gallons of syrup. Ada used sorghum as a substitute for sugar, to serve with pancakes or biscuits. With a little of it she sweetened water to make vinegar. And she made molasses cakes and cookies that pleased her children and many years later were to delight her grandchildren with a strange and tantalizingly ambiguous bitter-sweet taste.[11]

Before Warren had finished his sorghum making, Brother G.W. Southwell, the Methodist preacher newly assigned to the Hayes Center circuit, took the pulpit in the sod schoolhouse to preach his first sermon for them. He was a brother to the Clarks' sometimes irascible neighbor, Joe. Warren made no comment. Brother Hutchins came by to spend the night before he and his young family moved on to his new assignment in Red Willow County. In a day when seminary training was all but unknown on the frontier, the Methodist church reassigned its minister every two years. And in small rural charges, like Hayes Center, with two or more appointments on a circuit, the bishop was apt to assign the newest of the raw recruits. Both men began their ministry at Hayes Center, Hutchins as a "probationer," newly admitted to the conference, Southwell a "supply" who had not yet been formally admitted. Both men served their apprenticeship of two years and moved on. Late in the month, on a Tuesday, Southwell brought his family to call on the Clarks. Ada took the wife and children into the house and Warren gave up digging potatoes and for the rest of the day visited with the new preacher.[12]

With his threshing done and his sorghum sealed in jugs, Warren turned to the harvesting of feed for his stock. He cut the corn he and Ada had planted in the sod, late, not until the middle of June, but now mature enough to make excellent fodder. He cut cane for three more days, making a total of half a dozen altogether, and then, putting aside his corn knife, he mowed the rest. He gathered a little corn one afternoon, raked up his cane, shocked some of it in the field, hauled the rest and stacked it in the farmyard. Most of the corn he left standing in the field. He would pick it later over a period of a month or six weeks, some of it, perhaps, not until after the turn of the new year.

His diary came to an abrupt end on October 23, with his entry on the last page of the third of Dr. Pierce's little memorandum books. Presumably he filled a fourth booklet that is lost to us. We can infer from a later diary that in the last months of the year, with winter approaching, he began to put in his wood supply, hauling both from the Red Willow ten miles away and from the Blackwood only two or three miles distant. He no longer had to go for water every fourth or fifth day. No doubt he husked his corn, the most demanding of his winter work. He sold some grain in town, took grist to the mill, butchered a hog or a cow, built fence to pasture his cattle in one of his fields, and did such odd jobs as setting tires for his wagon, repairing and oiling his harness, cleaning out the barn and the hog and chicken houses, mending shoes, cleaning the clock, chopping wood for the schoolteacher. He faced the winter with plenty of feed for his farm animals, with his family well housed, his larder well stocked with meat, potatoes, flour and corn meal, beans, turnips, probably beets, plums and berries that Ada, Nellie, and Mary had picked from the canyon walls and dried. He had little money, but from the grain he sold he had realized enough to enlarge a bit his holdings in stock, add a piece or two of machinery, and to buy some condiments, some yardage, and a few items of clothing, most of it from the mail-order house, for Ada and the children. It had been a good year.

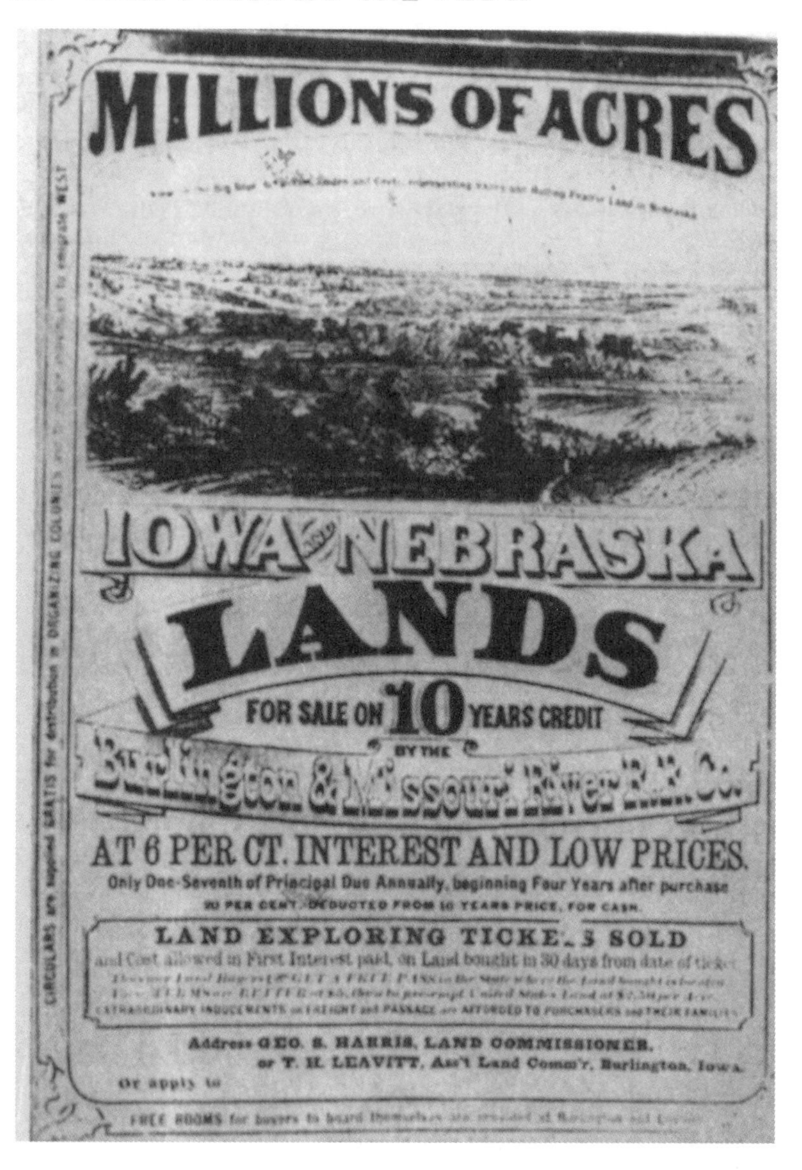


*Burlington and Missouri River Railroad Company's land poster, ca. 1873.*

# 15. METHODIST RIDGE

1888 had been a good year for Pleasant Ridge and all of Hayes County. The wheat Harvest was good, the corn never better, the Gruver brothers' millet four feet high at maturity. N.L. Wemple, who managed the Hope post office, put up the first windmill on the Ridge, followed in short order by Elisha Driscol and Oscar Gruver. Oscar had done well enough to put a new addition on his sod house, making the whole 17 by 40 feet, to build a new barn and blacksmith shop, and to lay down 350 feet of pipe to convey water from his new well and cistern to his house and barn.[1]

West of Hayes Center a mile, P.C. Iverson had "a truly remarkable" crop of corn, 66 acres with stalks averaging eight and ten feet high. The *Herald* did not estimate his yield per acre, but Iverson had raised three crops of corn on his land without a failure, in the first year enough to pay for his preemption fee of $200, and now before harvesting the new crop, he had 700 bushels in his cribs. Three miles from town another farmer offered his eighty-acre farm for sale at $450, four and a half times what it had cost him at the government price. He had 18 acres under cultivation.[2]

That September at the third annual county fair corn "occupied its usual place of prominence." It sat "enthroned." On the table were long lines of white and gold, "all of the most perfect and best qualities." The walls "were festooned with noble stalks with mammoth ears depending, a most gratifying sight." Oats, wheat, rye, and beans were "as fine as could be seen in any new country." Two farmers exhibited fourteen-foot corn and Henry Wiswall, showing three kinds of melons and nine varieties of corn, captured 11 blue ribbons. A month later at the state fair in Lincoln, two Hayes County farmers won blue ribbons, A.D. Moon for his wheat and Oscar Gruver on the Ridge for oats, and Henry Wiswall second place for watermelons. It was the third year in a row that Hayes County had won first place in wheat and oats.[3]

In all of the exultation over crops one note sounded triumphant above all the rest. Over near Carrico post office, in Valley Precinct, northeast of Hayes Center, some 20 miles from the Clarks, John Chavileer had four acres of corn in sandy loam that would average 75 bushels per acre. Said the *Times*, the new Democratic paper established to compete with Abbott's Republican *Herald*, "The sand hills are destined to be the farming country yet." Whether Warren Clark read the item or heard others talk about it, or whether it seemed important to him, we do not know. But it was an idea that in time, having grown to a conviction, would weigh heavily on him. He had already learned that the fine, powdery soil on Pleasant Ridge would seal over after a rain, and that a farmer had to break it up--harrow or plow it--or the next rain would run off like water on a rocky ledge. "Hard land," they called it, beautiful soil if you kept it loose--and if the wind didn't blow.[4]

Neither the people nor the two newspapers were much concerned with the comparative merits of sandhill and hard land farms. After four or five years of benign weather, good crops, and a great increase in population, it was time to appraise, even to rhapsodize. Miles Abbott, for the *Herald*, undertook the task on September 6, 1888, in a front page story, "Hayes County, Nebraska, Climate, Soil, Products."[5]

The county, he noted, had been organized in January, 1885, with a population of about 200. Now, three years later, it had a population of 4000. The first big wave of homesteaders began to arrive in the spring of 1885--the year that Warren Clark and Richard Roberts came--and to dot the gray buffalo grass of the prairies with the black sod of their houses and the small plots of land they plowed. Now, driving through the countryside "one passes broad fields of ripened grain and golden corn." In each of the last three years Hayes had proved "the banner county in the state." No other, he boasted, had yielded as much corn or grain per acre, none in this or any other state "is better adapted to agricultural pursuits than Hayes County." Appropriating the idea in Charles Dana Wilber's catchy maxim, "The Rain Follows the Plow," now become commonplace, he affirmed that "The rain-fall, once very light, is gradually increasing, and as it always increases with the cultivation of the soil and the growth of trees and shrubbery we need have no fear of drouth...." Warren and Ada and their neighbors had reason to be complacent as they read Abbott's words. The past four years had proved him right.

Abbott also had praise for the new county seat, Hayes Center. Charles E. McPherson of McCook, had platted the village in 1884 on 40 acres of government land near the center of the sparsely settled and not yet organized county. "Not a soul" lived within ten miles of the site. Now four years later it was a "thriving and energetic village," population 400. It had three general stores, two hardware stores, two drugstores, two banks, three land and loan agents, one of whom was Abbott, two newspapers, a millinery shop, a confectionery, a hotel, two blacksmith shops, two physicians, six attorneys, Abbott among them. It was as large as Ada's own Williamstown village in New York.

The town had a well, dug in 1885 at the main intersection by the first settlers who had quickly grown weary of hauling their water seven miles. They soon put up a windmill, "the waterworks," Abbott called it, grandiloquently. Dr. J.T. Meredith, one of the charter members of the Methodist church in Hayes Center and a friend of Warren's, had an office and drugstore on Main Street, and his three horses were constantly on the go, "substantial evidence," Abbott wrote, "of the Doctor's large and rapidly increasing practice." The Jacob Cases, Warren and Ada's friends from Pleasant Ridge, lived in the town and fellow Methodists, William Sears, George Barda, and Richard Mays, lived on their farms at the edge of town.

Abbott's highest praise was for the people and the climate. The settlers were most "of moderate means in the prime of life." They had grown weary of farming small acreages of high priced land and fighting floods and insect pests in eastern states. For Warren Clark he might have added, "and rocks and stumps." Their "intelligence," he wrote--voicing the pervasive doctrine of the time that later historians were to call Social Darwinism--was above the average of older settlements in the east, for they were "the plucky, bright ones . . . who had the energy . . . and the ambition to improve their condition." They had come to a beautiful country where the climate was "unsurpassed for healthfulness and purity." The atmosphere was "clear and bracing; so clear and transparent that language can not paint its splendor." Carried away in his own rapture he asserted that "the sunrise and sunset rival that of far-famed Italy." The climate was healthy, "free . . . from consumption, asthma, bronchitis, inflammation of the lungs, and kindred diseases." People who came into the locality felt "a general quickening and elasticity of spirits," their appetite and digestion improved, their minds and bodies lifted up.[6]

Most of the settlers would have been quick to affirm his judgments. There was, as Jesse Harris said, a grandeur in the setting, a sense of great distances that only the sweep of the plains and the clear atmosphere could engender. And as for Rome, none of them had been there, not even the editor, and the Nebraska sunrises and sunsets were certainly equal to any account they had read of that far-famed city.

The years 1889 and early 1890 brought little diminution in the optimistic spirit that prevailed in the county. The price of corn was low, 12 to 14 cents, but smart farmers were feeding it to their hogs and cattle. Henry Wiswall and his son, in Government Precinct, had one hog when they settled in 1886, and now had 120. William Black, in section 22, Blackwood, had 50 head of cattle, Charley Nichols 10 head of spring calves for which he had been offered $3.75 a hundred pounds--"a good way to dispose of cheap corn," the Pleasant Ridge correspondent moralized. Jake Wiggins was building "the finest hog house" for brood sows in the county, eight stalls on each side with an alley between. He had 60 head of hogs, mostly registered Poland China, and 36 head of cattle. Warren Clark had a "fine lot" of brood sows, some of them for sale, Jim Scott sold 12 head of eight-and-one-half-month-old pigs that tipped the scales at 258 pounds each. The Ridge was doing well.[7]

Irven Gruver, across the line in Logan Precinct, dug a new well, 190 feet deep, and cemented it from top to bottom. Ellsworth Jeffries went down 218 feet and installed a windmill to draw his water. Windmills were springing up all over the Ridge. George Scott dug 235 feet to reach water for his pump. Jake Wiggins took out a mechanic's lien for $75 to pay for his windmill and 215 feet of pipe; he attached a feed mill to it and bargained to pay off the lien by grinding grist for his neighbors. John Johnson, over in the Houghland district but still in Blackwood, borrowed only $35 to put up his windmill, and he signed an affidavit that his quarter section was worth $2,000. Wesley Gruver paid $500 for a quarter section, already proved up, in Logan Precinct. Miles Abbott, happy with the rise in land values, gloated: "Someone give ye pencil pusher such a bargain."[8]

In January, 1889, John Hughes, demonstrating the importance of the county in the State's agricultural production, was elected to a two-year term on the State Board of Agriculture. He was also placed on "one of the most important committees" of the State Fair Association. "The democratic statesman from Hayes County," the McCook *Democrat* called him. A year later Henry Wiswall joined him on the agricultural board. The county had begun to cash in on the ribbons it had won at the state fair.[9]

Despite the county's rising land values, or because of them, the community was restless. Someone was always on the go, selling the property on which he had earned title or relinquishing, for a fee, his rights to a claim. There were 36 quarter sections on the Ridge, or the part of it that was in Blackwood, everyone of them, by 1889, filed on or proved up. But two-thirds of the men who lived there were newcomers. Warren Clark could count on the fingers of his two hands his neighbors of four or five years before: Richard Roberts, Ellsworth Jeffries, Harlan Martin and his mother, Mary, Elisha Driscol, Harry Mansfield, all friends of his, Jake Wiggins in section two,Charley Nichols, and others whom he knew less well, Charles Andrews and Charles Boyd, his neighbors to the west in section 10, and Charley Coburger, a young bachelor down on the Blackwood.[10]

In 1885 Tom Scott had come out from Iowa and filed on a homestead in Highland Precinct, a mile east of Jacob Case's. He liked what he found on the high plains and urged his brothers, Jim and George, to come out and get some cheap land of their own. Jim came in the fall of 1887, liked Jacob Case's tree claim, in the far corner of section one, and took it over, for whatever fee Jake was able to exact and Jim willing to pay. He filed for a homestead which in the next four years he would change to a tree claim and back to homestead, a stratagem to reduce his immediate obligations and postpone the day when he received title and had to begin paying taxes. George in 1889 would purchase rights to two properties, a homestead in section two which he would preempt (buy), and a tree claim on the Ridge in section 14 which he would homestead. In the meantime, Jim had hastily constructed a dugout in the hillside to serve as his first living quarters and early in the spring, 1888, had brought out his wife, Ella, and their four children. Two of the children were of school age, Will, nine-years-old, and Ella seven, the same age as Nellie Clark. Jim was a drinking man, Nellie said, but he was hardworking, he had a good family, and he was always sober when he took them to church.[11]

Merady Williams in 1888 secured the rights to an unproved homestead in section two and preempted it. That same year Charles Rodgers, his sons and daughters already young adults or in their teens, homesteaded on an abandoned claim next to Charley Coburger's. All but Charles himself were recluses who attended neither church nor other community affairs. But one of them, Jesse, was to become intimately associated with the Clarks. That fall J.B.("Rome") Smith purchased a quarter section on the Ridge road, immediately east of Ellsworth Jeffries. He moved onto the property the next spring with his wife Mary, their daughter Nellie, 18, and three sons. They were Methodists, at least Mary and Nellie were. Nellie played the organ for the church, whether hers or one the neighbors bought for the church we do not know. Rome attended, but he was high tempered, drank sometimes, was blustery and loudmouthed. In a fit of anger he once threw a bucket at Mary; she dodged and it struck Nellie, cutting her face and leaving a scar that she was to carry to her grave. But for all of his bragging and bullying, Rome was a good farmer and his neighbors respected him. And now and then, he and his family went to the Clarks for dinner after church on Sunday. He had been on the Ridge scarcely six months before the neighbors elected him, along with Warren Clark and Richard Roberts, to serve as trustee for the cemetery association.[12]

Rome soon acquired a second property, a preemption just south of his own farm, across from Harlan Martin's, at a cost now lost to the record. He sold it to his brother, Edward, in September, 1889, for $1250, subject to a mortgage for $350, which was something of an index to inflated land values on the Ridge. Ed and his wife, Melissie, and their children moved to Blackwood at once. They were unequivocally Methodists, regular attendants at the church, soon good friends of the

Clarks and the Martins. Ed took over for Harlan as classleader, and even preached occasionally.[13]

Ed's place on the south bordered the tract Kate Weatherwax had purchased, the proximity of which to Charles Nichols' preemption, and the consequences thereof, had created such a scandal only a year earlier. Kate, with a threat of a $300 fine hanging over her, had appeared before the court. She had a way with officialdom, or her cause was just. The court forgave the fine and granted her the divorce. Now she and Charley, righting their relationship to the community, were married. Miles Abbott extended congratulations. "Charley," he wrote, "is one of the substantial farmers of Hayes County."[14]

That same fall James Abbott, a resident of Saline County southwest of Lincoln, not related to Miles but a friend of Rome and Ed Smith, came down at their urging to look over Blackwood and Hayes County. He found a tree claim that he liked, the southeast quarter of section two, bordering on the Ridge road. He struck a bargain with the man who held provisional title and paid the relinquishment fee. They went to the land office in McCook together, the one to cancel his claim, Abbott to file, also for a timber claim. He and his wife, Emma, and their several children would not move to Blackwood until the next spring, 1890, and would bring with them a carload of cattle, hogs, horses, farming implements, and household goods.[15]

Late in November, 1889, Blackwood and Hayes County were really set aflutter by the arrival of Brice McMullen. He and his wife, Eliza Jane, accompanied by their daughters, Anne and Ida May, had come from their home in Pennsylvania to see their daughter and son-in-law, Maggie and Ellsworth Jeffries, and to look over the country. Mr. McMullen, said the *Republican*, "is a man of considerable means." He was well pleased with Hayes County and "we are informed," the *Republican* continued, that he "will locate in this vicinity." And indeed he did. He took over the timber claim, in section 14, next to Harlan Martin, that Ellsworth Jeffries had been holding for a member of the family. Brice immediately began to build a sod house, he bought a new wagon and other machinery and provisions, and before the month of December was over, he and his family moved into their new home. By February he would plaster his house, an improvement most of the homesteaders did not make for several years, and the next month put up a windmill, all without borrowing on his property. He would soon be elected to the cemetery board, to serve with Rome Smith and Warren Clark, and to the school board with Harlan Martin and Warren Clark. And he had a sharp eye out, looking for a place for his son, Shaffer.[16]

There was no end of newcomers. The Rev. G.W. Southwell, a probationer, was the regularly assigned minister to Hayes Center and Methodist Ridge, but the Rev. R.S. Moore came into the county late in 1889. He had taken leave from his ministerial duties to try his hand at farming down at Red Cloud, in southeast Nebraska, apparently on a rented farm. In Hayes County to see if he could acquire a farm of his own, he was immediately drafted to conduct the winter's protracted meeting on the Ridge. Moore used tobacco, chewing tobacco, but he was devout and prayerful, he was a powerful preacher, much more experienced and effective than the young probationers who had been assigned to the circuit. And he had presence, he was a man among men, and a staunch Republican. Miles Abbott liked him at once, and so did the people. He was soon on the dinner circuit, visiting from Sunday to Sunday to "partake of the yellow leg chicken" at the Clarks, the Martins, the Driscols, a part of the larger circuit that took the Abbotts to the Smiths, the Roberts to the Jeffries, the Gruvers, the Theovalts, the Salings, the Jim Scotts, the George Scotts, the McMullens, the Clarks, to one another's household, all in good fellowship. Moore apparently reached some tentative agreement to buy a place.[17]

None of the newcomers outshone the Gruvers. George and Irven, younger brothers, each had a modest quarter section, homesteads. Levi, who had lost his life in the cave-in of a well, had left his widow a homestead and a tree claim to which she clung, with the help of the brothers. Levi's widowed mother, Mary, lived on her own homestead and had beside a tree claim and a preemption for a total of 400 acres. Her youngest children, Dock 19 and Orpha 15 in 1889, lived at home with her. Wesley, with a newly purchased farm, his homestead, which he had proved up in 1889, and his tree claim, had 480 acres. He was justice of the peace for Logan Precinct and, for a short time, succeeded Jacob Wemple, postmaster at Hope.[18]

Oscar outreached them all. His preemption, half of it in section four, Blackwood, the other half in Logan, was a show piece on the Ridge. An enterpriser, he took over the post office from Wesley in March, 1889, and opened a blacksmith shop. The Hope correspondent, "Dutchman," reported that he "hurd a mity big noize south mit de bostoffice" and found that O.C. Gruver "de blacksmit" was "makin de blows sharp fur de farmers." The next month he and Wesley purchased 96,000 "forest" trees and dispersed them to their neighbors who set them out on their tree claims and homesteads. That may have been the year Warren Clark planted, Nellie wrote, double rows of trees on three sides of his farmstead: ash, cottonwood, box elder, mulberries, and wild plums.[19]

In July the county superintendent of schools resigned, effective August 1. Friends and neighbors, whose children Oscar had taught at the Martin school, petitioned for him to be appointed. The commissioners complied with the request. That fall he ran on the Republican ticket for election to the regular two-year term and was elected by the handsome majority of 633 to 296. The *Republican* thought it a wise choice. "He is," said Abbott, "a straight upright industrious young man." He moved to town, rented a house, and began at once to call on the schools. The delighted parents on the Ridge found him "just as pleasant and sociable as he was before he was elected to office."[20]

Young Doctor Gruver had not yet made his mark. Only 19, he was still at home with his mother and his sister Orpha. Affable, smiling, bright, and a hardworker, he was a favorite, and something of a lady's man. He "like to go mit de girls," said Dutchman in the *Herald*. "He dakes dem oud buggy rides goot many times anyhow." But when Rome Smith's daughter, Nellie 17, moved to Blackwood, Dock soon came to tether. The opportunity for courtship could scarcely have been better. Not only were they the most eligible young man and woman on the Ridge, but Dock's sister, Orpha, was the one girl nearest to Nellie Smith's age. It was Nellie visiting Orpha or Orpha at Nellie's, and soon the correspondent was reporting that "Dock and Orpha Gruver were guests at Miss Nellie Smith's last Lord's day." The friendship ripened. January 1, 1890, they were married, Dock scarcely 20, Nellie not yet 19.[21]

The growing prosperity on the Ridge, the increase in the number of Methodist families, and the unsatisfactory condition of the little Martin school, prompted the neighbors on the Ridge to build a sod church on the plot Ezra McKenzie had set aside for a cemetery (later to be confirmed by Shaffer McMullen when he bought the rights to the property). The church was a substantial building, long and narrow, with a board roof, covered with sod, homemade pews, a central aisle with seats on one side for the men, on the other for the women and children. It was the first Methodist church building, perhaps the first of any denomination, in the county. The preacher reported at the yearly convening of the Southwest Nebraska Annual Conference that it was worth $225.[22]

The church stood, a stark wall of black sod on a lonely plain of buffalo grass, not a tree or a bush near it. But on Sunday morning it came alive with teams and wagons, men, women, and children, and the sound of the human voice in the preaching, the singing, the buzz of conversation, the laughter and cry of children. Even before the new building was erected the strength of Methodism in the community had prompted the settlers in surrounding areas to dub it "Methodist Ridge," a term that amused them and pleased the Methodists. Methodist Ridge the community became, and as Methodist Ridge it is still known a hundred years later.

*Top: Sod church after closure, Methodist Ridge, Hayes County, Nebraska.*
*Right: Interior of sod church, Methodist Ridge, Hayes County, Nebraska.*

# 16.
# The Prairie Looks Good

Miles Abbott of the *Republican* was troubled that Hayes County homesteaders too commonly put out hard-to-come-by cash for staple goods. A farmer came to Hayes Center, sold his corn for 15 cents a bushel and bought a bushel of apples for $1.50, a bushel of potatoes for 25 cents, three cans of corn for eight and one-half cents each, a side of bacon for 13 cents a pound. What had happened to the "old fashioned" farmer? Abbott wanted to know. He raised everything for himself and bought nothing.[1]

He wasn't talking to Warren and Ada. They knew from their childhood all about subsistence farming and the value, even the luxury for Ada, of a small cash flow that they need not spend for staples. They had their own meat, fresh, salted, smoked, plenty of potatoes and garden truck, all they wanted of sorghum for molasses, corn for meal, wheat for grist, chickens, eggs, and butter for the table and to trade at the store for what they could not themselves supply: salt, condiments, dry goods, buttons, hooks and eyes, thread. Warren had improved his assets: more acres under cultivation, more cattle and hogs, a second team of horses, a colt for the children to ride, Cola, they called her, hay and grain to feed the stock and fencing to pasture them.[2]

Ada added much to their sense of well-being. She left no journal account of her day-by-day duties, no diary entry for these years, but Nellie, in her reminiscences, tells the story, chiefly of food, clothing, and household duties. Ada made pumpkin butter and pie from the pumpkins Warren raised in his garden, preserves and sweet pickles from watermelon rinds, pickles from green and ripe tomatoes and vinegar from watermelon juice. She made cookies from the jugs of molasses Warren brought back from the mill that pressed his cane, and Nellie, nine-years-old that fall, 1889, could still savor the taste--"Oh, so good,"--when she wrote about them 75 years later. Ada gathered fruit from the canyons, wild plums, currants, chokecherries, grapes. The children went with her, delighted by the adventure, but pained and irritated when they stepped on or brushed against the poison ivy that crept along the bank and climbed the bushes and the trees. As she had done when she was a girl in New York and a bride in Iowa, an art that she had learned from her Dutch mother, and she from her Dutch forebears, and they from the Indians, she laid the fruit out in the sun to dry, turning the berries patiently until the hot sun sucked the moisture out of them. She packed cucumbers in salt brine and soaked them in vinegar and spice to make pickles.

She gave her family toast for breakfast, sometimes with hot milk, or she gave them pancakes raised with yeast, the flour from Warren's small patch of buckwheat, or she soaked wheat overnight and cooked it slowly for hours to make hot cereal. For dinner, served at noon, she almost always put meat and potatoes and gravy on the table, and often biscuits raised with soda. For supper she gave them bread and milk or corn bread and milk. And eggs for any meal, and often chicken, boiled or fried. Warren no longer hunted, but in the summer if in his box trap he could catch a cottontail or in the fall a young jackrabbit that had come to nibble at his corn pile, Ada would cook it as a special treat. When he butchered a young steer, he got the help of a neighbor, but Ada helped him scald and scrape and cut up a hog. They butchered in the fall and winter, when the cold would preserve the meat, and they salted down crocks of the pork for the summer months.[3]

Ada made most of their clothes, pants and shirts for Warren, dresses for herself and the girls, kilts for Earl until he was five. She knitted stockings and mittens for all of them. By the summer of 1889 she seems to have had her own machine, the one Warren had secured from Arza Nicholson, after his wife Kate left him. From an early time they had kerosene for their lamps and Ada no longer had to dip candles.[4]

Like most of the pioneer women, Ada made her own soap. She did more. Enterprising all of her life, she answered an advertisement by a chemical company that would, for the payment of one dollar, sell its carefully guarded formula for soap and certify her right to manufacture and sell Diamond Labor Laundry Soap. It must have caused her some pain to spend that dollar out of their meager resources. She received the certificate, printed and signed, with her name written on it, and the formula, the "receipt," for ingredients and process spelled out in detail. She must have had no expectation of selling the soap for cash, but she might have thought, indeed found it possible, to trade it at Culbertson or McCook for goods, or to distribute it to her neighbors in exchange for services or favors.[5]

For Ada, the most trying fact of homestead life, Nellie implies, was the dirt floor and the rough and sometimes crumbling sod of the interior walls. On a hot day the wind whipped in through the open door, loosening and swirling the dust, however tightly packed the dirt floors might have been. Ada put down throw rugs, braided of old clothes, until years later Warren could purchase wood flooring.

In those first years, like other homesteaders, they produced little for the market--Ada's eggs and chickens to trade for goods, a few hogs and some grain for cash. They were poor, but "we had fun," Nellie wrote, as she recalled not only her joy in the activities of children, but how she savored the simple, good food her mother served them. And Ada, when she visited the area in her old age, full of nostalgia for an earlier day, attested to the happiness they had known.[6]

Earl was three-and-one-half-years-old in November, 1889, the month that Warren and Ada's fourth daughter, Amelia Jane, named for Ada's mother, was born. Ada's parents, Pa and Ma, had seen the older girls, Nellie and Mary, when they visited in Iowa in 1884, but they had not seen their only grandson. And it had been ten years since Ada had left her family and friends at Stone Hill. She was homesick. Warren could not raise the cash to pay for a trip. Pa sent it, money enough to buy the ticket and pay for the meals along the way after Ada's carefully packed lunch ran out, perhaps enough to purchase a few new clothes.

Ada pumped the treadle of her sewing machine furiously. It hummed with the joy she felt. She made a new kilt outfit for Earl and an overcoat, cap, and mittens--it would be cold in New York--new clothes for the baby, Jennie, they called her, and no doubt a new suit for herself. And she had the dress she made for the family picture in 1889, still practically new. Just after New Year's day, 1890, Warren loaded their baggage into his wagon, hitched up his team, and drove them to Culbertson to catch the train for Oswego County, New York. Ada entrusted the three girls to Warren, Nellie almost 10, Mary seven, and Flora not yet two. She was to be gone for two months.[7]

Ada left no word of the trip for the record, nothing of the long and muscle-aching ride, three nights on the train with two babies, nothing of the joy in seeing her parents, of the return to the white house on the rocky hillside where she had grown up, of her trips to the village, the church, the old schoolhouse, of their walking 200 yards up the hill to Uncle Ratio's and Aunt Lydia's, the packed snow crunching under her feet, or of the snowbirds, the little dark-eyed juncos, the heads of the males black, gray for their mates, round and soft as a stuffed pincushion, or the black-bibbed chickadees she had written about so long ago, flitting in the bare branches of the trees, singing the song that gave them their name; nothing of visits with her family and with friends, or families of friends who were still in the neighborhood. Nellie remembered, long years afterward, only one fragment of Ada's talk when she got home--she had gone to see Papa's mother, Grandma Clark, and his sisters. That would have been by train, perhaps an hour to Sandy Creek, John and Bell Howe and Warren's mother at the depot to meet them. They would have driven out to the farm where she and Warren had lived those last exciting months--joyful and sad--before they left for Iowa. And in Sandy Creek they would have seen Warren's other sister, Dell, who had been with him down on Mr. Norton's farm that summer when Ada had come to pick hops.

Grandma Harris, writing to Earl when he was 15, also recalled one small incident. The snow was heavy that winter. Grandma Clark came down on the train from Sandy Creek to see Ada and the children once more. They all drove to the village to meet her, so many of them they had to take two sleighs. Coming home, Earl rode with his two grandmas, arriving some minutes ahead of the other sleigh. Grandma Harris proposed to help him off with his cap, mittens and coat. Earl declined. Grandma Clark made the attempt. Again he refused. He did not cry, but he stood there sturdily in cap, mittens, and coat until his mother arrived.[8] Afterwards he remembered only the snow and the rides in the sleigh.

How Papa managed when Mama was gone, Nellie could not remember when she came to write her reminiscences. But winter was the slack season. Warren had his corn in and had little more than the chores to do, and the annual routine maintenance: harness and shoes to mend, fences to fix, a door hinge or a loose board on the barn to repair, a trough to build for the pigs, a thousand and one things a farmer must do. And look after the children. He was good at caring for them. He could cook, bake bread and cupcakes, wash and iron their clothes. And he never complained, Nellie said. She thought that Mrs. Saling, who lived across the road, only three or four hundred yards away, or one of her nearly grown daughters, might have helped. No doubt. Ab Saling regularly spent much of the winter in Omaha where he found employment as a carpenter or mechanic. And Warren did much of Ab's routine chores, hauling and cutting wood, bringing supplies to Mrs. Saling from Culbertson or Hayes Center. He and Ab had a well established pattern of labor exchange.[9]

What Nellie did not remember is that Warren's sister, Hattie, came out from Trenton to spend a month with them. Hattie lived in town but she had taken a small timber claim, 40 acres in section 15, relinquished by the previous claimant, that Warren had selected and now farmed for her. Hattie had scarcely arrived from New York before she fell in love with and married a settler in Hayes County. The marriage had not worked out. In a matter of weeks she left her husband for reasons, the court judged, "of extreme cruelty." She was granted a divorce and the restoration of her maiden name, Hattie A. Clark. In Trenton, she worked, apparently as a housekeeper.[10]

Afternoons, when she got home from school, Nellie looked after Flora. Evenings Warren took over the care of the children. He probably read to them, watched them at their play, put Flora to bed. He seems not to have talked about New York. At least Nellie had no memory of such talk. But he sang to them in his deep bass voice, songs of the sea that he had learned from his sailor father, Anderberdeen, the bold robber from Scotland's shore, crying, "Stand by, stand by, for I'll have your ship and your cargo too, and your merrymen drown in the sea." And he sang hymns, too, *Sweet Hour of Prayer*, *Blessed*

*Assurance, Rock of Ages.* Twenty-five years later his grandsons, Earl's boys, would sit on his knee and peer upward past the white beard to his face and marvel that such a big and bell-toned voice should issue forth from a man who was so much smaller than their own father.[11]

Mornings Warren got the older girls up and off to school. He may have taken them, but most of the time they probably walked the mile and a half to the little soddy on the corner of Harlan Martin's place, on the Ridge road to Culbertson. It was not much of a school building. Hastily built with a straw-covered roof, it was poor shelter against rain or snow. Twice the roof caught on fire. The children grabbed their wraps and some of their books and ran out. Once the teacher discovered that she had left her watch on the desk. We cannot know what sacrifice it had cost her to buy the watch or what anguish she suffered when she realized that it was still in the building. She rushed in to get it, and was overcome by smoke. One of the neighbors, hurrying over to help put out the fire, pulled her out. They moved their school to the house of a bachelor who was gone and would not return to his claim until time to put in the spring crops. And the school board, giving up on the old building bought lumber to build a new schoolhouse for fall--also of sod, but with wooden floor and roof.[12]

The teacher that winter, 1890, was Nellie Duffield, who had her own homestead and her own sod house, a couple of miles away in Logan precinct, adjacent to her father's claim. Her younger brother lived with her. She was said to be a good teacher and "a lady of many fine qualities." Nellie Clark responded eagerly to her tutelage, won first prize for "standing highest in studies" in her school room, and got her name in the Hayes County *Republican.*[13]

Nellie forgot all about the prize when she wrote her reminiscences. But she remembered one of her schoolmates, Abe Mansfield, the most vivid memory from those weeks when her mother was gone. Abe was the son of James Mansfield whose lawsuit with his nephew, Harry, Warren had attended in 1888, and whose second suit, against his wife, Harriet, had dissolved his marriage. Jim and Abe lived with Richard Roberts and his wife Maggie, Ellsworth Jeffries' sister. Abe, 13, was the "kindest boy" in school, Nellie thought. He walked with Nellie and Mary and the Saling girls from school to their places and then went on alone for another mile and half to the

Roberts' homestead. He was sick one afternoon, early in January, on the way home. Nellie's mother was gone, so he did not stop there, and since the Saling house sat back from the road a quarter of a mile, Nellie thought he probably didn't stop there. Neither Warren nor Mrs. Saling knew about his illness, but he didn't come to school the next day. For nearly a week his fever raged and he died on January 7.[14]

His father, James, and Richard Roberts were away, over on the Red Willow, cutting wood. Maggie Roberts wrapped up her six-month-old baby and walked down to the Clarks. Warren was at home. He hitched up his team, left Flora with Mrs. Saling, drove Maggie and her baby back home and stayed with her until Richard and James came. He helped build the pine box in which Abe was to be buried, painted it black, lined it with muslin. Miss Duffield sent her brother to the Red Willow to cut cedar branches. She made a wreath for the coffin, gave a small green branch to each of the children, and they walked on either side of the open grave and dropped the green sprigs on the coffin as they passed. James put up a stone for his son that still stands in the tall grass on the stark plain at the Pleasant Ridge cemetery, engraved with the simple legend, "Abraham Mansfield, Nov. 25, 1876-Jan. 8, 1890.

Ada, with Earl and Jennie, came home the first week in March. Flora scarcely knew her, shied away from her at first and then, reconciled, clung to her, unwilling to share her with the older girls: "go away, this is my mamma." Ada was glad to be home. The Nebraska prairie looked good to her, she said. She was "better satisfied with Hayes County than ever."[15]

# 17.
# Brace up with the Thought

Eighty-nine owners resided in Blackwood in 1890, homesteaders who had earned title to their land, or soon would, or who had preempted it. Many of them, having experienced rising land values in eastern Nebraska, or other states, did not hesitate to borrow money to make their purchases. Much of the show of prosperity on Methodist Ridge depended upon mortgages: increased acreage, windmills, farm equipment--planters, drills, binders, barns, fences, livestock, plaster and floors for houses, paid for out of mortgage money more often than from the sale of crops. It was easy to borrow money. "Farm Loans Promptly Filled," the State Bank advertised, and soon its ad in block type read, "MONEY! MONEY!"[1]

No one in Warren Clark's place could have easily doubted that Blackwood was now a settled community. But for all the optimism, there remained an underlying sense of uneasiness that arose, for one thing, from the low prices for corn and wheat, and for another, the uncertainty of rain. Everyone complained about the low prices. And now and then a word from the country correspondent betrayed the anxiety over the rain--the Methodist Ridge reporter boasting about Rome Smith's profitable sale of livestock, with the defensive tag end, "Talk about it that you can't make it win in Hayes County. . . ." But no one wrote a word about the mortgages.[2]

Warren Clark undoubtedly knew that Richard Roberts had borrowed on a mortgage--although he probably didn't know that it amounted to $413--to purchase Annie Jeffries' commuted homestead, a long narrow strip that adjoined his homestead and tree claim in section 3. We can guess that Annie, Ellsworth's sister who was to marry James Mansfield, had also borrowed to pay the commutation fee, $200, just as she had borrowed to pay for her preemption in section 2. The addition gave Richard 480 acres and made him, after John Hughes and Russell Watts, one of the largest landowners in the township. Everyone knew that Oscar Gruver had to borrow money to put in his elaborate improvements: windmill, pipe, running water, an addition to the house, and a new barn. Everyone knew, too, or guessed, that John Hughes had borrowed on mortgages to purchase more land and to buy an expensive stallion, Marchmont, and a stable of horses.[3]

Jake Wiggins and Lish Driscol were probably candid enough to talk around the neighborhood about taking liens to pay for their windmills, but it is not likely that Lish told how much mortgage he had on his land to pay for other improvements. Nor is it likely that Jim Scott confided to anybody that he borrowed $800 to pay for the quarter section he bought from Jacob Case. Rome Smith might have boasted about his mortgage, as proof of how good his credit was. And friendly, outgoing George Scott probably confessed to his friends that he was a little worried about the big mortgages on his two properties. The fact is that nearly everyone on Methodist Ridge carried a mortgage. Not Warren Clark or Harlan Martin, or Mary Martin, or Ellsworth Jeffries, even after they took title in 1891. Nor Brice McMullen on his homestead--with his resources, he didn't need to. But everyone else on the Ridge, except the four absentee owners, had mortgaged or would mortgage his property. In all of Blackwood, in 1890, claimants had taken title to 96 tracts of land and had mortgaged 74 of them, and of the 22 unmortgaged tracts, nine belonged to absentee owners, seven to Russell Watts.[4]

The amounts of the mortgages ranged from $100 to $1,000, the average about $450. The interest rates ran from six percent to ten, with most of them clustered at seven or eight percent. Interest payments were due semi-annually, the mortgages not for five years. John Hughes had taken out the first in 1884, many had followed in 1885 and 1886, a few in the succeeding years.[5] The day of reckoning was at hand in 1890, but it did not seem ominous. A man could borrow again and postpone the date of payment. Warren Clark knew, from his father's little farm at Boylston, how inexorable that date was, when it finally came. He would have none of it.

The Blackwood settlers remained uneasy that winter of 1890, not because of any concern about the weather or the merits of Hayes County. They had had ample rain in the fall, some snow, a little rain in January and February, no appreciable change from the experience of the past five years.

It was the low prices for their produce that troubled them. The editor of the *Times*, Barney Hofer, rubbed their spirits raw, taunting them over the Republican tariff: "The Nebraska farmer looks out through window glass taxed fifty-six per cent upon his stupendous and solemn stacks of twelve cent oats and forty cent wheat, and, with a sigh heaves his brawny bosom against his rough flannel shirt taxed sixty per cent. . . ." Ten pounds of sugar cost him one dollar, nearly a bushel of oats for a pound of sugar, a bushel of corn and seven and one-half cents cash to boot to buy one pound of horseshoe nails. "Pleasant prices . . . pleasant protected prosperity." In late February the farmers on the Ridge gathered at Martin's schoolhouse and organized a grange. Thirty-one of them signed up as charter members. Warren Clark joined that night or a short time later, and so did Harlan Martin and Richard Roberts and Oscar Gruver, and the majority of the men on Methodist Ridge. They would soon build a grange hall, halfway between the church and the post office and children would learn the half-mile rule: from the new school (across the road from Shaffer McMullen's) to church, to grange, to post office, each a half mile.[6]

Abbott had a thought: 17 years ago, in 1873, corn was at the same low level, 13 or 14 cents. Farmers in Nebraska and Kansas burned it for fuel. Thousands of bushels went to waste. A year later farmers who had burned or sold their crop had to pay 75 cents to $1.00 a bushel for corn. They could not expect such a rebound in the market now, but prices would get better. Wisdom dictated hoarding the crops--"except in cases where the farmer is absolutely obliged to sell."[7]

It was "terribly windy" in late March, 1890, but by the first of April farmers, taking advantage of interspersed days of calm, were nearly done sowing wheat and oats. They could not have been more timely. On the second of the month rain fell, "a glorious rain." Nearly every farmer on the Ridge began to set out trees, fruit trees chiefly, Warren Clark 50, Harlan Martin and Ellsworth Jeffries, each 50, John Theovalt 30, Ed Smith 120. "We will soon have our own fruit," the correspondent boasted. Arbor Day, April 22, was reason for celebration on the arid plains, a legal holiday in honor of Sterling Morton, Nebraska statesman and publisher, who had urged setting aside a day to plant trees. It was a gesture of faith in the transformation of the land, not only in the beauty and utility of the trees, and in the fruit of the orchard but in man's role in bringing the rain. The *Times* urged "every property owner" to "observe Arbor Day by planting trees. . . ." Hope still burned brightly.[8]

But that week the wind once more began to blow, hard enough to tip over the mail carrier's wagon in Highland, and to blow loose dirt off the small grain, requiring some re-sowing. Every farmer on the Ridge was faced with the same dilemma: he must keep the soil loose enough to absorb the rain, but if he stirred it too much, it blew away. In a couple of weeks matters were right again, "gentle showers" on Methodist Ridge, "bright prospects" everywhere. Wheat was up. The reporter from Highland, registering a degree of caution, predicted that "with anything like a fair season [it] will make a fine crop." The farmers on the Ridge had broken 25 more acres of prairie that spring and had begun to plant corn. The next week it was "rain, rain, just lots of rain." Then another rain, a big rain, the second week in May, with a little hail, but the corn was "coming up fine," "everything growing nicely." Brother Moore, visiting again, decided that he would move to Hayes County. Harlan Martin had great success with the two acres of grama grass he had sown. It grew wild in Blackwood Canyon on William Black's place, standing two or three feet high, "thick as any timothy." The Rodgers brothers, Albert and Jesse, bought some blacksmith tools. It rained again, "a nice rain," the days were warm, "beautiful growing weather," the planting done, farmers in their fields plowing corn, "prospects for crops of all kinds were never better." Even the trees were "looking fine." And Abbott was right: last year's shelled corn, now getting scarce, had crept up to 25 or 30 cents a bushel. And yet more rain, "a copious rain," the last week in May, "worth thousands of dollars to Hayes county." Everything fine--save for one ominous note: the small grain and grass "need a little more rain," and two weeks later, mid-June, "dry, everybody wanting rain."[9]

It came a few days later, "a grand and glorious rain Sunday night," the farmers were all "happy," the corn "booming skyward." But the inexorable rhythm would not stop. The next two weeks were dry, "rather warm in these parts." The first week in July Methodist Ridge confessed that grass would be rather short to mow and that only "portions of the wheat" had "come out all right." But Richard Roberts, buoyed up in the general optimism, bought a binder that week, paid $180 for it. And a week later they had "a good rain" on Saturday and "Rain came down in torrents Sunday night." The *Times* was less cautious. The rains were widespread and "assure an abundant corn crop in Hayes county."[10]

The farmers knew well that the country correspondents, like themselves, were whistling in the dark to keep their hopes high. It was as if speaking the good words could conjure up the good crops. But the wind and moving dust and the hot dry days between the rains had their way. When it came time for harvest only Jim Scott and Warren Clark on Methodist Ridge had wheat tall enough to bind. Warren's crop, the only one reported on the Ridge that summer, threshed out at seven bushels to the acre. And sometime between the middle of July and the first week in August, the promise of the corn crop failed. Unreported, the hot winds came, searing the bright green of the young leaves, curling, yellowing, withering the edges, scorching the plants, cooking them into dry and lifeless stalks. The reporter advised the farmers to cut their corn for fodder--"let it dry a month, then stack [it] for feed." But the loss of a corn crop was no reason to quit. "Brace up with the thought that next year Hayes county will have the largest crop ever known."[11]

Abbott consoled the people by recounting the woes of others. The Rev. Moore had sold 70 acres of corn near Red Cloud for $20. "That's the kind of crop they have there." Imposing his will on nature, he intoned the incantation: "This is the fall to come west, next year we will have booming crops, there is no reason why the west won't produce good crops."[12]

Not all of the settlers on the Ridge were in a despairing mood. Ed Smith reckoned that he had 20 acres of corn and rye not injured by the drought, his brother Rome boasted that he had 40 head of cattle and enough feed from the year's crop to carry them over the winter. He had just bought up the rights to Emma

Saling's tree claim, adjacent to his own place, and had extra pasture. Charley Nichols had sold nine spring calves in April but come September he was "buying up a good many cattle." Ellsworth Jeffries had 22 fat hogs he thought would be "boomers" by November 1.[13]

Some farmers, a little more cautious, or short on cash or feed, began to sell off their livestock. Warren Clark took a load of fat hogs to Culbertson, and so did Harlan Martin. Richard Roberts had some "fine fat hogs" for sale. Jake Wiggins sold off some of his stock to conserve his supply of feed but in late January, 1891, still had a pen full of pigs "in good shape."[14]

For a few men, one dry season was enough. Juniper Slater in Highland sold out to Tom Scott, Jim's brother, for $700 and moved back to Iowa. By the end of August Ed Smith's optimism had withered with his dying corn. He sold off his livestock, rented his farm to the preacher, R. S. Moore, and headed for Seattle. The Methodist Ridge reporter lamented the loss of "an excellent citizen" and "his estimable family." The Rev. Moore had rejoined the Methodist conference and been assigned to Pleasant Ridge and Hayes Center, where he was to live. He would fill the void left by Ed Smith. A month later, John Theovalt, another of Warren's close friends, sold his farm, the Ridge correspondent reported, to Shaffer McMullen for $675. Shaffer, Brice's son, lived in Illinois but wanted to migrate to Nebraska.[15]

Two of the Clarks' neighbors to the west, in section 10, moved out, Charles and Thisbee Boyd to California, Charles and Kitty Andrews back to Illinois, from which they had come. Boyd owed $9.92 in delinquent taxes, Andrews $11.40 on his homestead, $10.33 on a preemption. There were a good many others whose taxes were delinquent, all publicly displayed in the columns of the *Republican*: John Hughes, for one, over $80 due on his five tracts, and Elisha Driscol, Merady Williams, George Scott, Charles Nichols, all on Methodist Ridge, and two of Warren's friends in the south and west areas of the township, Christ Landmark in section 21, $6.48, and George Houghland in section 19, $14.85. The list would have been longer save that many of the settlers, including Warren Clark, although they had been on their homesteads the required number of years, had not yet proved up. There was reason enough for the delay--the land was not taxable until they had taken title.[16]

Even the men who remained, or intended to remain, began to hunt jobs elsewhere, among them Dock Gruver and a friend. Dock went to Denver and soon found work in a sawmill back in the mountains. Nellie followed a week after Dock had settled into his job. But in six weeks they were back in Hayes County, Dock sick with "mountain fever." Nellie, who was with child, no doubt was glad to be home with family and neighbors. Several men found jobs on the Burlington and Missouri Railroad, building the grade near Palisade. One of them, William Wittwer, from the German community in the southern area of the township, and soon with his family to be friends of the Clarks, walked 14 miles to town every Sunday afternoon and back Saturday night after work so that he could be at home on Sunday and check up on how his family was doing with the chores.[17]

Warren Clark worked on the railroad, too, using his own team of horses, scraping and hauling the dirt to make the grade. He was gone for a month or six weeks, perhaps two months, with infrequent returns to the farm. "It was real lonesome with him gone," Nellie said. They sometimes saw neighbors who came by and on Sunday they went to church or Sunday school. Ada, Mary, and Earl, who was four, walked. Nellie rode the pony, Cola, holding Jennie in her lap, Flora clinging behind her. Abbott had carried a story in the *Herald* about women in Yosemite who rode horses astride. "When you come to think about it," he commented, "why should not women ride astride as well as men?" But proper girls didn't ride astride. And Nellie, who was almost eleven, was proper. She rode "sideways." They had no saddle for Cola, only a heavy blanket which was necessary, for she had a high sharp ridge of a backbone. They strapped the blanket to her and Nellie held the end of the strap with one hand, the reins with the other, and the baby cradled in her arms.[18]

Warren's earnings were most welcome. They were pretty short of food and supplies on the Ridge that winter. No one was "complaining of tired backs digging potatoes," the Hope correspondent joked. Jim Scott, the envy of the Ridge, received 32 bushels of potatoes from his parents in Iowa. A good many of his neighbors, said the reporter, "wish they belonged to the family.[19]

Still, bad as things were, Ed Smith found that they were worse in Seattle. No one could make money, he said, but real estate agents. He advised "every farmer in Hayes county to stay on his farm or else go east instead of west." He took his own advice and returned to Missouri for the winter.[20]

As the extent of the damage from the drought became apparent and the prices for farm produce continued low, the dissatisfaction of the farmers increased. And so did the appeal of the insurgent People's Party (Populist). The Eureka Grange had organized on Methodist Ridge in January, with 21 charter members. Warren Clark one of them. The State Farmer's Alliance, allying with the Knights of Labor, issued a call for a People's State Independent Convention to meet in Lincoln on July 29 to fight "ten cent corn, forty cent wheat, and two cent beef and pork." The issue was complex, as historians were to discover, but it seemed simple enough to many Hayes County homesteaders: too little rain to produce a crop, and too low a price on what they did raise. They called a meeting in mid-July; Henry Wiswall was one of the leaders. Both Democrats and Republicans were present. Oscar Gruver, Republican, was elected delegate to the convention to nominate a candidate for the state senate, Richard Roberts and Wesley Gruver, Republicans, and Henry Wiswall, Democrat, and Juniper Slater, who had not yet left the county, were chosen delegates to nominate a candidate for state representative.[21]

Miles J. Abbott was amused and impressed by the proceedings. "They were as free, independent and breezy as their own Nebraska zephyrs," he wrote in the *Republican*. "We are not making fun of them," he said. "It was as fine a looking body of men as ever met in convention in Hayes Centre," and they "meant business." Abbott was friendly enough to be accused of courting the favor of the Independents (Populists).[22]

With the approach of the election, he was not at all equivocal. He was especially critical of John Hughes, Democratic candidate for state representative, who was, he said, persona non grata in Hayes County, especially with leaders like Henry Wiswell and Jacob Wiggins who had "a scalping knife a yard long, already sharpened." He was friendly to John H. Powers, Hitchcock County farmer and Populist candidate for governor, and not unfriendly to other Populists. But he favored the Republican candidate for every office, from county surveyor to U.S. Congressman.[23]

For the Republicans the election was a disaster. James E. Boyd, the Democratic candidate for governor, eked out a narrow victory over the Populist, John H. Powers, with the Republican candidate running a poor third. The Populists won control of both houses of the legislature. In Hayes County, Powers out-polled the other candidates for governor. The single Republican victory was the election of Charles Ready as county attorney. To celebrate his party's victories Abbott had a block print of a great crowing cock, three columns wide, two-thirds of a page high. On this occasion he ran it upside down, its feet at the top of the page, with huge block headlines: "BLIZZARD," and in smaller type, "Republicans and Democrats in the soup."[24]

# 18.
# Glorious Rain

Long before the fall election in 1890 it was quite clear that the effects of the drought would be serious, devastating to some. S.P. Hart, registrar of the United States Land Office in McCook, notified settlers that if "by reason of a total or partial destruction or failure of crops" they could not support themselves or their families, they could secure a leave of absence, without forfeiting their provisional title or losing the time they had earned toward full title.[1]

The incumbent governor, John M. Thayer, who had not been a candidate for reelection, tried to wink at the problem. Neither he nor the legislature, nor the business community, wanted to take any action that would advertise the drought in Nebraska. It was well enough to talk about droughty Kansas and the suffering Dakotas, but not Nebraska. With the election over, winter approaching, and suffering of the people a grim possibility, he sent delegates to the several regions of the state to survey the damages. The Rev. George W. Martin, chaplain of the Kearney Reform School, toured the five southwest counties: Hayes, Dundy, Keith, Chase, and Perkins. He reported that 650 families would need help. One-third to one-half of them, for the most part west of Hayes County, could get along, he thought, if given clothing and coal; the rest, 300 to 400 families, must also receive food.[2]

From what he knew of human nature, Abbott was wary about how the farmers would react to aid. "Extend sympathy to some people," he wrote, "and they begin to cough all the more to show how bad they are." Nonetheless, he was enough concerned to go down to Lincoln to see what was going on. He talked with Governor Thayer, who said that the people in eastern Nebraska were ready to help if they could be sure that the needy, and not others, got the aid they sent. Abbott stayed on until one carload of goods had been shipped to George Gowing, Hayes County clerk. The governor stipulated that Gowing, and all county clerks, must give a receipt to the railroad, which was shipping the goods free, must organize their counties for distribution, must require a receipt from all receiving aid, and must keep accurate records. And he warned, "assistance cannot be given to counties that will not organize." Gowing promptly issued a call to justices of the peace to assemble in Hayes Center to prepare to distribute the goods.[3]

The Populist legislature, slow after the November election to get its program under way, finally in early March, 1891, appropriated $100,000 to supply fuel, provisions and seed to needy farmers and authorized the counties to pass bond issues to lend additional amounts to farmers for the purchase of seed. The Hayes County commissioners had appointed the Methodist preacher, R.S. Moore, to represent them in Lincoln. Moore was a big man, bearded, handsome, forceful. He lobbied for both bills and was, Abbott thought, largely responsible for the passage of the bond measure. He was effective, too, in getting some of the volunteer aid directed to Hayes County.[4]

The distribution of the goods, sent voluntarily without state funds, and transported free by the railroads, went smoothly enough. Warren Clark that year was not a justice of the peace, but each township was required to form a committee of three, two justices and one citizen, to be responsible for the distribution of the aid. Warren appears to have been the third member of the committee for Blackwood, serving with the two justices. The activity was centered at the homestead of William Black in section 22. From Warren's brief entries in his diary we know that he hauled goods to Black's for distribution, that he assisted Brother Moore in distributing a carload of goods sent to Beverly, and that he secured goods from Hayes Center for Alice Saling, whose husband Ab was in Omaha. On a trip to McCook, he got "some clothing" from Aid but whether for himself, Mrs. Saling, or the center at Black's he does not record.[5]

The daily routine of his life and farm work that winter and spring seemed little altered from past years. He and Harlan

Martin hauled, sawed, and chopped wood, he helped Harlan butcher a cow, he repaired his well rope, hauled manure, split posts to enlarge his pasture, hunted rabbits--which was unusual. He and Harry Mansfield drove to the mill at Culbertson, apparently taking some grist, and got feed for his stock. He did his chores, repaired his harrow and Ada's sewing machine. Ada got the meals, for seven of them, herself and Warren, the four girls and Earl. Nothing in Nellie's reminiscences suggests that they went hungry. Warren cut wood for Mrs. Saling, killed and dressed a pig for her. He went after his cattle when they wandered out of their pasture over to the Southwell's, who lived on the adjacent homestead to the south. Ben was a good neighbor but hotheaded. He had shut the cattle in his corral and would not release them until Warren paid for the damage they had done. Warren had to borrow the money, for he had none of his own that week or month. He did it at once, or as soon as he could round up Cola and ride to a neighbor's, probably Harlan Martin's. The children needed milk.[6]

He and Ada went to church regularly, only one of them or Nellie missing when one of the younger children was ill. If he had worked his teams in the field, the family walked. Brother Moore was a good preacher, powerful, and the services were well attended. Warren, himself, sometimes lead the singing, standing before the congregation, Nellie said, his deep voice ringing out in the gospel hymns they loved: *Sweet Hour of Prayer*, *Work for the Night is Coming*, *Blessed Assurance*. They remained unwavering in their daily devotions, grace before meals, the reading of scriptures and prayer, morning and evening, he and Ada taking turns, prayer meetings at their house or the homes of the neighbors. After church or Sunday school, as in past years, they frequently called on the neighbors, had dinner at their house, or the neighbors stopped for dinner with them: The Salings, Isaac Heater, his old Iowa friend now from the north part of the county, for a couple of days, the Martins, the Jim Scotts, the Rome Smiths, the Jeffries, the new settlers, the Jim Abbotts, all in the first two months of the year, 1891.

With the coming of March, Warren got out his cultivator and set it up, took some seed wheat (which apparently was from his own crop) over to Oscar Gruver's to clean. He was conscientious about the entries in his diary. No item suggests that he went to the Aid center to secure seed for himself. In April, he planted potatoes, in May he began the planting of corn, with no recorded assistance from Aid. He helped Harlan Martin haul corn to Culbertson, indicating a hold over supply. In mid-May he drove to Beverly for a load of Aid corn, but he hauled it to Black's for distribution. Now and then he took Earl, who was five-years-old, with him on his errands, referring to him simply as he did to adults, "Earl and I went to Palisade--all day." He bought a cow on credit, from Newton Wemple, he cultivated his trees and berries--which had survived the dry year without apparent injury--and hauled hay to mulch them. He borrowed Harlan's hog to breed the sows he had kept over the winter, he was fattening a cow which he would take to market, and he had several head of steers he would sell to Rome Smith. The drought had pinched him some, had worked a hardship on his family, made it impossible for him to increase his holdings in livestock, buy new machinery, or improve his buildings, but he got along. His family seems not to have suffered. And his neighbors were doing well enough so that he called on them, Jake Wiggins and Newt Wemple, among others, to ask for money to support Brother Moore.

Many in the county did not fare so well, and for some the need for supplies, food, and seed was acute. In March the county clerk, George Gowing, gave notice that persons wanting seed must go before the justice in their precinct to register their needs. The election on the bond issue, authorized by the legislature, was set for late April. Dr. F.H. Bostock of Estelle, who traveled into much of the county, argued in favor of the bonding issue. The county ought to pass it, he said. Eight-tenths of the farmers, he thought, "are literally without seed to plant and feed for their team to put a crop in." Some of the people on the Ridge were in favor, some opposed. It is better for the county to take care of its own, said the Hope correspondent, than to beg for help, thus "advertising Nebraska starvation to the detriment of population for several years." But others, who were struggling along without aid, were "indignant" at having to pay taxes to help neighbors "whose circumstances were no worse than their own." Rome Smith was opposed to the bond--and so was every man he had talked to in Highland and Logan precincts, and nearly every man in Blackwood. "I, for one, am going to stay in Hayes county," he wrote, "and would like to see the county build up and prosper." If any man would study the proposal "and see what that seed and feed is going to cost him he will never vote them kind of bonds." Ben Southwell, too, was outspokenly opposed. "We must keep the county out of debt," he argued. Brother Moore was in favor of the bonds. In a stirring appeal he argued that there were some who could not borrow from the banks to buy wheat and that their only alternative was to leave the county. Much to his surprise, some of the people who had received aid were now crying the loudest against the county's helping itself.[7]

Miles Abbott, in the *Republican*, was opposed to the bonds. He liked Moore and handled him tenderly, if a bit condescendingly. Hayes County, he said, was the only county in the state to have an active campaign in favor of the bonds. It was mainly because of Moore's "untiring efforts" that the legislature passed the bill. But the reason for Moore's advocacy was more deeply seated. Was it not possible "that the very nature of his profession" would cause him to be sympathetic, to look at only one side of the issue? The county could get along without the bonds. If the measure passed, many would borrow and not pay back. Even if the county could collect the money, the repayment would not begin for five years. The county could not afford it. Abbott had been a little more cynical a few months earlier. "Help a man out of a ditch, and if he does not pay you while the mud is still wet on his clothes, he never will." The bond measure lost, 203 for, 439 against. The vote was closer in Blackwood, where the Rev. Moore's influence was felt, 18 for, 27 against.[8]

Abbott felt a little remorseful about Moore. Some weeks after the failure of the bond issue, he and his rival editor Barney Hofer, the county officers, and about 70 citizens marched on the Methodist parsonage. They pressed through the doors and "took possession of the premises." The self-invited guests served ice cream and cake and presented the preacher with "numerous packages of groceries" and "a purse of money," value, $25.00 "We will always cherish this evening as a bright spot in the year of hardship and sorrow," Moore wrote in a thank you note to the *Republican*.[9]

Abbott's faith in Hayes County had not wavered since late in the fall, after the drought, when he had asserted that the "farmer who succeeds in raising a crop next year will strike it rich . . . The sky of the future is bright with the promise of prosperity."[10]

Abbott was right. The sky of the future had never been brighter than it was in 1891. A big snow fell shortly before Thanksgiving in 1890, causing "great encouragement among the farmers." They looked forward, or at least Abbott did, to the next year as "the most productive in Hayes County history." Warren Clark recorded snow for eight days in January, four in February, light snows for the most part, but several inches on January 8 and 9. He had to shovel paths to the outhouse, the barn, and his granary. It was nasty enough to keep him at home in the house on some days, with forays outside to do the chores. The snow fell intermittently, seven days in March, the largest fall of the season on March 24 and 25, a damp, heavy snow.[11]

By the third week in March "everybody" was thinking about sowing wheat "if they can only get the seed." Most of them got what they needed. Warren began to sow his fields on April 9. It was quite windy, reminiscent of 1890, but the next day was pleasant and mild, and so were the next ten days. And then the first rain came, on Saturday night and most of Sunday, April 18 and 19. Warren's timing was perfect. He had his wheat in and that Saturday afternoon finished sowing his oats. There was "plenty of water for the present," the Hope correspondent said, "and everybody is happy now." The Eureka Grange, on the Ridge, distributed packages of garden seed. There would be "a rush for gardening as soon as the ground is dry enough." After last year's drought and the wind-driven dust, that seemed an unlikely, even a ridiculous statement. It was time beyond memory when the Methodist Ridge folk had to wait for the ground to dry out before they could plant their gardens or their fields.[12]

By the first of May the bright green of the fields was "fair to gaze upon." In another two weeks there was "a glorious rain" on the Ridge, all day Saturday, and "a fine shower" on Monday. Everything was soaked, including sod on the roofs of houses. Water dripped through the cracks and soaked everything inside--beds, clothes, rugs, the dirt floor, despite Ada's scurrying about to get the clothes in the dry spots and pots and pans under the biggest drips. Warren recorded rain again in two days, and for much of that week, for eight of the next ten days. The big hollow on a farm northwest of Hayes Center filled up into a 60-acre lagoon, and the water was to remain and attract ducks all summer long. One wag said that he was going to build an ark to float out of the county, and every farmer who got to town had a "two-by-scantling" smile on his face.[13]

With the heavy rains, corn was late that year, "a little too much rain for corn," the Methodist Ridge correspondent complained. A hail storm did some damage on the Ridge, breaking out windows, pounding down some of the wheat and rye, but it was early enough for the grain to recover, too early to hurt the corn. That must have been the storm Nellie remembered when Earl, five, got caught out in the pasture where he had gone with the dog to drive home the cows. He sat on the ground, holding the dog in his lap, hunching forward to protect his head. The hail beat on his back, covered only with a thin summer shirt, and bruised him badly.[14]

John Low and his wife May came down from Saline County in eastern Nebraska that spring to visit the Jim Abbotts and the Rome Smiths. May was a sister to Emma Abbott. John was astounded to find the crops "looking so well after the drouth." He decided to locate if he could find a place. After some inquiry and negotiation he bought out Merady Williams, just across the Ridge road from the Abbott's, for $850. Williams, after paying off his mortgage for $650 and his back taxes and interest, had very little cash, but he was debt free. And after one dry year he was glad to get out. Ed Smith, having tried Seattle and found that his lungs were "not strong enough for that damp, swampy country," returned to his farm on Methodist Ridge, in time to take over the wheat his tenant had planted and to put in his corn.[15]

The other happy man on the Ridge that spring was Dock Gruver. He had turned 21 and promptly filed on a quarter section near his mother's place, land made vacant when the previous claimant's provisional title was canceled by the land office. Dock was lucky. He apparently avoided paying a relinquishment fee, and he got the property just in time to celebrate the birth of his and Nellie's son. Ever cheerful Dock was "stepping very high," the Hope correspondent reported. "A boy come to our house," he said, "and wants to stay for his board and clothes and he looked so pitiful that we concluded to let him stay." The correspondent thought that called for cigars. "Eleven pounds is pretty well for the first time."[16]

Dock's happiness was short-lived. The baby, born about the first of May, died the first week in November. Warren Clark, president of the Pleasant Ridge Cemetery Association, picked out the lot where they were to bury him. Dock was to grieve over the little boy for forty years, out there without family on that barren grass-covered slope. When his wife Nellie died and he buried her in Palisade, he moved the boy, to place him near his mother--but not until he had opened the little coffin, tremblingly, and looked in on the tiny form, remarkably preserved in that dry climate, he insisted, the features still recognizable, the little red jacket faded but not decayed.[17]

The harvest was as good as the promise, indeed, better. One farmer threshed out 38 bushels to the acre on a 45-acre field, one threshed oats at 78 bushels, another barley at 60. The pattern prevailed everywhere in the county. P.C. Iverson, from near Hayes Center, who had farmed in Nebraska for 25 years, said he had "never raised as fine a crop . . . as he did this year." Henry Wiswall harvested 2523 bushels of wheat from 100 acres, and he had 70 acres of fine looking corn. Abbott made a quick calculation. Prices had doubled. Wheat was selling at 60 cents a bushel, corn at 25. Given 2523 bu. @ 60c = $1,513; 350 bu. of corn @ 25c =$857. Grand total, $2388. "A pretty fair income." Jim Lakin, Warren's friend down in the southwest corner of Blackwood, had mortgaged his property to make improvements and purchase more land. The drought, he said, had "crippled him seriously." At the beginning of the year, 1891, he was in debt $1100. But after he had harvested his wheat and picked his corn, he paid it off, every dollar of it, and had a thousand bushels of corn still to market. "Mr. Lakin farms with his hands and not with his mouth," said Abbott, "and hence has no use for calamity howlers."[18]

That was the spring and summer of extravagant display of wildflowers and fruits on the canyon walls and of opulent gardens in the farmyards. Ada and the children loved the wildflowers. Nellie recalled them in her reminiscences, the delicate pink and the sweet scent of the five-petaled wild rose, the bluebells hanging from a tall slender stem, catching everyone who had eyes to see with surprise and wonder, the Jack-in-the-pulpits, the white spikes and clusters on the chokecherry bushes, and for her and Ada, too, the most lovely and exotic of the them all, the lavender to purple wild sweet peas. Mary, who had been the first of them to find delight in the wildflowers when she wandered about picking them in the fields of Gosper County, was to surround herself and her house with flowers for all of her life. Earl, too, loved the flowers, a delight he never lost. "He knew the name of almost every wildflower," said his daughter Mildred, "and interesting facts about them. He would touch them so tenderly when he showed them and told us about them." As for fruit, they picked plums by the tubful, and chokecherries, and currants, and thrust their hands into the poison ivy, which also grew rank that summer--"quite painful," Nellie said, remembering the smarting itch. The Clarks had so many watermelons that Warren hauled them in by the wagonload, piled them by the hog pen, and fed them to the pigs and the cattle. Ada and the children broke the melons and squeezed out the juice, which Ada then strained and made vinegar. They had a great abundance of pumpkins, squash, muskmelons, tomatoes, beets, cabbages, cucumbers, turnips, and the staple foods, beans and potatoes. And so did all of their neighbors.[19]

There were few reports from Methodist Ridge on the wheat harvest, but the average for the county was 32 to 35 bushels to the acre. The Ridge seems to have done as well as the rest. Warren had been able to thresh his wheat in a half day in 1888, but it took all day this summer, a day-and-a-half at Rome Smith's, a half day at Ed Smith's, all day at Harlan Martin's and Ellsworth Jeffries'. Only Jim Abbott, new on his homestead, had bad luck. His four beautiful stacks of wheat--Warren had stacked them for him--were struck by lightning and burned to the ground, with the loss of five or six hundred bushels of wheat. Fortunately, some of his crop was still in the field. He put his boy, Charley, with a team and scraper, to the job of cleaning up the ashes and charred straw from the land, to make way for new stacks. For one day Nellie Clark took Charley's place on the hayrack, loading rye. It was tough work. She stood there, a short slight figure in her long calico dress, sunbonnet, and high buttoned shoes, swaying to keep her balance, moving quickly to dodge the bundles or to fork them to their place, the hot sun beating down on her as she basted in her own sweat. It was easier when Jim Abbott tossed the bundles to her, because he placed them where they needed to be and she scarcely had to move them, but Richard Roberts, always in a hurry, "just thru them anywhere & often hit me." "I got awful tired," she said. She was eleven-years-old.

At the state fair in Lincoln that fall, Hayes County once again collected more than its share of premiums: first for spring wheat, second for oats, first for rye, first for beets. Abbott revised his encomium on Hayes County to include a section on the "average yield." It was, he said, "where ordinary good farming is done," about as follows: corn, 50 bushels to the acre, wheat 30, oats 50, rye 30, barley 35--averages very considerably above national levels, and above anything Hayes County had achieved, save in banner years.[20]

That fall John and Nellie Theovalt, and their children, disgruntled with Denver and the Rocky Mountains, returned to Hayes County. Warren moved them and their goods, temporarily to his house, then on to Nellie Duffield's homestead, only two miles from the Clarks. Nellie had proved up and either left the county or moved in with her parents. The Theovalts were very dear friends and Warren and Ada were delighted to see them. John needed goods and services, but he had nothing to offer in exchange, save cash. That was welcome enough, so Warren charged him $1.50 for transporting his goods from the train, $2.50 for hauling coal, $6.20 for 10 bushels of wheat, $5.00 for 15 bushels of potatoes, $6.80 for 170 pounds of beans, 60 cents for two bushels of beets, and 55 cents for two gallons of vinegar.[21]

In November, Warren made proof on his claim, six and one-half years after he had filed. With poor crops in 1890 and little enough money to buy the childrens' shoes and coats, and none at all to pay taxes, he had delayed a year and a half. And so had Harlan Martin and Ellsworth Jeffries, who rode in to McCook with him and made proof on the same day, both of them delaying as he had delayed, and for the same reason. But now they had title to their farms and crops big enough to pay the taxes and to promise a bright future.[22]

# 19.
# Stand Up for Hayes County

1892 was another joyous year for Blackwood and Hayes County. Warren Clark finished gathering the last of his big crop of corn from the previous fall on January 23, but two weeks later "a great deal" still stood in the neighboring fields. Farmers were hauling much of it off to town as soon as they could get it shelled, "anxious to settle all accounts against them." Warren was still marketing wheat in mid-January, and a load of hogs for which he got only $3.20 a hundred pounds. That was considerably less than he had received the year before, but with corn at 20 cents a bushel it was still a profitable sale as long as he could get more for a hundred pounds of hogs than he could for ten bushels of corn. The shellers pulled into his farmyard on February 1, broke down, another outfit came two weeks later, and Warren began to haul corn to Culbertson. With rain and snow in December and January and on into February, "the prospect for good crops" in the next year, said the Highland correspondent "never was better."[1]

There was almost a festive mood, a strong sense of communal well-being on Methodist Ridge that winter. On New Year's day, Friday, Warren and Ada went to see Brother R.S. and Sally Moore, and on "to see the sick," the Ed Smiths. The Moores now lived in the house and on the farm they had bought from Mary Martin (giving a note for $800 to Mary to pay for it). The house was on the Ridge road, a mile east of the Clarks' and almost directly across the road from the sod church. Ed and Lissie Smith had returned to their home a mile south of the Moore's, a half mile east of Harlan Martin's. The next morning Warren drove over to a neighor's to pick up a cradle for the Smith baby, "ett dinner," his noonday meal, with them, called on Brother Moore, and turned back to Harlan Martin's. Harlan went home with him to help sort some pigs. Not until late in the afternoon did he get into the field to pick a little corn. They went to Sunday school the next morning, all but Jennie who was sick and Nellie who stayed home with her.[2]

The Theovalts stopped overnight with them, moving from Nellie Duffield's to Bill Black's, a place they had just purchased in a second try at living in Hayes County. The whole distance was only four or five miles, but it was a good occasion to socialize and Warren and Ada and the children were glad to see them. Black's place, two miles south and a quarter mile west of the Clarks', but farther on the road around the canyons, was a convenient location for Warren. He drove past it on his way to Palisade. Several times that spring, on his way home, he would stop at Jim Lakin's, down in the southwest corner, drive on past the lone tree to Theovalts', sometimes staying overnight at one place or the other. After getting the Theovalts settled, the whole family drove into Culbertson to have the children's pictures taken. The third week in March, Moore began protracted meetings in the sod church, preaching every night but Saturday for two weeks. Warren missed only once, when he took a load of corn to Culbertson and got home too late to go. Brother Moore was a powerful preacher and the sod church was full, night after night. That was the year Nellie, not yet 12, was converted.[3]

In mid-January, Harlan came by and he and Warren drove to Hayes Center to W.I. Sears' sale. They were sorry to see him go. And so were the Methodists generally, to lose this charter member of the church in Hayes Center. And so was Abbott, who addressed him as "Judge," for he had been a justice of the peace. No one, for the record, offered an explanation of why he was leaving. He sold all of his horses, cattle, farm implements, and household goods, and with his family took the train to Orange Vale, California. He left his farm for Abbott, as land agent, to sell. It was heavily mortgaged, but both he and Abbott had confidence that the purchaser would assume the indebtedness. Joel Devereaux gave up about the same time and transferred his property to Hank and Nellie. But the transaction did not bring the younger Devereaux to Methodist Ridge as neighbors. They were still in Gosper County, but in a matter of months they were to sell their farm and they, too, would move to California, and Nellie out of Ada's life. John Hughes also was moving, taking his fine "string of stallions" from his ranch on the Blackwood to Culbertson where he would keep them at the fairground, make their services available to farmers, and train them for fairs. The *Times*, in reporting the news, said nothing about Hughes's possible financial troubles, but the *Republican* had noted, some months earlier, that John's wife had opened a boardinghouse in Culbertson.[4]

Jim Scott's brother, George, was another one in trouble. He had borrowed $800 in 1889, not due until September, 1894, but George, unable to keep up the semi-annual interest payments, despite the good year in 1891, was in arrears $130. In March, 1892, the district court ordered him to pay up in 20 days or face foreclosure and a sheriff's sale. George let the law take its course and lost his preemption in section two. He held on to his homestead. Jim's other brother, Tom, had bad luck of a different sort. His wife left him, had been gone for two years, and he was granted a divorce at the January session of the district court. He returned to Iowa.[5]

The misfortunes and the mistakes in judgment by men who had overreached themselves did not dampen the optimism of others. Jim Abbott was a neighbor of George's, and no doubt was sobered by his bad luck. But Jim had done well, despite the lightning fire that had cost him four stacks of wheat. With Charley to help him, and two younger boys coming on, he wanted more land. He bought Annie Jeffries' preemption, west of his place in section two, paid $550 for it and assumed the mortgage for $350 which Annie had taken to finance her purchase. That was reasonable, considering some of the other sales. Charles and Thisbee Boyd, in section 10, just west of Warren's, who had moved to California, sold to James W. Mansfield, Harry's brother, for $800. Harry and his other brother, John, had to pay only $20 for Charles Andrew's two quarter sections, but they assumed mortgages, unpaid interest, and back taxes totaling some $1200. Charles Hammond, in section 35, outdid them all. He converted his tree claim to a preemption, for a fee of $200, and promptly sold it for $1600. In land values, Blackwood was certainly prospering.[6]

Shaffer McMullen arrived that spring with his wife and four boys to take over the homestead adjacent to the Clarks, where the Theovalts had lived and where stood the sod church and the cemetery. They were a young family, Shaffer 30, Eliza Jane 28, lovely, vivacious, sparkling with her red-gold hair, and the boys, Earl not yet seven (a year older than Earl Clark), William (Bud) almost 5, Ray 3, and Bert a baby of three months. Shaffer was just in time to put in his spring crops. Warren Clark was already busy in his fields, manuring and plowing. In short order Warren sowed and harrowed his wheat and oats, planted his potatoes and garden, working when he could, with interruptions from rain, and even snow in the third week of April. He hauled more corn and two more loads of hogs to Culbertson--got $4.40 a hundred for the last load, a 30 per cent increase from January to June. He mulched his trees with straw, set out some more apple trees. He broke prairie for six days, getting another seven or eight acres under cultivation. For the first time he tried listing his corn--planting it down in the furrow in the manner that was to become standard on the plains. And for the corn that he planted in the old manner--cross-checked--he borrowed a roller from Brice McMullen to try Hardy Campbell's new method he had read about in the papers of packing the soil to hold the moisture. The correspondent for Methodist Ridge reported that those who had rolled their ground "hit the nail on the head, as it packed the ground so it held the moisture better."[7]

Twice he went to Charles Rodgers', in section 15, to get some blacksmithing done. The oldest son, Albert, 32, but still a bachelor at home, had opened a shop on his father's farm. Jesse, 24, the second of the sons, worked on the farm, and John, the youngest, both on the farm and in the shop. Charles was well liked in Blackwood, respected enough to soon be elected road overseer. The oldest daughter, Effie, was married to Frank Miller, who lived in section 8, and like Charles was well-known in the neighborhood. But the rest of the family were recluses, satisfied to be in their own little private community, the family. They did not go to church, they were too old to go to school, they did not visit in the neighborhood. Albert played the violin, Jesse the bass viol, and Nolia, one of the sisters, the organ. They played for themselves, at home. Although in early 1892 they had lived on their homestead for three years, no one, so far as Nellie was aware, had yet induced them to come out into the community to play. Among the Clarks, only Warren knew them.[8]

However demanding the farm work, Warren was not too busy for church and socializing. Even in the spring they were present for every service, and prayermeeting, too. He took off a day to help plaster the sod church, he and Ada found time to spend an evening with the Ross Beards, and Warren pulled his horses out of the field on a Tuesday afternoon when Jim and Martha Lakin, from down near Palisade, came to see them. Sundays after church they had company, the Theovalts, the Martins, the Driscols, the Southwells, or they went to their neighbors' for dinner. In May and June on Saturday and Sunday afternoons they met with other families to practice for Children's Day, first for the Grange, their service held at the sod church, and a month later for the Sunday school. Warren and Harlan spent a day building a pyramid for the program. They went to Hayes Center for Decoration Day, a cool and cloudy day. They went again to the Fourth of July celebration, taking their picnic lunches with them and joining their neighbors from Pleasant Ridge. For Miles Abbott it was a glorious day, "a hummer, and no mistake." Fully fifteen hundred "patriotic citizens" of the county were present. The town was "handsomely decorated with bunting;" the procession was led by the Martial Band of the Iuka Lodge of the G.A.R., followed by the Goddess of Liberty on a "tastily decorated wagon." But tragedy was in the making for Blackwood. Little Chauncey Beard, four-years-old, dashing about, laughing and playing with his friends, ran head on into another boy and fell, fainting. He lay unconscious in his mother's lap until he recovered enough for them to take him home.[9]

The harvest fulfilled the promise of the winter and spring. In July there was a moment's fright when "torrid" winds blew in from Kansas to bring the hottest days of the season, over 100 degrees in the shade. The corn was scarcely tall enough to tassel. Barney Hofer of the *Times* joked: "This hot weather will bring roasting ears in a very short time." But the rains came and Hofer reckoned that southwest Nebraska was prepared "to astonish the people again" with its big crop. It did not precisely astonish the world, but the crop was above average, some of the wheat 25 to 30 bushels to the acre, and the potatoes and corn average or better, "a full crop . . . and good quality." Some of the farmers on the Ridge were "discouraged" by the low price for grain, but hogs were bringing "a fancy price" in Culbertson, making "happy" those farmers with the luck or foresight to have some. Henry Wiswall counseled them not to put all their eggs under one hen. "Don't be afraid to raise a good deal of everything, for then you will be sure to hit something." In the six years he had been in the county, there had been a "full crop" every year but one, 1890, and that was not a failure. Henry was fighting a proposal to irrigate the land. Rather than pay those high costs, he said, they could "better afford a crop failure once every five years." But if they were to judge from the past, they could expect a failure "only once every ten years."[10]

All summer and fall Abbott had carried one-liners, interspersed among the other short items in his local news column: "Stand up for Nebraska," "Stand up for Hayes County." In the Republican party disaster of 1890, Abbott had editorialized that "when short crops" left the farmers "with nothing in particular to do," they tried to better their condition by blaming the party in power. It was, he wrote, "peculiar but a fact . . . that parties are almost as dependent on the weather as the crops . . ." He called his piece "Rain in Politics."[11]

If Abbott's thesis were correct, the rain and the good crops overwhelmed the Populists. In 1892 the Republicans won every statewide office, from governor to state superintendent of schools; they elected more members of the Senate and House than the Democrats or the Populists. Benjamin Harrison, Republican candidate for president, carried the state by a narrow margin over the Populist, James B. Weaver. In Hayes County, the Republicans won election in all but three contests. The "calamity howler" had been "knocked out." "Nebraska is all right," Abbott wrote. "There's no flies on Hayes county."[12]

For Blackwood, only a few small clouds hung on the horizon. The sheriff, J.A. Small, published notice of foreclosure and sale on Samuel Kinsinger, president of the county's Agricultural Association, and holder of a quarter section in Blackwood. And the Phoenix Insurance Company of Hartford, Connecticut, gave notice of suit against John Hughes, his wife Mary, and his mother Sophia, for the collection of $1120, plus interest, due on two quarter sections, in Blackwood.[13] Abbott made no editorial comment and included no news item on the plight of either the president of the Agricultural Association or of his old political antagonist, John

Hughes. It would not have been a good way to stand up for Hayes County.

# 20. When It Rains It Pours

Not without hope, 1893 would be a grim year, but dry enough to raise the specter of drought. It began auspiciously enough. Rome Smith, calling on editor Barney Hofer of the *Times*, who thought him one of Pleasant Ridge's "most enterprising farmers," boasted that five new families had settled in his neighborhood recently. Smith, like Abbott, was a booster, and for somewhat the same reasons: a natural disposition plus self-justification, in his case, for the high price he had paid for his property and for the two big mortgages he carried. Two of the five new settlers had come a year earlier, Shaffer McMullen, Brice's son, and John Low, Smith's friend and Jim Abbott's brother-in-law from Saline County. Two others, the Satchell brothers, were newly arrived from Iowa with five carloads of cattle, sheep, horses, farming tools and machinery, and household goods. They took up relinquishments in Highland precinct, just east of Rome's place on the Ridge. Who the fifth was we do not know, but the arrival of new men, able to pay or willing to take a mortgage for the property, was a good omen. The Satchells were Methodists and with their families helped to swell the attendance at the sod church.[1]

Another good omen to Miles Abbott was the election of Henry Wiswall as president of the County Agricultural Society. "A wise thing," Abbott wrote. Wiswall was "one of the ablest writers on farm topics in western Nebraska." A good farmer, too. And a strong booster for and able defender of

Hayes County. Naming him president was a vote of confidence in the county itself.[2]

Warren Clark, too, had a sense of well-being and confidence. Out of office for a term, he was once again justice of the peace. And that was the winter, after two good crops, that he put wooden floors into the two rooms of his sod house. Ada must have been happy with that, to get back into her Dutch ways with floors to sweep daily and mop on Saturdays. Warren bought a wringer for her, too--her hands and wrists were so lame that she could no longer twist the wet clothes to squeeze the water out of them. Nellie and Mary stood at the tub and turned the crank and helped hang up the clothes. She taught them how to fold the dry garments as they took them from the line, how to smooth out wrinkles with the iron they "het up" on the cook stove. She had long since taught Nellie to sew and knit. She did the cooking and housework, Nellie, almost 13, made the clothes for the children, pants and shirts for Earl, dresses for the little girls, for herself and Mary. She knit wool stockings and mittens for all of them, hoods for the girls to wear in winter and a stocking cap for Earl. Ada managed most of the time to have three dresses for each girl, a new calico one to wear to church and later--after the newness had gone--to school, a gingham dress for fall and winter, and sometimes a lawn dress for summer, and high-topped, button shoes. They changed from good dresses and new shoes to old as soon as they came home from school, not to get their clothes "dirty," Nellie said, while they did their housework and chores.[3]

That may have been the winter, too, when Warren built the extra room on the sod house, an extension of some eight or ten feet and 14 feet across, the width of the old house. Bud McMullen, a boy of six and new in the neighborhood, did not recall the building of that room but remembered that the Clarks' was a "big" house for a soddy. Warren did not have the cash to put in a floor. But now that Ada had the place to put it, he bought or traded for a loom. She wove rugs, sitting at the loom for hours, for herself and her neighbors, closely knit, tough fabrics. She had the children dig into the stack for fresh straw which she spread on the earthen floor. Then she put down her newly woven rug, stretching and tacking it at the corners and along the sides. They were very comfortable.[4]

In the years that he kept a diary, Warren was ill frequently, scarcely a month passing without his noting, often several times, "most sick," "sick today only done the chores." He was bothered, as he had for years gone by, with an upset stomach, biliousness, a churning within his body that left him half dizzy, crotchety, debilitated. Brother Moore, a powerful preacher, used tobacco and a physician, probably Dr. Meredith of Hayes Center, prescribed the smoking of a pipeful of it, after supper, for relaxation and calming of his stomach. Dr. Meredith was a Methodist, a charter member of the Hayes Center church, the most popular physician in the county. His West Side Drug Store was well stocked with patent medicines and "pure" drugs, but the doctor thought tobacco, at his fireside, was the best remedy for Warren's distress.[5]

Ada was upset. The use of tobacco was, for her, a sin, as it was for her mother. We do not know that she prayed for Warren, but we can be sure that she did, even as Amelia Jane, her mother, and Grandma Onderdonk had prayed that Uncle Arthur be saved from his smoking. In later years Ada was to testify that she once had a temper, fits of uncontrollable anger. Nellie makes no mention of it, nor did any of Ada's other children in years to come relate instances of their mother's temper. It may be that the anger welled up in her without boiling over into words, that Warren felt the force of it, and that she was afterwards remorseful. Whatever the case, Warren respectful of her feelings, was circumspect in his conduct and thoroughly self-disciplined in his practice. One pipeful only, after supper, no more. No smoking of the pipe with the men, nor carrying it to the field or on the long rides to town. It was prescribed. By the doctor, a Methodist doctor. He found it relaxing, peaceful. We can believe that he enjoyed it, devout though he was, for he did not fully assent to the pieties Ada imposed on herself and willed for others.[6]

Whatever concerns they had, weather remained the consuming passion. After two snowfalls in December, January had been beautiful, the skies clear, the atmosphere warmed by the bright sun. But nature was too benign. There was no moisture worth reporting, had not been since the coming of winter. Then in mid-February a "full-blown" snowstorm, with wind, a blizzard, struck the county, followed by another two weeks later, not so severe but "enough to satisfy the weather prophets." The rest of March and April was dry and windy. The Methodist Ridge correspondent was silent but "Vox", from neighboring Highland, on the eastern slope of the Ridge, was faithful in her reports. "Rather breezy," she wrote, "a good shower would be welcome." One of the boasts of Abbott, in his booster story, was that although Hayes County had little rain on the weather charts, what fell came at the right time, when the crops needed it. The rains began early in May and fell intermittently through the month and into the first week in June. The days were cold and damp, but warm enough to pull the bright green shoots of the corn out of the gray-black earth. The rains had "put new life into all nature, and humanity as well," wrote Abbott in the *Republican*, and Hofer in the *Times* thought them "worth millions to western Nebraska." "Vox" was skeptical. It had come too late. "There will be no small grain worth mentioning" in her neighborhood, she wrote.[7]

She was partly wrong. By mid-July the heads had filled out in the spring wheat field of her husband and he had 18 acres that were "very good." A neighbor, cutting his rye, thought he would get only enough to pay for his labor. Jim Scott threshed 301 bushels of rye off 35 acres, for a yield of nine bushels to the acre, but out of the 20 bushels of fall wheat he had sown he harvested only 27 bushels. A couple of men on the Ridge got ten bushels to the acre, one 15, Jim Abbott 8 on his fall wheat. Rome Smith, who planted big crops, had a total harvest (of how many acres we do not know) of only 102 bushels of wheat, 58 of rye. The reports said nothing of Warren Clark's harvest. But his crops did well enough for him to assert that there was nothing to worry about in Hayes County.[8]

The corn did little better. By the first week in August, some farmers had already begun to cut and bind it for feed. Rain on the Ridge late in the month brought out the almost lifeless cane and millet but it was too late for most of what corn remained in the fields. There were exceptions. Local showers, those capricious acts of weather that led men to personify the keeper of the clouds, dumped rain on one farmer's field while the sun shone on his neighbor's. Men began to murmur about who had charge of the spigots. A rainmaker appeared in Chase County to move about the countryside and bombard the heavens with his cannon, but with little effect--a few clouds, lightning, thunder, and a sprinkle, but "not enough rain to do any perceptible good." Boys in Hayes Center made their own cannon, overloaded it, lighted the fuse, and touched off a small earthquake when it blew up, and for some minutes, said Abbott, they dodged the shower of old metal with which they had packed the breech.[9]

But local showers were no joke to Lish Driscol. While his neighbors cut their corn for fodder, he cultivated his, nourished by abundant rain, and the next winter shucked out over 500 bushels. And Jim Lakin, down in the corner of the township, had corn that in mid-August he judged would make 40 bushels to the acre. But in general, farmers had a poor crop or a total failure, both in Hayes County and in the state. The price of hogs went up to $5.00 a hundred, twice what it had been a year or two earlier. "What shall it profit a man," asked "Van Winkle," the Baxter Ridge correspondent, "if he gain a whole raft of little pigs, and lose his corn crop?"[10]

In late July Ed Smith, having given up on his crops, drove north towards the Platte River to search for work. He was back in a few days, reporting that there were "two men for every job." Ten days later he and Ab Saling caught the train east, Ab to look for work in Omaha, where he knew his way around, Ed to go on to Iowa where he had sent his wife and children and where he had family. John Low, so recent a settler in the township, had sold out in April, while the crops still looked good. The buyer, Oscar Anderson, was his friend from eastern Nebraska and Jim Abbott's brother-in-law. The rest of the community stood fast.[11]

Harlan Martin had troubles of another kind: anger and embarrassment, and personal tragedy. Rome Smith got on his nerves. Nellie thought that Rome was abusive, "real mean." The scattered reports in the press and the reminiscences of those who knew him indicate that he was opinionated, loudmouthed, boastful. One Sunday night in May, at prayermeeting in the sod church, he was disruptive, breaking into the services either with the buzzing undertone of conversation with his neighbor or by direct comment on the exercises. He refused to be quiet. After the service they "flung hard words around promiscuously," then moved out of the church to the grass-covered churchyard. The words grew louder and in a moment Martin and Smith began to push and shove. Martin wrestled him to the ground and fell astride him, beating him with his fists. In some manner little Bud McMullen, aged six, excited and curious, got mixed up in those flailing arms and legs, he screaming his head off until his dad pulled him out of the melee. Ada herded her frightened children into their wagon, and no doubt other mothers did the same. Smith's boy, coming to the defense of his father, began to kick Martin until the men held him off and separated the fighting men, but not, said the *Republican*, until some "red blood had been shed." Martin drove his family home. A classleader and a devout member of the church, he was both angry and remorseful. He saddled up his horse, rode into Hayes Center, saw the judge the next morning, paid a fine, and had a warrant issued for Smith. The *Republican*, deploring neighborhood quarrels, admonished the men "to drop it right were it is, make up and fire the first one who tries to continue the disturbance."[12]

Martin's nerves may have been on edge, rubbed raw, beyond the point of tolerance, because of the illness of his wife, Emma. She had never been well, was in fact an epileptic, "a disease resembling apoplexy," the Methodist Ridge reporter said, either not knowing what her affliction was, or unwilling to put it down in writing. Nonetheless, Emma had managed very well, had borne two healthy, normal children, a boy Willie who was almost six that summer, a year older than Flora Clark, and a girl three, Jenny's age. Emma did all of her household duties, cooking, sewing, laundry, looking after the children. Harlan was gentle with her and helpful in the household tasks. They were the closest friends of the Clarks. Nellie stopped there often to see them on her way home from school. Emma had gem pans in which she baked her cornbread, each little muffin crisp on the ridged surface, with only a small soft center. That suited Nellie's taste and her fancy too, especially when Emma gave her a hot gem with cool applesauce. But it frightened her when Emma had a seizure and lay stretched out on the floor, still as death. Nellie was at her house one afternoon when Emma, apparently losing her balance from a slight seizure, thrust her hand into a skillet of hot gravy, burning it badly. Harlan dressed it for her, Nellie watching and never forgetting that act of tenderness. It was her right hand and "for a while," Nellie remembered, some days perhaps, Harlan had to help her with her cooking and household chores.[13]

Emma declined rapidly that summer and died on September 10. She was 33-years-old, not quite a year younger than Ada Clark. She was, said the *Republican*, "a consistent Christian and a loving mother." A "large concourse of friends and neighbors" gathered at the sod church on the Ridge. They buried her on the treeless slope, under the short gray-brown curling buffalo grass. Harlan's mother, Mary, having sold her place to Brother Moore and his wife, Sally, was living at Harlan's. She took over the household duties and the care of the children.[14]

There was more tragedy, illness, and the fear of tragedy on the Ridge that summer. Chauncey Beard had rallied slowly after his accident at the Fourth of July celebration in Hayes Center the previous summer, had failed to recover fully, and in the months that followed suffered from fainting spells and occasional paralysis that made it difficult for him to walk. The doctor said he had a tumor on the brain, that it seemed likely that he had had a severe bump on his head sometime. Eva Beard talked it over with Ada but said nothing of the accident when the children were at play in Hayes Center. Nor did Ada. Nellie pondered the reason for Eva's silence. Ada had instructed her children in a strict code of proper conduct for Christians. Probably, Nellie thought, it would have done no good to talk. It would only have hurt their friends whose little boy had run into Chauncey. The Beards, like the Clarks, were Methodists, and their reasoning, Nellie seemed to say, ought to have been the same. In May, 1893, nearly a year after the accident, Chauncey died. The *Republican*, lamenting the loss of the "bright little 5-year-old," expressed "the heartfelt sympathy of the community."[15]

Death struck again before the summer was over. Silas Briggs, a friend of the Clarks, had died in November, 1892. His young widow, Eva, moved to the Clarks' on November 21 and stayed with them until March 27. Warren charged her $1.50 per week, an amount presumably paid by the county. She was pregnant and gave birth to a daughter about the first of February. By that time, Ada too was pregnant. The Clark soddy, with six children, one of them an infant, and three adults, was crowded. Eva wanted her independence. When her baby was two-months-old and her own strength sufficient, she moved into Mary Martin's sod house, now owned by Brother and Mrs. Moore. Under the policy of the Methodist church, after two years in Hayes County, the Moores had been transferred that spring to the village of Elsie. Although they still planted their crops on the Blackwood farm, the house was vacant. The Clarks were concerned about Eva. She was not strong, could not nurse her child, and the baby was sickly. Ada sent Nellie over to the McMullens to arrange for Mrs. Briggs to buy milk from them. But the baby languished, grew fretful and weaker as the heat of the summer penetrated even the thick walls of the sod house. She died in mid-August, six months and 18-days-old. Mrs. Briggs asked Nellie and three other girls to serve as bearers of the tiny casket, the only time, Nellie said, that she ever saw or heard of girls serving as bearers for a funeral. They buried her in the Pleasant Ridge cemetery, across the road from the little house in which they had lived so briefly. Eva moved to the home of her married sister, and then out of the community. "I saw [her] no more," Nellie said.[16]

Neither grief nor drought denied the neighbors on Methodist Ridge the moments of joy, the exuberance of youth, the delight in social activity. Nellie plotted, whispering among her friends and her parents' friends, and writing notes, for how many weeks she does not tell us, to surprise her mother on her 34th birthday on July 28th. She brought it off, whether Ada was surprised or not. In some fashion Nellie got the word out, neighbors agreed to come and to bring food. In the regular course of events, with Ada's systematic schedule of work for everyone, the house was in order. The neighbors came and had a hilarious time, playing games, John Theovalt "the biggest boy in the crowd." They brought and set up a "sumptuous supper."[17]

A week later Maude Saling, Ab's daughter, conspired with her aunt, Mary Driscol, to surprise her mother, Alice, on her 38th birthday. Thirty persons gathered and they, like those at the Clarks' the week before, had a "sumptuous supper," an alliterative phrase that seemed to please the literary tastes of the Methodist Ridge reporter. Nellie always remembered that party. It was a lovely moonlit night. The crowd was too large for the two-room sod house, so they played outside, on the flat, bare surface in front of the house. Some one had a harmonica and played tunes, game tunes, *Skip to My Lou*, which Nellie played, and probably *Miller Boy*, *Pop! Goes the Weasel*, *Old Zip Coon*, and others. The Salings were Methodists, but the man with the harmonica played dancing tunes, square dances, Nellie thought, and the young people danced. Not Nellie. "I never danced," she said. Dancing was new to the Ridge, or at least it had not been reported until that summer when the correspondent, "Billy the Kid," under the caption "Methodist Ridge Items," listed the "hop" at the Phillipses', a family near the Ridge but not in Blackwood. He did not report any dancing at the Salings'.[18]

After successful and happy surprise parties two weeks in a row, the Ridge crowd tried again, on the next Friday night, August 11. They gathered at George Scott's to help him celebrate his 28th birthday. They had been too secretive, had kept their surprise too well. George was away. Not to be denied their fun, the well-wishers had the party without him. When he got home at midnight, they had long since departed. It was the last occasion they would have to celebrate George's birthday. To cover his unpaid mortgage the sheriff had sold his property in section two on February 11. And now, the investor who had loaned him money to preempt and improve his homestead in section 13, gave notice of suit to recover $700 due on his mortgage and interest. Shortly after the sheriff's second sale, George and his wife, Elizabeth, were on their way back to Iowa, whence they had come a half dozen years earlier.[19]

The Columbian Exposition, The World's Fair, opened that summer at Chicago. The *Republican* featured a story every week, in the ready print section, from April to fall. The fair was a marvel to behold, over 600 acres stretched along a mile and a half of Lake Michigan. The stories featured the controversial, the unusual, the sensational: the Liberal Arts Building, "the largest . . . ever roofed over," 1687 feet long; the court battle over Sabbath closing, won after six weeks by those who demanded that it be open; the race of the cowboys from Chadron, Nebraska, on relays of horses, 1400 miles to Buffalo Bill Cody's quarters at the fair; the exhibits--transportation, agriculture, electricity, mines and mining, music, art; the buildings of the states and of foreign governments, including the more exotic ones from Java, Samoa, China, Turkey, Japan; the giant upright merry-go-round, named for its inventor, George W.G. Ferris of Pittsburg, rising to a height of 250 feet, "a sensation akin to . . . a balloon ascent." And attractions without number, some of them scandalous--an Egyptian "stomach dancer," a Turkish girl "who palpably wore red stockings in lieu of trousers."[20]

Abbott admonished his readers not to go "unless you have the funds to spare." It was better to stay at home, read about it in the paper, and pay those "little debts . . . already contracted." Most of Hayes County obeyed the admonition--or stayed at home without need of it. The first to go was C. H. Eubank, president of the State Bank and dealer in real estate, followed by A.H. Hatch, "mayor" of Hayes Center, and his wife, and some weeks later, after the railroads had reduced fares by one-half, a few others, including Editor Barney Hofer of the *Times*, and his wife, and two of Warren's friends from Blackwood, Ross Beard who must have done well on his shipment of stock that summer, and Jim Lakin who had prospered more than most from the big harvests of 1891 and 1892, gone for a month with his whole family.[21]

Among the vast majority of stay-at-homes, those who read about the fair and paid their bills, and found some pleasure in both, were the Clarks. That November Ada gave birth to her sixth child and second son whom they named Jesse, for her brother and her mother's brother. The name pleased Nellie, too, for it was borne by the very tall, shy young man she had met that spring and dreamed about since--Jesse Rodgers.

# 21.
# Dust of the Earth

The calendar said 1894. The people of Hayes County could not get the weather off their minds. Their mood was ambivalent, ranging from hope to fear, from less than exultation to short of despair. Underlying both moods was an uncertainty that deepened into anxiety, that made them nervous, "touchy," quick to react to the subject of weather.

Abbott triggered their response on the last day of December, 1893. People were complaining about the dry year past and the "liability" of a dry year to come. They should "put their thinking caps on," he said. After the dry year of 1890, no moisture fell in the fall or early winter until February, 1891, "and all will remember what a great crop year that was."[1]

One of the country correspondents pounced on him in the next issue, happy to "call . . . our worthy Editor down." O.O.O. of Lucile, who kept a diary, had recorded six days of snow in January, 1891, totaling 12 inches. Warren Clark reacted almost simultaneously, his letter appearing the following week. "I beg to differ with you," he wrote. He had kept a record of all the snowstorms that winter and spring. Everybody would remember a day of dense fog in January, 1891. It began to snow that night, the 7th, "and snowed and blowed all the next day" and the next, several inches before the storm was over. And it snowed again on January 17th and all day on the 28th, several times in February and March, light snows, and a heavy snow, the best of the winter, on March 24 and 25th. Warren held out hope, not the threat of adversity: "I don't think we need to despair yet of raising a crop this year."[2]

In fact, they had "quite a blizzard" on January 5, the day after Warren wrote, freezing temperatures and a good deal of wind. "Vox" from Highland, reporting wind but "not very much snow," was ironic in her comment on the farmer's plight: Some good had come out of the dry year, 1893. The farmers could enjoy their rest this winter. They had no corn in the fields to pick, and few chores to do. And they weren't saying "so many bad words about the low price of grain as they would if they had it to haul to market."[3]

At last on Sunday night, the 23rd, they had snow, "some" at Eddy, an inch in Government precinct, two inches falling "very quietly" in Highland. Hope and Methodist Ridge were without regular correspondents but Highland was next door and "Vox" often included items about her Blackwood neighbors. She was not fully reassured by the snow. "Why not," she speculated, or reported the speculations of others, "talk up a plan to experiment for artesian water?" They could never irrigate the divide in any other way, but "no soil in the world could produce more abundant crops, if ours had plenty of moisture."[4]

Abbott, himself, whose confidence in the county had remained unabated, finally conceded on February 3 that the fall wheat would be a failure. But that very night, with his paper scarcely off the press, "a fine snow" fell and two weeks later three days of snow, enough to make "Vox" unbend: "Those who read disaster in the open winter, wear a more cheerful countenance."[5]

They had the first rain of the season on March 20, "Showers of Blessing," Abbott wrote, once again calling up the hymn he had heard as a boy in his father's church. The wind suddenly changed to the northwest and drove in a two-day blizzard. The roads were blocked, and travel and work in the fields came to a stop. Everyone on Methodist Ridge "feels happy," wrote Topsy, an infrequent correspondent.[6]

Wheat was at the lowest price in 77 years, the York, Nebraska, *Times* said, an item reprinted in the *Republican* for all Hayes County to read. But prices might improve--and what choice did a farmer have? James Abbott, on the Ridge, with his son Charley and a younger son or daughter to help him, began running three teams the first week in March. He would put in a hundred acres. The Rev. R.S. Moore came up from Elsie, "showing us little farmers how to farm," to sow wheat on the place he had bought from Mary Martin--all but 20 acres that he would save for corn. Over in Government precinct Henry Wiswall and his son John were putting in 160 acres of wheat. J.W. Theovalt began to think he might get a crop from his fall wheat. He said that he would "not trade his farm for spoiled butter, since the wet." And Rome Smith had so much small grain planted his neighbors thought he was trying to farm the whole Ridge. F.A. Jackson, "Vox" reported, one of the "early birds" who had begun sowing the first week in March, had a month later 150 acres of wheat. His crop would be big enough to help pay for his new threshing machine.[7]

The farmers were busy at their gardens, too, and other tasks. Warren Clark, with his wheat planted, set out a "fine plat" of raspberries. Oscar Anderson, new on the Ridge, was preparing a piece of ground near his well for shrubbery, gooseberries, pieplant (rhubarb), and some trees, all to be irrigated from his well. His wife, Lydia, by mid-March had cabbage plants with the fourth leaf showing and tomato plants with the third leaf. "Who can beat that?" asked "Billy Goat." Jim Abbott shingled the roof of his sod house, "making preparation for a wet spring." Shafe McMullen fenced his garden plot, Ed Smith, back from Iowa, was delighted to see the green in his field of spring wheat and Rome Smith, early in April, was already plowing for corn.[8] "Vox" remained anxious. "Two light showers last week," she said in her report of April 21, "but still the dirt is loose and still the wind blows." "No wonder," she added, "farmers ask what will the harvest be?" It was a question on everybody's lips. Every correspondent was writing about the weather, and all of the farmers were talking about it. "Billy" had put it bluntly for Methodist Ridge a month earlier. "Weather fine. Wheat sowing is progressing rapidly. A rain is needed badly . . . The ground is terrible dry."[9]

All of the talk about weather exasperated Editor Abbott. He begged his correspondents to refrain from writing about it. "It takes up room and time to put such items in type, and cannot be of interest. Besides it is not news. What everybody knows is not news." He quickly broke his own rule. In less than a month he confessed that "prospects for any kind of crops . . . are decidedly discouraging. All small grain will be a total failure for lack of rain." The farmers had planted a large acreage of corn, but most of them had pulled out of the fields until it rained. Some of them could still joke about it. Jim Abbott and Ben Southwell, from Methodist Ridge, joined Commissioner Frank Dye in "arresting" Charlie Keetch to bring him before the judge for disturbing the peace and quietude of the neighborhood--planting corn before it rained. Charlie was fined cigars and admonished not to let it happen again.[10]

Others saw nothing to laugh about. Before the end of May there was "a constant stream of white covered wagons" from the west where the drought was more severe, headed east along the valley road. "Lucky is the man who knows where to go to find work and relief," said Abbott. In the next issue "Vox" was back with a comment on the weather and the crops. "Long faces. No grain. Corn that got up, dead. Ground as dry as ashes." "Vox" continued: "We certainly are in a disagreeable 'fix' but as it is not the result of the tariff, the defeat of 'free silver,' 'Cleveland's orneryness' we wont complain. We'll just give ourselves a moderate kicking for being found here."[11]

The *Republican* carried an advertisement that week: "Homes in Arkansas," a state "exempt from extremes of heat and cold . . . salubrious climate. . . no blizzards, no drouth, never a crop failure . . ." Abbott, reflecting on the weather, the lack of rain, the ceaseless wind, could not suppress a wry comment; "The dust of the earth, from which you were originally manufactured, has been renewing relationship for sometime."[12]

Not much happened on the Ridge that winter and spring, "Vox" complained. If she were to send in a letter every week, she would have to make up the news, tell some "whoppers." Indeed, the country correspondents, or Abbott for that matter, had little to say about anything but the weather. Warren Clark, reelected justice of the peace, posted his bond. And so did Charles Rodgers, named road overseer for Blackwood township, and he promptly collected $40 for building a bridge. James Abbott, Ben Southwell, and Frank Hanks were selected for jury duty. Dock and Nellie Gruver had another son and Dock was once more radiant with happiness. Ab and Alice Saling, too, had a son, the first after eight girls. Ab was hilarious, said the *Republican*, his smiling face "not to be wondered at." Wintering in Omaha where he had a job, and unhappy over the dry summer in 1893, he had sold his farm in February for the handsome sum of $1,200, with the buyer assuming the mortgage. But he was in Hayes County for the birth of his son and he, Alice, and the children were staying on for the summer months before giving up the farm.[13]

Miles Abbott that spring offered the prize package of a combination subscription to the *Republican* and the New York *Tribune*, the nation's greatest newspaper, for $1.50 a year. The only takers on Methodist Ridge were Ellsworth Jeffries, James Abbott, and Shaffer McMullen. That was enough to circulate the news reported by the great metropolitan paper to all of the neighbors on the Ridge.[14]

In March, Harlan Martin went down to eastern Kansas to marry a widow, Cora, whose last name we do not know. He brought her and her young sons, one a year older than his boy, one a year younger, to Blackwood to make a home for him and all four of the children. The Clarks liked Cora and welcomed her into the church and the circle of close friends. Neighbors "charivaried" the happy couple and Harlan, having anticipated the ceremonial rite, distributed cigars to the men and oranges to the women and children. Eliza Jane McMullen, Shaffer's wife, had been seriously ill for several weeks and missed the party, but she was "rapidly recovering." The new Methodist preacher, C.A. Webster, seemed to be well-liked, but after the colorful and popular R.S. Moore, he attracted little attention. Nonetheless, he built a frame church in Hayes Center, valued at $2,000 (to which the sod church on Methodist Ridge contributed $25), and his daughter Stella captured the heart of young John B. Cruzen, president of the State Bank in Hayes Center. They were married in April.[15]

Two major topics, other than weather and crops, engaged the interests of the editor and the correspondents that winter and spring: thistles and poverty. Henry Wiswall lectured on the Russian thistle in January. It had flourished in South Dakota for 17 years and now had worked its way into five places south of the Platte River and was pretty well distributed through the central part of Hayes County. Abbott, commenting on the lecture, said that the thistle was the "worst pest" farmers had to deal with. His son Charles, employed in the Government Printing Office in Washington, D.C., said that the Senate Committee on Agriculture had reported favorably on a bill to appropriate $1,000,000 for "the destruction and extermination of the noxious . . . weed." "Vox" moaned that they had suffered two seasons (1890, 1893) "so dry that the perspiration would not start," and had been afflicted with a "third party," the Populists. Now they had "another worst foe in prospect"--the thistle. Lish Driscol made a trip to town to ask whether there was "some law to compel him and his neighbors to exterminate the Russian thistle" which was "holding the fort down" in his neighborhood. There was no law.[16]

On the question of poverty, Abbott had warned in November, 1893, that this was "going to be a particularly hard winter on the poor," and had urged the "more fortunate neighbors" to give work when they could and "help the needy in other ways, even to the giving of round dollars." As the winter months wore on he heard reports that several families in the county "are very destitute." He reminded justices of the peace that the law made them overseers of the poor and that no child should be allowed to suffer from hunger and cold. Since Abbott was both lawyer and that term the county judge, as well as editor, he spoke with authority. He also directed some remarks to the commissioners. He thought that they would be well advised to acquire a quarter section of land to be used eventually as a self-sustaining poor farm.[17]

The justices responded--with alacrity. In a matter of three weeks they had handed out numerous orders for merchandise and food, ranging from 35 cents to $14, and for medical services from $4 to $15. One of the country correspondents complained that justices were giving orders for "tobacco and such things." He joined Abbott in calling for the purchase of a poor farm. He did not favor paying $2 per week for boarding people who would work for their board if they had a chance.[18]

The commissioners, upset by the enterprise in good works at public expense, ordered the justices to make a personal examination of the poor to determine that their condition was destitute before issuing orders for goods or medical services. In addition, they instructed them to come to the next meeting of the board in June to report on the condition of the poor. The commissioners got tough. They would not pay for goods or services unless the justices had made a proper report to the commissioners. And they warned bondsmen that they were "likely to get stuck" unless the justices complied with the law. Abbott once again indulged in a witticism, spilling his type across the column:

Some
People
Have
Faith
to
Hope
That
Charity
Will get them through during the next year."

At its July meeting the commissioners announced their decision to buy a poor farm. They would receive sealed bids on August 20.[19]

By the first of June Abbott, heretofore the irrepressible optimist, was crying calamity with the best of his old political foes--but not for political reasons or political remedy. "There will be absolutely no hay or fodder of any kind," he wrote. The question that agitated the farmer was not the tariff or the railroad but how to obtain feed for his cattle and horses.[20]

There was a brief resurgence of hope. Rain fell throughout the county on June 14, an inch and a half in Hayes Center, two inches in the northern precincts. "The long drought was broken," Abbott exclaimed. The Hope correspondent reported that faces on the Ridge broadened to "a cheerful smile." "Vox" was skeptical. The rain would "not do much good unless we have more soon." But farmers on Methodist Ridge, and all over the county, hurried back to their fields, hoping that despite the late planting, they could get fodder at least. Quite a number of them, hastening to get their corn in while the soil was moist, planted on Sunday, arguing that the Bible "justified" their labor. Some farmers, who had had doubts, now began to think it would be worthwhile to celebrate the Fourth of July.[21]

The rains continued, little showers nearly every day for ten days. "Vox" still complained, "more wind than rain." One correspondent thought the epidemic of emigration "somewhat" checked, the spring wheat grew tall enough to make good pasture, the Hope correspondent reported that corn and weeds were making rapid progress on the Ridge, and even "Vox" in mid-July was "encouraged" by recent showers "to hope for some corn fodder." But she reported that two farmers in Highland, not taking any chances, had been up on the Dismal River to lease hay land to feed their stock the next winter.[22]

In an ironic twist of fate, the wild currants on the canyon walls, nourished at the right moment by the late, heavy showers in June and July, were luxuriant with growth, laden with dark purple, almost black berries. Everyone was picking them, filling buckets and tubs, heaping the fresh berries on pie crusts and short cakes, cooking them for jam, with what sugar they could spare, spreading them out on sheets and blankets to dry.[23]

Then came the hot winds, to Kansas first. The story was reported in the New York *Tribune* and talked about, no doubt, by the three subscribers on the Ridge, and all of the other men, as they squatted in the shade of their wagons at the sod church, after Sunday school or preaching. The corn looked good in Kansas in mid-July, the report said, the finest prospect in years. Three days of hot winds burned it up, "until every blade would break into a flame at the touch of a match," said the New York *Times* account. A reporter for the Omaha *Bee* was even more graphic. The wind "fairly blistered, scorched, withered everything endowed with life." The devastation was widespread, crops in the six counties of eastern Colorado bordering Kansas and Nebraska "a total failure," no corn on one-fourth of the acreage in Iowa, hot winds that ruined "what promised to be the finest crop" ever raised in northwest Missouri, "burned too dry to cut for fodder."[24]

There was no time for self-congratulation, no moment for a great sigh of relief that they had been spared in Hayes County. The hot winds struck. No one of the country correspondents, not Abbott himself, had the words to describe the disaster left in the fields. Months later a reporter for *Harper's Weekly*, travelling through the western counties of Nebraska, heard the story from the people: "Wind! Resistless, neverceasing, dry and penetrating, hot as from the bowels of a volcano. . . ." "Vox" was among the first to speak for Hayes County, on August 2: "King corn is dead and his subjects demoralized." Two weeks later "Busybody," writing from Methodist Ridge, reported that Jim Abbott had sold his pigs, a fine lot of "shotes," at $2 a hundred. The potato crop was short, the corn crop short, and there would be but half a crop of Russian thistles if the drought continued much longer. Rome Smith, whose neighbors had accused him of trying to farm the whole Ridge, had nothing to harvest, Jim Abbott with his 100 acres of wheat, Frank Jackson of Highland, with 150 acres and a threshing machine to pay for, nothing to harvest. The only threshing reported for the entire county yielded a little less than one bushel to the acre. At least one farmer had corn big enough to cut for fodder, some of it bearing roasting ears. And Shafe McMullen on the Ridge had roasting ears for a party, a Saturday night feast for his neighbors, the correspondent said, derisively, the ears "actually grown on his rich and fertile soil." Miles Abbott summed it all up, succinctly. The people of Hayes County "put in 29,163 acres of corn, 18,656 acres of wheat, 1882 acres of oats, 617 acres of barley, 552 acres of potatoes, and raised nothing." The county commissioners, confronted by the need for massive assistance and acknowledging the inconsequential aid a poor farm could provide, rejected the bids and postponed the matter indefinitely.[25]

Abbott thought the drought had served one good purpose. The rainmakers, wholly unsuccessful in their efforts, had been "knocked out completely." That "fake would never be heard of more." But magic and incantation had lost little of their charm. In mid-December "Billy the Kid" noted that there would be five eclipses the next year. That indicated "plenty rain and of course good crops."[26]

As the drought deepened in the early summer, men grew restless and began to talk about moving out, some for summer jobs, more to find new homes. On June 7 Abbott reported that Irven Gruver of Hope had sold his place and would remove with his family to Winfield, Iowa. The Hope correspondent had once commended him for having the finest well in the precinct, 190 feet deep, cemented, and yielding "an abundance of water." Abbott was shaken. "Hayes county can illy afford to lose farmers like Mr. Gruver. . . ." Two weeks later Dr. J.T. Meredith announced that he was closing out his practice and his drugstore and moving to Ontario, Oregon. "An excellent physician . . . very popular among those with whom he practiced," wrote Abbott. He "will be missed more than any other man who could leave Hayes county."[27]

By the first of August Abbott had named 17 families who were moving, "Vox" an additional 17, and other correspondents 16 more. "One by one, many of the best farmers are seeking work elsewhere," Abbott lamented. He hoped that they would return. Watching her neighbors pack up their goods, shut the doors on the empty house and barn, and drive off in their wagons, sometimes covered, sometimes not, "Vox" wrote, simply, "We begin to feel lonely."[28]

J.W. Theovalt, unwilling two months earlier to sell his place for "spoiled butter," gave up and moved to Sarpy County, just south of Lincoln. In mid-August, Warren and Ada Clark, with no field work and few chores to do, went on "an extended visit east in this state." Nellie, in her reminiscences, makes no mention of the trip. It was probably to have one last visit with the old New York friends, Hank and Nell Devereaux, before their departure for California. Brother R.S. Moore, his wheat and corn crops having failed, had no resources to pay his mortgage. Mary Martin was charitable. She "bought" back the farm at the price Moore had agreed to pay and tore up the mortgage. "Vox" listed Rome Smith as one of those leaving for the east and two weeks later "Busy Body" from Methodist Ridge reported that Smith was "the only happy man on the ridge;" he had sold his farm. Rome must have smiled grimly at that, knowing what "Busy Body" could not know: that he had sold to cover his mortgage. At least he was spared the ignominy of a sheriff's sale, at the front door of the courthouse, at one o'clock in the afternoon, as the sheriff's notice invariably said. But he had no intention of leaving. He would stay on the farm as a tenant, and he still had his timber claim.[29]

The second of the Gruvers, George, taking his family with him, left early in August for Missouri. He thought he might return in the future. Abbott hoped that "he may find it profitable to do so." Henry Wiswall and his son, John, with no wheat to harvest from the 160 acres of planted fields, went to Arkansas to explore the promises advertised in the *Republican*. Others were off to Arkansas with the intent to stay, among them Charles Rodgers and his family. Charley had proved up on his homestead in June. He resigned as road overseer--there undoubtedly was no more work to be done, or money to pay for it--, closed up his place, and set off in a covered wagon with his wife, their three grown sons, and two daughters. The horses belonged to his son Jesse, who had done the farming.[30]

The widespread devastation of the land and the suffering of the families prompted the Land Office in McCook, as it had in 1890, to relax regulations for homesteaders. They could suspend the residence requirement and take leave from the land without losing the right to prove up. But they would have to make up for the lost time before "making proof."[31]

Ten thousand people, it was said, left western Nebraska that summer. In the fall old friends of Methodist Ridge, Oscar and Wesley Gruver, gave up, loaded their goods on wagons and set off for Missouri. Oscar had once been superintendent of the Sunday school, teacher at Martin's school, and county superintendent of schools, and Wesley their postmaster at Hope after Newt Wemple, justice of the peace and road overseer for Logan Township. "They were among our oldest and most respected citizens," said Abbott, and, in the words he had used to comment on Irven Gruver's departure, "Hayes county can illy afford to lose such citizens." Dock that summer, with no crops to harvest, had gone down to Grand Island to attend the business college and would return in the fall. Only he, his wife, and their infant son kept the Gruver name in the county.[32]

One other departure that fall troubled Abbott. Late in November "Van Winkle" of Government precinct jocularly inquired, "What is the matter with 'Vox'?" whose reports had not appeared for some weeks. "Van" hoped that "he" had not "seceded on account of the poor postal facilities." Abbott answered soberly. "Vox" was a "lady," the "valued correspondent from Highland," whose identity had not heretofore been disclosed. She and her husband, Frank Jackson, had removed from the state, "much to our regret." She was, Abbott said, "one of the best correspondents the *Republican* ever had."[33]

# 22.
# In Agony Shape

Abbott was deeply concerned about the plight of the farmers. "The situation," he wrote, "is much worse than most people seem willing to believe." The commissioners ought to hold a public meeting and adopt a plan for relief. He had scarcely put his admonition in type before one of them handed him a notice calling the people together the next week, September 15.[1]

The meeting, although well attended, was inconclusive, the discussion loud, sometimes raucous, a good deal of it "intemperate and useless." Assessing the reports from around the county, the commissioners judged that they had funds enough on hand to meet the most needy cases for two months. They called another meeting for October 2, with only one representative from each of the precincts, twenty in all, a manageable group to develop a plan of action.[2]

Rome Smith, for the committee in Blackwood, met with his neighbors to find out what they "must have for the coming winter." What he learned from them was not reported in the press, but an occasional item, or reminiscence, provides some insight into their extremity. "Billy the Kid," writing from Methodist Ridge, reported that Elisha Driscol butchered "a fine hog." The neighbors knew whether he was speaking ironically or not. Warren Clark butchered a hog, a big one. It was so lean it had no fat to fry the meat; what they did not smoke they boiled or roasted, or salted down in crocks. But Ada still had her chickens. What she fed them, Nellie could not remember, probably "screenings" they got from the mill when they took what little grist they had to be ground. Jim and Ella Scott had coffee, or so Julius Blood from the State Bank thought, when he came to check on the mortgage payment long past due. Ella served him a cup of brew. How come, Julius wanted to know, that they could afford to drink coffee when they couldn't make a payment on their interest. Ella was amused, perhaps a little bitter. She had gathered the wild rye grass herself, shelled it, parched the seeds in the oven, brewed them in the pot on the kitchen stove. Coffee! If you want to call it that! But once again, the Scotts were the luckiest people on Methodist Ridge. Their son Will, just turned 16, went back to Iowa to work for his grandparents. He stayed all fall and winter and sent his wages home.[3]

They had a surprise birthday party that fall for Charley Abbott, Jim's son, to help him celebrate his 16 years. Thirty-seven neighbors came to greet him, "a pleasure both to the young and old." But "one very important thing was neglected," the correspondent said, "somehow supper was overlooked." Proud housewives had no delicacies they were willing to exhibit to their neighbors. Eliza Jane McMullen, "improving from her long siege of sickness," may have been there, but in two weeks she suffered a relapse, from pneumonia or "lung fever," the correspondent thought.[4]

Miles Abbott, distressed by the failure of the commissioners to act, went down to Lincoln in October to look into matters himself. Governor Lorenzo Crounce, whose term was about to expire, said that he was re-activating the relief commission of 1891. He might appeal to the legislature to appropriate funds. George Holdrege, general manager of the western division of the Burlington and Missouri, offered to ship, free of freight charge, any donated coal or goods. And someone, perhaps Crounce, told Abbott that aid was already available and a car would be shipped to Hayes County as soon as the commissioners appointed a relief committee to distribute the goods. The commissioners acted at once. By the middle of December, the first aid began to arrive. "Billy the Kid" advised all families in Blackwood wishing aid to go to Warren Clark's--"he has the goods."[5]

Even with the arrival of aid, the county was embroiled in controversy over the need for it and the best means of distributing what they received. Confronted by an unhappy dilemma, they wanted no one in eastern Nebraska, or in other states, to think ill of their land, but they needed help and to make a successful appeal, must confess their plight. In December a reporter for the Omaha *World Herald*, R. B. Peattie, after a swing around the western counties, wrote an account of the devastation and famine under the dramatic headline, "Hunger at Christmas Time." The story featured a "famine widow" in Hayes County whose husband was in Colorado looking for work and who had not returned before her supplies ran out. The Odd Fellows lodge in Palisade, wrote Peattie, sent her $10 worth of groceries and he went along with a member of the lodge to deliver them. The "famine widow" called on Abbott at the *Republican* office to deny that Peattie, or "anyone else," had brought goods to her from Palisade. What she said was true, literally, but she confessed that the Odd Fellows lodge from Hayes Center had brought her some supplies. She didn't need anything else. Peattie, she said, had "simply heard a romance and wrote it up in agony shape."[6]

Peattie undoubtedly made agony out of want, but the need was genuine, too acute, the topic too full of human drama and suffering, to ignore. The New York *Times* reported that farmers, in great need of food and clothing, must have help. It was rumored that some of them were eating prairie dogs. The dispatch cited the state relief commission as estimating that there were nearly 3,000 destitute families in western Nebraska, 200 of them in Hayes County. *Harper's Weekly* called it "utter destitution."[7]

The stories got results, and made easier the mission of the agents who fanned out across the country begging for help. Several Hayes County churches received goods, the first of which, three carloads from Baltimore, came to the Rev. Mr. Thomsen for the Lutherans in Germanville. The Free Methodists received a large box, the Methodists at Hayes Center and Methodist Ridge clothing and canned fruit, the Catholics 40 tons of coal. An Iowan from the town of Eagle Grove brought in a carload of flour to distribute to needy families; someone in Hayes County had word that the little town of Oneida, Illinois, had raised $500 to help destitute families; children in New York gathered up a barrel of clothing and a large box of toys, raisins, cookies, chewing gum, maple syrup, and sent it to Hayes County, hoping it would give "as much happiness" to the children who received it as it had to those who sent it. John Cooper, who owned "a fine home" east of Hayes Center, and who was a traveling salesman for the Mendota Coal and Mining Company, donated three tons of coal to the county. The state relief committee sent flour, beans, rice, dried fruit, and other groceries, shoes and bundles of clothing. The legislature appropriated $50,000 to purchase fuel, food, and clothing for needy families and laid down strict rules for distribution of goods received from the state funds or from the relief committee.[8]

The aid generated not only goodwill but anger and controversy. The Rev. Mr. Thomsen, his congregation abundantly supplied by the Lutherans of Baltimore, and under some local criticism for selfishness, brought some of his leftover goods to Hayes Center to be distributed. The Rev. J. C. DuVal, newly arrived on the scene as the Methodist preacher, speaking from his pulpit, charged Thomsen with deception. The goods, he suggested, had been intended not for the one congregation but for the county. Several hoodlums, aroused by DuVal's remarks, Abbott said, raided Thomsen's place and appropriated some of the goods for their own use or for distribution to people they considered needy. In consequence, it was rumored, additional aid intended for Hayes County was sent to other communities--20 carloads, said Abbott, ignoring the obvious exaggeration of the rumor. Incensed, he charged DuVal with "an absolute and unqualified falsehood;" he was a "clerical bilk full of misrepresentations."[9]

In the three months since DuVal's arrival, Abbott had grown to dislike, even despise, him. DuVal, from Chicago and Cincinnati, was a braggart and, some of his flock whispered, a liar. Abbott said that he was "loth to believe all of the ugly stories told of a certain minister." But it was clear that he had made "an egregious ass" of himself, particularly in his pursuit of a young woman on his circuit. "When the devil wants to catch a preacher," he added, "he bates [sic] his hook with a pretty woman." But DuVal was a go-getter. In two weeks' time he had organized an Epworth League, with 25 members, and had induced some of the leading citizens of the town to be its officers, among them Mrs. J.B. Cruzen, daughter of the previous preacher and wife of banker Cruzen, to be the president, Cruzen himself to be secretary, J.L. Blood, also of the bank, the vice president. He was a stem-winder of a preacher and in a short time boasted that he had converted 40 people, five of them the "hardest citizens in town." "That lets the rest of us down easy," Abbott said.[10]

Out on Methodist Ridge DuVal, as successful as in town, had also stirred up the people, organized an Epworth League with Warren Clark as president and made himself popular with the Methodists, including Warren and Ada. But he aroused a good deal of resentment among non-Methodists by his attack on a neighborhood party at the Grange hall. The Devil got loose, he said, and "set the feet of the people to dancing." If he had been there, he would have pulled off his coat and helped run the dancers out of the hall. Both "Billy the Kid" from Methodist Ridge and "Buffalo Grass" from nearby Logan joined Abbott in taunting the preacher for his falsehoods and posturings. They had added reason to be critical when DuVal boasted that he had received goods to distribute to the needy. The committee he had appointed issued an order on him for a "needy widow," but he had no goods to distribute. He had been "talking through his hat."[11]

Charley Nichols, long absent from the Methodist Ridge news, and Ben Southwell undertook to correct Brother DuVal's shortcomings. They solicited groceries from merchants in Hayes Center and took them to the "widow." "Billy" told it all, including the name of the widow. That infuriated her son who lived nearby. "Billy," he said, "had better investigate the matter" before he "advertises us as the most needy family in the neighborhood." He had taken the names of the donors and would repay them, "sooner or later." He had received some aid and "we don't care who knows it." It had come from the precinct committee, and "outside of that we don't need any more help than the majority of our neighbors."[12]

From the outset the State Relief Commission had required a strict accounting for goods, solicited from private sources, which it sent to local committees. But there were charges of favoritism, fraud, and inaccurate records. When the legislature appropriated public funds for relief it laid down the stipulation that every recipient must sign an affidavit for the goods he received. Those who swore falsely were subject to a fine of $100 or 30 days in jail. Farmers, gathered in the courthouse at Hayes Center to hear the details of the new bill and to elect a county committee, protested vigorously. "Unprincipled persons," they argued, "will not hesitate to make the affidavit." But "the more honorable people will go without that which is needed before they will comply with the red tape requirements. . . ." It was not the red tape that troubled them so much as the implication of dishonesty and the necessity of putting their names to a receipt for charity.[13]

There was much uneasiness in the county. One commissioner, J.E. Rhodes, went down to Lincoln to try to secure additional aid from the Relief Commission, and another, Frank Dye, caught the train for Missouri to solicit help. The people of Fairfield complained that they needed "only teacups or thimbles" to carry home the supply of molasses and kraut issued to them at the distribution center. In Blackwood there was "considerable dissatisfaction," no names called, but Warren Clark, justice of the peace, and his committee were in charge. In Hayes Center, Abbott, in a scarcely veiled allusion to Commissioner Frank Dye, noted that $500 a year in salary and aid coal "is one combination not to be sneezed at."[14]

Meanwhile, leading citizens of the county, following Dye's lead, scattered across the country to solicit feed and seed and other aid. In mid-March the *Republican* listed 23 persons who were in the east, or who would go that week. A dozen more names appeared in the reports of the country correspondents. Chapters of the local lodges, Independent Order of Odd Fellows, Modern Woodmen of America, G.A.R. (Grand Army of the Republic), began to promote a charity ball to raise money to purchase seed and feed. With Abbott as chairman and Barney Hofer of the *Times* as secretary, they printed 12,000 tickets and a circular explaining the purpose of their appeal and mailed them to their chapters across the country.[15]

Mrs. Bell Dye, Frank's wife, in an effort to help, concocted a letter of fact and fiction--hungry children, so many without shoes or clothing that a Sunday school had to be closed; women in confinement with no doctor and without clothing for the new born child, and Bell coming to the rescue as midwife, taking off her skirts and aprons to "cover the nakedness" of the babies. The Omaha *World-Herald* published it on the front page with a note saying that many packages of clean warm baby clothing had been forwarded to Mrs. Dye and that other packages should be sent to her at Hayes Center.[16]

When the *World-Herald* with Bell's letter reached Abbott's desk, he perceived the exaggeration at once and no doubt smacked his lips and noised the word about the community. Dye was a Democrat with Populist sympathies and Abbott thought him an extravagant spendthrift and irresponsible commissioner. Frank, too, saw the letter and hurried to the *Republican* office to demand that Abbott not publish it, perhaps to threaten him. Bell followed her husband to the editor's office. Admitting that she had overstated the facts, she argued that "people out here have to exaggerate in order to induce people of the east to contribute supplies." Abbott printed the letter, with a single editorial comment: "We leave it to our readers to say how much of it is fact and how much pure fiction."[17]

Frank Dye was furious. Cocky, high tempered, he was as quick with his fists as with his tongue. We have only Abbott's version of what happened. As he was walking along the street Dye "slipped up behind us and made a vicious assault on us." Friends pulled Dye off Abbott's back and he rushed to his office to write up the incident. The letter "was a tissue of falsehoods," a slander on the women of Hayes County. Abbott taunted Dye. If he tried to whip every man in the county who denounced him, "he will have an all summer's job on his hands."[18]

He had scarcely cleared his columns of Bell and Frank Dye before Abbott once more had trouble with DuVal. The minister had gone to Chicago, among his old friends, to appeal for aid. Back home, he quickly disposed of "hundreds of pounds of flour, meat beans and oatmeal." He had found on his return, he wrote to his Chicago brethren, that the suffering among the people was "intense, one mother and two children a few miles from his home having died of starvation and cold." The preachers, deeply moved, took up a collection at their annual conference and agreed to appeal to the people in their local congregations. The item was published and widely circulated.[19]

Abbott was contemptuous. "The *Republican* would give $50 for the name of a mother and two children who had died of starvation and cold anywhere in Nebraska. "These tales of woe from diseased imaginations make interesting reading for people who don't know anything about the situation in Nebraska."[20]

By then the need for exaggeration had passed. The many agents had brought in aid from the east, particularly feed and seed, some in carload lots. The appeal of the charity ball proved irresistible. Donors from across the nation, 176 lodges, 374 businessmen and wholesale merchants, from Maine, New York, New Jersey, Pennsylvania, Maryland, North Carolina, all of the Midwest states, Utah, Oregon, and California purchased tickets, chiefly for one to two dollars but ranging among the merchants up to ten dollars. The grand total was $1,137.41, enough to supply seed for 75 farmers. Said the Wallace *Herald*, "The Hayes county people are hustlers and are always capable of holding their own against all conflicting incidents and difficulties.[21]

Late in March the legislature at last appropriated $200,000 to purchase feed for the horses and seed for the fields of the farmers. The commissioners, on the basis of volunteer and anticipated state funds, contracted for 4,000 bushels of corn, 1,000 of oats, 1,000 of potatoes; they would begin distribution as soon as the shipments arrived. That, said Abbott, should "fix the farmers pretty well for seed." And, he added, "if the rain will only come everybody will soon be on their feet again." No conjuring this time.[22]

The rains came but they were capricious, as they had been in the winter and early spring: two good rains in May, then dry days, hot winds, and dust. On May 30 Abbott moaned, "an absolute and complete crop failure again confronts the people."[23]

He scarcely had the paper off the press before the rain returned, falling steadily for twelve hours all day Thursday, two inches that moistened the ground to the depth of plowing. Saturday rain fell again, three inches. "No such amount of water has fallen in the same length of time in the memory of the oldest inhabitants," said Abbott. Jubilant, he published a series of one-liners, a dozen of them: "Plow corn!" "Now watch the vegetation grow!" "Wheat and oats revived--farmers say half a crop." "Grass, millet, sorghum for feed assured." And "'That melody of nature, that subdued, subduing strain,' the concert of bullfrogs singing welcome to the rain."[24]

There was one tragic consequence. Fred Nurnberger, son of a German settler in Blackwood, on his way home from Culbertson, got his wagon caught in the angry waters of the creek. He tried to unhook his horses, his neighbors surmised, but one of them kicked him in the head, knocking him into the roaring water. He drowned, and his horses, too.[25]

There was another tragedy in Blackwood that summer, only three weeks later. For more than a year the Methodist Ridge correspondent had reported periodically on the illness of Eliza Jane McMullen, who lived on the homestead adjoining the Clarks. The rhythm of hope and despair was one with the weather. In January she was improving. "It is hoped," wrote "Billy the Kid," "she is out of danger." A week later she was "improving nicely," and in another month she was "able to be around some." She was pregnant that winter and spring, but it was not the carrying of the child but some deep-seated and to the country doctor unfathomable malady that laid her low. Vivacious, energetic, attractive with her blue eyes and reddish blond hair, she had quickly made her way into the community after their coming in 1892. On May 20 she gave birth to a boy, her fifth son. Two months later she was dead, at 31 years of age. She died, said the report in the *Republican*, "in the triumph of a Christian faith." They cut away the sod and buried her in the churchyard on Methodist Ridge, among a dozen of her erstwhile neighbors.[26]

There was intermittent rain in July and August, but not much of it and the dry spells were long. A few farmers got 20 bushels of wheat to the acre, one 30, but in general the range was from six to 12. The best yields were in the sandhill country where Dock Gruver and his partner threshed 1000 bushels of wheat. They had a county fair that fall, not large, but good, "fully up to the standard of prolific years." Down at the state fair Hayes County once again won first place for winter wheat. At least the county did not need aid that fall. When the elections came the people in Blackwood, no matter how dissatisfied a few of them had been with the distribution of aid supplies, reelected Warren Clark as justice of the peace. And in the second district, however instructed and urged by Editor and Judge Abbott, the jury of the people returned Frank Dye to the Board of County Commissioners, the first man in the history of the county to win reelection to that office.[27]

A few of the settlers returned to the county, and to Blackwood. Jesse Rodgers had come back on the train in December. Hayes County was "not so bad a place afterall." Arkansas had "nothing but timber and rock." Grass did "not even grow there." Henry Wiswall, after his trip to Missouri, made it known that he would remain in the county. Frank and Emma ("Vox") Jackson returned to Highland in the fall, Emma taking up her duties in the schoolhouse and Frank planting his fields. Wesley Gruver and his family came back from Missouri in November, "pleased to get back to Hayes county," and the same week Charles Rodgers and his family arrived, driving Jesse's horses and hauling their furniture. Arkansas, Charley said, "is no place for a Nebraska man." John Theovalt, too, and his family, came back for a third try at farming on Methodist Ridge, the people at the sod church happy to see them. J.B. Smith purchased his brother Ed's farm. Ed was gone, but Rome would stay."[28]

Abbott had become a realist, of sorts. No longer arguing that the crops could not fail or that rains would certainly come, he printed an exchange from the *Nebraska Farmer*. Too much was said about the "immense crops in Nebraska as a whole," when there was "not a word of truth in it." In some sections the crops had been "extra good," in others they raised "very little" grain or corn.[29]

A big snowfall in mid-November led country correspondent "Rustler" to utter again the old incantation. The snow would "insure a good crop for '96." Many hoped but few believed. It is likely that they found more sense in "Van Winkle's" grim humor when he had predicted no drought for 1895, "for the same reason old Barney McPherson used to assign for his disbelief in that place of fire and brimstone; `Sure a man couldn't stand it.'"[30]

# 23.
# Nellie Grows Up

Nellie Clark, 15-years-old in 1895, the year after the drought, was in love. She had grown up quickly. One day she was a schoolgirl and the next a romantic teenager, still in school, but yearning for the love of a very tall young farmer and dreaming of the day when he would be her husband and she keeping house for him. She was, if we can judge from her own account and the attitude of her parents, a very mature young lady.[1]

She had first encountered the young man who attracted her beyond all the other boys of her acquaintance in the spring of 1893, a month or so before she was thirteen. Eva Briggs, who had lived with the Clarks that winter, wanted a place of her own and had arranged to move into the vacant soddy of Mrs. Martin, across the road from and halfway between the McMullens and the church. Ada sent Nellie to the McMullens to arrange for Eva to get milk from them for her child. There in the kitchen, Nellie met Jesse Rodgers. He was a young giant of a man, six feet, one inch tall, towering far above Nellie and short, small-framed Shaffer McMullen, his head reaching toward the low ceiling of the sod kitchen. He was 25-years-old, but he was shy, extremely shy, and his shyness, his open embarrassment, must have made him seem to Nellie much younger than he was. The Rodgers did not go to church or to social affairs, but in some fashion Nellie and Jesse managed to see each other in the course of the months. The next year, when she was 14, they began "to go together."

The children of the early years of settlement were growing up, they were young people now, full of the zest of living, the exuberance, the vitality, the gregariousness of youth. They met at church, the literary society, parties, sing songs. In good years they had taffy pulls in each other's houses, melting the butter, adding the molasses, sugar, and vinegar, watching the pot bubble, pouring the viscid brownish-yellow mass on a greased pan to cool, picking up a ball of it in buttered hands, stretching, folding it over and stretching again, pulling, stretching and folding until the cords turned light golden yellow and hardened into chewable, delicious taffy. And all the while, chattering and laughing and teasing. Warren and Ada must have recalled the boiling of the maple sap and the sugaring off in old New York.[2]

Occasionally they had a box supper at the church or school. Each woman or girl made her own box, filled it with goodies, decorated it, and put it on the table for the auctioneer to sell. The proceeds were used to buy a piece of much needed furniture, or books for the school. Nellie took her first box when she was 13 or 14-years-old, after she had met Jesse Rodgers. Perhaps she hoped that he would be there to bid on it. But he did not come. A young boy bought it, Harlan Martin's new stepson. He was "a real little gentleman," got a cup of water for her, "no man could have been more polite or courteous."

Those were the years when the generation of the young, taking over their own entertainment, introduced the dance to Methodist Ridge. And prompted Brother DuVal to denounce it and threaten to drive the dancers out of the hall and the devil out of the community. "C.A." of Hopewell heard "much talk" against "the religious reformers" of the Ridge. The church had been treated with respect even by those who did not agree with it. He was sorry that some of its members, "wanting in common sense," would bring "a fight against their church." "Billy the Kid," who had mocked Brother DuVal for fighting the devil, was relieved when a dance on the Ridge "went off," and "no bloodshed either." He did not favor dances and hoped that there would be no more of them, but "under the circumstances," he was "glad to see the program carried out."[3]

Nellie did not dance, but she loved parties. That fall when the young people gathered at a neighbor's house, it was too cold to play outside. The host had a big house, with three rooms, so they pushed the furniture back and played inside. Nellie got kissed. She was especially embarrassed because it was ladies' choice and she chose her partner. She really didn't know him. She had seen him a time or two at church and at literary, but never at a party or with a girl. His sister was an invalid and Nellie, going after the mail, had stopped several times to see her. The boy was always in the field. They lined up that night, the girls in one row, boys in the other, partners across from each other. At a given signal the girl at the head of the line started running for the rear, her partner after her. If he caught the girl he got to kiss her--if he could. When it came her turn, Nellie ran and the boy caught her. "I got it on the cheek," she said, and "oh how they did laugh at me."

It is not likely that Jesse went to the parties. He was too shy, and had he gone Nellie would have recounted it. But he did go, at least occasionally, to literary and to school exercises, "exhibitions," where not only the children recited but adults sometimes provided "entertainment." The literary society met once a month, on Friday evenings, from late fall until early spring. The whole community came out, 52 "active" members one winter. Charley Nichols, now a stable young farmer, his breach of conventional ways long since forgotten--or forgiven, was president in 1894-95. They had spelling bees, ciphering matches, songs, dialogues, debates. And one evening James Mansfield successfully prosecuted an accused criminal and sent him to the penitentiary "for life." Now and then someone persuaded Albert and Jesse Rodgers to play, Albert his violin, Jesse his bass viol.[4]

Nellie had enjoyed school, both being there and the coming and going. It was a mile from their house, a little more, to the schoolhouse. The Saling girls from across the road often walked with them, and the Abbott children, walking south along the property line between the Clarks and McMullens, joined the others for the last half mile, east to the Ridge road and the schoolhouse. One afternoon Mary and Nellie and the Saling girls encountered a rattlesnake on the way home. They knew the stories of the poisonous snake, death to those who were struck, people or stock, if not treated quickly, and they knew the folk remedies, too, a piece of salt pork or a freshly killed chicken to draw the poison, or the application of kerosene or turpentine. But no one ever let a rattlesnake get away. So the girls stood in a circle around it and Mary or Nellie (each girl remembered having done it) ran to the house, almost a half mile away, to get Ada. She couldn't come but she sent the hoe and one of the older Saling girls killed the snake.

Nellie remembered, too, the time they teased the Abbotts. They had parted at the corner, the Abbotts turning north, the Clark children continuing west. After they had gone some distance, the Abbotts stopped, stooped over or dropped to their knees, apparently hunting for something. Nellie and Mary were hard put to guess what the Abbotts were doing. And the Abbotts wouldn't say. Nellie and Mary guessed: they were hunting and catching grasshoppers to put in their soup for supper. That was a good joke, evocative of much bantering and no explanation, but good for 50 years.

It was fun, one day at school, when Rome Smith's boy, Otto, gathered up a handful of snow at recess, stepped into the school room where three or four girls were sitting, tugged at Nellie's collar and put the snow down the back of her neck. She and other girls ran him down "and really washed his face with snow." It was no fun when, running down the slope adjacent to the schoolhouse, she twisted her foot and fell, badly spraining her ankle, perhaps breaking the bone. Her leg turned blue from her toes to her knee. Her mother put hot hops and vinegar packs on it each evening and wrapped it in a bandage each morning. She missed school for a few days and then Papa let her ride the pony, Cola. She stabled it at the McMullens', across the road from the new schoolhouse, and had only a short distance to walk. She played no more running games. The ankle was tender and sore for several years. For the rest of her school days, Nellie kept tally for the games, helped the teacher, or knit for herself. They called her teacher's pet.

Nellie was 14 when she began going with Jesse Rodgers in the summer of 1894. She could not have gone often. Literary had closed for the year, the school term had ended, and in that dry summer there were very few social functions. Nellie was working for the Ross Beards who lived three miles to the west of the Clarks. Methodists and friends of Warren and Ada, they attended the Hougland Sunday School which was closer to them and more accessible--fewer canyons to cross. Nellie knew them well from other church functions, picnics, meetings in town. The Beards had the measles: Ross and his wife, Eva, and their two little girls. The hired man, who had brought the disease to them, had scarcely recovered enough to do the chores. The Beards hired a German girl, Amelia Wittwer, whose parents were homesteaders four or five miles south of the Clarks. Amelia was 17, but the work was too much for her, so they sent the hired man to get Nellie.

The girls became fast friends, and remained friends for life. And we can guess that working at the Beards gave Nellie some opportunity to be with Jesse Rodgers. Jesse's sister Effie, and her husband, Frank Miller, lived on the homestead to the west, probably less than a half mile from the Beards. Nellie tells us only that she went with Jesse and that his mother "fussed & fussed" about it. She didn't want any of her children to get married and five of them, all adults, were still at home, single. Again we must guess how Nellie knew that Mrs. Rodgers "fussed and fussed." It is not likely that big, shy, quiet Jesse said much, or anything, about it. Very probably Effie, the oldest child and the only married one, talked, and talked a-plenty, her eyes flashing and her tongue clucking, not to Nellie, but to Mrs. Beard when she dropped in to see her and to inquire about the family. And no doubt she encouraged Jesse to break out of the maternal bondage, to see the Clark girl if he wanted to.

Jesse saw her, took her to church or Sunday school, or to whatever social function might have occurred in that dreary summer. But not many times. Nellie was not 14 until the middle of May. It was later that month, or June, when she worked for the Beards. About the first of September the Rodgers closed up their place, loaded some of their household goods into wagons, and like many others in Hayes county, left for more hospitable country, for them, Arkansas. Mrs. Rodgers had a niece down there. The reason for their going, Nellie believed then, and believed all of her life, was not to escape the drought but that "she could break us up if she got him away."

That was the fall when the Rev. J.C. DuVal reported to Hayes Center, Palisade, and the country churches, as the newly appointed Methodist preacher. He took up his duties about the first of October and quickly established himself as a powerful preacher and an energetic leader. The Clarks, Nellie said, always took in any minister who preached for them. DuVal came often. He was a widower, perhaps 35-years-old. Nellie was grownup for her age, a mature young lady and a teacher in the Sunday school. He found her attractive and wanted her to go out with him. Warren and Ada, whatever reservation they may have had about Nellie's age, made no objection. After all, he was the preacher. No critical word about him had yet appeared in the *Republican* and the gossips had not yet begun to talk.[5]

Nellie didn't like him, didn't want to go out with him, but given his urging, probably his teasing, she went "a few times." Just before Christmas, six weeks after DuVal had come to the circuit, Jesse Rodgers returned to Hayes County, thoroughly disenchanted with Arkansas. He stayed with Effie and Frank Miller, his sister and brother-in-law. Nellie "quit the preacher real quick." Two months later DuVal was married to a young woman in Palisade.[6]

Nellie and Jesse quickly resumed their courtship. Under Nellie's tutelage, Jesse soon learned, as she put it, to be "the social type." They went together, as the sparse social fare of Blackwood permitted--to Sunday school, literary, school exhibitions, parties, and down to see Amelia Wittwer. Nellie had come to regard Amelia as her closest friend. To call on her satisfied both her desire to be with Jesse and her wish to see Amelia.

For six months Jesse worked for a neighbor, then rented a farm. His family, having been gone a year, came back from Arkansas in the fall of 1895, bringing with them their household goods and Jesse's horses.[7]

Jesse and Nellie continued to keep company for another six months, a year and a half altogether after his return, until May, 1896, when they were married. Nellie was 16, Jesse 28. Warren Clark, Nellie's father, as justice of the peace, read the ceremony. Mary Clark and Amelia Wittwer signed the certificate as witnesses. Amelia was the only non-family member present. The Rodgers declined to attend, said "they didn't have clothes fit to come in." Nellie thought that a poor excuse. "It was no fine affair," she said. Jesse wore the pants and coat he had been wearing to church. Grandma Harris had sent her a flowered lawn dress, one that she had worn herself, "very pretty," Nellie thought. She altered it to fit her, put on a lace collar, a ribbon sash, and ribbon bows on the shoulders. Papa bought her a new pair of low shoes, the first she had ever owned.[8]

Ada must have been full of memories, recollections of her own wedding, the fine new clothes her father had bought for her, the Hamburg lace, the ear drops, the gold pendant at her throat, and the chest of clothing she had for her trousseau. She may have experienced a touch of anguish, suppressed an urge to call down the wrath of heaven on such a harsh land. It is more likely that she had long since made her peace with the land as it was, and that if she suffered some anguish, she avoided exacerbating her spirit by not calling in the neighbors to look on their poverty. She said no word to shatter or mar the happiness of her daughter. But she had not forgotten those days long past. A decade later when Earl married and she saw his lovely bride in her wedding gown, Ada remembered and sent to her new daughter-in-law a snippet of lace and a bit of cloth from her own wedding finery.[9]

They settled on Jacob Wiggins' homestead, that Jesse had been farming on shares, only a mile and a half north of the Clarks. Jake and his family had moved to Culbertson where he had established or taken over a business of selling farm wagons and machinery. He had done much to improve his place--had put in a windmill with attached gear and stones to grind corn, put up good barns and sheds, and purchased and bred good livestock. He supplied cows to milk--Nellie got the butter--, he gave Jesse a percentage of the increase in hogs, furnished him with horses and machinery. Ada gave Nellie six hens and eggs to set two of them. Nellie bought more eggs and soon had a hundred chickens, young roosters to sell or eat and "a nice bunch of hens."

They had a great time together in those first months. They always attended Sunday school and church and parties, and when winter came, the literary society. They drove down to see Amelia Wittwer and her fiance, Frank Miller, a German who had anglicized the spelling of his name. Amelia and Frank came to see them. They drove to the Wittwers' again for Amelia and Frank's wedding. The party began in the morning and lasted all day, until after supper, when the wedding ceremony at last took place. The merry company sang, drank beer, danced to the tune of an accordion and two fiddles. But not Nellie and Jesse. After the ceremony Frank passed out cigars, even to the women. Nellie kept them, wrapped and stored them away. Twenty-five years later, when Amelia and Frank came to call, Nellie got out the cigars and Frank and Jesse sat on the porch and smoked them.

Some crises broke into the carefree routine and were difficult for a young bride to handle, not easy for anyone in Blackwood or Hayes County. In October a three-day blizzard struck. Jesse was sick. Nellie did the chores, one cow to be milked, others to be fed, and eight horses to be fed and led out to water twice a day--she dared not release them lest they bolt for the pasture, get lost in the storm, and freeze to death. Half of her chickens died in the drifting snow and the cold. She was almost sick herself.

That was the storm when Mary and Earl, who was 10, almost got lost on the way home from school. The wind came up in the afternoon, whipping the snow, threatening a blizzard. The teacher dismissed the children. He boarded with the Clarks but he sent Earl and Mary on their way while he secured the windows and door. They followed the fence for a half mile before the teacher caught up with them. Holding hands, the three of them cut across the field, the wind blowing the snow in their faces, half blinding them. They misjudged their direction, veered off towards the south, when they should have gone northwest. At length they encountered a fence, followed it to the corner post, and knew where they were. They turned north, following the west boundary fence to its end at their dooryard, and found the house, scarcely visible in the thick and swirling snow.

At last, with a break in the storm, Dock Gruver came by, looking for a lost calf. He helped Nellie do the chores, went on home and finding Jim Scott's boy there on a horse, sent him to the Clarks. They got word to the Rodgers. Albert and John came at once, and one of them went for the doctor. Jesse had typhoid fever. He was sick for weeks. Some one of the Rodgers stayed to help Nellie--Albert, John, Mrs. Rodgers briefly, and Charles, Jesse's father. The old man caught cold, was sick for several weeks, was removed to his daughter Effie's home, and suddenly died. It was Nellie's first encounter with death in the family. The neighbors gathered, Warren helped build a coffin, someone furnished a sheet to line it, others bathed and dressed the deceased. The family asked Nellie to cut a curl from the back of his neck, where his hair was soft and beautiful. They buried him in the churchyard on the Ridge.[10]

The next year Nellie went back to school. She had little to do at the house, only Jesse and herself to cook for, not much more chores or housework than she had done at home. Mr. Wiggins had a pony she could ride, and she liked school. For two months she was back in the classsroom with Earl and her sisters and neighboring young people. "I took," she wrote in her memoirs, with a touch of pride, "what would now be called 9th grade work."

Then Mr. Wiggins decided to build a new barn to protect his stock. He hired Albert and John to help Jesse. Nellie had to cook and keep house for all of them. Her school days were over. Thereafter she was a farmer's wife. It would be another half-dozen years before she would become a mother.

# 24.
# Nubbin Ridge

1896 was a year of great hope, the most promising since 1891. Six inches of snow had fallen in late November, 1895, enough, up in the sandhill country to "insure good crops for '96." In Germanville precinct, the cribs had filled up even in the dry year of 1895. Warm weather and a big rain in January set farmers all over the county to plowing fields and breaking prairie to get more land under cultivation. For the most part the days were sunny, an "open winter," "Italian skies from September to February." It was like the winter of 1890-91, the editor of the Arapahoe *Mirror* thought, "unusually mild and such a crop year as followed was never known in the state of Nebraska before or since." The rains continued into February and March, more rains in three months than in any one of the past three years. It rained again in April, "clear from the top down," Abbott said, falling steadily from Saturday noon to Sunday noon, two inches altogether. Barney Hofer of the *Times* vowed that the grass grew so fast that "it actually scared the live stock." "Fact," he added. Ben Southwell, Warren Clark's neighbor on Methodist Ridge, boasted to Abbott that he had 40 acres of corn "big enough to show three leaves."[1]

Disaster fell so quickly and so unexpectedly that the country correspondents, in their exultation over the rain, had no foretaste of it. A short hot spell in May damaged the wheat and it suffered again when the first ten rainless days of June reduced extravagant predictions to hope for "a fair crop." Abbott confessed that "the crop will be extremely short." Harvest confirmed his fears. Even in Germanville, where the yield was nearly always good, the best of the wheat threshed out at 12 bushels to the acre.[2]

More rains came in June, in time for the corn, "the finest rain of the season" in early July. The corn in Hopewell, just west of Blackwood, "never looked better." On Methodist Ridge it grew so rapidly, the correspondent boasted, that farmers hurried to complete their final plowing before they got lost in the field. The reporters stepped up their chant of exultation: "Great corn weather," "the corn looks fine and the farmers look finer."[3]

It was a great summer for other produce, domestic and wild. Henry Wiswall picked 17 quarts of cherries, his first crop, from a tree he had planted in 1890. Plums and wild grapes were plentiful, the watermelon crop "immense." One farmer brought into Hayes Center a squash that weighted 71 pounds, another a gallon of plums for editor Abbott.[4]

Temperatures soared the first week of August and no rain came. The corn in Hopewell, just west of Blackwood, soon was "badly sunstroked." In nearby Thornburg, where the corn "roasted on short notice," the reporter was despairing and contemptuous. "The simple possibility of frail mortality subsisting eternally upon faith and south wind is too egregious for even our venturesome Yankee nature." He would leave Hayes County, "henceforth and forever." It was the second week of August. The farmers had already begun to cut their corn for fodder.[5]

Ben Southwell, his 40 acres of promising corn burned to a crisp, took off for northeast Nebraska to find work. And so did John Wiswall, Henry's son, and to look for a more propitious place for them to farm. John Theovalt, good friend of Warren Clark, left the county for the third time and a month later sent for his wife and children to join him at Holdrege. He would not return. Others were on the move, "a great exodus" from all southwest Nebraska, the Palisade correspondent reported. Henry Wiswall, after a favorable report from his son, announced his intent to move to Buffalo County, east of Kearney. He packed up his goods and he and his family, with two wagons and a herd of cattle, headed east in mid-November. Miles Abbott mourned. He was "one of the most thorough, up-to-date farmers that Hayes county ever had."[6]

On Methodist Ridge the fall was "nice weather for gathering corn," observed the correspondent, "but where, O, where is the corn in the south half of the county." Selecting his country name place from undeveloped ears of corn, he wrote under the ironic caption **Nubbin Ridge**. Whatever the failure in Blackwood, the corn crop was good in the sandy loam of the county's northern townships, 20 to 40 bushels to the acre in Germanville, "a large crop" in Valley precinct. Warren Clark went north to Germanville, Jim Abbott and his son to Fairfield, John Spickelmier from the Highland slope of Methodist Ridge to Lincoln County, all to pick corn.[7]

1897 was the wettest year since 1891. The *Times* declared droughts "a thing of the past." Harlan Martin boasted that he had a fine piece of fall wheat that would make "at least 15 bushels to the acre." A week of dry, hot weather damaged the small grain and the farmers were happy to settle, as Miles Abbott put it, for "a full half crop." The corn, booming in early July, wilted for want of rain before the month was over. Local showers saved some of it and none was a failure. No one on Methodist Ridge had reason to boast. Nor was there much reason to rejoice even among the successful farmers, for what they harvested brought only 15 cents a bushel at Palisade. And that fall Hayes was the only county without a display at the state fair.[8]

The rainfall in 1898, less than in the two preceding years, was timely. The wheat averaged about 17 bushels to the acre, the best since 1891. And in the pattern now well established, corn was good in the northern precincts. (Harry McGinnis, in the sandy loam of Valley Precinct, raised 5,000 bushels), but it was light on Methodist Ridge and in the southern townships. And so it was in succeeding years. No crop failures, but no bountiful yields. When the weather was damp they had cutworms, when it was dry, the corn burned. They had grasshoppers every year, "millions of the little pests," "totally destroying" gardens and some of the fields.[9]

And every year they had wind, in March and April, chiefly. It swept across the level plain, brushing lightly over the short buffalo grass, its force broken in the canyons by the irregular walls. But it roared across the fields, whipping the dust into great clouds, driving the tiny pellets into a farmer's face, stinging, half blinding, choking him, smarting in his nostrils, bitter on his tongue. Warren hadn't noticed the wind much in the first years when he had plowed only a few acres, for the newly turned sod, bound by roots of the grass, did not blow. Now he saw his good top soil swept from his field. "Plenty of real estate changing hands," a country correspondent joked.[10]

The women may have suffered more than the men, in spirit at least, with no one in the lonely house but children, often cross and fretful in the choking dust. When they stepped through the door the wind struck them, sent their skirts and petticoats swirling about them, clinging to their legs as they plowed their way to the chickenhouse for eggs, or to the well or the outhouse. Within, they could hear it in the incessant slapping of a loose board, the banging of an unfastened barn door or window shutter, in the clanging and groaning of the windmill, and for a few of them, in the crash of the falling tower. When the wind blew less angrily, it sought out the hollows of the sod walls, the irregular fittings of wood and earth, and whistled and moaned over the apertures, an unharnessed and harassing ghost. There is a sad tale, still told in Blackwood, of a young bride, unable to cope with the great spaces, the wind, and the loneliness, who now lies, and has lain since those early years, in the German cemetery near the Lutheran church, not far from the Lone Tree. Most of the women endured, conquered the wind and the solitude, as long as their husbands could hold on.[11]

Whether the farmer suffered anguish or built up a growing sense of hostility and injustice because of the loss of his crop, he had no idea of the devastation he himself wrought when he plowed so deeply, with such pride in the cleanness of his field, its freedom from weeds and stubble, no thought of the dust bowl in the making. It would be two generations or three before his children's children, and their children, would learn the techniques of soil conservation, of terracing to hold the moisture, stubble mulching, chiseling to leave a crop residue, a ground cover, all to check the blowing dust. The early settler could only pull out of the field until the rain settled the dust, as it always had save that one disastrous year, and replant what he must.[12]

Warren and Ada did not prosper but they got along. They had warm and serviceable clothes and plenty to eat--chicken and eggs, beef and pork, butter and cheese, potatoes, beans, green vegetables and melons in the summer, fruit from the canyon walls, corn meal and wheat flour from their fields. They suffered from no more droughts like that of 1894. Having grown up on subsistence farms, in families largely self-sufficient, they did not ask for much. They traded Ada's hens and eggs and young roosters for provisions at the store, sold some butter, cheese, and occasionally a beef, and Warren marketed his young steers. The cow and the hen, said the *Times*, "are the standbys in hard times to furnish the wherewith for the comfort of a family. . . ."[13]

But Nebraska was not upstate New York. Hayes County was too far from market, the weather too uncertain for truck farming or small cash crops. With the persistently light yields in wheat and corn, and the narrow margin between success and failure, Warren needed to increase his production. He could do it only with better machinery and more horses to cultivate more acres. After 1894 the rain was sufficient and timely enough for the native grasses to flourish. It was enough, too, for the wheat to make fair pasture and the corn good fodder, even when the grain shriveled and the stalks dried up. Warren rented extra pasture from Saling and when Ab sold out and moved away, from the new owner. He borrowed against the future to buy machinery--he was always in debt, his son was to say--, but he borrowed prudently, only enough to get his most needed tools, never enough to require a mortgage or a lien on his property. He replaced his eastern corn planter with a walking lister which, with its deep furrow to collect and hold the rain, was better suited to this dry climate. Then, to conserve his own energy, he bought a riding lister. "Too near the 20th century to walk," said a country correspondent. He bought a mowing machine and at haying time left his scythe hanging in the barn while he sat on the machine that the horses pulled across the canyon floor, dropping the tall grass in flat windrows. He traded his labor to Harlan Martin for the use of a binder. In 1896 Earl was 10-years-old and big for his age. Warren put him in the field, cultivating corn, nearly doubling his work force in the busiest of the summer months.[14]

Some in the neighborhood did quite well, made little splashes of prosperity. Frank Dye, the county commissioner from Logan precinct, bought a new buggy. That should not have been surprising, for with a salary of $500 a year, he could afford it, but it was unusual enough for the *Times* to exclaim, "such is life in Hayes county." It was news when Grandpa McMullen traded for one and more surprising when Harlan Martin, in 1897, bought "a fine new top buggy" to drive his new wife about the neighborhood. Even a grade B buggy from Sears Roebuck, with freight, cost nearly $50 and one in that class retailed at wagon dealers for about $75. Jim Abbott had enough enterprise and help from his boys to plaster his house and to build a "mansion" for his hens. He was going to feed them kaffir corn, get two eggs a day from them, "by gum," and sell the eggs by the bushel basket. Moreover, he had acquired enough stock for the editor of the *Times* to think him "quite a cattle king."[15]

Warren Clark, whatever his struggles with the land, stood well with his neighbors. He remained a leader in the church, a member of the school and cemetery boards. In 1897 he was re-elected justice of the peace, his third successive two-year term, eight years in that office since 1887. Before the year was well advanced, the Blackwood assessor resigned and moved to Oklahoma. Neighbors carried a petition for Warren and the commissioners appointed him to the office. It carried a small compensation for services rendered. In anticipation of the income and to aid him in getting around the township, he bought a small road cart, a topless buggy, which cost him, probably, twenty to twenty-five dollars. In June he turned in a bill for $36. The commissioners allowed him $33, enough to pay for the cart. That fall he was elected to the office and the next summer collected $30 for his services.[16]

Ada began the year 1896 in sorrow. Her father, Nathaniel Harris, had died in late December. She must have received the word about New Year's day. For weeks she had waited anxiously for every report from home. Her mother, Amelia Jane, had written down "things as they happened," day by day, and Albert's wife Julia had helped--what Pa had to say, how he had led family prayer up to November 29 and then, too weak to kneel, had asked Ma to pray; what songs Ma sang to him at his bedside--*Our Weary Days Will Soon Be Over*, *Safe in the Arms of Jesus*, *More Like Jesus Would I Be*--that, he said "is a good hymn." A few days before his death he lost his voice and when Amelia Jane questioned him could respond only with a slight movement of his head. Three hours before he died she asked if he could hear what she said. He motioned yes. She asked, "Are you trusting in the Savior?" He moved his head forward in response. He was only a month past his sixty-third birthday when he died. Ada read it all in anguish, cherished every word, relived her childhood on the wooded hillside. There was no way that she could have joined her mother and her brothers. Warren could not afford it. Amelia Jane would not have expected it. Nathaniel had gone in triumph, he had earned a "calm sleep and a sweet rest." "Rest for [his] spirit, glad and free."[17]

Ada had no cause for grief at home. Other families among her friends and neighbors had lost a child: the Roberts, the Beards, the George Scotts, the Dock Gruvers, or children had lost a mother or father: Eliza Jane McMullen, Emma Martin, Eva McKenzie, Levi Gruver. Ada's children, six of them, were well and strong. Mary was in school through the spring of 1897, when she was 15, perhaps through 1898 when she began to spend much of her time at Nellie's. That annoyed Ada. If Mary would stay at home and do the housework, Ada wrote to Ma, she could, herself, work out for women who were ill or had babies, as she had done for one neighbor, and earn $5.00 a week. But Mary would not do it. Little Jesse was still at home, Earl, Flora, and Jennie all in the Pleasant Ridge school in 1898. The school was well attended with the Clarks, the Abbotts, the McMullens, the Scotts, Asa Smith, Rome's son, the Martins, Rose and Bertha Jeffries, Ellworth's nieces who were living with him and Maggie, and others, 28 children in all, the oldest, Charley Abbott, nearly 20. Shaffer McMullen, J.H. Martin, and W.F. Clark were the board members, Hiram Picket, a United Brethren preacher, the teacher.[18]

That winter Warren and Ada took the children who were still at home to Culbertson for a photograph, the four of them solemnly facing the camera. Flora and Jennie were in twin dresses, wool plaids with plain tops, long sleeves, braid trimming at the wrists, on the shoulders, and looping down to form a necklace below the high collar; and black stockings and high-buttoned shoes. Earl, 11-years-old, stood stiffly in his three-piece suit, his dark wool coat buttoned at the top under the short lapels, parting to show his vest, a man's black stock against his white collar. Jesse wore a boy's coat of somewhat the same cut, knee pants, a big patterned bow tie, and buttoned shoes. They were a handsome lot.[19]

With the big school and the children growing up, Pleasant Ridge was a lively neighborhood. They had a fine closing exhibition in 1897 with exercises in spelling and ciphering and well-delivered recitations. Spelling was fun for the adults, too, at the literary society where Rome Smith proved that he could spell "ax" and someone discovered that Webster said there were two ways to spell "syrup." Debates vied with spelling bees for popularity. At Thornburg the question was: "that the present tariff is a detriment to the American people." In that Republican community, the decision was for the negative. At Hougland schoolhouse, where Jim Lakin was the society chairman, they argued the proposition "that Curiosity will lead a person further than Necessity will drive him." Methodist Ridge debated a romantic issue, "that a man will go further for the love of a woman than for the love of gold." Young people attended not only their own societies but those at neighboring schoolhouses, "quite a number" from Methodist Ridge at Hougland school, young people from Sunny Hill at Methodist Ridge.[20]

At the Eureka Grange's annual Children's Day, in 1897, 140 people were in attendance, most of them from Methodist Ridge. Wesley Gruver presided, Grandpa McMullen gave the prayer, a schoolteacher an address, Mariette Wemple and Nellie Gruver, recitations. They started early in the morning, a choir sang, the Methodist Ridge banjo and violin club rendered "fine selections," which were "especially appreciated." Such a "grade of music," said the correspondent, was "seldom heard in western Nebraska." The climax was an address by the master of the state Grange. The program went on nearly all afternoon until the women unpacked their baskets and spread the food on the table for a late dinner: chicken, boiled ham, light bread, pie, cakes, coffee, "in great abundance." And then ice cream, group singing, and a "social time," meaning talk, until almost six o'clock and time for chores.[21]

Much else that was exciting went on in the county these days. Palisade had a new half-mile racetrack that could "accommodate the fastest horses in the country." With an early balloon ascension, immediately after the midday dinner, and with Hayes Center and Trenton joining, the promoters expected to have a thousand people for the Fourth of July celebration. Sometime in these years a touring company brought a big tent, probably to Culbertson, and played *Uncle Tom's Cabin*. The Clarks went to see it. They had already read the book. The Driscol boys, from Methodist Ridge, bought a graphaphone and entertained crowds of people in Hayes Center, Palisade, and even Culbertson where they took in "a neat little sum." About the same time, February, 1898, someone brought a moving picture--*Edison's Kinetoscope Show*, to the Methodist church at

Hayes Center, admission for adults, 25 cents, children 15 cents. "Very seldom, said the *Times*, in giving notice of the event, does "a little berg [sic], like Hayes Center, have an opportunity to witness such a wonder." Viewers would see "every scene as it would take place before your eyes." The next week's *Times* thought the show "a grand success. The pictures were as natural as could be."[22]

The Methodist church in Hayes County suffered some loss of membership and was, R. S. Moore, the presiding elder, reported to the annual conference, "a difficult field." But it remained vigorous. The "supply" pastors, for the most part young, unmarried men, not yet educated for the ministry, seemed to do quite well. The *Times* thought one "a good talker" who would "do good here," another delivered "an excellent sermon," and one "fit like an old shoe." One of them succeeded in raising enough money to build a parsonage in Hayes Center, the sod church on Methodist Ridge contributing $25 for the enterprise. On the Ridge, Newton Wemple held an ice-cream social to raise money for the preacher. Quarterly meetings remained an attraction to many in the neighborhood, including Rome Smith. Warren Clark, Shaffer McMullen, and Dock Gruver were delegates one spring--probably were often delegates, but this time reported by the correspondent--and drove, with Ada accompanying them, northwest of Hayes Center to the meeting at Elmer. That was some 25 miles, not too far in one of the new light wagons. When R.S. Moore, as Presiding Elder, came to Hayes Center to hold the quarterly meeting the *Republican* praised him as "an able man." He was, said Abbott, "greeted by many old friends who were much pleased to meet him again." But membership at the Ridge had declined and the sod church, a decade old, had begun to sag a little.[23]

For many, in these years, fraternal organizations, lodges, began to take over the functions of the grange and informal social gatherings. There were four of them in Hayes Center: the Odd Fellows, the Masons, the Ancient Order of United Workmen (AOUW), and Modern Woodmen of America (MWA). Abbott thought the town needed "about 40 barrels of paint" and not so many lodges. The community paid over $100 a month to lodges and couldn't raise $10 for the minister and the Sunday school. They should paint the school and the church, grade the streets, and kill half the lodges.[24]

The appeal was in the secret order, the prescribed ritual, and the good times. Men reasoned that the lodges were insurance groups, organized for the mutual aid of their members at time of death. For a man of Warren Clark's age, the assessment was about $5.00 a year for a $500 benefit. It was the only group insurance available and a godsend to those who could not afford life insurance. And Miles Abbott, despite his criticism, belonged to all four of the orders and boosted them regularly in his columns, citing examples of benefit payments to widows.[25]

The MWA quickly won the support of Methodist Ridge. Ross Beard was the first to join, followed by Dock Gruver, James Abbott, J.B. Smith, and a little later Shaffer McMullen, N.L. Wemple, Warren Clark, and doubtless others not named by the correspondent. The "camp" met twice a month, on the first and third Saturday evenings. Officials stood at stations, members whispered the password, made the secret signs, and reenacted a drama of the order's charitable giving. Initiation was often hilarious, bantering before and after about "riding the goat" and branding the candidate by pressing a piece of ice against his naked back. The solemn rite concluded with the formation of a "hollow" square about the urn in the center of the room, the recitation in concert of the "Woodsmen's honors," and a brief, "inspirational" speech from the presiding Consul, all saved from the ludicrous by the common love of secrecy and ritual, the warm feelings of friendship, and the undeniable testimony of charitable services rendered. The social functions improved when the women's auxiliary, the Royal Neighbors, was formed in 1897 or 1898.[26]

Warren Clark, surveying his neighborhood in the spring of 1899, must have looked about him with troubled eye. The community, like the sod church, was crumbling. Ab and Alice Saling and their eight girls who had lived across the road, Ab who had dug his well and plastered it, and for whom he had done so much farm work and chores in exchange, Ab and Alice were gone, had been gone for four years. And Ben Southwell, his impulsive, sometimes hotheaded neighbor on the south, faced with the prospect of another crop failure, had in March two years ago taken off for Plainview in northeast Nebraska. This spring Ross and Eva Beard had moved to Kansas. Harlan Martin made a trip to Washington state and returned "not liking the country." But he soon purchased land in eastern

Kansas and prepared to move. That was the greatest blow of all. From the first, Warren had loved Harlan like a brother, had worked with him more than with any other man on the Ridge. And Ada and the girls had been close to Emma Martin and to Mary, Harlan's mother, and to Cora, his second wife, often in each others' homes to sew, mend clothes and talk while the men worked. They had been guests for Sunday dinner, ridden together to quarterly meeting and children's day picnics. That was a loss beyond repair.[27]

Disaster had struck Rome Smith, an old curmudgeon, a sinner and a troublemaker, but likeable in his own way, a frequent associate in the community's business and the affairs of church, grange and school, and now and then a guest at the Clarks for Sunday dinner. In 1897 his wife, Mary, sued him for divorce--for "cruel and inhuman treatment." She won the case and custody of their young daughter. Rome stayed on, trying to make the best of it. He was often in the "Nubbin Ridge" news for attendance at literary, Sunday school, quarterly meeting, with his neighbors or with his grandchildren, Nellie and Dock Gruver's children. He brought out a widow from Missouri as a housekeeper and squired her to church, school exercises and literary functions. But it was no use. Unable to handle the mortgage on the farm he had acquired from his brother Ed, he let the creditor take his course. He relinquished his tree claim, got what he could from it, and left the community.[28]

Many others could not cope with the mortgages and uncertain crops. Jim Scott lost the quarter section he had bought from Jacob Case, but he held on to his homestead. Charles and Kate Nichols, after having redeemed their social standing, suffered the foreclosure of the mortgage and the sale of their property. Of the 36 men and women who before 1890 had taken claims in the northeast corner of Blackwood, Methodist Ridge, only six remained: Elijah Driscol, Richard Roberts, Ellsworth Jeffries, Jim Scott, Brice McMullen, and Warren Clark, and two who had filed after 1890, Jim Abbott and Shaffer McMullen.[29]

J. Sterling Morton, a gold-standard Democrat, leading Nebraska statesman, Secretary of Agriculture in Grover Cleveland's administration, successful farmer, and editor of a monthly journal, the *Conservative*, traveled on the Burlington through southwest Nebraska in 1899. He was surprised and pleased to see, along the Republican River Valley, "the substantial improvements and evidence of thrift," the "comfortable, tasty homes, commodious barns, and acre after acre of alfalfa, corn and other cereals." He reflected, somewhat bitterly, on the first settlers, many of whom he judged "worthless, shiftless citizens . . . men who could not earn a living in the Garden of Eden, with free silver at the ratio of 16 to 1." Morton was right about the early speculators and even about the well-intentioned men of high hope and poor judgment. But he spoke harsh words, savage ones, to apply to men like Oscar Gruver, Ross Beard, Harlan Martin, Henry Wiswall, and two score others in Blackwood who had spent eight to ten, even twelve years, on the divide, under climatic conditions they could not cope with, on land they could not convert into profitable farms. As for Warren Clark, he had no intention to leave. He went up to the sandhills for corn, put out Paris green to fight the grasshoppers, and built more fence to pasture his cattle.[30]

# 25.
# The Sandhills Are Destined

In the first years of the new century, the Clarks were much in the eye of the Hope correspondent, the most frequently mentioned family on Methodist Ridge. The items about them are so much more intimate and detailed than those about others that one is compelled to believe that the correspondent was a Clark--it was not unusual for the reporter to favor her own family, as Emma Jackson had when she wrote for Highland over the name "Vox." The most likely candidate is Ada, herself. Mary, now called Mamie, was living with Nellie and Jesse Rodgers, near Palisade; Flora 13 and Jenny 12 were too young to take responsibility for the numerous and regularly appearing items. Ada, if indeed it were she, reverted to the simple style of her teenage diary, reporting who did what, when.[1]

Shaffer McMullen and his new wife, Mary Jacobs from nearby Thornburg, and the Ellsworth Jeffries were at the Clarks for Sunday dinner, the Rev. B. L. Gaither, and his wife and little daughter Audra, called one afternoon, the Clarks went to the Satchells for dinner, to the Jim Abbotts, to the Driscols, the Jim Scotts. The Satchells, the Abbotts, the Scotts called on the Clarks, most of them for Sunday dinner. There were new people in the community, the Jacob Brights, the William Effenbachs, the Thomases, all renters, at least initially, and all Methodists or friends of the Methodists, whom the Clarks quickly drew into their circle.[2]

Warren was sick a few days with the grippe, Richard Roberts hurt his hand and for several weeks was unable to work in the field, scarcely able to do his chores. Earl, 15, out in the stable before daylight to get his horse, hurt himself "quite badly" when he tripped over a calf sleeping on the floor. He fell forward, striking his stomach across the manger, but after a day or so he was "able to be around." Little Arley, last of the Clark children, born in June, 1900, was sick twice in the summer of 1901 and in August, 1902, he fell backward into a pail of hot water that Ada had just taken off the stove and put on the floor to scald a chicken. It was Arley who was "badly scalded--very painful but not serious." But it was traumatic--in his old age, Arley could reach far back in his memory--more than eighty years--to that unhappy event. In April, 1901, the Clarks and the Abbotts went together to the Jacob Bright's to see and admire their new baby, a fifth child and second son. Two and a half months later they joined their neighbors to bring solace to the weeping parents as they buried the tiny boy in the cemetery on Methodist Ridge.[3]

Warren helped Roberts put up a frame stable, he built some fence, and so did Jim Abbott and "most of the farmers," all working at the same time, perhaps helping each other. He and Charles Satchell hauled a load of coal from Culbertson to Hayes Center for the Rev. B.L.Gaither, and Warren hauled a load for himself--coal had come to replace wood as a fuel.[4]

And so the news, and the round of events, continued. One Saturday in July Grandpa McMullen, Bertha Jeffries--Ellworth's niece--, Warren and Ada Clark, Jim Abbott and his daughter Etta and son Calvin, Shaffer McMullen and his son Bud, and Cleve Scott were all in Hayes Center. Warren and Jim Abbott stayed Saturday night for a meeting of the MWA lodge, the rest went home to do the chores. The lodge brought Warren to town frequently, sometimes Ada with him for a supper or entertainment. In the summer of 1902 she joined the women's auxiliary and at the initiation "enjoyed a ride on the Royal Neighbor goat." That was quite a burden for the little beast, for Ada was rapidly gaining weight and had reached nearly 200 pounds.[5]

The Jim Scotts were great ones for parties--oyster stews in the winter, ice cream in the summer, or even in the spring, as in March, 1901, when "several of the friends and neighbors, both old and young" at their house "enjoyed a good time." We can judge that, with Ada the correspondent, the Clarks were in the party. A few weeks later Jesse, eight-years-old, was the only Clark in a company of grownups at the Scotts' for Sunday dinner. He, no doubt, had gone from Sunday school to play with Glen Scott, who was two years his junior.[6]

Despite the succession of dry years and partial failure of crops, Warren and Ada had, by the slow process of accretion, gained a little in possessions that added to their comfort and pleasure and to the efficiency of their work. Warren's old horse, Mage, brought from Iowa in 1885, an "old settler" by 1901, died and commanded a couple of lines in the Hope news items. Warren had already bought a replacement, and several other horses, too. In addition to his cart, he apparently bought a light ("spring") wagon or a buggy. Ada acquired a new freedom, and the children, too. She went alone, or with the little boys, Jesse and Arley, to call on her neighbors, or to visit Nellie and Mamie in Palisade. She and Claracy Bright drove over to Ella Scott's to help her quilt. She went into business herself, in a minor way, much more productive than the soap-making adventure of a dozen years before: using her loom to weave carpets, lovely, tight, tough fabrics, that she sold to ladies far and near--on the Ridge, in Hayes Center, and about the county. She became known and was acknowledged in the *Times* as "The Hope carpet weaver."[7]

With the increased mobility the Clarks extended their social exchanges beyond the tiny square that encompassed the Blackwood portion of Methodist Ridge: to the Charles Satchells in Highland, the William Effenbachs in Logan, the Franklin Hanks, down in section 26 of Blackwood precinct, the William Shupps in section 23. The Shupps did not enter into the jottings of the Ridge correspondents or Warren's diaries in the early years. Bill Shupp had taken out a tree claim in 1888 and converted it to a homestead four years later. But he was too far removed from the Martin school for the children to attend and the family had apparently gone to Sunday school and preaching at Sunny Hill in Highland. In these latter years the Methodists had given up Sunny Hill and the Shupps had come to the sod church. When Brother Gaither could not be present, Bill Shupp sometimes preached for them. The correspondent referred to him as "Brother" Shupp, a term the Methodists in their reports ordinarily reserved for the clergy, including local preachers licensed by the church to exhort.[8]

The extra horses emancipated the Clark children, too. So Earl, Flora, and Jennie, free from school one Friday, could visit Oresta Satchell where she was teaching in a neighboring district. Flora and Jennie could drive alone to visit the Satchell girls on Sunday afternoon or, with Jesse, to the Wittwers, five or six miles away, in section 26, and Jennie with Jesse and Arley, some 20 miles to Palisade to see Nellie and Mamie. Their friends had equal freedom: May Scott, Girty Thomas, Molly Hanks, and others, together or alone, making their way to the Clarks. Ada must have thought of her own girlhood on Stone Hill, walking, not riding, from one house to another.[9]

Jennie had a spill one day, riding the horse for the mail, probably hurrying him a little. He stumbled, she was thrown from his back, fell on her arm and broke it. Papa took her to Hayes Center to have Dr. Bostock set it and back again a few days later for him to check. Callers "too numerous to mention" came to the house to ask about her.[10]

Earl had even more freedom than his sisters, probably his own horse to ride. One Sunday he and the Satchell boys called on Arthur Shupp, just before he was to leave for Colorado to work on a ranch. Earl was only 15, the Satchell boys a little older, and Arthur a grownup 22, but they knew each other from church; Earl was large for his age, and old beyond his years. Another Sunday three Earls, Clark, McMullen, and Bright, all spent the afternoon with Cleve Scott, each no doubt on his own horse. Earl worked away from home that summer, 1901, for a month near Palisade, for the remainder of the summer and early fall for Frank Roe in the sandhills of Government precinct, a dozen miles north of his parents' homestead. He was home nearly every weekend, down on Saturday night, back Sunday night, either on his own horse or one he borrowed from Frank Roe. Warren and Ada drove up to see him one Saturday in September. It rained so hard they had to stay over until Sunday but Earl, anxious to see his friends, rode home through the storm. The drought did not dry up, nor did the rain dampen the spirits of the young.[11]

If there were social events those years, box suppers, literary, spelling bees, the correspondent did not write about them, or wrote in those weeks for which the record is no longer extant. There were dances in Hayes Center and in the country--so many in Thornburg, three in a two-week period, that the correspondent pleaded "why not have literary instead of so many dances?" When the Methodists held a protracted meeting in the sod church in the winter of 1902, Brother Gaither brought in his son from Scottsbluff to help in the preaching. Young Gaither left his text one Sabbath night "long enough to score the ballroom and dances, to a frazzle." But no matter. The Clark children at home were too young to be interested. Mamie who was at Nellie's was much enamored of Jesse Rodgers' brother, John, and John was too shy to go to church, let alone dance."[12]

Earl had been converted the year before in a Baptist meeting--"given his name to the church and been dedicated to the service of his creator by baptism," his grandmother, Amelia Jane Harris, Ada's mother, wrote in the stilted language of her generation. Earl was baptized by immersion but he held to the family loyalties and joined the Methodist church.[13]

Brother Gaither was well liked in Hayes Center and on the Ridge. "Few ministers and their families so endear themselves to this community," the *Times* said when it was announced that he would be reappointed for a second year, with his circuit enlarged to include Palisade. "The whole community welcomes his return."[14]

These had been good years in the church for Warren and Ada: their affection for the Gaithers, Earl's conversion, the faithfulness of the other children, protracted meetings both winters, camp meeting at Curtis, quarterly meetings conducted by their former pastor and neighbor, the Rev. R.S. Moore, now presiding elder for the district, the best of the preachers they had known on the Ridge, the best of their ministerial friends.

The bright dream of a better day on the plains had faded a little. The country correspondents, and Abbott, too, had given up on their expectation that men's activities could change the weather, that the rain would follow the plow. Many of them still possessed the hope that the good days of the eighties would return. A few of those who remained in the county might have been ready to curse God and, if not die, move on to a better place. In the fall of 1901 Miles Abbott, for political reasons, gave voice to the sentiment. He cited an aspirant for county office, "Peruvian Pete," a "godless character" who had cursed the recent heavy rains because they didn't come earlier. Said Pete: "Ol' God has got too old to govern the world. He don't attend to business anymore, and we will have to get a younger God in

His place one that will look after things better and make it rain at the right time."[15]

Abbott thought the idea too "blasphemous" to print, save that the old sinner ought to be exposed and defeated. Nearly the whole county would have thought it blasphemous. Certainly Warren and Ada. They did not view the failure of crops as a judgment of God. The rain falls on the just and the unjust. They painted the God of history in broader strokes, in the great promise and unhappy fate of the Chosen People, in the Manifest Destiny of America, the land now favored of God, not in the petty triumphs of little men or the tribulations of the poor. Two of their granddaughters, young adults with their own families, came to know their grandmother well, and to understand her views. If there were a fault, it was in the land, not in God. Men could move in the faith, as Harlan Martin had done, to improve their condition. Warren and Ada, remaining on their homestead, found solace in their faith, strength to bear the adversity, confirmation of their own faith in the preaching of the Word at the sod church and in the faith of their neighbors and the children. Above all, their children.[16]

Conditions were not much better for the Clarks or Methodist Ridge in the early 1900s than they had been in the last years of the old century. The snows and the rains came in the winter and early spring, once again bringing "broad smiles" and dreams of Hayes County as "the garden spot of creation." The hot winds followed, baking the soil, shriveling the kernels, sucking the life out of the once-green stems. If there were more rain and hope for the corn, hot winds returned or, as in 1902, September frost nipped the kernels before they had matured. With the crops, such as they were, already in, rains flooded the county in October and Blackwood Creek was "so swollen," wrote the Highland correspondent, "as to be uncrossal by the mail carrier."[17]

The thistles, however, flourished. Alex Smith, from Hope, it was reported, had about 80 acres of them he was cutting for hay. Warren Clark had less acreage, but one of his neighbors, J.C. Bright, spent a full day cutting "thistle hay," for him. And always there were "plenty of hoppers," one of the reasons being, the McCook *Tribune* complained, that city hunters from Denver and Omaha "killed birds by the wholesale," two or three thousand of them "slaughtered." The *Republican* copied the item. Farmers on Methodist Ridge had already posted their land, among them, R.R. Roberts, J.P. Scott, Frank Miller, W.B. McMullen, Ellsworth Jeffries, J.S. McMullen, W.F. Clark: "to protect ourselves from the inordinate shooting of game, [we] do hereby forbid any person or persons from shooting or killing in any manner, any [prairie] chicken, grouse or quail, on any land owned or controlled by the undersigned."

In a typical fall, with no crops to harvest, they went up into the sandhill country, W.F. Clark to Eddy in Fairfield Township, where they got 30 bushels to the acre, to pick corn and haul enough to supplement the fodder and provide meal for their tables. A photograph taken in the summer of 1902 shows the Clark farmstead almost barren of trees and shrubs, with no evidence of the grove, orchard or berry bushes Warren had so hopefully planted.[18]

Still, Warren had pigs to sell, a load of them in July, 1901, when the hog market had gone "straight up" to $6.75 and $6.90 a hundred pounds (only $2.80, a year or two earlier). And he had a fat cow and a small herd of steers for sale the next winter. Ada had chickens and eggs--merchants of Hayes Center shipped out 2500 dozen eggs one week in May, 1901. And in the fall of 1902, Hayes County at the state fair in Lincoln, with its samples chosen from the sandhill country, won the first premium on rye, first on onions, first on table beets, second on muskmelons, and 905 points on its total exhibit, eleventh among the counties exhibiting.[19]

If the sandhills prospered and Warren Clark and some of his neighbors survived, the poor crop years nonetheless had a devastating effect on Methodist Ridge. The disintegration of the community was apparent on every hand, empty farmsteads, people gone, buildings deteriorating. Sod houses ordinarily lasted only a dozen or fifteen years. Richard Roberts, building a new one, tore down Harlan Martin's soddy to get lumber for the floors. The grange hall on the Ridge began to fall apart, the walls to cave in. The grangers tore it down and salvaged the boards from the floor and the roof. That was the summer of 1901. Children would no longer learn the half-mile rule: from schoolhouse to sod church, to the grange hall, to the post office.[20]

The sod church, too, was in poor condition but the neighbors met to clean, refurbish and brace it up for more years of service. Shaffer McMullen dismantled Grandma Martin's place to get lumber to build a milk house and he and Dock Gruver took the lumber from the old schoolhouse for some unnamed improvement--but not until the neighbors, holding on to their community, put up a new building the third for the district. Warren Clark's sod house was one of the oldest remaining on Methodist Ridge, 17-years-old in 1902. He did not attempt to replace it, but he worked doggedly at the task of trying to improve his farm--building new fences and planting more trees.[21]

The new century brought a new exodus from Methodist Ridge. Wesley Gruver had returned in 1895, George and Harvey a year later, bringing their mother with them, and Orpha's daughter. They were all gone by the spring of 1901, George and Harvey back to Missouri where they located near Oscar, Wesley to McCook and then Culbertson to open a farm implements store. As in 1894, among the living, only Dock remained.[22]

Jim Lakin pulled out, too, in 1901, Warren's friend from the southwest corner of Blackwood, the good Methodist with whom he liked to stay when his business in Palisade kept him late. Jim had had a couple of bumper-crop years, one in 1891 that paid off his whole mortgage of $500, but his harvests in these last years seemed to have been no better than those on Methodist Ridge. He and his family moved to Hood River, Oregon. Six months later he reported happily on the big red apples and the strawberries, on towering Mt. Hood and Mt. Adams, rising above the valley, and the good living people were able to earn on two to five acres.[23]

Ross Beard, stock raiser and cattle buyer, and good Methodist, gave up sometime in these years and, unnoticed by the local papers, moved to Coffey County, Kansas. In 1902 he sold his tree claim to Richard Roberts, whose property joined it. Frank Miller, whose wife Effie was Jesse Rodgers' sister, sold his homestead and moved to rental property. Bill Shupp, six months after the departure of his son Arthur, packed up his goods and followed him to Colorado. The congregation had a farewell service for him at the sod church and Bill preached his last sermon to his friends of many years.[24]

The climax of blows came to the Clarks in the fall of 1901. Jim Abbott, their neighbor on the north, sold out. For ten years the families had been closely associated, the children in school, all of them at church, Warren and Jim in the exchange of work, in recent years the men active in the MWA lodge, and their wives in Royal Neighbors. Warren had helped Jim put up his sod house and plaster it, build a chicken house, a hog pen, a fence, they had harvested together and together had gone north into the sandhills to pick corn and haul it to their stock. Hardworking and enterprising, Jim had 320 acres and he fed a good number of cattle and hogs. He had paid off the mortgage of $350 which he assumed when he bought the farm and it now stood free and clear, except for the last year's taxes. If anyone on the Ridge could succeed, he should have. But he was tired of hauling corn from the sandhills. He bought land up in Lincoln County, near Gandy, in the sandy loam, where he could raise his own corn. He sold his Blackwood place to Jake Wiggins, who still lived in Culbertson but held his property in Hayes County, for $800, the Hope correspondent said. It was a good price for a half section, even including the windmill, the sod house, the outbuildings, and the pasture fence, the best price recorded on the Ridge in these years. Jim would not move to his new place until time to put in the crops in the early spring.[25]

Warren Clark gave no indication of an intent to move, probably had no such intent. Life went on as usual. He cultivated his crops, repaired and built more fence and, on October 1, 1902, put up a new windmill.[26]

That summer Earl was working in the sandhills, for Harry McGinnis, up in Valley precinct, near the border of Frontier County. Family legend has it that he came home one weekend and said: "Papa I believe if you would sell out and go to the sandhills and rent you would do better." And the family, the legend has it, followed his advice. That a boy of 16 should have been so persuasive seems unlikely. Warren knew all about the sandhills, from his very first year on the homestead. Could he have forgotten the words Barney Hofer had written in the *Times* so many years before? "The sandhills are destined to be the farming country yet." He knew all about the bountiful crops, even in the dry years when the corn shrivelled and died on Methodist Ridge. What seems likely is that Harry McGinnis, first suggesting the idea to Earl, had urged it on Warren and Ada that summer when he spent a night with them in Blackwood. A month or so later, the Clarks, visiting Earl at the McGinnis farm, had a chance to observe how well the crops were faring in the sandhills.[27]

The first indication now available to us that they might be talking about moving occurred in September when the Jacob

Dambachs of Hayes Center called on them at Methodist Ridge one Sunday afternoon. Jake had little in common with Warren. He was a druggist and a Catholic. But he was also a landowner whose holdings were farmed by tenants. In January the Clarks spent the weekend with the Dambachs in Hayes Center and had another opportunity to talk about rentals.[28]

In the meantime, life went on, the routine unchanged save by the season. Earl returned from his summer's work to enter school. With Nellie and Mamie at home to help, Ada put up sweet corn, for herself and for them. She wove a carpet for Jim Scott's daughter, Ella Barker. Flora and Jennie called on the neighboring girls and they came to the Clarks. The Dock Gruvers and Ada and Warren went to the MWA and Royal Neighbors lodge meetings in Hayes Center and an oyster supper afterwards. The Clarks drove over to Curtis for camp meeting and to a neighboring schoolhouse for quarterly meeting where they heard their old friend, R.S. Moore, preach. Mamie was married in November, to John Rodgers, Jesse's brother. Two weeks later, on December 5, Warren and Ada celebrated their twenty-fifth wedding anniversary. All of the children were there, said the Hope correspondent, and a "few friends" for a "fine supper." The friends brought presents, "not numerous but all useful articles." Ada, the probable correspondent, had a good eye for all things practical.[29]

A month passed. In her first report of the new year, the Hope correspondent announced that Warren had rented a place in the sandhills, ten miles west of Maywood, in Frontier County, a few miles beyond Harry McGinnis'. The family would move in the spring. In a few days the correspondent reported the sale of the Clarks' farm to Shaffer McMullen for $200, a young mare, and two cows, perhaps $300, altogether. Warren retained possession of the improvements, including the windmill, most of the fence, and the buildings for whatever boards he could salvage. For $200 he could have preempted the place eighteen years before, when he had filed on it. But he had done as well as many others. Frank Miller sold for $150, with all improvements, Dock Gruver bought a quarter section for $90, and Ross Beard sold to Richard Roberts for $200.[30]

There was another round of social calls: the McMullens, the Gruvers, the Driscols, the Effenbachs, and others. Warren and Ada went to Culbertson on business and stayed overnight with Wesley and Alma Gruver. Nellie, reluctant to have her family move across the county, came out frequently, lingering a day or two, Mamie, newly married, came less often. Warren with Jesse's help began to haul their goods to the rented place. Earl, working on the big ditch at Palisade, kept at the job. In mid-March the neighbors, "old and new" friends, "administered a surprise" party on the Clarks, games for the young, "social chat for the older ones." At midnight the guests served a "fine supper."[31]

In another week the Clarks were gone, their homestead deserted. Their names no longer appeared in the newly merged *Times-Republican* and for months to come no one reported the goings-on at Methodist Ridge.

*Gandy's Store, Hayes Center, Nebraska, ca. 1898.*
*Courtesy of Nellie Clark Rodgers.*

*Hayes Center, Nebraska, ca. 1917.*
*Courtesy of Nellie Clark Rodgers.*

# 26.
# A Beautiful Day

The Clarks lived that first year in Frontier County, east of Hayes Center fifteen miles or so, in a dugout on the side of a canyon, boarded up to make a front wall into which were cut a door and a window. The arrangement was temporary, until Warren could find something better. He plowed and cultivated his fields, Jesse at ten big enough to help. So far as we know Flora and Jenny were at home, busy with housework and chores.[1]

Earl worked for a neighbor, perhaps again for Harry McGinnis, and in the fall quit in time for school. He was a big boy, in his eighteenth year. There was nothing unusual for a boy his age to enroll for another term to complete his elementary education. The next spring he made the highest marks in the county examination and earned a scholarship to the preparatory department of anyone of a half dozen colleges in the state. He chose York, a United Brethren school, and after a summer's work enrolled in the fall. With his summer's wages and odd jobs in town--waiting tables, doing chores, wearing a sandwich board to advertise a merchant's wares--he made his way that first year.[2]

Warren found a better farm, back in Hayes County, in Germanville precinct, and he needed Earl's help. He promised him the harvest from one of the fields for his summer's work. When the harvest came, Warren needed the proceeds to meet his own obligations. Perhaps he remembered the years when without protest, he had poured his own earnings into the payments of his father's mortgage. But it was a new day out on the Western frontier where a boy thought his wages were his own. Earl never quite forgave him--or never quite forgot--and he never went back to school.[3]

But it did not matter much. That year, or the year before, he had met a girl across the line in Frontier County, Kathryn Jewel, newly arrived with her parents from Iowa. She was tiny, about the height of his mother, but slight, scarcely ninety pounds in weight. She had honey blond hair and white skin and heavenly eyes--bright blue sparkling gems that might have been plucked out of the Nebraska sky. She was vivacious, an endless chatterer who left this big, dark, shy boy no embarrassed silences to fill. And she sang, in a high, clear soprano voice, hymns when the occasion required, or jaunty, irreverent tunes when it suited her mood: "My name is Morgan, but it ain't J.P.", "If you knock the l out of Kelly, he'll knock the 'ell out of you." Earl was madly in love with her.

Her family called her Kate, her father Kitty. Her parents, John and Mattie, were Methodists--at least Mattie was. John favored the Methodists and was as strict in his conduct as they, but he never joined: "too many hypocrites," he said. And he left the praying to Mattie, including grace before meals. Whatever the religious preferences of her family, and her own in serious moments, Kate had flying feet. She loved to dance. It was not long before Earl learned.

In September, 1906, they were married. For the first time since she and Warren had moved to Nebraska Ada felt in a position to entertain. Warren had moved them a second time, again in Germanville, to a frame house, a lovely, square, substantially built, hipped-roof house, still standing four decades later. Ada's mother, Amelia Jane, had come out from New York to spend several months and was with them. Ada held a reception after the wedding, a gala occasion with great numbers of Clarks and Jewels and their friends, and with supper and wedding cake. With a touch of elegance for this frontier community, that Kathryn remembered years afterward, Ada had molded the butter in the shape of a pineapple. But one little episode marred the event for her. Earl, in keeping with the practice of the community, and his friends, passed cigars. Ada might have overlooked that, regretfully, perhaps, but silently, had not Warren taken one of them. She came on him while he was smoking it. Anger welled up in her.

"Papa," she said, "I am surprised." Warren defended himself. "This is my son's wedding," he answered. It's probably the only time he'll ever get married. I'm going to help him celebrate." He took another puff on his cigar.[4]

The next fall, in 1907, Warren heard from Jim Abbott who had moved from Methodist Ridge to Lincoln County. Jim had found just the right place for them, 80 acres which they could homestead. Under new legislation, sponsored by Senator Moses Kincaid of Nebraska, farmers on the high plains were allowed to homestead 640 acres and those who had proved up on less were eligible to file for additional acreage. The land Abbott had in mind had been homesteaded, several times in fact, but never proved up. Each man had relinquished his rights to another, for a fee, and the rights were again for sale. Warren looked at the place, liked it, found that he could rent adjacent land for more pasture and cultivation, bought up the relinquishment, and filed on the property.[5]

In the early spring of 1908 he put their surplus goods up for sale. It was remarkable what they had accumulated, could dispose of, and still have enough to start over again on a new farm: plows, a two-row cultivator, a mowing machine, a walking lister, a riding lister, a grinder, lumber, posts, harness, corn, potatoes, chicken coops, hog troughs, chickens, hogs, cattle, horses, totaling just over a thousand dollars--enough, no doubt, to pay the relinquishment fee, his debts, and buy what he needed.[6]

Only the two younger boys, Jesse and Arley, moved with them. Jennie in 1907 had married Wiley Jewel, Kate's brother, and Flora, remaining in Trenton, near Nellie, soon married a local boy, William Craw. Warren and Ada were comfortable on their new homestead, not prosperous but they had enough. The land was productive, the crops did not fail. They were better off than they had been on Methodist Ridge. Warren was 53-years-old in the fall of 1908 and not well. He was, in fact, worn out, old before his time, "an old man as long as I can remember," his son, Arley, was to write about him. Photos show him slightly stooped, his face thin, the top of his head bald, the beautiful black curly hair gone, save for a fringe on the side and back. Unable to do the heavy farm work, he did the chores, maintained the fences and buildings, repaired the harness and tools and machinery. Jesse, who was 15, did most of the fieldwork until 1912 when he got married. Arley, then 12-

years-old, big and strong for his age, nearly full grown, took over the fieldwork. The small farm, giving them what they needed for comfort above subsistence, suited them well. It was not the white cottage of the early dreams, with a picket fence and red barn, but the sod house was new, it had three rooms, board floors, and a good roof. Warren planted a grove of trees and a small orchard.[7]

Jesse located close to them, and so did Jennie, for a brief period, after the death of Wiley, with her second husband, Bert Jewel, another of Kate's brothers. Earl in 1909 homesteaded fifteen or twenty miles north of their farm in Logan County and in the four or five years he lived there came by now and then with his family. Nellie, in 1911, with her daughters Leah and Rena, eight and four, driving a team of horses, visited them. It took the better part of three days to get there, and as long to return home. Once they had automobiles, Jesse and John Rodgers, took Nellie and Mamie and the children up to the new homestead for an occasional visit.[8]

The grandchildren were not there often, but Warren and Ada enjoyed them when they came. Ada tempted them with molasses cookies--with that strange sweet and bitter taste--which she doled out one by one. Warren held them in his lap and, in his deep bass voice, welling up from a great hollow chamber, sang to them the songs of the sea that his father had sung to him, and he to his children: "'Stand by, stand by', cried Anderberdeen." It was a good life.[9]

Warren and Ada were hardly settled into their new home before they found their way to Methodist services in the nearby Whittier schoolhouse. It was a station on the circuits of both the Methodist and the Free Methodist preachers who took the pulpit on alternate Sundays in the afternoon. They were soon caught up in the activities of the Sunday school, Ada a teacher of the boys' class, Warren president of the Lincoln County Sabbath School Association, Garfield District.[10]

The Free Methodists were Methodists, split off from the parent body in 1860, much more conservative, more deeply committed to John Wesley's doctrine of Christian perfection, "holiness," they called it, more restrictive in rules of conduct. For the first time Warren and Ada heard the story of Wesley's heart "strangely warmed" at Aldersgate. They listened to instruction on the second grace, sanctification after the new birth, and they sang with new understanding Augustus

Toplady's great hymn, *Rock of Ages*: "Be of sin the double cure, Save from wrath and make me pure."[11]

Ada knew she had been converted. That was the substance, the touchstone, of her Christian life. But she was skeptical about the new doctrine of sanctification. The Free Methodist preacher said that she could be free from sin, free from anger. She did not think that possible. How could she be free from her fierce temper, her occasional outbursts of anger? But she sought the experience, prayed, knew the blessed sense of release, of deliverance, of peace and serenity, of strength and security, in a new life. She promptly joined the Free Methodists. Warren remained with the old church.[12]

It was true that her spirit was flooded with a new sweetness, a gentleness beyond what she had known before, a freedom from censoriousness. It was also true that her piety grew more proscriptive, she was more prone than in years past to measure the quality of the Christian experience by rules of conduct, by simplicity in dress, freedom from ostentation and adornment, commitment to the exercises of the church and the language of the Scriptures. It was a re-assertion, with a new intensity, of the old Dutch pietism to which her mother, and her mother's mother and grandfather before her, and seven or eight generations before them, had given expression.[13]

She applied the same discipline to her physical well-being. Troubled by her great weight, she answered an advertisement in a newspaper or magazine, sent for the nostrum, followed directions rigorously, with what pain or struggle, and for how many months, or years, she does not record. But she lost weight, forty or fifty pounds, or more, and would never regain it, and never excuse others who did not take themselves in hand.[14]

Warren and Ada prospered enough so that by 1915 they could afford a trip back to New York, to Williamstown and Oswego County. They had come west 35 years before and Warren had not returned. It had been 25 years since Ada had gone, taking Earl and baby Jennie with her. Jesse and his wife, May, came home to do the chores and look after the farm. Warren secured a place in Gandy for Arley to work for his board and room while he went to high school. On September 20, he and Ada took the train for New York.[15]

Their journey was sentimental, nostalgic, adventuresome, nearly every moment brimming with memories or filled with exciting wonders of the eastern cities. They stopped in

Cleveland to see Jesse Harris, his wife Carletta, and their daughter, Ada May. Marveling at the sights of a great city, they visited the zoo, saw the baby elephant purchased by the coins of school children, the bears and the monkeys, the sea "lyon" and the mountain "lyon," even prairie dogs and coyotes. They looked at the shipyards, for the first time rode on a street car. Ada May gave her aunt a school notebook and Ada began a journal, backposting it to the first day of the journey and recording, as she had done when she was a teenager, where they had been, whom they saw, what they did, and what the weather was like. But she wrote, too, with a much fuller record of her impressions. They "visited," meaning that they reminisced, undoubtedly about their childhood and Nebraska, the first winter on the homestead when Jesse was there, finishing the sod house, the big snow while they were still in the stable, Jesse's teaching at Blackwood, the first term of the new school.

In Williamstown they stayed with Ada's brothers, Albert and Elmer, and with old friends, changing every two or three days "so we visit them all." Ada thought Albert's son James "a great big noble boy," and she was pleased with "little Venila," the three-year-old daughter of Albert's second wife, Jennie. Ada's cousin, Retta, who had grown up in the Harris household, was in the village with her husband, Lewis Stone, out from their home in New Jersey, their trip planned to coincide with Warren and Ada's.

They remained in the village all week, visiting with Ma, Albert and Elmer, Retta and Lewis Stone and friends who came and went. One day Jennie took photographs, "snapshots," of them, Warren standing tall beside Ada's short-statured brothers, his white beard neatly trimmed, his shoulders broad and his frame sturdy in his heavy, double-breasted coat. Ada, too, looked well, stern, her hair brushed back severely from her face, slender for her age and much younger than Warren. One day was stormy, very hard rain, another cold with a heavy white frost. Ada heard crows cawing in the woods "every morning." They drove about looking in on old neighbors, went past the place where Grandma Onderdonk had lived before she and Retta moved to the Harrises.

On the second Sunday Albert and Jennie took them out to Stone Hill, to see Uncle Horatio and Aunt Lydia Harris. The cousins gathered, Uncle Ratio's children, Ella who was just younger than Ada, Henry whom they had banished from their girls' talk and play, and their families, and unmarried Cora who lived with and took care of her parents.

After dinner, and again the next morning, they walked around the old place, across the road and down the hill from Uncle Ratio's, where Ada had grown up. The house was empty and "going to pieces very fast," the dooryard fence gone, the stone wall crumbled, a road cutting across the corner of the lot. The orchard, young when Ada was at home, was "much neglected," with only a few "nerly" [gnarly] apples on the ground. They saw the pile of stone that Pa had cleared from the fields, the wood lot where he sawed logs, the sweetbrier bush she and the boys tried to dig out.

They stayed overnight and had "genuine maple syrup" for breakfast. Ada read from the fortieth chapter of Isaiah and they had family prayers. Uncle Ratio, 79, and Aunt Lydia, 82, too feeble to kneel, bowed their heads on their canes. Ada and Warren walked down the road, saw peppermint growing in the brook, spearmint on the edge of the road, plants long forgotten. They stopped for a few minutes at the schoolhouse, still in use, they walked past Mr. Stone's old place where they had seen so much of Warren and Mary and others when they all were young. And back to Williamstown when Jennie came for them.

Uncle Arthur Onderdonk, Ma's brother, came down from his old soldier's home that week to spend a few days with Elmer. The rest of them, Ada and Warren, Ma, Albert and Jennie, went to a temperance lecture but Elmer and Emma had to remain at home. Uncle Arthur didn't like temperance lectures. The next day they all gathered at Elmer's to help Uncle Arthur celebrate his eighty-fourth birthday. Did Ada remember that evening, over forty years ago, when she and Retta "whipped" him on his birthday?

Friday they went down to Camden where they stayed with Cousin Vina, Aunt Charlotte's daughter, who had lived just down the hill. They saw Ann Mott whom Ada and Warren had gone to see the week after they were married. Warren Stone lived in Camden, Ada's childhood friend whom Warren Clark had come to know in the hopfields down in Oneida County and whose friendship and residence at Stone Hill had given him a base from which to court Ada. On Sunday they went to the Free Methodist church with Vina and others of their old friends, to class meeting, preaching and Sunday school in the morning, to preaching again at night, Ada delighted to find her cousin and friends in the way that John Wesley had marked out. Back at Williamstown on Tuesday, they stayed the remainder of the week and on Friday started for Mannsville to see Warren's family and friends. Albert and Jennie drove them in their automobile.

They rode past Ricard, past the place where Uncle Porter and Aunt Calista lived, and Cousin Wallace, past the little farm where Warren had lived as a small boy, the hill rising steeply behind it, now after the first frost, brilliant with red on the trees. They saw Warren's sisters, Dell, Nettie, and Bell, spent two weeks with them and their families, drove to Mannsville to the cemetery where Warren's father and mother lay, and John Howe, Bell's husband, a single red granite stone engraved with their names marking the site. They drove past the house where Warren's parents had lived and welcomed Warren and Ada after their marriage, past Uncle Walter Greenwood's place, past the Boylston church where Warren had been converted and the creek where he was baptized. Ada, after the years on the wide, sparsely settled plains, was astounded to stand at Nettie's window, look out over the rolling hills and count thirteen farm houses, the farthest not more than a mile away. First of the family up on a pleasant Sunday morning, she heard an old and almost forgotten song, a chickadee endlessly chanting his name.

At Nettie's they went to the Methodist Protestant Sunday School in the morning, to prayer meeting at night, "a glorious meeting." Bell took them to the Congregational church in the morning, the Baptist at night. Everywhere Ada did her laundry, washed out "Papa's black shirt," helped with the household chores, and "moped" the floors, spelling the word as she had spelled it when she was a girl.

They returned to Williamstown and stayed another week and a half, Ada, her cup running over, scarcely able to get enough of past joys. Uncle John and Ellen Foil, Pa's youngest sister and Ada's favorite aunt, came to see them. They went to Altmar to see George Harris, little George, born the summer Ada was fourteen, and his wife Lucy Stone, younger sister of Warren and Mary, and their three daughters, Margaret, Marian, and Helen. They were with Ma day by day, at Elmer's, or at Albert's when she came to dinner or supper, and when they went together to church or prayer meeting. At last, on

November 17, almost two months from the beginning of their journey, they started for home, with two week-long stopovers ahead of them, in Syracuse and again in Cleveland.

In Syracuse they stayed with Wallace and Vick Harris, Cousin Wallace, Uncle Porter's son, of whom they had seen much in their courting days--trips to Uncle Porter's, a July 4th celebration at the Sand Banks, sugaring off at Stone Hill. They spent nearly a week with them, saw Aunt Charlotte, Vina's mother and Uncle Justin's widow who had lived at the foot of the hill, and several Williamstown friends, among them Ada's cousin, Emma Smith Chase and her husband, Herschel. Emma's parents were Uncle Ham Smith and Aunt Sarah, Pa's sister. Herschel and Emma lived in a grand house with electric lights, a furnace, bath and toilet both upstairs and down, a sitting room, and a parlor "nicely furnished" with three solid mahogany chairs "nicely upholstered," each of which had cost $45, as much as a farm hand could earn in two months. Emma and her daughter served an elegant dinner that Ada itemized in three "courses:" beef soup and crackers; boiled beef, mashed potatoes, macaroni and tomatoes; apple pie, jelly roll, and tea.

But the great experience at Syracuse was the Billy Sunday revival. Having made the most urgent of their family calls on the first day, they went on the next to hear the flamboyant evangelist in his huge tabernacle. They heard him every day for their remaining time in the city, some members of their family always with them. On Friday afternoon they walked home in the rain and got wet. But they changed their clothes, ate supper, and went back to the evening meeting. They went again on Saturday and on Sunday morning before the elegant dinner at Cousin Emma's.

In Cleveland they stayed another week with Jesse and Carletta before catching the train for Chicago and Nebraska. They arrived in McCook December 3, changed to the local train, and reached Beverly before noon. John and Mamie were at the station to greet them.

They spent the next four weeks savoring the trip, recounting their experiences, "visiting" with Nellie and Mamie and their families at Beverly, with Jennie and Bert who that winter were on a farm in Hayes County, and with Earl and Kate who lived nearby in a little house on Kate's father's farm. Earl, his homestead proved up, had sold it for a handsome profit, $1,000 and 50 horses and mules. That winter he was teaching at Greenfield school in Hayes County, marking time until he could buy the farm he wanted. Warren and Ada spent Christmas with him and Kate, and with Kate's parents and the Jewel clan, and then a few more days at Jennie's. On January 5, 1916, Mr. Jewel drove them to North Platte, and on the next day to their farm. Mr. Jewel returned home and Ada "cleaned things all day."

They had been gone nearly four months, three months for the trip, one to unwind and catch up. Life had come full circle: childhood, youth, courtship and marriage in New York, and the great dream: a homestead in Nebraska, the high hope, the despairing struggle, and the sustaining faith, a brood of children now grown, unschooled in the wants that only money can buy, happy in what they had. In these few months Warren and Ada had relived it all: the vision of things past, fragrant with happy memories, suffused with a sense of loss, an awareness of events and loved ones forever gone. And a return to reality, to present wants and demands, the unstoppable flow of life itself. Ada had no word for her feelings, save for the day when they came into McCook, a little after sunrise, and she looked out on the great expanse of the plains, glad to be home, and wrote, with what seemed to be a sigh of pleasure,"a beautiful day."

*Clark's second homestead, Lincoln County, Nebraska, ca. 1916. Left to right: Warren Clark with Ray Craw [Mamie's son], Jenny Clark Jewel with son Wiley and Ada Clark.*

# 27.
# Oh, the Canyons

Warren and Ada remained on the farm, the Lincoln County homestead, for two more years. In the spring of 1916 little Ray Craw, six-years-old, came to live with them. Flora, his mother, Warren and Ada's third daughter, had died in 1915, out in Idaho where she and her husband had gone to live, the first break in the family circle. Ada grieved, not at the death only, but because Flora had died alone, far from her family. Ray loved his grandmother--"she was like a mother to me"--, he said, but he found his grandfather old and sick, irritable and impatient with the ways of children. Ada comforted him, folding him in her great skirt when he ran to her, wrapping her arms around him, holding him in her lap.[1]

In the spring of 1918 they sold out to retire to Kansas and make a home for Arley while he attended school. Arley had been converted in a revival at the schoolhouse when he was 14 or 15-years-old. It was his mother, he said, "who led me to the Lord." She was his Sunday school teacher in a class of boys, not much of a teacher, he thought--she had gone only through the fifth grade. But she had a strong hold on the boys in her class and everyone of them "sought the Lord" in that revival.[2]

In the course of a few months, the joy of the religious experience faded and Arley, in the language of the evangelicals, "backslid," lost his faith. He went back to partying and having a good time. One night after he had been out until the early hours of the morning, he found his mother on her knees, where she had been all night, praying for him. That brought him back. He was only 16, but he began to preach "some."[3]

He went to high school in Gandy that fall, but the next year, 1917-18, he attended the Free Methodist preparatory school at Central College in McPherson, Kansas. He liked it and was persuaded that his parents should sell out and join him. He arranged a trade, the farm for a house in McPherson. They had a sale in April, livestock and farm machinery, keeping only one team of horses, two cows, and most of the household furnishings. Arley came up from Kansas to accompany the livestock and the household goods in an emigrant car and Warren, Ada, and Ray took the train.[4]

They were greeted by the president of the school, taken into the home of one of the sisters of the church, welcomed into the neighborhood by men and women of like mind, absorbed into their community of Christian fellowship. Ada, already a Free Methodist, presented her letter of transfer. Warren, reasonably at home among these fellow Methodists, however ardent they might be, joined the church, mindful, no doubt, that the discipline required, as a condition of membership, not the experience of Christian perfection, but the intent to diligently seek it.[5]

Warren was not well that summer and fall. He did his chores, a few odd jobs in the town, planted and tended his garden, puttered about the house. He took to his bed in November with an illness he did not understand, a general debility, a painful swelling of his feet. There was much flu in the town but no deaths in the church or the college and he did not believe that he had it. He was up on November 13, "gaining a little," he wrote to Earl, walking about in the yard, but it would be some time before he could get around much; "wish you could come and see us while I am shut in." Five days later he died, November 18, 1918, one month and 19 days beyond his sixty-fourth birthday.[6]

Ada had almost no resources. Years before Warren had given up his insurance in the MWA lodge--annual assessments had increased so much he could no longer afford to pay them. He told Arley that he could have what was left after their death if he would take care of them in their old age.[7]

Arley finished high school, completed a reading course for ordination in his church, married his sweetheart whom he had met in the church, Grace Carley, and, in 1923 moved to

Lawrence, Kansas. He had taken the civil service examination and joined the postal service. He began his life's vocations, to carry mail to support his family and to evangelize in the church as time permitted. Ada and Ray remained in McPherson, in the big house, full of students, for two or three years, and then moved to a smaller one. She had a boarder or two, sold little household gadgets, mend-its for sewing, and other notions, for pin money and income from the sale of her house. Her life, beyond her household duties, was completely absorbed in the church and the college. She could scarcely have been happier. The very terms of address in the church, "Brother," and "Sister," expressed the intimacy of the members, and the constancy of religious discourse bound them together in a tight little community.[8]

Ray, when he was 16, went to live with a Free Methodist farmer in western Kansas and thereafter came home only to visit. Two years later, in 1928, Ada suffered a slight stroke. Arley moved her to Lawrence where he and Grace provided a place in their home, a small apartment in the first years, and subsequently a room. There she was to live out the remaining years of her life.[9]

In moving, Ada discovered Warren's old diaries and read them with reminiscent pleasure, now and then commenting in pencil on an event, or identifying a person. On the blank lines she began to make her own entries, once again after all of these years, posting her own diary.[10]

She was happy at Arley and Grace's and, with their household of children, needed and welcome. Arley, a mail carrier during the week, a preacher on Sundays, dedicated to the church, held views congenial to Ada. In her apartment she maintained a degree of independence, taking her meals alone, but she worked with Grace in the household tasks. "Her sewing basket was always full," a granddaughter said. Grace did a 'big ironing," Ada wrote, "I mended & sewed on buttons & changed new shirts so they fit boys (Wesley, six, Arley, three)." While Grace sewed on Opal's dress, "I moped [sic] the bed room." "Nice day. I was all done out from sweeping and cleaning so much dust." "Grace and Arlie & the children [Arley, Jr., and Maxine] went to the prayer meeting. I staid with Wesley & Opal." She had her own stove and kept a fire all night when it was cold, cooked her own food, canned apples, pears, pie plant (rhubarb), and tomato pickles.[11]

She held on to her old-fashioned ways: pulled her hair straight back and tied it in a knot. Why girls would comb their hair over their ears she couldn't understand, she said to Mildred, "unless their ears were dirty." She refused to use electric lights. The kerosene lamp was good enough, and it was cheaper.[12]

Above all, she loved the church. She went to Sunday services, prayer meetings, revivals, camp meetings, always with a brother or sister of the church, or with Arley and Grace who often took her to her own church before they drove to the country where Arley preached. It might be cold, but if it did not snow, they "all went to church." She was at church on a Friday for "All World Prayer to lift Christ up to all people," on another day to the State WCTU Convention, on a Sunday night to hear Arley preach, to the Nazarene Church with her older grandchildren, Edna and Wiley Jewel, to Ottawa to a revival, the sermon "deep and Gloryous," to the local church to hear Brother McKay who preaches "wonderfull stirring sermons." Her entries glow with satisfaction and happiness.[13]

Ada went back to Nebraska several times to see her family and friends, the most notable journey in 1933, a long and reminiscent one, not unlike the trip she and Warren had made to New York in 1915. She spent three weeks in Beverly, saw Nellie and Mamie, and Nellie's married daughters, Leah and Rena and their children. Most of her old neighbors in Blackwood were gone. The township, with a population of 282 in 1890, had scarcely half that number, 148, in 1930, few of whom Ada knew. She wrote a postal card to Dock Gruver and he came to see her. They talked about his family and the old neighborhood. Dock still owned the Harlan Martin place and he had bought James Mansfield's homestead in section 23, on the Blackwood, and lived there. Dock's wife Nellie was dead, had died the year before at 59. Dock, himself, was 61. His mother had died in Iowa. Oscar, too, was dead, and so was Mary Smith, Nellie's mother. Of Nellie's father, Rome, Dock had nothing to say, or Ada nothing to record. Harvey Gruver lived in Kansas City, Wesley and his wife Alma, the Driscols' daughter, in Idaho. Ada wrote it all down and what the children were doing and where they lived. Shaffer McMullen, Dock said, was dead. His second wife, Mary, lived in Culbertson. Their daughter Silva, married to a newcomer, Victor Fagerstone, lived on the Grandma Martin place. Earl

McMullen lived in Arthur County, Bud north of Hayes Center, on the Repass place, the farm he had bought from his wife's parents. Richard Roberts was dead but Maggie, his wife, remained on the homestead. A few days later Maggie came to see her, confirming many of the details Dock had already reported. Jim and Ella Scott still lived on their homestead, too old to farm but Glen, their youngest son, who lived on the Wemple place, farmed their fields for them. Of all the homesteaders who had filed on Methodist Ridge in the 1880s, only Jim and Ella Scott and Maggie Roberts remained.[14]

It was all small talk, but it encompassed the destiny of the men and the women, and their children, whom Ada had known on the Ridge: where they were, who had married whom, who was yet alive and who was dead, who suffered what infirmities, who prospered and who did not. She must know what had happened to her neighbors--that Richard Roberts was buried in McCook, that Maggie, still sorrowing over the loss of their infant daughter, Elsie, in 1897, had removed her body from the grave on Methodist Ridge and placed it by the side of her father; that Dock Gruver's son, Archie, had married Cy Smith's daughter, Florence, that Maggie Jeffries, widowed in 1907 by Ellsworth's death, had married "a good man" and had "a good home" out in Colorado. It was a joy to "visit," a satisfaction to learn all that she could, every little detail, about her old friends and neighbors. She was not simply curious. She needed the bits and pieces to fill our her own life, to fit into that vast jigsaw puzzle of her own past, to give a sense of completion, of the approaching wholeness of life.

John Rodgers drove her from Palisade north into the sandhills of Keith County, north of Paxton, to see Jesse Clark, his wife May, and their children. It was far west of where she and Warren had lived, some 50 miles, and she knew no one in the neighborhood. The country was sparsely settled, isolated. They did not believe in Sunday school and had no preaching on the two Sundays she was there. Jesse belonged to the "two-by-two" sect, Christian "workers" who, refusing to join a church, did their evangelizing, two by two, as Jesus had instructed, calling at homes or preaching in rented halls, schoolhouses, or tents.[15] Ada missed the church services but "visited" with Jesse and May and busied herself about the house. They had a terrible dust storm, the "awfulest sand storm I ever saw," and "the blackest darkness I ever remember seeing before sun down."

They had lightning and hail and a little rain. Then the clouds rolled back, the sky cleared, and all over was a "beautiful pink."

After twelve days Jesse took her to the railroad at Madrid and she caught the train to Maywood, phoned Earl, and went over to her old friends, the Harry McGinnises, who now lived in town, to wait for his arrival.

Earl, after a dozen years in one town or another, managing grain elevators and purchasing livestock, had returned to the farm, to the McGinnis place where he had worked as a boy. Ada was back in a neighborhood she knew well, both from the dugout where they had lived after selling the homestead, and from the Germanville precinct where they had lived for three years.

Earl and Kate had a big household, their only daughter, Mildred, 19, their younger boys ranging in age from four years to 13, Bill, Ken, Jim, Kate's sister, "Tommy," her husband, and daughter Margaret, 14, and Jennie's daughter, Ada, her grandmother's namesake, 16. Jennie had died in childbirth in 1924. Mamie took the baby and Earl the three older children. Only Ada was still at home. Earl managed the farm, Jim and a hired man planted and cultivated the crops, Kate oversaw the household and with her father's help did the gardening, Tommy the cooking, young Ada helped the men in the fields, Mildred and Margaret did most of the housework.

Earl was a big man, strong in body and spirit, quiet, competent, respected by them all, loved by his children and nieces, adored by his daughter. He ruled his motley household less by command than by his presence.[16] Ada marveled at how smoothly it all went and how Kate and the girls kept the house "so nice and clean . . . with so much dust blowing." She liked Tommy's food, praised her for "a nice dinner" for "fresh beef boiled and potatoes and dumplings with it." But she was troubled that Tommy was so "fat," a battle she had fought with herself and won. The girls hugged and kissed her--"they act like they love me," she said. One or another of them was constantly at the piano, playing hymns for the most part. Earl had family prayers and grace before meals, Kate gave her religious books to read, and they went to Sunday school at the schoolhouse.

One night she had a long talk with Kate, her non-conforming daughter-in-law whom she had never really understood. Earl had taken Tommy and the young people to

Hayes Center for school exercises. Ada lay on her bed resting and Kate came in, stretched out on the girls' bed beside her "and we just had the best visit until way late." Kate, for all her wild laughter and the wild songs she still sang, or whistled, at her work, for all that strange un-Methodistic prayer she prayed every night at family worship--unmindful of the sinless life John Wesley had taught--"forgive us our sins of omission and commission," Kate was clearly in the fold, committed in her own peculiar and irregular way.

On "Decoration Day" all of them drove to Maywood to place flowers on the graves of Kate's mother and of Jennie and her first husband, Wiley Jewel, and other members of the family who lay buried there. Ada saw several, "quite a lot," of her old friends and talked with them. But for all of the welling up of sorrow, she was clearly very happy with the memories of days past. As she rode home her thoughts were not on the dead but on the land, the countryside, "Oh, the canyons," she wrote, "the hills and the prairies are beautiful." The sweet peas and the wild roses on the canyon walls were in bloom and the corn in Earl's fields was "coming on nicely." What, indeed, of man's work on the plains was more beautiful to the eye, more uplifting to the spirit, than row upon row of young corn, the stalk sturdy, the dark green leaves stirring in the wind, a symbol of hope.

In the days that followed Earl took her to see others of her friends. She had, altogether, "a great good visit." And yet she was vaguely uneasy. Mr. Jewel, for no good reason, or no reason that he chose to state, refused to go to Sunday school. Tommy stayed home to cook. Ada and Mildred had bobbed hair, Kate and the girls wore short sleeves and no stockings, the girls often wore sleeveless dresses, arms bare to the shoulders. What was it that Paul had said? That women should "adorn themselves in modest apparel, with shamefastness and sobriety." Mildred knew the problem. She had stayed a few weeks with her grandmother in McPherson and had been astonished when she refused to accept payment for goods until a neighbor girl who had first appeared at her door in jeans came back dressed in a skirt. And she had seen her grandmother hurt, offended, when a young woman on whom they called, a professing Christian, a member of their church, met them at the door wearing a sleeveless blouse, and how much pleased grandmother was when the girl, excusing herself, returned in a moment in a blouse with sleeves. With the passing years her piety had grown more proscriptive. She did not preach or scold but everyone who knew her understood her code and knew that she suffered without words, was pained visibly, when they violated it. Some of her grandchildren were to think of her as austere, remote, oppressively religious. One of Arley's sons thought her "stern," Leah's daughter, Lois, was puzzled when Grandma reproached her for being "vain," setting her hair on curlers," but all of them loved her, thought her kind, "sweet," Leah said. Those who knew her best, Mildred among them, and Maxine, reared in the same household, and her favorite grandchild, smiled at her foibles, were tolerant of her unbending pietism. They thought of her as warm and gentle and protective, "loving," Maxine (Peggy) said, perhaps saintly, undeniably religious.[17]

She had much to comfort her. All of her children, daughters and sons alike, after brief years of rebellion for most of them, were faithful to the church. They gave credit to their Christian family, praised their father, but acknowledged, with gratitude, the dominating influence of their strong-willed mother. All her sons were leaders in their churches, one a mail carrier-evangelist, one a farmer-Christian worker, one a devout layman, and all of them had followed her into the Wesleyan experience of Christian perfection. She was the bearer, in the ninth generation, of that remarkably strong and persistent tradition of Dutch pietism, and the transmitter of that tradition to her sons and daughters and they to many of her grandchildren.

She spent 18 days at Earl's. Leah came for her, drove her through Hayes Center and along the road on Methodist Ridge. They stopped to see Jim and Ella Scott. They looked old, especially Ella, and they were old, too old, Ella said, for her to do the milking anymore. Did Ada remember the years when Jim hit the bottle and the old mule brought him home while he slept on the floor of his rig? No matter. He sent his kids to Sunday school or, cold sober, brought them himself. In a brief half hour they reached back to the early years and events that bound them together. They could not know that a later generation, too, would bind them, that Earl's young son, Billy, would some day marry Jim and Ella's granddaughter, Glora, Glen's daughter. Old Jim would have cackled: "My granddaughter marry one of the pious Clarks?"[18]

Back at Leah's Ada dreamed a dream. She was walking alone on the prairie, looking for Earl and Arley. It was quite dark and she could not find them. Soon Warren, "Papa," came, took her by the arm and walked with her. She felt a great sense of peace and happiness, and awakened to moralize: "We are traveling on to God in the way our fathers trod. We are happy now and we soon their happiness shall see." It was the **happy now**, and in the years past, that seemed to engulf her and to verify the hope for happiness to come.

Five years later, in 1938, Ada came back to Nebraska for her final visit. Earl was gone, like his father before him driven out by the drought. But his daughter, Mildred, remained, she and her husband, Homer Richter, still living in Hayes County. Homer was young and tough, bred on the rhythm of hope and despair, on the mixed elements of the rain, the drought, the wind, the driven dust, and the good earth, the rich top soil of the county. And he was soon to learn the new techniques for subduing the rain and the wind and fighting the drought: contour planting, terracing, shallow plowing, alternate strips of ground cover. He had made a down payment on a farm in Blackwood precinct, the farm house in section 20. It was not far from Methodist Ridge, five or six miles from Warren Clark's homestead. It bordered on what now seems to have been the road, or trail, from Culbertson to John Hughes' homestead, the route Warren followed that fall in 1885 when he brought his family to his new sod stable and partially constructed house.[19]

Ada was pleased to be in Hayes County, so close to the old homestead and other landmarks. Day after day she stood, minutes at a time, on the back porch, looking off to the northeast, toward Methodist Ridge and the old homestead. How many times she stood there, gazing into the distance without seeing the tree in Homer's field, no one now remembers. But one day she saw it, a green, shimmering tower, a cottonwood, standing alone, apart from the clusters of trees that marked the farmsteads. "Why that's the lone tree," she exclaimed.[20]

And so it was, or a shoot from the old landmark now grown into a new tree, here on her granddaughter's farm. It was the one object, yellow-brown then in its fall colors, that broke the vast expanse of plain when Warren's horses drew the wagon out of the canyon that day so many years ago. It was the landmark her eyes had sought that first morning when they turned south at the corner of their homestead, after spending a night with John and Mary Hughes. And it was the tree that through the years she could see on a clear day from her dooryard, that marked the road they took from Methodist Ridge to Palisade or that they could see off to the west when they went to Culbertson.

She rejoiced in the tree. To possess it, here on her granddaughter's farm, was to possess the past, to bind it to the present and the future, to bind her and her family to the land she had long ago come to love.

She fell ill at Mildred's, had a stroke, her second or third. Nellie said she must be moved to Leah's, near the doctor at Trenton. Ada resisted. She wanted to remain on the farm. To Mildred she seemed to be saying, without words but quite plainly: "If I am going to die, let me die here, in the midst of my memories." But they moved her to Leah's.[21]

She rallied and returned to Arley and his family at Lawrence, Kansas. She lived another year and died, November 19, 1939, three months after her eightieth birthday.[22]

Back in Hayes County the lone tree still stood in her granddaughter's field and again that summer the pink roses and the wild sweet peas had blossomed on the canyon walls.

*Warren and Ada Clark at their homestead in Lincoln County, Nebraska. Photo dated April 18, 1912.*

*Ada Clark with her son Arley Clark, ca. 1924.*

*Four generations, 1931.*
*Standing left to right: Nellie Clark Rodgers, Leah Rodgers Hidy.*
*Seated: Ada Clark, Lois Hidy.*

*Left to right: Warren Clark, Ada Clark, Etta Harris and Jesse Harris, Cleveland, Ohio, 1915.*

*Ada Clark, 1920.*

*Clark family, ca. 1903. First row, l. to r.: Warren, Arley, Ada. Second row: Jesse. Third row, l. to r.: Mary, Flora, Earl, Jenny, Nellie.*

*Kathryn and Earl Clark, wedding photo, 1906.*

*Ada Harris Clark, Williamstown, New York, 1915.*

# NOTES

## PROLOGUE
### *Notes to Pages xv to xix*

1. United States Censuses, 1860, Population Schedule for Oswego County, New York.

2. The diaries are in the possession of the writer.

3. New York State Census, 1855, Population Schedule, Oswego County, Town of Orwell.

4. New York State Census, ibid.; *Oswego County Book of Deeds*, Vol. 63, pp. 23-25, September 20, 1852; United States Census, 1860, Population Schedule, Oswego County, Orwell precinct, p. 62; Crisfield Johnson, *History of Oswego County, New York*, (Philadelphia, PA., 1877), pp. 300, 301.

5. Oswego County, New York, Book of Deeds, Vol. 111, p. 496, September 13, 1866. The writer's father, Earl Clark, son of Warren, also sang one of the songs of the sea to his children, Anderberdeen: "Stand by, stand by," cried Anderberdeen, "For I'll have your ship and your cargo, too, and your merrymen drown in the sea."

6. New York State Census, 1875, Agricultural Statistics for Amboy, Oswego County, p. 20; Amelia Jane Onderdonk Harris, manuscript "Journal." One of the three known copies of the journal is in the possession of the writer.

7. Harris Journal.

8. Harris Journal; Elmer Onderdonk, *Genealogy of the Onderdonk Family in America* (New York, 1910); Robert D. Clark, "Ada Harris, Teenager: Oswego County, New York, 1873," *New York History*, LXVI (January, 1985), 29-47.

9. J. H. French, *Gazetteer of the State of New York* . . . (Syracuse, NY., 1860), p. 520; Ada Harris Clark,"Journal of a Trip from Nebraska to New York," September 20 to December 8, 1915. The writer, guided by Ada's niece and nephew, Mrs. Venila DeStephen of Oswego and John Harris of Camden, visited the site of the Harris home in 1980 and again in 1984 and can verify the details of topography, soil, and flora. Remnants of the farmstead still exist--the foundation walls, the apple orchard, the sugar maples marking the lane, but the land has returned to its natural state.

10. Ada Clark, Journal; Matthew Simpson, Ed., *Cyclopedia of Methodism* . . . Rev. Ed. (Philadelphia, PA., 1880), p. 603.

11. Harris Journal; James Tanis, *Dutch Calvinistic Pietism in the Middle Colonies: A Study in the Life and Theology of Theodorus Jacobus Frelinghuysen* (The Hague, 1967), p. 44; David Cole, *History of the Reformed Dutch Church of Tappan, New York* (New York, 1894), pp. 8-20.

## Chapter 1. Ada Harris, Teenager
## *Notes to Pages 1–12*

1. Ada Harris, Diary, 1873, is the principal source of information for this chapter. Other sources will be cited.

2. Briggs Brothers were among the major seed merchants in Rochester, "The Flower City." The merchants scattered thousands of their catalogues across New York and neighboring states, all elaborately illustrated, some with two or three hand-colored plates. Blake McKelvey, Ed., *The Rochester Historical Society Publications*, XVIII, Part II: *Nurseries, Farm Papers, and Selected Rochester Episodes* (Rochester, 1940), pp. 153-54, and McKelvey, *Rochester on the Genesee: The Growth of a City* (Syracuse, NY., 1973), p. 87.

3. The location of households is recorded in the *New Topographical Atlas of Oswego County, New York* (Philadelphia: C. K. Stone, 1867; reprinted by B & E Printers, Rochester, NY., 1974), pp. 13, 79.

4. The age of Ada's friends was determined from the United States Census, Population Schedule, 1870, and the New York State Census, Population Schedule, 1875, Oswego County, Williamstown and Amboy.

5. Amelia Jane Harris, Journal; The New York State Census, 1875, Oswego County, Table II, "Marriages in First Election District." Henrietta's name was Onderdonk; the clerk mistakenly enters it as "Underdonk," perhaps reflecting the way it was often pronounced. Henrietta's father deserted the family before her birth.

6. Harris Journal.

7. Elmer Onderdonk, *Genealogy of the Onderdonk Family in America* (New York, 1910), p. 185.

8. Harris Journal.

9. Onderdonk, pp. 187-88.

10. An advertisement in the Mexico, NY., paper asserted that Santa Claus had his quarters in L. L. Virgil's store. News stories from neighboring villages reported that he had deposited presents in children's stockings and that their parents had parties and received beautiful gifts. Mexico, NY., *Independent and Deaf Mutes' Journal,* Jan. 2, 1873.

## Chapter 2. Warren Clark, Farmhand
## Notes to Pages 13–26

1. Warren Clark, Diary, 1876, is the principal source for this chapter; United State Census, 1870, Population Schedule, Oswego County, Orwell and Amboy.

2. Warren's family belonged to the Methodist Protestant Church, Ada Clark, Journal, 1915.

3. Crisfield Johnson, *History of Oswego County, New York* (Philadelphia, PA., 1977), p. 381.

4. Charles Davies, *University Arithmetic* . . . (New York, 1870); *The National Cyclopedia of American Biography* (New York, 1893), III, 26.

5. Blake McKelvey, *Education in Rochester*, Part I, in The Rochester Historical Society *Publications*, XVII (Rochester, NY., 1939), 80-81,114-15.

6. Ralph M. Faust, *The Story of Oswego County* (Oswego, NY., 1948), p.85; the distance between stations (but not the timetable) for the Watertown and Rome railroad is given in J. H. French, *Gazetteer of the State of New York* . . . (Syracuse, NY., 1860), p. 73.

7. United States Census, 1870, and New York State Census, 1875, Population Schedules for Oneida County, town of Marshall.

8. French, pp. 458, 465, 467. New York State Census, 1875, Oneida County, Town of Marshall, Agricultural Statistics.

9. Jay S. Morris, "Old Time Hop Pickers," *St. Lawrence County Historical Association Journal*, X (Oct., 1965), 12.

10. United State Census, 1870, Population Schedule, Oneida County, New York, town of Marshall.

11. French, p. 467.

12. *Constitution and Discipline of the Methodist Protestant Church* . . . (Pittsburgh, PA., 1877), pp. 146-48.

13. Mary S. Bowers, "Hop Growing in the Town of Seward," *Scholarie County Historical Review*, XXIX (Oct., 1965), 12-18; Clayton E. Risley, "Hop-Picking Days," *New York Folklore Quarterly*, V (Spring, 1949), 18-23.

14. Liberty Hyde Bailey, *The Harvests of the Year to the Tiller of the Soil* (New York, 1927), pp. 25-27.

15. Bowers, "Hop Growing;" Risley, "Hop-Picking."

16. Thomas Hillgrove, *A Complete Practical Guide to the Art of Dancing* (New York, 1863), pp. 23, 77, and passim.

## Chapter 3. I Went with Ada Harris
## *Notes to Pages 27-36*

1. Warren Clark, Diary, 1876, is the major source for this chapter. Other sources are noted. United States Census, 1870, Population Schedule, Oswego County, Orwell. For the train schedule see J. H. French, *Gazetteer of the State of New York . . .* (Syracuse, NY., 1860), p. 73.

2. Oswego County Records, Mortgages, Vol. 108, p. 263, Oct. 21, 1875. Warren's advance to his father is recorded in his diary on Feb. 14, 1876.

3. Ada in 1929, reading Warren's old diary for Feb. 9, 1876, penciled in a note saying that he threshed with a thrail. Leo Rogin, *The Introduction of Farm Machinery in Its Relation to the Productivity of Labor in the Agriculture of the United States during the Nineteenth Century*, University of California Publications in Economics, IX (Berkeley, CA., 1931), 179; Clarence H. Danhof, *Changes in Agriculture: The Northern United States, 1820-1870* (Cambridge, MA., 1969), p. 221.

4. New York State Census, 1875, Oneida County, Vol. 3, Bridgewater, III, Deaths.

5. Ibid., 1875, Population Schedule, Oswego County, Amboy and Williamstown.

6. The description is derived from Warren and Ada's wedding photograph, a copy of which is in the possession of the writer. Warren's height is recorded by Ada in the journal of a trip to Nebraska, June 3, 1933. The average height of males was 5' 7.5": see Robert Fogel, "Physical Growth as a Measure of the Economic Well-being of Population: The Eighteenth and Nineteenth Centuries," in Frank Falkner and J.M. Tanner, Eds., *Human Growth: A Comprehensive Treatise* (New York, 1986), 3 Vols., Vol. 3, p. 271.

7. United States Census, 1870, Population Schedule, Monona County, Iowa, Sherman Township.

8. James M. Buckley, *A History of Methodism in the United States* (New York, 1898), II, 214.

9. Vira (Secor) in Ada Harris, Autograph Book, n.d. (ca. 1875). The booklet is in the possession of the writer. Vira (Elvira) was the daughter of Ma's (Amelia Jane's) sister, Eleanor Onderdonk Secor, Elmer Onderdonk, *Genealogy of the Onderdonk Family in America* (New York, 1910), pp. 184-85.

## Chapter 4. A Ring That Binds Me
## *Notes to Pages 37-48*

1. Warren Clark, Diary, 1877, and Ada Harris, Diary, 1877, are the principal sources for the narrative.

2. J. H. French, *Gazetteer of the State of New York . . .* (Syracuse, NY., 1860),p. 73.

3. Clarence H. Danhof, *Changes in Agriculture: The Northern United States, 1820-1870* (Cambridge, MA., 1909), pp. 262, 263.

4. Elmer Onderdonk, *Genealogy of the Onderdonk Family in America* (New York, 1910), p. 125; United States Census, Population Schedule, Oswego County, 1870.

5. Testimonies and examination of the class by the leader were regular features of the early Wesleyan class meeting that still prevailed in rural areas in the late 19th century, Matthew Simpson, Ed., *Cyclopedia of Methodism . . .* (Philadelphia, PA., 1880), pp. 228-9.

6. Ralph M. Faust, *The Story of Oswego County* (Oswego, NY., 1948), p. 85.

## Chapter 5. A Long Farewell
## *Notes to Pages 49-60*

1. Ada Harris, Diary, for the last months of 1877; Warren Clark Diary, 1877, 1878, 1879. These diaries constitute the principal sources for this chapter. The spelling is consistent with the entries in the diaries.

2. J. H. French, *Gazetteer of the State of New York . . .* (Syracuse, NY., 1860), p. 527; Crisfield Johnson, *History of Oswego County, New York* (Philadelphia, PA., 1877), p. 379.

3. The certificate of marriage is in the collection of the Hitchcock County Historical Society.

4. Note to "Kate" enclosed in birthday card for Earl Clark, May 23, 1932, Earl Clark Papers.

5. Letter from Ada's son Arley Clark to Robert D. Clark, June 13, 1980.

6. Oswego County Records, Mortgages, Vol. 102, p. 331, Feb. 4, 1874, Vol. 108, p. 203, Oct. 212, 1875. See Chap. III, note #2.

7. Oswego County Records, Deeds, for Chauncey and Alma Clark: Vol. 63, pp. 23-25, Sep. 20, 1852; Vol. 109, p. 489, Mar. 14, 1866; Vol. 111, p. 486, Sep. 10, 1866. For Nathaniel and Amelia J. Harris: Vol. 221, p. 235, Nov. 12, 1895; Vol. 222, p. 49, Nov. 4, 1895. The custom of fathers favoring sons over daughters, in the bequeathing of property, is illustrated by Mary P. Ryan, *Cradle of the Middle Class: The Family in Oneida County, New York, 1790-1865* (Cambridge, London, and New York, 1981), pp. 28-31.

8. Henry Nash Smith, *Virgin Land: The American West as Symbol and Myth* (Cambridge, MA., 1950, Reissued, 1970), "Garden of the World," pp. 123-136, "Desert as Garden," pp. 174-211. Warren's move to the West in search of land, not unlike that of many other sons of eastern farmers, does not, of course, imply the "safety-valve" theory, which Shannon called a "long-exploded myth," whether applied, as it was originally, to laborers in the city, or later, to the surplus of farm

youth in the East. Fred A. Shannon, "A Post Mortem on the Labor-Safety-Value Theory," *Agricultural History* XIX (Jan., 1945), pp. 34-36.

9. The beseeching call to "come to Christ" was initiated in America by George Whitfield in the early 18th century and has continued among revivalists to modern times. Joseph Belcher, *George Whitfield: A Biography with Special Reference to his Labors in America* (New York, ca. 1857), p. 49.

## Chapter 6. First Year in the West
## *Notes to Pages 61–72*

1. Warren Clark, Diary, 1880, is the principal source for the details of this chapter.

2. S. B. Maxwell, *Centennial History of Guthrie County, Iowa . . .* (Des Moines, IA., 1876), pp. 11, 147; United States Census, 1880, Guthrie County, Iowa.

3. Coal was an important industry in Iowa, ranking, in the early 1890s, fifth in production among the states. Samuel Calvin, Charles K. Keyes, G.E. Patrick, *Iowa Geological Survey, First Annual Report for 1892 . . .* (Des Moines, IA., 1893), I, 122.

4. This shaft was on the farm adjacent to John Kunkle's, George A. Ogle and Co., Compiler, *Standard Atlas of Guthrie County, Iowa* (Chicago, IL., 1900), p. 41.

5. Maxwell, p. 12.

6. Allan Bogue, *From Prairie to Corn Belt: Farming on the Illinois and Iowa Prairies in the Nineteenth Century* (Chicago, IL., University of Chicago Press, 1963), p. 60.

7. Maxwell. p. 14.

8. U. S. Census, Guthrie County, Iowa, 1880.

9. In the spring of 1880, the Plains, including Iowa, suffered "probably the worst dust storm of the nineteenth century" on March 26 and 27. R. Douglas Hurt, *The Dust Bowl: An Agricultural and Social History* (Chicago, IL., 1981), p. 6. On the 26th, in Guthrie County, Warren noted that "the wind blew a gale all day." He began working in the field but "it blowed so hard I quit."

10. Nellie Clark Rodgers, "A Nebraska Pioneer," typescript of reminiscences. The original document is lost; a copy of the typescript is on file at the Nebraska Historical Society Library.

11. U. S. Census, Guthrie County, Iowa, 1880.

12. Nebraska State Census, 1885, Gosper County. The Devereaus moved to Nebraska in 1879, and filed on a timber culture claim on April 8, 1879. United States Land Office Tract Books for Nebraska, Vol. 76, T6N R23W, Sec. SW$^4$.

13. U. S. Census, 1880, Population Schedule, Oswego County, New York.

14. Ada Harris Clark, "Journal of a Trip from Nebraska to New York," September 20 to December 8, 1915.

## Chapter 7. For My Independence
## *Notes to Pages 73–82*

1. This chapter is based on Warren's diaries for 1881, 1882, 1883, unless otherwise noted.

2. The note was drawn to Randall & Dickey, Agricultural Implements, Mar. 23, 1882; Stuart *Locomotive*, Jan. 4, 1883.

3. S.B. Maxwell, *Centennial History of Guthrie County, Iowa . . .* (Des Moines, IA., 1876), pp. 114-147.

4. Ada Harris Clark, "Journal of a Trip from Nebraska to New York, 1915." John Ise, *Sod and Stubble: The Story Of A Kansas Homestead* (First Bison Book printing, Lincoln, NE., 1967), pp. 179-188, 196-200. Ise describes a dry period in 1880-81, about 40 miles west of John Howe's place. See also, Craig Miner, *West of Wichita: Settling the High Plains of Kansas, 1865-1900* (Lawrence, KS, 1986), pp. 128-29.

5. Oswego County, New York, Records, Deeds, Vol. 227, pp. 222-24, Nov. 29, 1897.

6. Rodgers, "A Nebraska Pioneer."

7. H. H. Mowry, "The Normal Day's Work of Farm Implements, Workmen, and Crews in Western New York," U.S. Department of Agriculture, *Bulletin No. 412*, Sep. 22, 1916, p. 9, in *Department Bulletins, Nos. 401-425* (Washington: Government Printing Office, 1919); Stuart *Locomotive*, Jan. 13, 1882.

8. Receipt dated Sep. 22, 1882, and signed by E. C. Mount, Agt. for Esther Porter, Owner.

9. U.S. Census, 1880, Population Schedules, Monona County, Sherman Township, p.1; *Blencoe Centennial, 1871-1971* (Blencoe, IA., n.d.), p.[182].

10. Rodgers, "Nebraska Pioneer".

11. *Blencoe Centennial, 1871-1971*.

12. United States Census, 1900, Population Schedule for Guthrie County, Iowa, p. 59.

## Chapter 8. Rain Follows the Plow
## *Notes to Pages 83–90*

1. This chapter is based largely on Warren Clark's diaries for 1884 and 1885.

2. Nellie Clark Rodgers, "A Nebraska Pioneer."

3. *Blencoe Centennial, 1871-1971*, Blencoe, IA., n.d., pp. 167-69; *History of Monona County, Iowa* (Chicago, IL., 1890), pp. 481-2. Only a few Indians, probably Sioux, remained in northwest Iowa after the

1850s--see Joseph Frazier Wall, *Iowa: A Bicentennial History* (New York and Nashville, TN., 1978), p. 15.

4. Everett Dick, *Conquering The Great American Desert: Nebraska,* Nebraska State Historical Society *Publications*, Vol. XXVII (Lincoln, NE., 1975), pp. 328-330.

5. Charles Dana Wilber cited by Henry Nash Smith, *Virgin land: The American West as Myth and Symbol* (Cambridge, MA.,1950, Reissued, 1976), pp. 182-183; L.D. Burch, *Nebraska As It Is* (Chicago, IL, 1878), p. 145. For a comprehensive survey of promotional efforts, see David M. Emmons, *Garden in the Grasslands: Boomer Literature of the Great Plains* (Lincoln, NE., 1971), pp. 25-77.

6. Everett Dick, *Conquering*, pp. 175-177, 328-336; Dick, *Sod-House Frontier 1854-1890 : A Social History of the Northern Plains from the Creation of Kansas and Nebraska to the Admission of the Dakotas* (Lincoln, NE., c. 1954), pp. 417-19; Monona County *Gazette*, Nov. 3, 1884, Feb. 23, 1885; Ada's pencilled note, made in her old age in Warren's Diary for Jan. 18, 1883.

7. See f.n. #4, Ch. VII.

8. Henry Nash Smith, *Virgin Land*, pp. 179-188, 196-200; Burch, pp. 25-29; Dick *Conquering*, pp. 12-20; Samuel Aughey *Sketches of the Physical Geography and Geology of Nebraska* (Omaha, NE., 1880), pp. 43, 44; James C.Olson, *History of Nebraska* (Lincoln, NE., 1966), pp. 166-68;

9. Thomas M. Davis, "Building the Burlington Through Nebraska--A Summary View," *Nebraska History*, XXX (Dec., 1949), 317-47; Gene O. Morris, *Portraits of the Past: McCook's First Hundred Years* (McCook, NE., 1982), pp. 35-36; *Hayes County Bicentennial Book* (Hayes Center, NE., ca. 1976), pp. 2, 4.

10. John O'Neill, *Northern Nebraska as a Home for Immigrants . . .* (Sioux City, IA., 1875), p. 13.

## Chapter 9. Finding a Homestead
## *Notes to Pages 91-100*

1. Warren Clark, Diary, 1885.

2. Nellie Clark, "A Nebraska Pioneer." Unless otherwise noted, the details of this chapter are based on Warren Clark's diary and Nellie' narrative.

3. "Furnas County Centennial, 1873-1973, "Supplement" to the McCook *Daily Gazette*, May 3, 1973.

4. Citing James C. Olson, without source, Bruce H. Nicoll, *Nebraska: A Pictorial History* (Lincoln, NE., 1967), p. 110.

5. United States Census, 1870, Population Schedule, Oswego County, New York, Williamstown. Joel Devereaux was 45-years-old; "Richard M. Roberts and Margaret Jefferies [sic] Roberts," *Hayes County Bicentennial Book* (Hayes Center, NE. ca. 1976, p. 82.

6. Old Jules, in northwest Nebraska, received $25 for locating a claim--see Mari Sandoz, *Sandhill Sundays and Other Recollections* (Lincoln, NE., 1971), p. 5. United States Land Office Tract Books for the State of Nebraska, Vol. 81, Blackwood Township, T5N, R32W, section 3. The *Kansas Farmer* recommended the upland to new settlers "for this land was better than bottom land for wheat and fruit orchards," as reported by Lawrence Bacon Lee, *Kansas and the Homestead Act, 1862-1905* (New York, 1979), pp. 204-5. Allan Bogue reports the same reaction among settlers in Iowa, *From Prairie to Cornbelt: Farming on the Illinois and Iowa Prairies in the Nineteenth Century* (Chicago, IL., University of Chicago Press, 1963), p. 47. In modern times a visitor from New York to Hayes County, looking at the canyons, voiced her "surprise at all the wasteland," Mildred Clark Richter to Robert D. Clark, Sep. 7, 1979.

7. Tract Books, sections 4, 5, 9; Addison E. Sheldon, *Land Systems and Land Policies in Nebraska Homesteading* . . . in *Publications of the Nebraska State Historical Society*, Vol. XXII (Lincoln, NE., 1936), 181.

8. Tract Books, section 11.

9. Tract Books, Section 11.

10. Tract Books, Logan Township, T6N R32W, Sec. 34.

11. Everett Dick, *Conquering the Great American Desert: Nebraska*; Nebraska State Historical Society *Publications*, Vol. XXVII (Lincoln, NE., 1975), pp.31-36.

12. Dick, ibid., pp. 31-36; Everett Dick, *Sod-House Frontier, 1854-1890* (Lincoln, NE., 1954), pp. 113-114. For further descriptions of sod houses see Frances Jacobs Albert, Ed., *Sod House Memories*, Sod House Society (n.p., 1972): Mr. and Mrs. P.J. Almquist, I, 6-8; Mrs. Clarence McNeal, I, 47, et.al.

## Chapter 10. The Lone Tree
## *Notes to Pages 101-110*

1. Nellie Clark Rodgers, "A Nebraska Pioneer." The details of this chapter, unless otherwise noted, are based on Nellie's account.

2. Gene O. Morris, *McCook's First One Hundred Years* . . . McCook, NE., 1982, pp. 35, 63, 67-69, citing the McCook *Tribune*.

3. The location of Hughes' homestead is recorded in the United States Land Office Tract Books for the State of Nebraska, Vol. 81, Blackwood Township, T5N, R32W section 5. Records of the Bureau of Land Management, National Archives (Washington, D.C.), microfilm.

4. Francis Parkman, *The Oregon Trail: Sketches of Prairie and Rocky-Mountain Life* (Boston, 1880), p. 61.

5. Amelia Jane Harris, Notebook, p. 71.

6. Ada Clark, Journal, May 30, 1933.

7. The writer has explored the possible route and discussed it with the late Homer Richter who, in 1980, lived three miles directly south of Hughes' homestead, on the land claimed by Christian Schielke and on the

probable route that Warren took. A "Lone Tree" at what is now Central City was a famous landmark on the California (Mormon) Trail in the early years of migration to Utah and the West Coast. See P.S. Heaton, "The Lone Tree," *Nebraska History*, XXXI (June, 1950), 147-50.

8. Tract Books, section 20.

9. 10th U.S. Census, 1880, Population Schedules, Hayes County, reprinted with minor errors in *Hayes County Bicentennial Book* (Hayes Center, NE., ca. 1976), pp. 22-23.

10. Hayes County *Herald*, Oct. 18, 1888; Hayes County *Times*, Oct. 24, 1888; Hayes County *Republican*, Aug. 15, 1889.

11. Ada Clark, "Journal of a Trip from Nebraska to New York," Sunday, Sep. [3], 1915.

12. Nellie Snyder Yost, *The Call of the Range: The Story of the Nebraska Stock Growers Association* (Denver, CO., 1966), pp. 75-76; Tract Books, sections 3, 4, 5, 9, 10, 11.

13. Conversation with Willard (Bud) McMullen, Oct. 1, 1978; Warren Clark, Diary, April 9, 13, 25, 29, 1891, locates his fields north, south, and east of his house.

14. Nellie gives enough detail about the house to verify its careful construction; further details are taken from Everett Dick, *The Sod-House Frontier, 1854-1890* (New York, 1937), pp. 113-115; Dick, *Conquering the Great American Desert:Nebraska*; Nebraska State Historical Society, *Publications*, Vol. XXVII (Lincoln, NE., 1975), p. 329, quoting Keith County *News*, (Ogallala), March 19, 1886; *Hayes County Bicentennial Book*, p. 25.

## Chapter 11. Hope
## *Notes to Pages 111-120*

1. Nellie Clark Rodgers, "A Nebraska Pioneer." Details of this chapter, unless otherwise noted, are based on Nellie's account and Warren Clark, Diary.

2. United States Land Office Tract Books for the State of Nebraska, Vol. 81, Blackwood Township, T5N, R32W, sec. one.

3. Tract Books, ibid., sections 11, 15; Sidney A. Ahlstrom, *A Religious History of the American People* (New Haven, c. 1972), pp. 439-40; William Bert McMullen, *The McMullen Family Book* [Kansas City, MO., 1953], p. 20; "Robert M. Roberts and Margaret Jefferies [sic] Roberts," *Hayes County Bicentennial Book* (Hayes Center, NE., ca. 1976), p. 82.

4. Tract Books, sec. 11.

5. Methodist Episcopal Church, *Minutes of the West Nebraska Conference,* (University Place, NE., 1888), pp. 56, 61.

6. Kathryn Jewel Clark related this incident to her children, including the writer; Arley H. Clark to Robert D. Clark, Aug. 30, 1982.

7. Hayes County *Herald*, Sep. 6, 1888.

8. "A Normal Day's Work for Various Farm Operations," *Bulletin* of the U.S. Department of Agriculture, No. 3, Sep. 23, 1913, in *Contributions from the Bureau of Plant Industry* (Washington: Government Printing Office, 1914), Nos. 1-25, p. 10, Table II, p. 15, Table VI; Hamlin Garland plowed two acres of stubble in a day, *Son of the Middle Border* (New York, 1922), p. 88. The plains agriculture, James C. Olson wrote, "was not corn and 'tater' patch farming, but a commercial enterprise," in *History of Nebraska* (Lincoln, NE., 1966), pp. 169-70. Fred A. Shannon, *The Farmer's Last Frontier: Agriculture, 1960-1897* (New York, 1968), pp. 165-169.

9. James C. Olson, *J. Sterling Morton* (Lincoln, NE., 1942), p. 191; Hayes County *Republican*, Jan. 30, 1890.

10. United States Census, 1900, Population Schedule for Nebraska, Hayes County, Blackwood Precinct, records Mary Martin's age as 70 years; Everett Dick, "Water: A Frontier Problem," *Nebraska History* 49 (Autumn, 1968), 234. For the shipment of kerosene, "coal oil," "in large wooden barrels," see "Edsal and Harrie S. Potts," *Hayes County Bicentennial Book*, p. 76.

11. Everett Dick, *Conquering the Great American Desert: Nebraska*; Nebraska State Historical Society *Publications*, Vol. XXVII (Lincoln, NE., 1975), 107; Charles S. Reed, "Life in a Nebraska Soddy, A Reminiscence," *Nebraska History*, XXXIX (Mar., 1958), 63.

12. Beth Sims Frasier, "The Blizzard of Jan. 12, 1888," *Hayes County Centennial Book*, p. 35.

13. "Gruver Family," *Hayes County Bicentennial Book*, p. 83.

14. Warren Clark, Memorandum Book, n.d., ca.1888.

15. Methodist Episcopal Church, *Minutes of the West Nebraska Conference* (University Place, NE., 1888), pp. 56, 61.

## Chapter 12. We Finished the Well
## *Notes to Pages 121–128*

1. The narrative in this chapter is based largely on Warren Clark's Diary for 1888 and Nellie Clark Rodgers, "A Nebraska Pioneer." Mortgages for Case and Driscol were entered in the Hayes County Mortgage Records, Vol. I, pp. 155-56, May 24, 1889; Vol. II, p. 221, May 28, 1887.

2. United States Land Office Tract Books for the State of Nebraska, Vol. 81, Blackwood Township, T5N, R32W, Section 10, Records of the Bureau of Land Management, National Archives (Washington, D.C.), Microfilm, Sep. 24, 1884, Aug. 22, 1887, Sep. 17, 1887. Robert D. Clark, "The Settlement of Blackwood Township, Hayes County, Nebraska, 1878-1907," *Nebraska History*, 66 (Spring, 1985), 80.

3. Tract Books, Logan Township, T6N, R32W, Section 35.

4. "Our Old Newspaper Tells Interesting Pioneer Stories," *Atlas of Hayes County*, compiled by Western Cartographers (Sioux City, NE., 1980), n.p.

5. Friedrich Wach's well in Hayes County was four feet square: "Life Was Great Life Was Dear For This Dedicated Pioneer," *Hayes County Bicentennial Book* (Hayes Center, NE., ca. 1976), p. 66. Charley O'Kieffe, *Western Story: The Recollections of Charley O'Kieffe, 1884-1898* (Lincoln, NE., 1960), p. 34, says that in his neighborhood, Sheridan County in northwest Nebraska, wells were usually three feet square.

6. R.L. Ardrey describes the harrow in *American Agricultural Implements . . .* 1894, Reprint Edition, Series, *Technology and Society*, Advising Editor, Daniel J. Boorstin (New York: Arno Press, 1972), p. 21; Hamlin Garland, *Son of the Middle Border* (New York: The Macmillan Company, 1922), p. 100.

7. Garland, *Middle Border*, p. 88.

8. The child of one western Nebraska settler recalled that, near Lexington, farmers were still sowing by hand in the 1890s: see Frances Jacobs Albert, Ed., *Sod House Memories*, Sod House Society (n.p. 1972), Alva T. Anderson, Vol. 2, p. 97.

9. Hayes County Court Journal, May Term, 1888, p. 32; Hayes County *Times*, Jan. 30, 1889.

10. Court Journal, May Term, 1888, p. 23.

11. Hayes County Deed Records, Vol. IV, p. 399, Mar. 17, 1888; Court Journal, ibid., pp. 20-21, 30-32.

12. Conversation with Mrs. Glen Scott, Sep. 9, 1878; William Bert McMullen, *The McMullen Family Book* (Kansas City, 1953), p. 30.

## Chapter 13. Summer
## *Notes to Pages 129-140*

1. The principal sources for this chapter are Warren Clark, Diary, 1888, and Nellie Clark Rodgers, "A Nebraska Pioneer."

2. Lena Mae Madely, "Joseph G. Smith, A Pioneer," *Hayes County Centennial Book* (Hayes Center, NE., ca. 1976), p. 47.

3. Hayes County Mortgage Record, Vol. 19, p. 227, Feb. 13, 1901.

4. The duty of the justice is clear from Warren's brief note and is made explicit by orders to the justices for the distribution of aid to drought sufferers in 1894, see Hayes County *Republican*, Mar. 31, 1894.

5. Arley H. Clark to Robert D. Clark, June 13, 1980.

6. *Republican*, Feb. 13, Apr. 10, 24, May 21, Jun. 26, 1890.

7. *Republican*, May 4, 1893; Hayes County *Times*, May 21, 1890, Jan. 21, 1891. It was believed not only in Nebraska but elsewhere on the plains that settlement and cultivation of crops brought increased rain; the actual increases in the 1870s and again in the 1880s seemed to confirm the belief. See Craig Miner, *West of Wichita: Settling the High Plains of Kansas, 1865-1890* (Lawrence, KS., 1986), p. 47 and Paul Travis,

"Changing Climate in Kansas, A Late 19th Century Myth," *Kansas History*, (Spring, 1978), pp. 48-58, particularly, p. 52.

8. Ada's undated (ca. 1935) penciled note in Warren's diary for Jan. 18, 1883, supports Warren's entries about the Heaters for 1888. U.S. Census Population Schedule for Nebraska, Hayes County, Harrison Precinct, 1890.

9. Kleven's Grove, in Highland Township, was on the Blackwood. Mrs. Gladys Godtel to Mildred Richter, February 26, 1991.

10. *Herald*, Sep. 13, 1888.

## Chapter 14. Harvest
## *Notes to Pages 141-152*

1. Warren Clark, Diary, 1888, is the principal source for this chapter.

2. May, who held a mortgage on the Hayes County *Republican*, took it over when Abbott defaulted. McCook *Tribune*, Dec. 12, 1902. The George Barda in Warren's diary may be George Buda, cited in the Hayes County *Republican*, Aug. 14, 1889, as one of the organizers of a short-lived Presbyterian Church.

3. Joel lived on the SW$^{4}$ of section 34, T6N R32W. Emma's tree claim was on the SE$^{4}$ of section 12, T5N R32W. United States Land Tract Books for Nebraska, Vol. 81.

4. Tract Books, NW$^{4}$ of section 6, T5N R31W.

5. For descriptions of threshing see Charley O'Kieffe, *Western Story: The Recollections of Charley O'Kieffe, 1884-1898* (Lincoln, NE., 1960), pp. 86-88; Everett Dick, *Sod-House Frontier, 1954-1890* (Lincoln, NE., 1954), pp. 291-293. That it was a horse-powered machine is affirmed by the fact that a neighbor, Frank Jackson, bought such a machine four years later, see Hayes County *Republican*, Aug. 18, 1892.

6. John T. Schlebecker, *Whereby We Thrive: A History of American Farming, 1687-1922* (Ames, IA., 1975), p. 192.

7. Hayes County *Times*, Oct. 3, 1888. Warren's diary, which stops soon after this entry, contains no record of payment of the second note.

8. Hayes County *Herald*, Dec. 6, 1888.

9. Hattie's tree claim, on which she filed in October, 1889, was in sec. 15, SE$^{4}$ of NE$^{4}$. See United States Land Office Tract Books for the State of Nebraska, Vol. 81, Blackwood Township.

10. Howard Ruede, *Sod House Days: Letters from a Kansas Homesteader, 1877-78*, John Ise, Ed. (New York, 1937), p. 145.

11. Everett Dick, *Conquering the Great American Desert,: Nebraska*; Nebraska State Historical Society *Publications*, Vol. XXVII (Lincoln, NE., 1975), 142-145.

12. *Times*, Oct. 10, 1888.

## Chapter 15. Methodist Ridge
### *Notes to Pages 153-162*

1. Hayes County *Herald*, Aug. 16, 23, 30, Sep. 6, Dec. 6, 1888.
2. *Herald*, Sep. 13, 1888; Hayes County *Times*, Aug. 29, 1888.
3. *Times*, Sep. 5, Oct. 3, 1888.
4. *Times*, Aug. 15, 1888; Conversation with Homer Richter, Oct. 11, 1978.
5. *Herald*, Sep. 6, 1888.
6. Richard Hofstadter, *Social Darwinism in American Thought*, rev. ed. (New York, 1959), pp. 178-79; *Herald*, ibid., Sep. 6, 1888. James C. Olson, *History Of Nebraska* (Lincoln, NE., 1966), p. 195, points out that the abundant rainfall in the eighties "appeared to be demonstrating" the validity of "the theory that 'rainfall follows the plow.'"
7. *Times*, June 5, 1889; Hayes County *Republican*, Jan. 9, 30, Feb. 13, May 1, 29,1890.
8. *Herald*, Mar. 2, Apr. 18, 1889; *Republican*, May 16, 1889, Mar. 20, Dec. 4, 1890; *Times*, May 21, 1890; Hayes County Mechanic's Lien Record Vol. 1, p. 82, Mar. 18, 1889, ibid., Vol. 1, p. 85, Jan. 30, 1889.
9. *Times*, Jan. 2, 23, 1889.
10. United States Land Office Tract Books for the State of Nebraska, Vol. 81, Blackwood Township, T5N R32W. For changing ownership see Allan Bogue, *From Prairie to Cornbelt: Farming on the Illinois and Iowa Prairies in the Nineteenth Century* (Chicago, IL., University of Chicago Press, 1963), pp. 51-52.
11. Tract Books, Secs. 1 and 13, and Highland Township, T5N R31W, Sec. 6; Conversations with Mrs. Glen Scott, Sep. 29, 1978; Willard (Bud) McMullen, Oct. 12, 1980, and Charles Mansfield, Oct. 12, 1980; Nellie Clark Rodgers, "A Nebraska Pioneer."
12.Tract Books, Secs. 2, 15; Rodgers, ibid.; *Republican*, May 30, Dec. 12, 1889; Willard McMullen, Oct. 18, 1980.
13. Hayes County Deed Record, Vol. 4, p. 289, Sep. 6, 1889.
14. Hayes County District Court Journal, Vol. I, p. 39, Oct. 9, 1895; Hayes County Marriage Record, Vol. I, p. 128, Nov. 26, 1889; *Republican*, Nov. 24, 1889.
15. U.S. Tract Books, Sec. 2; *Republican*, Feb. 13, 1890.
16. U.S. Tract Books, Sec. 14; *Republican*, Nov. 24, 1889, Jan. 9, 1890; *Times*, Jul. 2, 1890.
17. Methodist Episcopal Church, *Minutes of the West Nebraska Conference* (University Place, NE., 1889), pp. 35, 41; *Republican*, Jan. 23, Mar. 20, Jul. 23, Oct. 9, 1890, Apr. 14, 1894.
18. U.S. Tract Books, Logan Township, T6N R32W, Secs. 27, 32, 33; *Herald*, Jan. 31, 1889; *Republican*, Jan. 31, May 16, 1889.
19. *Herald*, Mar. 28, Apr. 18, 1889; *Times*, Apr. 16, 1890.
20. *Republican*, Jun. 20, Jul. 14, Aug. 1 and 8, Nov. 7, 1889, Jun. 12, 1890.

21. *Herald*, Jun. 6, 27, 1889; Doc and Nellie's ages were determined by reference to the United States Census, 1900, Population Schedules, Hayes County, Nebraska.

22. Methodist Episcopal Church, *Minutes*, 1889, pp. 35, 41.

## Chapter 16. The Prairie Looks Good
## *Notes to Pages 163–170*

1. Hayes County *Republican*, May 8, 1890.

2. Nellie Clark Rodgers, "A Nebraska Pioneer," manuscript. Much of this chapter is based on Nellie's account.

3. Rodgers. For an excellent account of the homesteader's domestic life see "Home," Chapter XII in Craig Miner's *West Of Wichita: Settling The High Plains Of Kansas, 1865-1890* (Lawrence, KS., 1986), pp. 145-159. Everett Dick, *Sod-House Frontier, 1854-1890* (Lincoln, NE., 1954), pp 232-43, and "Sunbonnet and Calico: The Homesteader's Consort," in *Nebraska History*, XLVII (Mar, 1966) has graphic descriptions of domestic duties and hardships. See also Glenda Riley, *Frontierswomen: The Iowa Experience* (Ames, IA., 1981), Ch. II, "Women's Workplace," pp. 29-55. Riley (p. 30) is justly critical of earlier writers who overstate, mythologize, the hardships women faced and the way they met, or retreated from them. For other colorful details, and enterprises of the women, see Julie Roy Jeffrey, "A Maid of All Traids," Chapter 3, pp. 51-78, *Frontier Women: The Trans-Mississippi West, 1840-1880*, American Century Series (New York, 1979).

4. Robert D. Clark, "Ada Harris, Teenager: Oswego County, New York, 1873," *New York History*, XVI (Jan., 1985), 33.

5. Certificate from the L. Chase & Co's Chemical Works, New Bedford, Mass., Aug. 26, 1886, for soap making, in Warren and Ada Clark's papers.

6. *Republican*, Jan. 9, 1890.

7. Scenes in Oswego County are from Ada's diary, 1873 (Clark) and Ada Harris Clark, untitled manuscript Journal of a Trip to New York, 1915.

8. Amelia Jane Harris to Earl Clark, Sep. 19, 1901.

9. Rodgers, "Nebraska Pioneer."

10. *Republican*, Feb. 20, 1890, from the Trenton *Register*, n.d.; *Republican*, May 23, 1889; United States Land Office Tract Books for the State of Nebraska, Vol. 81, Blackwood Township, T5N R32W, sec. 14; Hayes County Court Journal, May Term, 1889, p. 57.

11. Rodgers; Clayton Clark to Robert D. Clark, Oct. 18, 1980.

12. Rodgers; *Republican*, Aug. 14, 1890.

13. *Republican*, Feb. 6, Mar. 13, 1890.

14. Rodgers; *Republican*, Jan 23, 1890.

15. *Republican*, Mar. 13, 1890.

## Chapter 17. Brace Up with The Thought
## *Notes to Pages 171-180*

1. United States Land Office Tract Books for the State of Nebraska, Vol. 81, Blackwood Township, T5N R32W; See, also, Robert D. Clark, "The Settlement of Blackwood Township, Hayes County, Nebraska, 1878-1907, *Nebraska History*, LXVI (Spring, 1985), 90 ff; Hayes County *Times,* Apr. 30, 1890; Hayes County *Republican*, Aug. 11, 1892.

2. *Republican*, April 10, 1890.

3. Hayes County Mortgage Records, Vol. IX, p. 46, Dec. 9, 1889; Deed Records, Vol. V, pp. 479-80, Sep. 28, 1892; *Times*, May 22, 1889. Annie Jeffries' title by commutation is recorded in the United States Land Office Tract Books, Section 3. The record of any possible mortgage and of her sale of the property to Roberts apparently was destroyed in a fire in 1891; Hayes County *Times*, Jun. 19, 1889, citing McCook *Tribune*, n.d.

4. Hayes County Mechanics Lien Records, Vol. I, p. 71, Nov. 19, 1888, p. 85, Jan. 30, 1890; Deed Records, Vol. IV, p. 226, Aug. 23, 1890, Vol. X, p. 181, Jan. 13, 1898; Mortgage Records, XII, pp. 196-199, Sep. 1, 1889; *Republican*, Nov. 24, 1889; Clark, p. 91. Although many records were destroyed in the fire of 1891, some information, e.g., Scott's mortgage, can be determined from entries of subsequent transactions. Except for the low prices on farm produce beginning in the good year of 1889 and the disastrous droughts of 1890 and 1894, the mortgages might have proved a good investment for farmers trying to increase their production; see Allan G. Bogue, *Money at Interest: The Farm Mortgage On The Middle Border* (Ithaca, NY., 1955, reissued, New York, 1969), pp. 1-6, 267, 274.

5. Clark, p. 92.

6. *Times*, Jan. 1, 1890; *Republican*, Feb. 27, 1890. Willard (Bud) McMullen, reported by Mildred Clark Richter to Robert D. Clark, [Jan. 21, 1978].

7. *Republican*, Mar. 20, 1890.

8. Ibid., Apr. 18, 1889, Mar. 27, Apr. 10, 24, 1890; *Times*, Apr. 2, 16, 1890. Forest trees for timber claims sold for $1.20 per 1,000, Hayes County *Herald*, Jan. 31, 1889. James C. Olson, *J. Sterling Morton* (Lincoln, NE.: University of Nebraska Press, 1942), pp. 162-166. Morton argued, not for the spurious claim of manipulating the weather, but for the "beauty" of trees, for orchards as "missionaries of culture and refinement," for fruit and forest trees to make Nebraska "the Orchard of the Union, the Sylvan Queen of the Republic."

9. *Republican*, Apr. 10, 17, 24, May 8, 22, 29, Jun. 5, 1890; *Times*, Apr. 16, 23, 30, June 18, 1890.

10. *Republican*, June 12,19, Jul. 3, 10, 1890; *Times*, Jul. 2, 1890.

11. *Republican*, Jul. 24, Aug. 7, 14, 1890.

12. *Republican,* Jul. 31, 1890.

13. *Republican*, Apr. 10, May 8, Apr. 10, Aug. 14, Sep. 4, 1890.

14. *Republican*, Apr. 24, Aug. 7, Sep. 4, 1890, Jan. 29, 1891; *Times*, Jan. 28, 1891; Deed Record, Vol. 5, p. 147, Nov. 21, 1891.

15. *Republican*, May 22, Aug. 14, Sep. 4, Oct. 9, 16, 1890; Deed Record, Vol. V, p. 147, Nov. 21, 1891. Lucy McMullen, Shaffer's sister, acquired the property from Theovalt for Shaffer to whom she transferred it later. Tract Books, Blackwood Township, T5N R32W, sec. 11, Oct. 20, 1890, Mar. 5, 1892.

16. *Republican*, Oct. 8, 1891.

17. *Republican*, Oct. 9, 16, Nov. 20, 1890; Conversation with Mrs. Fred Wittwer, Oct. 13, 1980.

18. Nellie Clark Rodgers, "A Nebraska Pioneer;" *Hayes County Herald*, Nov. 15, 1888.

19. *Republican*, Oct. 16, Nov. 13, 1890.

20. *Republican*, Dec. 18, 1890.

21. *Republican*, Feb. 27, Aug. 7, 1890; James C. Olson, *History Of Nebraska* (Lincoln, NE., 1966), pp. 221-222; Ronald Briel, "Preface to Populism: A Social Analysis of Minor Parties in Nebraska Politics, 1976-1890," Ph.D. thesis, University of Nebraska, 1981, Microfilm of Typescript, (Ann Arbor, MI.,1981), pp. 283-285; David S. Trask, "Nebraska Populism as a Response to Environmental and political problems," in Brian W. Blouet and Frederick C. Luebke, Eds., *The Great Plains: Environment and Culture* (Lincoln, NE., 1979), pp. 70-72.

22. *Republican*, Aug. 7, 1890.

23. *Republican*, Jun. 26, Nov. 20, 27, 1890.

24. *Republican*, Nov. 6, 1890.

## Chapter 18. Glorious Rain
## *Notes to Pages 181–190*

1. *Republican*, Jul. 31, 1890.

2. *Republican*, Nov. 13, 27, 1890.

3. *Republican*, Nov. 20, 27, Dec. 4, 1890.

4. *Republican*, Feb. 12, 26, Mar. 12, 1891; Albert Watkins, *History of Nebraska* (Lincoln, NE., 1911), III, 236; Everett Dick, *Conquering The Great American Desert: Nebraska*, Nebraska State Historical Society *Publications*, XXVII, 322-34.

5. United States Land Office Tract Books for the State of Nebraska, Vol. 81, Blackwood Township, T5N R32W, Sec. 22.

6. Nellie Clark Rodgers, "A Nebraska Pioneer." Further references to Nellie are from this source.

7. *Republican*, Mar. 5, 12, Apr. 9, 1891; *Times*, Mar. 11, 1891.

8. *Republican*, Nov. 27, 1890, Apr. 23, 30, 1891.

9. *Republican*, Jun. 25, 1891.

10. *Republican*, Nov. 27, 1890.

11. *Republican*, Nov. 13, 1890; Warren Clark, Diary. Further references to Warren Clark, unless otherwise noted, will be from this source.

12. *Times*, Apr. 29, 1891.

13. *Times*, May 6, 27; *Republican*, May 21, 1891; "Charles C. & Phebe C. Troxel," *Hayes County Bicentennial Book* (n.p. ca.1976), p. 48.

14. *Times*, Jun. 24, 1891; *Republican*, Jun. 11, 1891.

15. Hayes County Deed Record, Vol. 4, p. 32, Aug. 31, 1891; *Republican*, Jun. 4, 1891; Dec. 18, 1890, Jul. 9, 1891.

16. Tract Books, Logan Township, T6N R32W, Sec. 28, Jun. 13, 1891; *Times*, May 6, 1891.

17. Warren Clark, Diary, Nov. 5, 1891; Ada Clark, Journal of a Trip to Nebraska (Untitled), May 6, 1933.

18. *Republican*, Jul. 30, Aug. 6, 27, Nov. 19, 1891, May 12, 1892; *Times*, Jun. 24, Dec. 16, 1891.

19. Mildred Clark Richter to Robert D. Clark, Jun. 18, 1980.

20. *Republican*, Sep. 17, 1891, Jun. 16, 1892.

21. Warren's references to Theovalt are recorded in both his diary and in an undated account book.

22. *Republican*, Nov. 19, 1891.

## Chapter 19. Stand Up for Hayes County
## *Notes to Pages 191-198*

1. Hayes County *Republican*, Feb. 4, 1892; Warren Clark, diary for 1892. Further references to Warren's activities, unless otherwise noted, are to this source. For discussion of the corn-hog ratio see Fred A. Shannon, *The Farmer's Last Frontier: 1860-1897*, Vol. V, *The Economic History of the United States* New York, 1945), pp. 165-69; also, James C. Olson, *The History of Nebraska* (Lincoln, NE., 1966), pp. 197-98.

2. Hayes County Deed Record, Vol. 4, p. 296, Aug. 6, 1891.

3. Hayes County Deed Record, Vol. 5. p. 152, Jan. 15, 1892; Nellie Clark Rodgers, "A Nebraska Pioneer." Further references to Nellie's activities and narrative are to this source.

4. Hayes County *Times*, Jan. 13, Apr. 13, 1892; *Republican*, Jun. 26, 1890, Jan. 21, 1892; Hayes County Mortgage Record, Vol. 14, pp. 232-5, Jul. 1, 1892, pp. 257, 259, Jul. 4, 1, 1892. Deed Record, Vol. 7, p. 532, Jun. 13, 1897, cites Los Angeles, CA., as the address for Henry and Nellie Devereau, the only report we have of their removal.

5. *Republican*, May 2, 1893; Deed Record, Vol. 6, pp. 19-20, May 22, 1893; Hayes County District Court Journal, Vol. 1, p. 197, Nov., 1891.

6. Deed Record, Vol. 4, p. 347, Dec. 8, 1891 (He purchased it from Annie's parents, Brice and Eliza Jane McMullen--how they acquired it from Annie is lost in the record, undoubtedly because of the fire). Deed Record, Vol. 4, p. 431, Mar. 18, 1892; Mortgage Record, Vol. 5, pp. 81-84, Mar. 20, 1888, Vol. 6, p. 418, Oct. 22, 1888, etc.; United States Land Office

Tract Books for the State of Nebraska, Vol. 81, Blackwood Township, T5N R32W, sec. 35, Feb. 9, 1891, and Deed Record, Vol. 7, p. 27, Apr. 3, 1891.

7. William Bert McMullen, *The McMullen Family Book* (Kansas City, MO., 1953), pp. 23-24; *Republican*, June 12, 1890; Everett Dick, *Conquering The Great American Desert: Nebraska*, Nebraska State Historical Society *Publications*, Vol. XXVII (Lincoln, NE., 1975), pp. 355-362; Mary W. M. Hargreaves, *Dry Farming in the Northern Great Plains, 1900-1925* (Cambridge, MA., 1957), pp. 85-86; *Republican*, Jun. 12, 1890.

8. Clark, Diary; Rodgers, "Pioneer."

9. *Republican*, Jul. 7, 1892, Sep. 14, 1893.

10. *Times*, Jul. 20, 1892; *Republican*, Aug 11, Nov. 10, Dec. 8, 15, 1892.

11. *Republican*, Nov. 3, 10, 1892, Aug. 13, 1891.

12. *Republican*, Nov. 10, 1892; James C. Olson, *History Of Nebraska* (Lincoln, NE., 1966), pp. 234-237.

13. *Republican*, Aug. 25, 1892, Jun. 28, 1894.

## Chapter 20. When It Rains It Pours
## *Notes to Pages 199–208*

1. Hayes County *Times*, Jan. 18, 1893, Apr. 22, 1891; Hayes County *Republican*, Jan. 26, Mar. 16, 1893.

2. *Republican*, Jan. 19, 1893.

3. *Times*, Dec. 6, 1893; Nellie Clark Rodgers, "A Nebraska Pioneer."

4. Conversation with Willard (Bud) McMullen, Oct. 23, 1980; *Republican*, Dec. 21, 1893, reports that Mrs. Y. E. Benton, 4 miles east of Hayes Center has a new loom and "will do carpet weaving." The date when Ada Clark acquired her loom is not known.

5. Mildred Clark Richter to Robert D. Clark, Jan. 11, 1978, confirmed by L. Kenneth Clark to Robert D. Clark, Jun. 26, 1982 and Arley H. Clark to Robert D. Clark, Aug. 30, 1982. Abbott, in the *Republican*, Apr. 14, 1894, said that Moore "eats more tobbaco [sic] than all the other preachers in the conference."

6. Arley H. Clark to Robert D. Clark, Jun. 13, 1980.

7. *Republican*, Dec. 8, 22, 1892, Jan. 26, Feb. 16, Mar. 2, Mar. 23, Apr. 27, May 11, Jun. 29, 1893; *Times*, May 10, 1893.

8. *Republican*, Jul. 13, Aug. 3, 10, 1893, Jan. 13, 1894.

9. *Republican*, Jul. 27, Aug. 3, 17, 1893.

10. *Republican*, Aug. 3, 31, Sep. 7, Dec. 14, 1893. The phenomenon of local showers, which gave encouragement to rainmakers, is referred to in Dick, pp. 336-345.

11. *Republican*, Apr. 13, Jul. 27, Aug. 3, 1893.

12. Nellie Rodgers. Further reference to Nellie's narrative is made without notation. Conversation with Willard (Bud) McMullen, Oct. 23, 1980; *Republican*, May 4, 1893.

13. *Republican*, Sep. 14, 1893.

14. *Republican*, Sep. 14, 1893.

15. *Republican*, May 11, 1893.

16. *Republican*, Aug. 24, 1893. Warren Clark's account with Mrs. Briggs is listed on a loose sheet in his diary for 1893.

17. *Republican*, Aug. 3, 1893.

18. *Republican*, Aug. 10, 1893.

19. *Republican*, Mar. 2, Aug. 17, 1893; Hayes County Deed Record, Vol. 6, p. 19, Feb. 11, 1893; Deed Record, Vol. 8, p. 66, Aug. 22, 1895.

20. *Republican*, May 4, 11, 18, Jun. 29, Jul. 20, 1893.

21. *Republican*, May 18, Jun. 29, Jul. 20, Aug. 17, 31, Sep. 7, 14, Oct. 5, 26, 1893.

## Chapter 21. DUST OF THE EARTH
## *Notes to Pages 209–220*

1. *Republican*, Dec, 28, 1893.

2. *Republican*, Jan. 6, 13, 1894.

3. *Republican*, Jan. 13, 20, 1894

4. *Republican*, Jan. 20, 27, 1894

5. *Republican*, Feb. 10, 24, 1894

6. *Republican*, Mar. 24, 31, 1894

7. *Republican*, Mar. 10, 17, 31, Apr. 7, 14. 28, 1894

8. *Republican*, Mar. 17, 31, Apr. 7, 14, 1894

9. *Republican*, Mar. 17, Apr. 21, 1894

10. *Republican*, Apr. 21, May 19, Jun. 7, 1894

11. *Republican*, May 31, 1894

12. *Republican*, May 26, Jun. 7, 1894

13. *Republican*, Jan. 13, Feb. 3, Mar. 17, Jun. 14, Jul. 5, 1894. Hayes County Deed Record, Vol. 6, p. 342, Feb. 24, 1894.

14. *Republican*, Feb. 3, Mar. 3, 17.

15. Nellie Clark Rodgers, "A Nebraska Pioneer." *Republican*, Jul. 27, 1893, Mar. 17, Apr. 28, Aug. 3, 1894; Methodist Episcopal Church, *Minutes Of The West Nebraska Conference* (University Place, NE., 1890), n.p.

16. *Republican*, Jan. 27, Feb. 10, Jul. 12, 1894

17. *Republican*, Mar. 31, 1894

18. *Republican*, May 12, 19, Jul. 26, 1894

19. *Republican*, May 12, Jun. 7, 1894

20. *Republican*, Jun. 7, 1894

21. *Republican*, Jun. 21, 28, 1894

22. *Republican*, Jun. 21, 28, Jul. 5, 19, 1894

23. *Republican*, Jul. 26, 1894

24. New York *Tribune*, Aug. 1, 8, 1894; New York *Times*, Aug. 5, 1894; Omaha *Evening Bee*, Jul. 26, 1894, cited in an able and comprehensive study by Everett Dick, "The Great Nebraska Drouth of 1894: The Exodus," *Arizona And The West,* 15 (Winter, 1973), pp. 333-334, and particularly p. 340.

25. "The Destitution in Nebraska," *Harper's Weekly*, 39 (Jan. 19, 1895), 62; *Republican*, Aug. 2, 16, 23, 1894, Feb. 14, 1895.

26. *Republican*, Sep. 20, Dec. 20, 1894.

27. *Republican*, Jun. 7, Jul. 5, 1894, Dec. 4, 1890.

28. *Republican*, May to August, 1894, particularly, Jul. 12, 19, 1894. Robert D. Clark, "The Settlement of Blackwood Township, Hayes County, Nebraska, *Nebraska History*, 66 (Spring, 1985), 94-96. Everett Dick, *Conquering The Great American Desert: Nebraska*, Nebraska State Historical Society *Publications*, XXVII (Lincoln, NE., 1975), 347-48.

29. *Republican*, Aug. 2, 23, Oct., 18, 1894; Hayes County Deed Record, Vol. 7, p. 532, Jun. 13, 1897; Vol. 7, p. 222, Mar. 23, 1895; Vol. 6, p. 270, Aug. 14, 1894. Hayes County Deed Record, Vol. 7, p. 532, Jun. 13, 1897.

30. *Republican*, Aug. 2, 16, 1894

31. *Republican*, May 31, 1894, Aug. 1, 1895.

32. *Republican*, Aug. 23, Oct. 25, Nov. 8, 1894.

33. *Republican*, Nov. 22, 1894

## Chapter 22. In Agony Shape
## *Notes to Pages 221-230*

1. Hayes County *Republican*, Sep. 6, 1894.

2. *Republican*, Sep. 20, 27, 1894.

3. *Republican*, Dec. 20, 1894; Nellie Clark Rodgers, "A Nebraska Pioneer;" conversation with Mrs. Glen Scott, Oct. 29, 1978.

4. *Republican*, Dec. 20, 27, 1894.

5. *Republican*, Oct. 18, Dec. 27, 1894. It was the practice of the railroads to ship the aid goods without charge, Everett Dick, *Conquering The Great American Desert: Nebraska*, Nebraska State Historical Society *Publications*, XXVII (Lincoln, NE., 1975), 352.

6. *Republican*, Jan. 10, 1895; Omaha *World-Herald*, Dec. 25, 1984.

7. New York *Times*, Dec. 24, 1894; "Destitution in Nebraska," *Harper's Weekly*, 39 (Jan. 19, 1895), 59. Dick, ibid., p. 344-46, 349-52.

8. *Republican*, Nov. 15, 1894, Jan. 17, 24, Feb. 21, 28, 1895.

9. *Republican*, Nov. 29, 1894, Jan. 3, 1895.

10. *Republican*, Oct. 25, Dec. 6, 20, 27, 1894.

11. *Minutes of the First Annual Conference of the Epworth League*, bound with the Methodist Episcopal Church *Minutes of the West Nebraska Conference* (University Place, NE., 1890). Rodgers, "A Nebraska Pioneer;" *Republican*, Dec. 20, 27, 1894, Jan. 3, 10, 24, 1895.

12. *Republican*, Jan. 17, 24, Feb. 7, 1895.

13. *Republican*, Feb. 7, 1895.
14. *Republican*, Jan. 17, 31, Feb. 14, 21, 28, Mar. 7, 14, 1895.
15. *Republican*, Mar. 14, 1895, and succeeding issues.
16. *Republican*, Mar. 28, Apr. 4, 1895.
17. *Republican*, Apr. 4, 1895.
18. *Republican*, Apr. 4, 1895.
19. *Republican*, Apr. 18, 1895.
20. *Republican*, Apr. 18, 1895.
21. *Republican*, Feb. 21, Mar. 14, 21, 28, Apr. 25, 1895.
22. *Republican*, Mar. 21, 28, Apr. 11, 1895. Dick, pp. 350, 352.
23. *Republican*, Apr. 18, 25, May 2, 9, 16, 30, 1895.
24. Jun. 6, 13, 1895; Hayes County *Times*, Jun. 12, 1895.
25. *Republican*, Jun. 6, 1895.
26. *Republican*, Jan. 3, 10, Feb. 7, 21, Mar. 14, Jul. 18, 1895.
27. Jul. 18, Aug. 8, Sep. 5, 12, 26, Oct. 10, 24; *Times*, Nov. 6, 20, 1895.
28. *Republican*, Sep. 26, Nov. 21, Dec. 12, 1895.
29. Dec. 12, 1895; *Times*, Dec. 18, 1895.
30. *Republican*, Nov. 28, 1895, Mar. 28, 1895.

## Chapter 23. Nellie Grows Up
## *Notes to Pages 231–240*

1. Nellie Clark Rodgers, "A Nebraska Pioneer," manuscript, 1967. This chapter is drawn largely from Nellie's story. Other sources are noted.

2. See Everett Dick, *Sod-House Frontier, 1854-1890* (Lincoln, NE., 1954), pp. 364-385 for an interesting account of frontier social activities, many, but by no means all, of them engaged in by settlers on Methodist Ridge.

3. Hayes County *Republican*, Feb. 14, 21, 1895.

4. Hayes County *Republican*, Jan. 3, Feb. 21, 1895.

5. Hayes County *Republican*, Oct. 18, 1894.

6. Hayes County *Republican*, Jan. 3, 1895.

7. Hayes County *Republican*, Nov. 21, 1895.

8. Hayes County Marriage Book, I, 299, May 14, 1896; *Republican*, May 21, 1896; Hayes County *Times*, May 20, 1896.

9. Ada Clark to Earl Clark, May 23, 1932, in Earl Clark papers.

10. *Republican*, Dec. 24, 1896; *Times*, Mar. 10, 1897.

## Chapter 24. Nubbin Ridge
## *Notes to Pages 241–252*

1. Hayes County *Times*, Nov. 27, 1895, Jan. 10, Apr. 22, 1895; Hayes County *Republican*, Nov. 21, 28, 1895, Feb. 6, 20, Mar. 12, Apr. 2, 16, May 7, 1896.

2. *Republican*, Jun. 11, 25, 1896; *Times*, Jun. 17, 1896; *Republican*, Sep. 17, 1896.

3. *Times*, Jul. 1, 1896; *Republican*, Jul. 2, 9, 16, 30, 1896.

4. *Republican*, Jul. 9, Aug. 20, 27, 1896.

5. *Republican*, Aug. 6, 13, 1896; *Times*, Aug. 12, 1896.

6. *Republican*, Aug. 20, Nov. 19, 1896; *Times*, Sep. 16, 1896.

7. *Republican*, Oct. 8, Nov. 12, 19, 1896; *Times*, Dec. 16, 1896.

8. *Times*, Jun. 17, 1897; *Republican*, Jul. 1, 8, Oct. 7, 21, 1897.

9. *Times*, Sep. 1, 1898; *Republican*, Dec. 21, 1899, May 21, 28, 1896, Jun. 30, Jul. 7, 21, Aug. 4, 1898.

10. *Times*, Feb. 10, 1898.

11. *Times*, Mar. 28, 1901; Kathryn Clark to her children; Mildred Clark Richter to Robert D. Clark, Oct. 23, 1977; Everett Dick, *Sod-House Frontier, 1854-1890* (Lincoln, NE., 1954), pp. 236-37.

12. R. P. Beasley, James M. Gregory, Thomas R. McCarty, *Erosion and Sediment Pollution Control* , 2d. Ed. (Ames, IA, 1984), pp. 33-41, 153-160; Observation with Homer Richter of practices in Hayes County, October, 1980.

13. Nellie Clark Rodgers, "A Nebraska Pioneer;" *Republican*, May 27, 1897.

14. The subsistence farmer, said Allan Bogue, "had little place in the plains states," *Money At Interest: The Farm Mortgage On The Middle Border* (Ithaca, NY., 1955, reissued, New York, 1968), p. 274. Warren Clark's memorandum of sales when he moved from the homestead in 1903 lists machinery and stock, valued at more than $1,000, which he sold. Warren Clark papers; *Republican*, Jun. 23, 1898; James C. Olson, *History of Nebraska* (Lincoln, NE., 1966), pp. 169-70.

15. *Republican*, Apr. 29, 1897; *Times*, Jan. 1, May 5, 19, Jun. 3, 1897, Feb. 24, 1898; Sears Roebuck and Co., 1897 *Catalogue*, (Chicago, IL., 1897), pp. 710, 712, 726.

16. Warren, school and cemetery; *Republican*, Jan. 13, Jun. 23, Nov. 17, 1898; *Times*, Apr. 14, Jun. 30, 1898.

17. Ada Harris Clark to Albert Harris, Nov. 5, 1923, in John Harris, Album, Camden, New York.

18. *Times*, Apr. 7, 1897; *Republican*, May 11, 1893, Sep. 12. 1895; Warren Clark, Diary, Nov. 5, 1891; fragment of a letter from Ada to her mother, Amelia Jane Harris, Apr. 14, 1898, Warren Clark papers; "Souvenir: Pleasant Ridge School, Hope District No. 8, Oct. 3, 1898-Mar. 31-1899" lists pupils, teacher, and board members. Earl Clark papers.

19. The photo, from the Warren Clark papers, is in the possession of the writer.

20. *Republican*, Jun. 3, Jul. 1, Jan. 28, 1897; *Times*, Feb. 10, 24, 1897, Jan. 6, 1898.

21. *Republican*, Jun. 3, Jul. 1, 1897, Jun. 6, 1901.

22. *Republican*, Jun. 25, Jul. 2, 1896, Jun. 23, 30, Jul. 7, 1898; *Times*, Feb. 17, 24, Mar. 24, 1898.

23. *Republican*, Feb. 3, 24, 1898, Sep. 21, Nov. 16, 1899, Oct. 4, 1900; *Times*, Jan. 27, Sep. 29, 1898, Sep. 12, 1901; Methodist Episcopal Church, *Minutes of the West Nebraska Conference* (University Place, NE., 1900), p. 51.

24. *Republican*, Sep. 21, 1899.

25. Arley H. Clark to Robert D. Clark, Jan. 24, 1979; Noel P. Gist, *Secret Societies: A Cultural Study of Fraternalism in the United States, University of Missouri Studies: A Quarterly Research Journal*. XV (No. 4, Oct. 1, 1948), pp. 39-40; *Republican*, Aug. 26, 1897, Oct. 6, 1898.

26. *Republican*, Oct. 26, 1899, *Times* Jan. 6, 20, Apr. 1, 1897, Mar. 21, 1901; Gist, pp. 83, 87, 89, 102, 105, 108-9.

27. *Republican*, Aug. 3, 1893, Apr. 1, 1897, Dec. 28, 1899; Hayes County Deed Record, Vol. 6, p. 342, Feb. 24, 1894; ibid., Vol. 11, pp. 372-3, Dec. 30, 1902.

28. Hayes County Court Journal, April Term, 1897, Vol. 2, p. 624., Apr. 6, 1897; Hayes County Deed Record, Vol. 7, p. 262, Dec. 7, 1895; ibid., Vol. 10, pp. 246-7, Jun. 2, 1900; *Times*, Jan. 27, 1898; *Republican*, Feb. 17, 1898.

29. Robert D. Clark, "The Settlement of Blackwood Township, Hayes County, Nebraska, 1878-1907, *Nebraska History*, 66 (Spring, 1985), 88; Hayes County Deed Record, Vol. 10, p. 181, Jan. 13, 1898; ibid., Vol. 8, p. 280, Apr. 16, 1901. The sheriff's sale was ordered by the Nov., 1897, term of the court, and effected on Mar. 21, 1898, for $267.00.

30. *Republican*, quoting Morton, Sep. 21, 1899. Warren's use of Paris Green is reported in the *Republican*, Jul. 25, 1901.

## Chapter 25. The Sandhills Are Destined
## *Notes to Pages 253-264*

1. The Hope correspondent's reports appeared in the Hayes County *Times*.

2. *Times*, Jan. 31, May 2, Jun. 13, Aug. 8, 29, 1901; Hayes County *Republican*, Feb. 14, 1901, Jan. 26, 1902.

3. *Times*, Jan. 31, Feb. 14, Apr. 18, Jul. 4, 18, 1901, Aug. 21, 1902; Arley H. Clark to Robert D. Clark, Oct. 22, 1977.

4. *Times*, Mar. 7, May 2, Jul. 4, Sep. 19, 1901; *Republican*, Feb. 25, 1901.

5. *Times*, Jul. 25, 1901, Jul. 10, 1902; Arley H. Clark to Robert D. Clark, [Dec.] 15, 1977.

6. *Times*, Mar. 14, Oct. 3, 1901, Sep. 18, Nov. 27, 1902.

7. Ibid., May 9, Jun. 27, Sep. 19, Oct. 24, 1901, Jul. 10, Oct. 16, 1902.

8. *Republican*, Feb. 14, 1901; *Times*, May 2, Jun. 27, 1901, Aug. 21, 1902. Effenbach, as in this citation, is often spelled Effenbeck. The United States Census, 1900, Population Schedule for Hayes County, spells it Effenbach, and indicates that both Will and his wife, Anna, were born in Germany.

9. *Republican*, Jan. 24, Jun. 6, 1901, Jul. 31, Nov. 20, 1902.

10. *Republican*, Aug. 8, 15, 1901.

11. *Republican*, Apr. 11, May 2, 9, 30, Jun. 6, 27, Sep. 12, Nov. 14, 1901.

12. *Times*, Nov. 14, 1901; *Republican*, Feb. 27, 1902; Nellie Clark Rodgers, "A Nebraska Pioneer."

13. Amelia Jane Harris to Earl Clark, Sep. 19, 1901, Earl Clark Papers.

14. *Republican*, Oct. 11, Nov. 1, 1900; *Times*, Oct. 3, 1901.

15. *Republican*, Sep. 19, 1901.

16. Mildred Clark Richter to Robert D. Clark, Sep. 30, 1979; Leah Rodgers Hidy to Robert D. Clark, Oct. 17, 1979; Ada Harris Clark, untitled journal of a trip to New York, 1915, Warren and Ada Clark Papers. The view is clearly expressed by T. De Witt Talmadge, pastor of the Brooklyn Tabernacle and one of the most popular preachers of the era. He offered God's "grace" as the means to bear the world's tribulations. His sermons were published weekly, at different periods, in both the *Republican* and the *Times*. See, particularly, his sermon on "Plain People," *Republican*, Aug. 1, 1895.

17. *Republican*, Apr. 2, 25, 1901, Dec. 13, 1900; *Times*, May 2, 23, Jul. 4, 1901, Sep. 18, Oct. 2, 1902.

18. *Times*, Jun. 26, Jul. 10, 1902; *Republican*, Nov. 15, Dec. 13, 1900, Jun. 6, 20, 1901. Photograph, Warren and Ada Clark Papers.

19. *Times*, Feb. 24, 1898, Jul. 11, 18, 1901, Feb. 24, 1898, Sep. 11, 1902; *Republican*, May 16, Aug. 22, Sep. 26, 1901, May 15, Jul. 3, 1902.

20. *Times*, Jun. 6, Oct. 31, 1901.

21. *Republican*, May 2, Sep. 12, 1901; *Times*, May 1, Aug. 28, Oct. 8, 1902.

22. *Times*, Jan. 24, 1901; *Republican*, Feb. 28, Apr. 4, May 16, 1901, Apr. 10, 1902.

23. *Republican*, Feb. 28, 1901; *Times*, Nov. 28, 1901.

24. Hayes County Deed Record, Vol. 11, pp. 372-3, Dec. 30, 1902, Vol. 9, p. 230, Mar. 30, 1903.

25. *Times*, May 19, 1898, Nov. 7, 1901, Jan. 30, 1902.; Hayes County Deed Record, Vol. 12, p. 233, Jan. 11, 1902.

26. *Times*, Oct. 1, 1902.

27. *Times*, Aug. 14, 1902; Arley H. Clark to Robert D. Clark, Jun. 13, 1980; *Times*, Aug., 15, 1888, Jun. 5, Aug. 14, 1902.

28. *Times*, Sep. 4, 1902.

29. *Times*, Oct. 24, 1901, Aug. 28, Sep. 11, Oct. 16, Nov. 6, Dec. 4, 11, 1902.

30. *Times,* Jan. 15, 29, 1903; Hayes County Deed Record, Vol. 9, p. 235, Jan. 29, 1903; Vol. 9, p. 230, Mar. 30, 1903;, Vol. 11, p. 307, Jun. 23, 1903; Vol. 11, pp. 372-73, Dec. 30, 1902. *Times,* Jan. 15, 29, 1903. Land values generally in the state dropped after the droughts; see Addison Sheldon, *Land Systems And Land Policies In Nebraska,* Nebraska State Historical Society, *Publications*, XXII (Lincoln, NE., 1936), 145-48.

31. *Times,* Jan. 22, 29, Feb. 19, 26, 1903; *Republican*, Feb. 27, Mar. 12, 1903; *Times-Republican*, Mar. 19, 26, Apr. 2, 1903.

## Chapter 26. A Beautiful Day
## *Notes to Pages 265 to 274*

1. Arley H. Clark to Robert D. Clark, Sep. 12, 1978.

2. "Certificate of Scholarship," May 31, 1904, signed by D.W.C. Huntington, President, Nebraska Association of Colleges and Academies; York College Entrance Card for Earl N. Clark, Fall, 1905; Certificate, "Highest Honor Graduate of Frontier County," signed Clara L. Dobson, County Superintendent, all in Earl N. Clark papers.

3. Arley H. Clark, ibid.; Conversations with Clayton Clark and Mildred Richter Clark, confirming reports of Kathryn Jewel Clark to her children.

4. Kathryn Jewel Clark to her children, ibid.; Arley H. Clark to Robert D. Clark, Aug. 30, 1982; Mildred Clark Richter to Robert D. Clark, Sep. 28, 1982.

5. Arley H. Clark to Robert D. Clark, Jun. 24, 1979, Aug. 26, 1980.

6. Memorandum of goods sold, with prices, 4 pp. [1903], Warren and Ada Clark Papers.

7. Arley H. Clark to Robert D. Clark, [Dec.] 15, 1977, Jun. 13, Aug. 26, 1980, Oct. 23, 1982.

8. Confirmed by bill of sale [1917]. Both Jesse Clark and Bert Jewel were present for the sale and made purchases; Leah Rodgers Hidy to Robert D. Clark, Dec. 31, 1977.

9. Recollections of a visit to the grandparents, December, 1916, confirmed by Clayton Clark in conversation and to Robert D. Clark, Sep. 20, 1983.

10. Conversation with Ray Craw, Sep. 23, 1978; Letterhead for Lincoln County Sabbath School Association, North Garfield District, Nebraska, Mr. Clark Whittier, President; Arley H. Clark to Robert D. Clark, [Dec.] 15, 1977, Jun 13, 1980.

11. Arley H. Clark to Robert D. Clark, Jun. 13, 1980; *Doctrines and Discipline of the Free Methodist Church* (Chicago, IL., 1915), pp. 3-23, 34-36, 37-39.

12. Arley H. Clark, Jun. 13, 1980.

13. Mildred Clark Richter to Robert D. Clark, Apr. 18, 1978; Opal Clark Dean to Robert D. Clark, Sep. 17, 1985.

14. Arley H. Clark to Robert D. Clark, [Dec.] 15, 1977; Ada Harris Clark, Diary, May 29, 1933.

15. Ada Harris Clark, untitled journal of a trip to New York, 1915. The journal is the source for the remainder of this chapter.

## Chapter 27. Oh, the Canyons
## *Notes to Pages 275–284*

1. Conversation with Ray Craw, Sep. 23, 1978.

2. Memorandum of sale, with prices, [1918]; Arley H. Clark to Robert D. Clark, [Dec.] 15, 1977.

3. Arley Clark, [Dec.] 15, 1977.

4. Arley H. Clark to Robert D. Clark, [Dec.] 15, 1977, Jan. 24, 1979, Jun. 13, 1980, Mar. 12, 1984.

5. Ibid., [Dec.] 15, 1977. *Doctrines and Discipline of the Free Methodist Church* (Chicago, IL., 1906), p. 4.

6. Warren Clark to Earl Clark, Nov. 13, 1918, Earl Clark Papers; Record of Warren's death in Warren and Ada Clark Papers.

7. Arley H. Clark to Robert D. Clark, Jun. 13, 1980, Mar. 12, 1984.

8. Arley H. Clark, Oct. 23, 1982, Mar. 12, 1984.

9. Conversation with Ray Craw, Sep. 23, 1978.

10. Ada began posting a diary on Aug. 8, 1929, after she moved to Arley's, and continued for four of the next five years, through 1933, using her old diary for 1877 and Warren's for 1876, 1877, 1878.

11. Diary entries; Conversations with Mildred Clark Richter, Oct., 1978.

12. Mildred Clark Richter to Robert D. Clark, Sep. 16, 1979; Opal Clark Dean to Robert D. Clark, Sep. 17, 1985.

13. Diary entries.

14. Untitled journal of a trip to Nebraska, 1933; the journal, unless otherwise noted, is the source for the remainder of this chapter; *Eleventh United States Census, Population*, I (Washington, DC., 1891), 229; *Fifteenth United States Census, Population*, I (Washington), 675.

15. Leah Hidy to Robert D. Clark, Dec. 4, 1982; Arley H. Clark to Robert D. Clark, Oct. 23, 1982. The name "two-by-two" is derived from Jesus' admonition to his disciples in Mark 6:7.

16. Clayton Clark to Robert D. Clark, Oct. 10, 1983, confirms this judgment of Earl Clark, expressed by others in conversation.

17. The Scripture cited is I Timothy, 2:9; Letters to Robert D. Clark: Mildred Clark Richter, Apr. 18, 1978; Arley H. Clark, Jr., Nov. 23, 1982; Lois Hidy Penner, May 29, 1979; Peggy French, Mar. 5, 1983.

18. Mildred Clark Richter to Robert D. Clark, Jan. 28, 1980.

19. Homer Richter and Mildred Clark Richter to Robert D. Clark, Sep. 7, 1979.

20. Mildred Clark Richter to Robert D. Clark, Oct. 23, 1977, Sep. 7, 1979, Jun. 24, 1982. See Chapter X, note #7, on the lone tree.

21. Mildred Clark Richter to Robert D. Clark, Apr. 18, 1978.

22. Record in Warren and Ada Clark Papers.

# Bibliographical Sources

## The New York Years

The principal sources for the New York years are the diaries of Ada Harris for 1873 and 1877, her journal of a trip to New York, 1915, and Warren Clark's diaries for 1874, and 1876-1879. Also important is the handwritten scrapbook-journal of Amelia Jane Onderdonk Harris, Ada's mother, which contains brief histories of the Onderdonk and Harris families and a large number of Amelia Jane's poems, most of them about members of the family. Elmer Onderdonk, *Genealogy of the Onderdonk Family in America* (NY., 1910), gives precise information about that family.

The United States Census reports, Population Schedules, from 1830 through 1880 are valuable sources not simply for ages, but for location of family members. Especially useful are the Agricultural Statistics of the New York State Census, 1875. Also valuable in the location of families is the *New Topographical Atlas of Oswego County, New York* (Philadelphia, PA.,1867, reprinted by B & E Printers, Rochester, NY., 1974). The Oswego County Records of Deeds and Mortgages list property holdings, sales and purchases, and obligations incurred by the many members of both the Clark and Harris families.

Crisfield Johnson, *History of Oswego County, New York, 1789-1887* . . . (Philadelphia, PA., L.H. Everts & Co.,1877), is not only a history but a compendium of information about the towns and villages, with short biographical sketches of leading citizens. Also helpful for background are John Church, Ed., *Landmarks of Oswego County, New York* (Syracuse, NY., D. Mason & Co., 1895) and Ralph M. Faust, *The Story of Oswego County* (Oswego, NY., 1948). Very useful for quick and detailed reference is J.H. French, *Gazetteer of the State of New York . . .* (Syracuse, NY., R. Pearsall Smith, 1860). Mary P. Ryan, *Cradle of the Middle Class: The Family in Oneida County, New York, 1790-1865* (Cambridge, England, Cambridge University Press, 1981), provides insight into family life and values in upstate New York.

For background in some specialized enterprises and activities, see: R. L. Ardrey, *American Agricultural Implements* (Chicago, IL., 1894); Leo Rogin, *The Introduction of Farm Machinery in Its Relation to the Productivity of Labor in the Agriculture of the United States during the Nineteenth Century,* University of California *Publications in Economics,* IX (Berkeley, CA., 1931); Clarence H. Danhof, *Changes in Agriculture: The Northern United States, 1820-1870* (Cambridge, MA., Harvard University Press, 1969); Ulysses Prentice Hedrick, *A History of Agriculture in the State of New York,* Introduction by Paul W. Gates, American Century Series (New York, Hill and Wang for the New York

State Historical Association); John T. Schlebecker, *Whereby We Thrive: A History of American Farming, 1607-1972* (Ames, IA., Iowa State University Press, 1975); Jared Van Wagenen, Jr., *The Golden Age of Homespun* (Ithaca, NY., Cornell University Press, 1953).

For accounts of hop growing and harvest, Mary S. Bowers, "Hop Growing in the Town of Seward," *Scholarie County Historical Review*, XXIX (Oct., 1965), 12-18; Jay S. Morris, "Old Time Hop Pickers," *St. Lawrence County Historical Association Journal*, X (Oct., 1965), 12-13, and Clayton E. Risley, "Hop-Picking Days," *New York Folklore Quarterly*, V (Spring, 1949), 18-23. Two accounts of sugar making are Rowland E. Robinson, "Old Time Sugar-Making, *Atlantic Monthly*, LXXVII (Apr., 1896), 466-471, and Neil Morton, "When the Sap Begins to Flow," *Colliers*, XLIV (Mar. 12, 1910), 18-19. The rules of the Methodist churches are set forth in their disciplines: Bp. William L. Harris, Ed., *The Discipline of the Methodist Episcopal Church, 1872* (Cincinnati, OH., and New York, 1872), and *Constitution and Discipline of the Methodist Protestant Church* (Pittsburgh, PA., 1877).

## Iowa Interlude

Most helpful in the interpretation of the American Dream, the yeoman on the farm, and motivation for the westward movement in search of land, are A. Whitney Griswold, *Farming and Democracy* (New York, 1948); Henry Nash Smith, *Virgin Land: The American West As Symbol and Myth* (Cambridge, MA., Harvard University Press, 1950); Richard Hofstadter, *The Age of Reform: From Bryan to F.D.R.* (New York, Alfred A. Knopf, 1955). Hofstadter, p. 29, says of *Virgin Land*, "a remarkable exposition of the fate of the agrarian myth as a source of political measures and strategies."

The diaries of Warren Clark from January 1880 to March 1885 are the chief source for the narrative in this period. Also helpful are the first pages of Nellie Clark Rodgers (the Clarks' first child, born in May, 1880), "A Nebraska Pioneer," in typescript. Useful local histories, with descriptions, anecdotes, and biographical notes of Guthrie County settlers are Mrs. S.B. Maxwell, *Centennial History of Guthrie County, Iowa . . .* (Des Moines, IA., Carter, Hussey & Curl, Printers, 1876); *History of Guthrie and Adair Counties, Iowa . . .* (Springfield, IL., Continental Historical Company, 1884; *Past and Present of Guthrie County, Iowa . . .* (Chicago, IL. The S.J. Clarke Publishing Co., 1907); and Geo. A. Ogle & Co., Compilers, *Standard Atlas of Guthrie County, Iowa* (Chicago, IL., 1900). For discussion of the topography, soil, and coal deposits, see Samuel Calvin, Charles K. Keyes, and G.E. Patrick, *Iowa Geological Survey*, Vol. I, *First Annual Report, for 1892 . . .* (Des Moines, IA., 1893).

Donald L. Winters, *Farmers Without Farms: Agricultural Tenancy in Nineteenth Century Iowa* (Westport, CT., Greenwood Press, 1978), helps to define the social and economic status of the Clarks; Allan G.

Bogue's exhaustive and definitive study, *Money at Interest: The Farm Mortgage on the Middle Border* (Ithaca, NY., Cornell University Press, 1955), particularly, "Introduction", "Illinois", and "Iowa," provides the background to explain why it was all but impossible for them, with their limited resources, to secure an Iowa farm. Equally indispensable to an understanding of the era, and the problem of tenancy, is his *From Prairie to Corn Belt: Farming on the Illinois and Iowa Prairies in the Nineteenth Century* (Chicago, IL., University of Chicago Press, 1963). R. Douglas Hurt, *The Dust Bowl: An Agricultural and Social History* (Chicago, IL., Nelson-Hall, c. 1981) reports the occurrence of dust storms in Iowa in 1880, confirming Warren's diary entry of an experience that was to help prepare him and Ada for their Nebraska homestead trials. H.H. Mowry provides the basis for estimating the number of acres a farmer might cultivate, in "The Normal Day's Work of Farm Implements, Workmen, and Crews in Western New York," U.S. Department of Agriculture, *Bulletin No. 412*, Sept. 22, 1916 (Washington, DC., Government Printing Office, 1919).

Useful sources for Blencoe and Monona County are *History of Monona County, Iowa . . .* (Chicago, IL., National Publishing Co., 1890); *Progress and Resources of Monona County, Iowa*, (n.p. [188_]); *Blencoe Centennial, 1871-1971* (Blencoe, Iowa, n.d.). The newspapers, Stuart *Locomotive*, 1880-1884, and the Monona County *Gazette*, 1884-1885, yield interesting and sometimes important bits of information for the two communities.

Leland L. Sage, *A History of Iowa* (Ames, IA., Iowa State University Press, 1974), and Joseph Frazier Wall, *Iowa: A Bicentennial History* (New York, Norton 1978), give an overview of events and issues. Glenda Riley's *Frontierswomen: The Iowa Experience* (Ames, IA., The Iowa State University Press, 1981), is a lively and discerning account of women's role in the settlement of the frontier. Riley challenges the stereotypical image of woman as overburdened and unhappy, either "saint in a sunbonnet" or one victimized and broken by hardships.

## Rain and the Plow

The narrative in this section is based on Nellie Clark Rodgers "A Nebraska Pioneer," and Warren Clark's diary: March, 1885, until it stops, abruptly, on March 15, 1885; it is resumed January 11, 1888, and continued through October 23, and again from January 1, 1991, through the remainder of the year. The Hayes County *Republican*, which began publication as the *News* in 1885, and was issued briefly as the *Herald*, is available in scattered numbers from 1888 at the Hayes County *Times-Republican* office in Hayes Center, and in an almost complete file from 1892 at both the *Times-Republican* office and at the Nebraska State Historical Society Library in Lincoln. Some issues of the Hayes County *Times* are also available. These contemporary newspapers, including the

McCook *Tribune*, help to establish the setting for Warren and Ada's homesteading and to verify and illuminate their experiences.

Augmenting these sources are the many accounts of Hayes County pioneer life in the *Hayes County Bicentennial Book* . . . [Hayes Center, *Times-Republican*, 1976] the *Supplement to Hayes County Bicentennial Heritage Book* . . . [Hayes Center, *Times-Republican*, 1977], and *Atlas of Hayes County in Nebraska*, Compiled by Western Cartographers (South Sioux City, NE., 1980). Further details were derived from the writer's interviews of and correspondence with local residents, including ninety-three-year-old Willard (Bud) McMullen, who had lived on a homestead adjacent to the Clarks for ten years, and others who were children or grandchildren of the homesteaders, including Mrs. Glen Scott, Charles Mansfield, Mrs. Fred Wittwer, Mrs. Archie Gruver, Homer Richter, Mildred Clark Richter, Leah Rodgers Hidy, Donald and Glynn Fagerstone, Robert and Neva Korell.

The McCook *Daily Gazette*, May 3, 1973, the "Centennial Souvenir Edition," is an unusually comprehensive and informative report of pioneer days in several southwest Nebraska counties and villages, including areas relevant to the story of Warren and Ada Clark: Gosper County, Arapahoe and Furnas County, Hitchcock County, McCook. Gene O. Morris, *Portraits of the Past: McCook's First One Hundred Years* . . . (McCook, NE., High Plains Historical Society, 1982), succeeds in shaping a mass of historical facts into an engaging narrative.

The United States Land Office Tract Books for Nebraska, Vol. 81, Township T5N, R32W, are indispensable for the locating of the Clarks and their neighbors in Blackwood Township, and for determining the nature of their land claims, their success or failure, in "proving up," and the probable intent to farm or speculate. Of equal importance are the Hayes County Deed Record and Mortgage Record books. The United States Census reports for 1880 and 1900 aid in identifying members of families. The author has analyzed and reported on these data in Robert D. Clark, "The Settlement of Blackwood Township, Hayes County, Nebraska, 1878-1907, *Nebraska History*, LXVI (Spring, 1985), 74-110. Steven A. Schienst reports on the soil in the county and its suitability for agriculture, *Soil Survey of Hayes County, Nebraska*, USDA Soil Conservation Service, in cooperation with University of Nebraska, Conservation and Survey Division (Aug., 1982).

Many narratives, autobiographical and biographical, record the homestead experience in Nebraska and Kansas and provide information useful in understanding the enterprises, successes and failures, of the Clarks. Among them are: *Cass Grove Barns*, *The Sod House: Reminiscent Historical and Biographical Sketches Featuring Nebraska Pioneers, 1867-1897* (Madison, NE. 1930); John Ise, *Sod and Stubble: The Story of a Kansas Homestead* (Lincoln, NE., University of Nebraska Press, 1936, First Bison Book Printing, Mar., 1967); Charley O'Kieffe, *Western Story: The Recollections of Charley O'Kieffe, 1884-1898*

(Lincoln, NE., University of Nebraska Press, 1960); Howard Ruede, *Sod House Days: Letters from a Kansas Homesteader, 1877-1878,* John Ise, editor (Lawrence, KS, University of Kansas Press, 1983, reprint of Columbia University, 1937); Mari Sandoz, *Old Jules* (Lincoln, NE., University of Nebraska Press, A Bison Book, 1962, reprinted from Boston, Little, Brown & Co, 1935); Mari Sandoz, *Sandhill Sundays and Other Recollections* (Lincoln, NE., University of Nebraska Press, 1970); Nellie Snyder Yost, *The Call of the Range: The Story of the Nebraska Stock Growers Association* (Denver, CO., Sage Books, 1966); Frances Jacobs, editor for the Sod House Society's *Sod House Memories* (n.p., 1972).

Henry Nash Smith, in his "Rain Follows the Plow: The Notion of Increased Rainfall for the Great Plains, 1844-1880," *Huntington Library Quarterly,* X (February, 1947), 169-193, and "The Garden and the Desert," Chapter XVI, pp. 174-183, *Virgin Land,* ibid., sets forth the thesis, now widely accepted, that the mythologizing of goals and values gave great impetus to the settling of the plains; the thesis provides a clear rationale both for Warren and Ada Clark's decision to file on a homestead in 1885 and for their sense of triumph in the first years, a triumph that was frequently trumpeted by the Hayes County newspapers, the *Republican* and the *Times*. In an able exposition, David M. Emmons, *Garden in the Grasslands: Boomer Literature of the Central Great Plains* (Lincoln, NE., University of Nebraska Press, 1971) explores in depth and evaluates the tactics used to promote the myth and encourage settlement of the plains: "Rain follows the plow," he writes (p.129), "was the single most important promotional device to come out of the boomers' frontier." Craig Miner, *West of Wichita: Settling the High Plains of Kansas* (Lawrence, KS., University of Kansas Press) pp. 46-49, shows the force of the idea in western Kansas. Smith and many other scholars summarize the views of Powell and his chief opponents, Samuel Aughey and Charles Wilber Dana (Dana, the author of the famous epigram "Rain follows the plow)." The second edition of Powell's book is readily available: John Wesley Powell, *Report on the Arid Region of United States . . .* (Washington, DC., 1879), pp. 1-55. Samuel Aughey, a professor of natural sciences at the newly organized University of Nebraska, presented what he believed to be scientific proof for the theory on increasing rain in his *Sketches of the Physical Geography and Geology of Nebraska* (Omaha, NE., 1880); Leslie Hewes, "The Great Plains: One Hundred Years after Major John Wesley Powell," in Brian W. Blouet and Merlin P. Lawson, eds., *Images of the Great Plains* (Lincoln, NE., University of Nebraska Press, 1975), pp. 203-214, challenges the view that Powell was right and points to the successes of dryland farming--acknowledging dependence on government support. Martyn J. Bowden, "Desert Wheat Belt, Plains Corn Belt: Environmental Cognition and Behavior of Settlers in the Plains Margin," Blouet and Lawson, ibid., pp. 189-201, question the view that the idea of an American desert was widespread among the travelers or the homesteaders. Lawrence D. Burch, contemporary with Aughey, extolled the virtues of Nebraska and urged settlers to come in his *Nebraska As It Is: A Comprehensive Summary of the Resources. Advantages, and Drawbacks of the Great Prairie State* (Chicago, IL., 1878). John O'Neill, *Northern Nebraska as a Home for Immigrants* (Sioux City, IA., Sioux City *Times* Print, 1875), is something of a guidebook, with sketches of the northwest counties and an estimate of the homesteader's costs.

One of the first scholarly and useful treatments of the settlement of Nebraska, is Addison E. Sheldon, *Land Systems and Land Policies in Nebraska . . .*, in *Publications* of the Nebraska State Historical Society, Vol. XXII (Lincoln, NE., 1936). Everett Dick's two comprehensive surveys of pioneer life on the plains are mines of information: *The Sod-House Frontier, 1854-1890: A Social History of the Northern Plains from the Creation of Kansas and Nebraska to the Admission of the Dakotas* (New York, D. Appleton-Century Co., 1937) and *Conquering the Great American Desert: Nebraska*, Nebraska State Historical Society, *Publications,* Vol. XXVII ([Lincoln], 1975). Dick's "Sunbonnet and Calico: The Homesteader's Consort," *Nebraska History*, XLVII (Mar., 1966), 3-14, is a colorful, if somewhat romanticized, account of women's suffering on the plains. Julie Roy Jeffrey narrates in engaging detail the varied duties and experiences of women in her "A Maid of All Traids,", Chapter 3, pp. 51-78, *Frontier Women: The Trans-Mississippi West, 1840-1880,* American Century Series (New York, Hill and Wang, 1979); James C. Olson, *History of Nebraska* (Lincoln, NE., 1966) in an excellent one-volume history is attentive to social and economic as well as political factors. Also valuable is his biography of *J. Sterling Morton* (Lincoln, NE., University of Nebraska Press, 1942).

Among the many other studies helpful to an understanding of public land policy and settlement of the plains are: Benjamin H. Hibbard, *A History of the Public Land Policies*, Foreword by Paul W. Gates (Madison, WI., University of Wisconsin Press, 1965), pp. 347-423, 547-570; Paul W. Gates, *History of Public Land Law Development* (Washington, DC., U.S. Government Printing Office, 1968) pp. 387-494; and Gates's two critical and incisive essays on the success or failure of the homestead policy, the latter modifying the first and finding, despite weaknesses in the law and administration that led to corruption, much to praise in the homestead law as a mechanism for transferring ownership of public lands to farmers: "The Homestead Law in an Incongruous Land System," *American Historical Review*, XLI (Jul., 1936), 652-81, and "The Homestead Act Free Land Policy in Operation, 1862-1935" in Howard W. Ottoson, Ed., *Land Use Policy and Problems in the United States*, Homestead Centennial Symposium, University of Nebraska, 1962 (Lincoln, NE., University of Nebraska Press, 1963). Homer E. Socolofsky reviews both Hibbard and Gates in evaluating the homestead policy in "Success and Failure in Nebraska Homesteading," *Agricultural History*

XLII (Apr., 1968), 103-108. Among others: Walter Prescott Webb, *The Great Plains* (New York, Ginn and Company, 1931), pp. 270-431; Roy Robbins, *Our Landed Heritage: The Public Domain, 1776-1936* (Lincoln, NE., University of Nebraska Press, 1962), pp. 216-298; Fred A. Shannon, *The Farmers' Last Frontier: Agriculture, 1860-1897* (New York, Harper Torchbooks, 1968). Chapter III, "Disposing of the Public Domain," pp. 51-75. Lawrence Bacon Lee's *Kansas and the Homestead Act,* (New York, Arno Books, 1979), in an excellent section on homesteading in western Kansas, pp. 368-591, relates experiences somewhat parallel to those in southwest Nebraska.

## Drought and Exodus

Warren's diary, covering only the six months from January 1, 1892, to June 25, contains little of importance to this period of his homestead years. Nellie Clark Rodgers, "A Nebraska Pioneer," is the chief source for the personal narrative. Also informative, generally routine but occasionally colorful, are the weekly reports of the country correspondents to the Hayes County newspapers, the *Republican* and the *Times*. Fragmented notes in a pocket memorandum and account book add some information as does the record of sale of part of Warren and Ada's farm equipment and household goods in 1903.

The hot winds of 1894 came so quickly and devastatingly that the editors and country correspondents hardly took note of the disaster. They gave much attention to the consequences, the exodus from the region and the county and the desperate plight and need for assistance of many of those who remained. Newspapers and journals outside the county and state gave at least one-time attention to the tragic story, among them: Omaha *Bee*, Jul. 26, 1894, Nebraska *State Journal* , Aug. 29, 30, 1894; New York *Tribune*, Aug. 1, 8, 9, 1894; New York *Times*, Aug. 4, 5, 6, 7, 8, 1894. Lincoln, *Nebraska State Democrat*, Oct. 6, 1894. The Omaha *World-Herald* ran a series of 15 reports by Robert B. Peattie, who had traveled in the area, beginning December 14, 1894, and running through December 30. The one on Hayes County, "Hunger at Christmas Tide," appeared on December 25. The newly elected Fusion (Populist-Democrat) Gov. Silas A. Holcomb, as reported in the *World-Herald* for Jan. 4, 1889, urged the legislature to enact relief measures: "every government is duly bound to provide at public expense the necessities to sustain life to its own needy inhabitants, and especially is this the case when the needy are without fault on their part." Another contemporary account, in two issues, is vivid in detail: *Harper's Weekly,* "The Drouth in the West," 39 (Jan. 12, 1895), 39-40; "The Destitution in Nebraska," 39 (Jan. 19, 1895), 59-62; the reply of James H. Canfield, Chancellor of the University of Nebraska, is highly defensive, arguing that matters were not so bad as depicted--"Destitution in Nebraska," 39 (Feb. 9, 1895), 142. See also, Everett Dick, *Conquering the Great American Desert: Nebraska,* pp. 335-354. The problem of mortgage and foreclosure did not concern Warren Clark directly, nor was he involved in the Populist uprising, but both issues affected his neighbors, and his own family indirectly. See James C. Malin, "The Turnover of Farm Population in Kansas," *Kansas Historical Quarterly* IV (Nov., 1935), 339-372; Allan G. Bogue, *Money at Interest: The Farm Mortgage on the Middle Border* (Ithaca, NY., 1955,) pp. 1-6, 60-75, 262-276. And for Populism: John D. Barnhart, "Rainfall and the Populist Party in Nebraska," *American Political Science Review*, XIX (Aug., 1925), 527-540; John D. Hicks, *The Populist Revolt: A History of the Farmers' Alliance and the People's Party* (Minneapolis, MN., University of Minnesota Press, 1931), Richard Hofstadter, *The Age of Reform*; and later studies critical of earlier views: David Stephen Trask, "Nebraska Populism as a Response to Environmental and Political Problems," Brian W. Blouet and Frederick C. Luebke, *The Great Plains: Environment and Culture* (Lincoln, NE., University of Nebraska Press for the Center for Great Plains Studies, c. 1979), pp. 61-80; Luebke, "Main Street and the Countryside: Patterns of Voting in Nebraska During the Populist Era," *Nebraska History* L (Fall, 1969), 257-275.

## The Final Years

The narrative for this section is derived largely from personal papers: a few fragments of letters, memoranda, a list of items sold at auction in 1918, when the Clarks retired from the farm; Ada's journal of a trip to New York in 1915, and one to Nebraska in 1933; Ada's diaries for 1929, 1930, 1931, 1932, posted in the unused lines of the diaries she and Warren had kept in New York in the 1870s; and letters to the writer, chiefly from her son, the Rev. Arley H. Clark, and her granddaughters, Mildred Clark Richter, Leah Rodgers Hidy, and Peggy G. French, and notes from, or conversations with, others of her grandchildren: Ray Craw, J. Clayton Clark, Wiley Jewel, James Wesley Clark, Opal Clark Dean, and Arley Herbert Clark.

*Warren Clark, Williamstown, New York, 1915.*